W9-BNT-293

AMERICA'S PEACEMAKERS

America's Peacemakers

The Community Relations Service and Civil Rights

A new edition of *Resolving Racial Conflict*

Bertram Levine and Grande Lum

UNIVERSITY OF MISSOURI PRESS

COLUMBIA

Copyright © 2020 by
The Curators of the University of Missouri
University of Missouri Press, Columbia, Missouri 65211
Printed and bound in the United States of America
All rights reserved. First printing, 2020.

Library of Congress Cataloging-in-Publication Data

Names: Levine, Bertram J., author. | Lum, Grande, author.
Title: America's peacemakers : the community relations service and Civil
    Rights / by Bertram Levine, and Grande Lum.
Other titles: Community relations service and Civil Rights
Description: New edition. | Columbia : University of Missouri Press, [2020]
    | "A new edition of Resolving Racial Conflict." | Includes
    bibliographical references and index.
Identifiers: LCCN 2020019504 (print) | LCCN 2020019505 (ebook) | ISBN
    9780826222169 (hardcover) | ISBN 9780826274519 (ebook)
Subjects: LCSH: United States. Community Relations Service--History. |
    United States--Race relations. | United States--Ethnic relations. |
    United States. Civil Rights Act of 1964. | Race discrimination--United
    States--History--20th century. | Race discrimination--United
    States--History--21st century. | Civil rights--United
    States--History--20th century. | Discrimination--United
    States--History--20th century. | Civil rights--United
    States--History--21st century. | Discrimination--United
    States--History--21st century.
Classification: LCC E184.A1 L467 2020 (print) | LCC E184.A1 (ebook) | DDC
    323.1196/073/009045--dc23
LC record available at https://lccn.loc.gov/2020019504
LC ebook record available at https://lccn.loc.gov/2020019505

♾™ This paper meets the requirements of the
American National Standard for Permanence of Paper
for Printed Library Materials, Z39.48, 1984.

Acknowledgment of permissions for this volume appears on page 449

Typefaces: ITC Galliard Pro and Mr Eaves Modern

First Edition (Bertram Levine)

To Muriel

Who decorated my life

New Edition (Grande Lum)

In Gratitude to Bertram Levine's children: Neil, David, and Susan Rae

In a time of unnecessary trouble and disorder, the members of CRS had the capacity and courage to cool the tensions of a Nation. You helped to bring order where there would have been chaos. You helped bring peace where violence would have ruled the day.

On behalf of a grateful Nation, on behalf of a grateful people, on behalf of those who gave all they had in this fight, I stand here to say thank you for all that you did to help to get us to where we are today.

As a Nation, we are deeply indebted to the Community Relations Service at the Department of Justice for helping to create a more perfect Union. I say to each and every one of you who continue to work at CRS, never give up. Never give in. Keep the faith. Keep your eyes on the prize. We are going to build a beloved nation.

—Congressman John Lewis at
CRS's Forty-Fifth Anniversary, 2009

CONTENTS

Note: The introduction and chapters 1–10 are by Bertram Levine, the author of the original edition. Chapters 11–15 are by Grande Lum. Chapter 16 has sections by both authors.

NONVIOLENCE, CONFLICT RESOLUTION, AND SOCIAL JUSTICE

THE LANDMARK CIVIL Rights of Act of 1964 is most known for its historic legislative enshrinement of civil rights, something African Americans struggled for centuries to achieve. Lesser known than the more publicly celebrated sections of the act is Title X, creating the Community Relations Service (CRS).

Bertram Levine and Grande Lum have written a compelling book describing more than five decades of service. The authors' work is a "must read" for anyone who seeks a better understanding of the historic magnitude of what the act sought to redress and achieve. It provides insight into the value of nonviolent negotiation of what could otherwise, in the absence of such negotiation, become instances of violence and setbacks to the intent of the act. In summary, the book is about over fifty years of racial conflict in America, and what was done by federal conciliators to help resolve it.

As the former political adviser, personal lawyer, and draft speechwriter for Dr. Martin Luther King Jr., I am honored that former CRS director Grande Lum asked me to write a foreword to what is a superb new edition of this book about the operation of CRS created under the Civil Rights Act of 1964. I feel especially so given the deep polarization in this country in 2020 and the need for conflict resolution experts to aid in the cause of social justice. Since Levine's book covered CRS's history up until 1989, it is particularly important to shed light on CRS's amazing work since then, which includes:

- throughout the country post-9/11, preventing backlash violence against innocent people targeted by xenophobic racists;
- in Miami, a valiant attempt to create a peaceful handover of Elián González from his Florida relatives to his Cuban father;
- in Ovett, Mississippi, mediating after local residents harassed occupants at Camp Sister Spirit, a lesbian retreat center;

- throughout the South, helping to protect African American churches from arson following President Bill Clinton's signing of the 1996 Church Arson Prevention Act;
- in Sanford, Florida, easing tensions after the tragic 2012 killing of Trayvon Martin, where the state's "Stand Your Ground" law enabled violence with a "Get Out of Jail Free" card;
- and in Oak Creek, Wisconsin, in 2012, enhancing communication after a white supremacist entered a Sikh gurdwara and murdered six congregants.

Grande's focus on CRS's work from 1990 forward adds to how we think about how American society has evolved as a whole in terms of civil rights. What is striking is that as other minority groups—whether Native American, Hispanic, Muslim, LGBTQ, or Asian American— increased their civil rights advocacy, they also began utilizing CRS, especially when the situation involved governmental actors. The Matthew Shepard and James Byrd Jr. Hate Crimes Prevention Act opened up CRS's ability to work in situations beyond race for the first time, mirroring the changes in the country as a whole.

Neither the author of the first edition, Bertram Levine, nor anyone working on civil rights immediately after the assassination of President John F. Kennedy on November 22, 1963, could have known that this event would result in Martin Luther King developing what may have been the most important strategic decision during his leadership of the civil rights movement: that there would be no major material improvement on the issue of race in the United States unless it occurred under the political leadership of a white, southern political leader. A description of the genesis of this political thesis by Dr. King is described in greater detail in my own forthcoming memoirs.

Just what role does nonviolent conflict resolution play when conflict resolution and civil rights programs enacted under the Civil Rights Act end up at cross-purposes? This is one of the challenging issues Levine and Lum bring to our attention. One of the most profound and prescient observations from Levine is that from its earliest days, it was apparent to CRS's leaders that the roots of racial animosity lay deep beneath the surface of American society.

This seems to be right on the money with the issues that our country's political leaders are confronting today. For example, in competing for the Democratic Party's nomination to prevent President Donald Trump's reelection, former vice president Joe Biden has faced challenges to his civil rights credentials because when he was a senator, he worked with segregationists from the South to enact various pieces of legislation, including civil rights, during his more than thirty-five years in the Senate. This is exactly what President Lyndon Johnson had to do to enable the successful passage of the Civil Rights Act of 1964.

President Johnson, in the creation of CRS, was politically savvy. He appointed white business, civil, and political leaders, who themselves at one time or another had supported racial segregation. Johnson recognized that effective politics often requires working with people who once held racist views.

This book makes clear that both President Johnson and former Governor LeRoy Collins of Florida saw CRS as an indispensable "fountainhead that would reach out to opinion molders and community leaders across the nation" following the enactment of the 1964 Civil Rights Act, "to create a climate in which civil rights and racial amity would flourish."

Johnson is appropriately heralded for his historic leadership in the enactment of the Civil Rights Act of 1964 and Voting Rights Act of 1965. Bertram Levine's and Grande Lum's book about the work of CRS makes it clear that substantial nationwide compliance with these landmark civil rights achievements would not have been possible without the largely unknown work of CRS.

The authors have written a compelling narrative of the agency's history. It is a "must read" for anyone who seeks to better understand how we as a nation largely peacefully complied with the greatest civil rights revolution in our country since the Civil War. Thus, as mentioned earlier, it is a special moment for me to have been asked to write this foreword.

As Grande Lum writes, "The work of CRS is ultimately to help the country sustain harmony in all its diversity." President Johnson was so politically tuned in to the soul and body issues of the average white person from the South that he uniquely created CRS "to help the medicine go down." The Civil Rights Act of 1964 was strong medicine.

Neither President Johnson nor Dr. King in their wildest imaginations could have predicted that CRS would become the federal statutory framework for nonviolent resolutions of disputes arising in communities following its enactment. Its existence became tantamount to a prescription for nonviolent pursuit of social justice, embodying Dr. King's philosophical commitment to nonviolence based on the legacy of Mohandas K. Gandhi, who used nonviolent resistance so effectively to free India from British colonialism.

Dr. King, in an article that appeared in the magazine the *Christian Century* on February 6, 1957, stated, "The basic question which confronts the world's oppressed is: How is the struggle against the forces of injustice to be waged? There are two possible answers. One is resort to the all too prevalent method of physical violence and corroding hatred. . . . The alternative to violence is nonviolent resistance. . . . [It] does not seek to defeat or humiliate the opponent, but to win his friendship and understanding." Nonviolent resistance seeks to "awaken a sense of moral shame in the opponent. The end is redemption and reconciliation."

In a new chapter written by Grande Lum for the second edition, he reminds us that the advent of "smartphone videos of police officers' actions against citizens changed the landscape by providing immediate, visceral, visual documentation that kept the narrative going." What is particularly troubling as I write this is the resurgence of white nationalism and xenophobia in this country. I am appreciative that Grande went back in time and wrote about CRS's early 1970s work in Skokie, Illinois, when a small American Nazi group threatened to come to Skokie, with its numerous Jewish and Holocaust survivor residents. The work that CRS's Dick Salem and Werner Petterson did to help prevent violence is nothing short of incredible.

As we face the social media and fake news–driven extremism of the twenty-first century, social justice requires culturally skilled dispute resolution experts like those at CRS more and more. The work that Grande and his staff did in Sanford after Trayvon Martin, Baltimore after Freddie Gray, and Ferguson after Michael Brown is crucial if we want to both make our minority communities safer and build trust again between minority communities and law enforcement.

In sum, this book about the history of CRS is an essential historical reference to obtaining an accurate understanding of just how prescient President Johnson was in his requirement that CRS be a constituent part of the 1964 Civil Rights Act.

We all owe a debt of gratitude to the authors and to the staff, both past and present, of the Community Relations Service.

Thank you.

Dr. Clarence B. Jones
Scholar in Residence
Martin Luther King Jr. Institute
Stanford University

> We can't expect to solve our problems if all we do is tear each
> other down. You can disagree with a certain policy without
> demonizing the person who espouses it.
>
> President Barack Obama, May 1, 2010

JUST WEEKS BEFORE President Barack Obama articulated this sentiment
at his May 1, 2010, University of Michigan commencement speech, I
made the decision to join his administration. I was especially proud to
do so because, throughout his career, Obama had often advocated a
passionate and balanced approach to conflict- and problem-solving. I
had spent my career in conflict resolution, mediating numerous types
of issues with a wide range of parties, and I had been a clinical professor
and ran a center on negotiation and dispute resolution at the University
of California Hastings College of the Law. Two years later, I would
be leading the one federal agency that was legislatively mandated to
resolve disputes and reduce tension, and doing so as the United States
entered its most challenging period of social discord since the 1960s
civil rights era. This later period started with the killing of Trayvon
Martin, an unarmed African American high school student visiting his
father, by neighborhood watch captain George Zimmerman in Sanford,
Florida. The unrest spiked with further tragic deaths of unarmed African
American citizens, primarily by the hands of police officers in Ferguson,
Missouri; New York City; and Baltimore, Maryland.

When the possibility of joining the Community Relations Service
(CRS) presented itself to me, I found the one and only book that provided a complete narrative of its first twenty-five years of existence. I
tracked down a copy, and as I read the book, even though I had been
familiar with CRS's work, I was awestruck by the agency's unique and
critical service to the country. Much of its history I did not know. The

book, *Resolving Racial Conflict: The Community Relations Service and Civil Rights, 1964–1989,* floored me on that first read. I learned for the first time how CRS was the brainchild of President Lyndon Baines Johnson and how future Supreme Court justice Arthur Goldberg formulated the agency in order to mediate community civil rights issues. Through compelling writing about an urgent time of our country's history, the book's author, the late Bertram Levine, a longtime CRS staff member, detailed how Johnson then stewarded CRS into being through the 1964 Civil Rights Act, arguably the most important American legislation of the twentieth century. CRS mediators played a critical role after Bloody Sunday in keeping successive marches from Selma to Montgomery safe, in creating biracial parent coalitions during the Boston Public Schools desegregation, in bringing the American Indian Movement takeover of Wounded Knee to an end, and in mediating a dispute between Vietnamese and white fishermen in Galveston, Texas, where the Ku Klux Klan was actively engaged.

After President Obama nominated me as the ninth director of CRS and the Senate confirmed me by unanimous consent on June 29, 2012, the book took on new importance. It became the touchstone that I would turn to regularly to understand how the agency responded in similar past situations. My start as CRS director on August 1, 2012, was low-key, as I was in the process of moving my family from the San Francisco Bay area to Washington, D.C. I met with a single human resources employee at the San Francisco U.S. Attorney's Office, who swore me in so I could officially start working. I then walked over to the federal building where the CRS San Francisco Field Office was located, and the single conciliator there, Carol Russo, welcomed me to the agency.

My real introduction to the world of CRS came three days later. On Sunday, August 5, I was about to board a flight to Dallas, Texas, to meet my entire staff for the first time. As I stood at the gate, the CNN broadcaster on the airport television monitor reported that there had been a mass shooting in a Sikh gurdwara in Oak Creek, Wisconsin. After landing in Dallas, I rode to my hotel with CRS staff members who were all on their cell phones to Sikh leaders throughout the country and to Department of Justice colleagues to understand the situation, share information, and strategize next steps. Tragically, the shooter, a white supremacist, had killed six people and wounded four others. Within hours, we were in contact with the Federal Bureau of Investigation; the Bureau of Alcohol, Tobacco, Firearms, and Explosives; and the White House Office of Faith-Based and Neighborhood Partnerships, enhancing communication between law enforcement and community members by providing critical information for key law enforcement personnel.[1]

That Wednesday, August 8, CRS conciliators—along with Jim Santelle, then the U.S. attorney for the Eastern District of Wisconsin—ran a community session to discuss anxieties over the shooting, better understand hate crime definitions, coordinate law enforcement response, and problem-solve funeral arrangements. There were rumors of a second shooter that needed to be dispelled and desires to have the Oak Creek gurdwara revert to a place of worship rather than a closed crime scene. We were also able to help shooting victims who did not have relatives close by receive out-of-town visitors to support them. CRS coordinated and facilitated a larger community meeting the following day at Oak Creek High School with more than 250 people. I personally briefed the staff of First Lady Michelle Obama in preparation for her visit to the Oak Creek gurdwara on August 23. Thus began a whirlwind three and a half years in which CRS played both a first responder role as well as a preventive one, with me at its helm.

After the initial post-tragedy work, CRS continued to work with Sikh community leaders and law enforcement to reduce fears and ultimately enhance safety for the Sikh community. This work included the revision and national launch in September 2012 of resources to prevent hate crimes against Sikhs, notably a cultural awareness training program for first responders to inform and educate communities still experiencing tension. In 2013, CRS contributed to the inclusion of the Sikh religion in the FBI's Uniform Crime Reporting (UCR) form in order to measure bias-based incidents targeting Sikh community individuals. Those killed and injured in Oak Creek could not be counted as victims of anti-Sikh violence because the option was not available on the form. CRS and the Civil Rights Division of the Department of Justice convened religious leaders, civil rights advocates, and Department of Justice representatives to address shortcomings of the UCR form and determine changes that could improve it. The inclusion of Sikhs and additional groups on the UCR form was approved by FBI Director Robert Mueller and went into effect on January 1, 2015.

Throughout my time at CRS, I found myself flipping through the pages of the first edition of this book to see how early CRS conciliators worked with Martin Luther King and negotiator Andrew Young (later Atlanta mayor, congressman, and UN ambassador) of the Southern Christian Leadership Conference; Alabama state trooper Colonel Al Lingo in Selma; or Russell Means and the FBI at Pine Ridge, South Dakota. I also used the book for inspiration and grounding in discussing CRS's illustrious history. For example, when I spoke to Department of Education employees, I shared the courage of CRS conciliator Silke Hansen during her work in the Boston Public Schools to facilitate court-ordered desegregation.

Levine's book provided the historical context to the contemporary work, which came to the forefront in 2014 when CRS celebrated its fiftieth anniversary. Attorney General Eric Holder presided as the entire staff and alumni showed up for the commemoration. It was a moment where past and present met to reflect on a half-century of peacekeeping accomplishments. In the Great Hall at the Robert F. Kennedy Main Justice Department Building we were honored to have Andrew Young interviewed by me as well as former CRSers Ronald Gault, Rose Ochi, Stephen Thom, Grace Flores-Hughes, and Joan Trumpauer Mulholland sharing their memories.

When I left CRS in February 2016 after directing the agency during the George Zimmerman trial and the Ferguson and Baltimore tragedies, I felt gratified to have completed some of the most important work of my life. After I left, I became the first director of the Divided Community Project at the Ohio State University Moritz College of Law, whose mission it was to complement CRS work by focusing on prevention and helping communities transform conflict into cooperation. As I unpacked my boxes, I reopened the Levine book. Bertram Levine's motivation for writing the book jumped out at me: "The Community Relations Service of the Justice Department had provided the nation with a unique and important service during a critical—and dangerous— period of history, and virtually nobody knew anything about it. Here was a book that cried out to be written." It struck me in that moment that the decades of CRS work since 1989 also needed to be captured for future generations.

During my time at CRS, I met with Bertram Levine's sons, Neil and David. They both were excited and supportive of the idea of a second edition of the book. I spoke with the editors at the University of Missouri Press, and they agreed that a new edition made sense given both the expanded work CRS was doing to address community conflicts beyond race and the worldwide attention to the protests in Sanford, Ferguson, Baltimore, and numerous other cities.

Having worked during these most recent crises, I was disturbed by the parallels with what had transpired in the civil rights era of the 1960s and 1970s and saddened to see Levine's sense of "monumental progress" in police-minority relations not borne out. Modern-day tools Twitter, Facebook, and social media as a whole made Sanford and Ferguson into worldwide phenomena. Smartphone videos of police officers' actions against citizens changed the landscape by providing immediate, visceral, visual documentation that kept the narrative going. While newspaper photos and network television news transformed conflicts in the 1960s, information from witnesses and family members was now being shared directly on new, faster, farther-reaching platforms.

The context of CRS had also evolved due to its decision to expand its mission beyond issues of race, color, and national origin. This shift came about as a result of the Matthew Shepard and James Byrd Jr. Hate Crimes Prevention Act, which was signed into law by President Obama on October 28, 2009. For the first time in its then-forty-five-year history, CRS worked on issues involving gender, gender identity, sexual orientation, religion, and disability. CRS was again breaking new ground in using conflict resolution to address pressing civil rights matters. For example, I was proud to initiate CRS's production of the first federal video training on transgender issues.

To appreciate the unique contribution CRS makes, it is important to understand that the fields of social justice and conflict resolution intersect sparingly. This separation is largely due to inherent tension between advocacy and neutrality. It is a complex dynamic to simultaneously strive to uphold civil rights while serving as a conciliator or mediator trusted by both sides of a conflict. Only recently have researchers and academicians begun to analyze the work of those who navigate this intersection. Allowing for greater examination of the groundbreaking work of CRS requires creating a record, which is what I seek to do here.

I sought to honor the original book by walking the same path that Bertram Levine took toward composition. I read through all of the CRS annual reports. I perused the interviews of CRS conciliators by

Richard Salem and Heidi and Guy Burgess, especially those concerning their work after 1989. Many of the choices for a second edition were clear-cut. I prioritized CRS's work in Mississippi after neighbors harassed a lesbian community; throughout the country on hate and violence against Muslims, Sikhs, and others post-9/11; in Miami, Florida, after two fisherman saved Elián González; and in Sanford, Florida, after George Zimmerman shot Trayvon Martin. I also honor the confidentiality provision of the 1964 Civil Rights Act by only sharing information in the public record or provided to me with no confidentiality expectation.

The importance of capturing the record of CRS's involvement since 1989 particularly hit home when I read Bernard Mayer's excellent 2004 book *Beyond Neutrality*. In that volume he stated, "Years later, when the Elian Gonzalez case was in the news, I wondered why there was no serious attempt to mediate that situation."[2] As this new edition makes clear, there were in fact serious, extended mediation efforts led by CRS to find a peaceful resolution to Elián's custody crisis. If CRS's work was unknown even to renowned dispute resolution experts, there was an obvious need to fill that gap with this publication.

The harder choice was what to leave out regarding all the tremendous work that CRS did from 1990 to the time of writing this book. CRS conciliators Stephen Thom, Silke Hansen, and others spent significant time in Los Angeles after the police brutality against Rodney King.[3] Thom and Julian Klugman did groundbreaking work in California mediating disputes on Native American repatriation of remains and artifacts.[4] Also, CRS was closely involved with communities after Hurricane Katrina hit Louisiana and the Gulf Coast. A large team of CRS conciliators, including Silke Hansen, Azekah Jennings, Pascual Marquez, Rosa Melendez, Carmelita Pope-Freeman, and Synthia Taylor, were dispatched by Director Grace Flores-Hughes and spent weeks away from home, working with tragedy-stricken communities, mediating numerous disputes, and facilitating help and support. Conciliators worked diligently in Jena, Louisiana, after six young African American students were initially charged with attempted murder of a white student. After I departed CRS, my successor, Acting Director Paul Monteiro, and a conciliation team did crucial work in the Dakota Access Pipeline protest in maintaining safety and helping marginalized voices be heard. I wish there was room to explore all of this work in depth, and I hope this book encourages others to document and analyze more CRS efforts in the future.

I made only one substantial pre-1990 addition to this book. When I started at CRS, I reached out to legendary CRS mediator Richard Salem, and he mentioned his work with a neo-Nazi group in Skokie, Illinois. It rang a bell, as it was a well-known constitutional case I had read in law school, which effectively set the precedent that the First Amendment right of freedom of speech is for all, even Nazis. I then read a journal article by Salem that went into detail on how CRS's work fundamentally changed the events in Skokie.[5] Given the 2017 Charlottesville tragedy in which white nationalist protests resulted in the death of a young woman, Heather Heyer, and the continuing national struggle with race and memory, I thought it would be immensely beneficial to add a chapter on how CRS helped avoid bloodshed in Skokie.

In some of Levine's original chapters, I provide a few additional paragraphs and endnotes to provide insight from the last thirty plus years of change in the country and CRS experience. Per my respect for the first edition, I have kept them to a minimum. Nonetheless, it was important to update chapter 6, "Police-Minority Relations," given how this issue has surged in the American consciousness in the decades following where the first edition leaves off, on an optimistic note for the future. The final chapter reflects more editing, primarily to acknowledge the addition of numerous CRSers since 1989 and to give a fuller overview of its history.

In that vein, I wanted to be as respectful as possible of the original text, particularly as Bertram Levine had passed away and I was unable to seek his counsel. In writing a new edition, I was confronted with how terms to describe different racial groups have evolved over time. For today's reader, terms like "Negro," "Asian," and "ghetto" can be jarring at best and offensive to many, and the new chapters use today's common terms like "African American" and "Asian American." I consulted with Neil and David about whether to leave the original text undisturbed, and David made the point that the changes in terminology "reflect trends that are meant to enhance equality and respect," which is certainly my goal as an author and that of CRS in its work. We also agreed that the book would be a more unified whole if we changed this terminology. Thus, I made the final decision to update the terms in the earlier text, though of course not in quotations or proper names of organizations.

My editor and I also discussed at length whether to leave the N-word in given the highly offensive impact the term has. The word was used four times in the first edition, and in each instance it is in quotations. Three of the instances were usages of the term by police officers and one was a usage in the Boston Public Schools integration controversy. We made the decision to leave them in to better reflect the context of the situations the communities and CRS faced at the time.

I also faced the same personal quandary as Bertram Levine in that, like the original author, I had worked at CRS. While I was not there nearly as long, I was involved in the period 2012–16 and led the agency during the Oak Creek tragedy, through the Sanford, Ferguson, and Baltimore work. This work is not an autobiography, so I do not delve into my involvement in great detail but mention it only where I believe it is helpful in sharing the narrative of events. I added five new chapters: chapter 11, "Nazis, Free Speech, and Hate: Preventing a Bloodbath in Skokie and Beyond"; chapter 12, "Arabs, Muslims, and Sikhs: Preventing and Responding to Unfounded Violence after 9/11"; chapter 13, "Not Only Race: Confronting Other Types of Hate"; chapter 14, "Crossing Borders: The Elián González Custody Dispute"; and chapter 15, "Back to the Future: Law Enforcement and Race Takes Center Stage in Sanford, Florida." I updated and added sections to the final chapter of the first edition, "The Quest for Value" (now chapter 16), to reflect events and trends since the book was originally written, as well as additional analysis.

The work of CRS is ultimately to help the country sustain harmony in all its diversity. The American story has always involved diversity, which has been both a source of strength and a basis for discord. From the moment the Native Americans who first occupied the land encountered European settlers, there has been conflict and tension. Later, whole economies were founded on the work of enslaved people brought to the country from Africa. The social repercussions of this economic model have reverberated throughout American history. Secession and the Civil War were fought over slavery, while the denial of rights in the Jim Crow South and segregation continued for a hundred years afterward.

The country's diversity—and need for civil rights protections—encompasses not only differences across race and ethnicity but also religion, gender, gender identity, and sexual orientation. Religion was a reason why many who came to the United States fled their home countries. Many found support in America, while some found themselves at odds with others' beliefs or religious identity. Women have been fighting for equality since the country's founding, and the recent Me Too movement reveals how much further there is to go on inclusion. Issues involving sexual orientation and gender identity have come to the forefront of national consciousness. This continuing struggle toward equality for all has, in fact, come far since 1989, where Bertram Levine's original edition of this book left off. This new edition covers this more recent era to continue to document that journey and provide social justice and conflict resolution insight for an even more inclusive—and hopefully more harmonious—future ahead for all Americans.

A LOOK AHEAD

The first edition of this book was completed in 2004, fifteen years after the period it covered. In that edition Bertram Levine noted that patterns of racial conflict and the Community Relations Service's response were the same and yet different.

In 2004, Levine observed that police-minority friction was still the number-one source of conflict in which CRS became involved. While the frequency of such incidents appeared to have diminished, acts of police abusiveness still had the power to inflame an entire community. Many scenarios were unchanged: a young African American man was shot by police who thought they saw a gun; a Hispanic man died in police custody. To these examples have been added the practice of racial profiling by police, which to many appears to be an adaptation of the notorious, racially biased stop-and-frisk excesses that were condemned by the Kerner Commission more than three decades earlier.

In 2019, when I reread Levine's original final chapter, I was quite chastened by how the situation seems to have worsened dramatically in the last fifteen years. The tragic shooting of seventeen-year-old Trayvon Martin by a self-appointed neighborhood-watch captain sparked the Black Lives Matter movement. Martin's death was soon followed by those of Michael Brown in Ferguson, Missouri; Eric Garner in New York; Philando Castile in Minneapolis; Walter Scott in Charleston, South Carolina; Laquan McDonald in Chicago; Antonio Zambrano-Montes in Pasco, Washington, and a further stream of unarmed African American and Latino males shot to death by police officers, often caught on smartphone or police camera videos. The George Floyd tragedy in the midst of the COVID-19 pandemic has unleashed a dramatic new round of protests in the United States calling for defunding of police and fundamental change. A new civil rights era driven by technology and social media has shined a brighter light on such incidents than has been seen in decades.

In 2004, Levine also noted that hate violence cases had been making up an increasing portion of the CRS caseload. This second edition devotes a chapter to the 9/11 tragedy. From that moment forward, CRS significantly increased its work with Muslim, Sikh, and other Arab communities targeted since 9/11. The second edition also contains a new chapter on the hate crimes jurisdiction work CRS has done since the 2009 Matthew Shepard and James Byrd Jr. Hate Crimes Prevention Act.

This new edition was finished in 2020. It is troubling to see that these last few years have seen a rise in anti-immigrant, anti-Semitic, and nativist rhetoric and violence both nationally and internationally. Presidential candidate Donald Trump spearheaded a "birther" campaign against President Obama, falsely promoting the idea that Obama was born in Kenya, and portrayed Mexicans seeking entry into the United States as "criminals and rapists." Since Trump's election, he has insisted that "very fine people" were among the white supremacists participating in demonstrations in Charlottesville, Virginia, that led to the death of a young liberal protester; referred to immigrants involved in gangs as "not people" but "animals"; and made barriers to the entry of people from Mexico, Central America, and Muslim-majority countries a cornerstone of his ambitions.[6] The COVID-19 pandemic gave rise to scapegoating of Chinese and Chinese Americans and increased hate crimes against Asian Americans. President Trump insisted on calling the coronavirus disease a "Chinese virus."

A Pew Research Center survey shows that regardless of who is president, the political divide in the country has steadily worsened in the twenty-five years since the poll was first given. That same trend applies to political differences, which are now seen as a bigger conflict than race or gender ones.[7] Major legislation on critical issues like immigration, infrastructure, taxation, and trade have been nearly impossible to pass in the past two decades. While politics is not within its legislative mandate, politics is the crucible by which CRS was created and the landscape in which it has operated. CRS's impartiality and confidentiality serve CRS well in that regard. Mediation, facilitation, and other conciliation services have and continue to serve this country well when dealing with political gridlock and enmity.[8]

In this political climate, since 2016, hate crimes have occurred at greater frequency. The 2017 FBI Hate Crimes Report revealed a 17 percent increase in hate crimes that year, which was the third year in a row that hate crimes have risen. A 37 percent increase in anti-Semitic crimes also took place in 2017. Note that FBI data has often been criticized for underreporting, as only 12 percent of law enforcement agencies submitted reports regarding hate crimes in 2017.[9] While the FBI reported 7,175 criminal hate crime incidents that year, the Bureau of Justice Statistics estimates upward of 250,000 hate crimes. The Southern Poverty Law Center reported in 2019 that the number of hate groups operating in the United States has reached an all-time high.[10]

What Levine observed in the first edition may be even truer today, given the stoking of nativist, anti-immigrant, and race-based fears. In the first edition, Levine observed that the impact of America's changing population had triggered a rising number of hate crimes and provided a foretaste of future stress as the nation adjusts to the transition from being predominantly white to being a country in which whites will be in the minority.[11] Demographic changes involve not only immigrants from Asia, Eastern Europe, Mexico, and other Latin American countries. The problem is compounded by a major population shift within the country, as "new Americans" follow jobs and relatives to areas of new settlement. Many of these formerly "untouched" communities are in outlying suburbs and in small cities outside major metropolitan areas. These population movements have generated a variety of clashes between newcomers and other ethnic groups, and between the newcomers and the Immigration and Naturalization Service. Anxiety about newcomers, particularly when it comes amid growing economic uncertainty, has reawakened nativist fears. Preventing and responding to hate crimes have become major CRS priorities.[12]

CONFLICT RESOLUTION AND SOCIAL JUSTICE

As I read and reread Levine's book, as I led the agency, and finally as I wrote the chapters for this new edition, the theme that came back to me over and over again was the perceived tension between conflict resolution and civil rights. The fundamental question is on the relationship between peace and justice. Skeptics of CRS working from a social justice perspective would focus on how its conciliators tamp down protest and conflict, and those are the primary tools of marginalized groups. This is reflective of an understanding of social change as resulting from conflict-applied pressure, that is, a hydraulic model of social justice.[13]

Wallace Warfield, a theorist on the nexus between social justice and conflict resolution who worked at CRS for many years, wrote, "Any intervention that diverts or bleeds off pressure does so at the expense of social change and should not be encouraged. The critical measurement of conflict resolution processes then is whether they interrupt, increase or direct the pressure."[14] In this book, the reader can reflect on this measurement for every CRS case. For example, in Sanford, Florida, conciliators helped protestors like the National Action Network and Dream Defenders work with local and state government officials and law enforcement to enable voices to be heard while preventing injury and possibly worse.

Neutrality is at the heart of this question too. CRS conciliators, both historically and certainly in my experience as the agency's director, have to be seen as impartial and unbiased in order to work in the highly polarized and politically charged environments CRS works in. Add to that the fact that CRS is within the Department of Justice, the only federal agency whose title is a moral value, so following rules and regulations is imperative. Yet the reality is also that CRS's stated goals and jurisdictional mandate are provided by the 1964 Civil Rights Act and the 2009 Hate Crimes Prevention Act, laws that advanced social justice dramatically. All of this informs a complex, nuanced role for CRS conciliators. As you read this book, you will find that the third-party conflict resolution role is much broader than what we conventionally think of for court-based mediation and other types of dispute resolution, which focus on procedural rather than substantive justice.

This reflects a similar dynamic that exists for international conflict resolution, that is, peace and human rights. It should be no surprise that so many of the actors in this book went on to international diplomacy, including James Laue, Andrew Young, Wallace Warfield, and Richard Salem.

Change comes through confrontation and conflict. Just as I was finishing this book, I walked through the Menlo College Bowman Library and saw a poster for Black History Month. It contained a quote by Martin Luther King that reads, "True peace is not merely the absence of tension; it is the presence of justice." This speaks to the goal of CRS's work in that it has always been an amalgamation of those two invaluable cornerstones of American society. Effective CRS conciliation work has been about both the short term and the long term, bringing parties together, enabling them to solve critical problems on their own, reflecting that American democratic ethos, and advancing toward more truly just outcomes while prioritizing nonviolence.

Clarence Jones, in the foreword to this book, captures the best of CRS strategy to reach that goal of achieving both justice and peace, saying the Community Relations Service may have been the federal statutory embodiment of the "nonviolent pursuit of social justice, embodying Dr. King's philosophical commitment to nonviolence based on the legacy of Mohandas K. Gandhi." Even the term CRS workers go by, "conciliator," captures the quest each one of them has taken to advance the cause laid out by the 1964 Civil Rights Act and the 2009 Shepard and Byrd Hate Crimes Prevention Act. The Latin root *conciliare* means to unite, and in a world where people are torn apart, the need for uniting peace and justice continues.

A NOTE ON SOURCES

To maintain consistency with the original book by Bertram Levine, I consulted many of the same sources as the original author. For example, I went through all the CRS annual reports. While I focused on annual reports for the years Levine did not cover, beginning with 1990, I also consulted all the preceding ones. The Civil Rights Mediation Oral History Project by former CRSer Richard Salem and University of Denver's Heidi and Guy Burgess was likewise particularly helpful, as they conducted in-depth interviews with CRS conciliators who worked after 1989. I extensively utilized these recollections of events, such as those articulated by Reinaldo Rivera concerning the 9/11 tragedy. Like Levine, I conducted a number of interviews, primarily with CRS conciliators, to gain insight on how the work was done.

While Levine noted using the internet, many more sources were available online by the time I began this second edition. Like the first author, I started with the *New York Times* and *Washington Post* to provide details, background, and context for CRS work discussed in this volume. I also drew not only on articles and books but also on videos that have been produced about these conflicts. Because this edition, like the first, is intended for a general rather than a purely academic audience, I follow my predecessor's restrained approach to endnotes. In addition, I searched for photographs, which the first edition did not have. I felt it was important to show photos of the conciliators who labored in these conflicts in anonymity and little, if any, fanfare.

Grande Lum

NOTES

1. Community Relations Service, *America's Peacemaker Community Relations Service Annual Report Fiscal Year 2012* (Washington, D.C.: Department of Justice, 2012), v, https://perma.cc/A8LA-KYUB.

2. Mayer, *Beyond Neutrality*, 102.

3. For firsthand accounts of CRS work in Los Angeles after the police beating of Rodney King, see "Stephen Thom," Civil Rights Mediation.org, February 6, 2002, https://perma.cc/PSN2-ZUZH, and "Silke Hansen," Civil Rights Mediation.org, August 3, 1999, https://perma.cc/BV5E-2J92.

4. For firsthand CRS accounts of Native American repatriation work, see "Stephen Thom" and Klugman, Thom, and Myers, "Mediation and Native American Repatriation of Human Remains."

5. Salem, "Mediating Political and Social Conflicts."

6. The Trump Administration has called for the elimination of CRS. For more, see Monroe, "An Attack on America's Peacemakers."

7. "In a Politically Polarized Era, Sharp Divides in Both Partisan Coalitions," Pew Research Center, U.S. Politics and Policy, December 17, 2019, https://perma.cc/WUN9-BT3X.

8. Menkel-Meadow, "Why We Can't 'Just All Get Along.'"

9. "2017 Hate Crime Statistics," U.S. Department of Justice, Federal Bureau of Investigation, https://perma.cc/K5QK-F7H3.

10. "Majority of Hate Crimes Victimizations Go Unreported to Police," U.S. Department of Justice, Office of Justice Programs, Bureau of Justice Statistics, June 29, 2017, https://perma.cc/SRX3-4JLT.

11. Minorities already outnumber whites in many urban school systems and in a number of cities. The shift is projected to occur for the nation as a whole by the middle of the twenty-first century.

12. Community Relations Service, U.S. Department of Justice, Bulletin, "Hate Crime: The Violence of Intolerance," 1998, https://perma.cc/8L4L-QE3K.

13. L. A. Coser, *The Functions of Social Conflict* (London: Routledge and Kegan Paul, 1956).

14. Wallace Warfield and Mara Schoeny, "Is Maintaining Peace Always Right?" in Pfund, ed., *From Conflict Resolution to Social Justice*, 117.

TWO LINES OF American graffiti explain the impulse that generated this book. "*Pasado por aqui*—I passed by here" is how the awestruck conquistadores recorded on canyon walls their wonderment at being the first Europeans to behold the magnificence of the American Southwest. "Kilroy was here" is how the American GI chose to attest his presence as a participating witness to the cataclysmic events of World War II.

From 1964 to 1989, I was a participating witness to a different kind of American adventure—not comparable in scale, but certainly worthy of a footnote in history, which it did not seem likely to get. This book was written to provide that footnote—and because I wanted to record that I was there.

Sometime in 1988, about a year before my retirement from the Community Relations Service (CRS) of the Justice Department, Calvin Kytle called to ask if I had ever considered writing a book about CRS. Kytle was then a book publisher. We had first met when I joined CRS, a pinpoint of a federal agency, during the year of its birth, when he was the deputy director. That call fertilized the seed of an idea that had just begun to tease me. The Community Relations Service of the Justice Department had provided the nation with a unique and important service during a critical—and dangerous—period of history, and virtually nobody knew anything about it. Here was a book that cried out to be written.

The brainchild of President Lyndon Johnson, CRS was created to work behind the scenes to reduce racial violence and to speed peaceful acceptance of the changes that the new civil rights laws demanded. The strictures of the law that created CRS, and the modus operandi of the agency, which included respect for confidentiality and the avoidance of unnecessary publicity, fostered a self-effacing style of operation. As a result, CRS became one of Washington's best-kept secrets.

My original idea was to tell the story of a small band of men and women—Black, white, Hispanic, Asian American, and Native American—whose duty every day was to rush to the heart of racial controversy to lessen the violence and move the scene of action from the streets to the conference table. These were the conciliators and mediators through whose efforts CRS addressed more than a thousand hostile encounters a year in hundreds of cities and towns in every state of the union. But it soon became apparent that the story was larger than the sum of individual achievements and adventures.

During its first twenty-five years the agency had done more than calm troubled waters in individual locales. The weight of so many healings in so many places for so many years clearly affected many behavioral patterns as well as the quality of intergroup relationships nationwide. In the process, the agency itself had developed a unique ethos and persona that had to be depicted, and a record that needed to be brought to light.

From the outset I wanted to avoid making this a personal memoir. I had not been hired to be one of the peacemakers. My job was to aid and abet. The "I" began to crawl into the narrative only when my own infrequent ventures into "the field" provided me with the best available data about a particular circumstance. My use of the first person also crops up when my duties as a "chairborne commando" made me central to certain operations essential to the story.

My relative anonymity, however, left a gap in the book that was pointed out by Robert Dentler, one of the outside scholars called upon by the publisher for an evaluation of the manuscript. Dentler, whose long involvement in civil rights matters had made him familiar with the Community Relations Service, suggested that "Levine describe his own role in the CRS, his relation to the actors in his book, and above all his methods in preparing this history." I took his point to mean that the reader deserved to be informed just how the author derived the authority to write what he wrote. Hence this preface of how I became qualified to relate the life and times of the CRS.

That requires a trip behind the scenes.

I joined the Community Relations Service early in 1965 when a still-skeletal staff of conciliators was rocketing from crisis to crisis, mostly in the rural South. My job was to provide liaison with the private sector. That meant to cultivate a symbiotic relationship with national membership organizations whom we might be able to help and who might be able to help us. Religious social action agencies and civil rights organizations needed to let their local constituents know that federal troubleshooters were available, and we needed to have access to their local leaders. Organizations like the U.S. Chamber of Commerce could put us in touch with influential local business leaders who knew that racial controversy was bad for business. This linkage with national organizations, so important when the infant CRS needed to develop resources, was always a useful tool. The American Jewish Committee, the National Urban League, the International Association of Chiefs of Police, the AFL-CIO, the National Council of Churches, and the National Education Association were typical of groups that partnered with CRS on various projects to reduce racial bias and support compliance with civil rights laws.

Within months, I was part of a CRS team that became the spearhead of a special multiagency federal effort, headed by Vice President Hubert Humphrey, to help the most troubled cities get through the summer of 1965 without the civil disorder that had flared up the previous summer. In less than a year my boss, Roger Wilkins, was appointed by President Johnson to be the director of CRS. Roger picked me to fill his old position as assistant director in charge of the Office of Community Action. "Community Action" was a euphemism for "doing whatever it takes to speed compliance with civil rights law beyond what the conciliation staff did in local communities." Mostly we worked to find, motivate, assist, and help target the resources of potential allies. We enlisted other federal agencies in the fight and helped local governments to create and improve human relations commissions. We joined with private sector organizations in national programs to support human rights objectives.

I continued to work for CRS for the next twenty-three years, mostly as assistant director or associate director. While titles and portfolios changed, at one time or another I directed almost every area of activity that supported the conflict resolution program, except for the conciliation staff itself. The following description of three of these management systems may illustrate the extent and variety of my exposure to racial conflict in America and how CRS addressed it.

(1) Information flow. In a typical year CRS might be alerted to about two thousand racial confrontations in four to five hundred communities. After an initial assessment of causes and

possible consequences, we tried to resolve about half of them, recording the effort in carefully structured case reports. All of these data were accumulated in the Management Information System, where it was studied to monitor case process and staff performance and analyzed for insight into what was happening in America. The data were also mined for information that enabled CRS to use its experience to develop training activities that continually upgraded our conflict resolution abilities.

(2) Program development. Since the demand for CRS's services always exceeded its capacity to perform, limited resources had to be focused in areas and on problems where they would do the most good. Annual work plans for each region, and nationally, identified needs, set priorities, and made choices as to program emphasis: a short-range focus to quell violent symptoms or a long-range focus to address causes of conflict; working for a quick settlement and then moving on or striving for a problem-solving process that would build relationships and enable antagonists to work out future problems on their own; responding to a freedom-of-residence conflict in one town or to a Ku Klux Klan demonstration in another. For many years the information and program development activities were supplemented by the Annual Assessment of Racial Tension. When the nation was concerned with the high incidence of urban civil disorder, CRS eschewed the popular guessing game of riot prediction. Nevertheless, for our own planning purpose, veteran conciliators, in and out of troubled areas all year long, were called upon to hone their intuitive judgments with supporting data, to help identify places of concern. In the eighties this process evolved into a fairly accurate system of identifying cities of greatest risk. It required that every field representative study a specially constructed battery of quantifiable social indicators that, in their aggregate, CRS had found to be significant in distinguishing risk levels. These data were used by regional offices in preventive planning for work in critical cities. The findings were always treated with great secrecy to avoid self-fulfilling prophecy or political exploitation.

(3) Accountability. The CRS field representative has been likened to the Lone Ranger, the stranger, armed with nothing but

his own resources, who comes to help a beleaguered community. An apocryphal story from CRS's early years has a neophyte conciliator calling on the titan of American police chiefs, William H. Parker of Los Angeles—ace crime fighter, dominating administrator, national political mogul. The conciliator said, "Chief, I'm here to help with your police-community relations. Tell me your problems, and then give me a list of your worst troublemakers so that I can get their side of the story." Parker immediately phoned the attorney general and said, "General, this is a courtesy call to thank you for the man from CRS— whom I'm about to throw out of my office."

Literally, there are just three degrees of separation between a CRS field representative and the attorney general. The relationship is symbolized by a black leatherette ID folder with gold lettering: "Department of Justice." While it rarely needs to be shown, this badge of office conveys great authority. It is a license to intervene, on the agency's own motion, in the affairs of a community and to act as a catalyst that may alter the community chemistry. This short chain of command (attorney general—CRS director—regional director—field representative) imposes a heavy responsibility on the CRS actors to be worthy of the trust.[1] Systems were emplaced to guide the exercise of discretion and assure accountability. An Operational Planning System clarified the rules of engagement, determining criteria for opening and closing cases and specifying how progress would be reported and monitored. Various quality-assurance programs were employed to make sure that fieldwork accorded to the highest standards of case practice. Peer review panels were used to backtrack a sampling of cases, reviewing paperwork and interviewing antagonists and observers in the field, so that when the director reported to the attorney general or to Congress he knew he could rely on the quality of the casework and the accuracy of its reporting.

This rendering of account by the director was an institutionalized ritual that CRS always approached as though its life depended upon it—as it sometimes did. As a tiny agency, working outside the limelight, with no significant constituency or political sponsor, it often had to struggle for political and budgetary support. With every new administration, with the accession of every new attorney general, with every annual budgetary submission, there came an opportunity and a requirement for the director of CRS to analyze the state of race relations in America, to recount CRS's record in ameliorating racial violence and resolving conflict, and to define the continuing need for its services. For many years coordination of the task of making the case for the director's presentation fell within my portfolio.

With this background as my base, writing the book should have been easy. From the outset I knew the themes I wanted to touch on and was informed about many of the cases that could illustrate them. I knew the personalities of most of the CRS actors and had worked side by side with many of them. I understood the community dynamics that impacted on the CRS mission and that, in turn, were impacted by CRS.

In one way, I felt hampered by information overload. Selection of material was painful, involving the reduction of an original outline of eighteen chapters to a book with eleven. Another hazard was the need to distinguish between memory and lingering impression. The burden of my research, therefore, was to confirm or correct what I thought I knew, to find enriching detail, and to better inform my understanding of the social climate in which events took place.

My principal resources for CRS activities were of three types. One was the interviews I conducted, specifically for this purpose, with many of my CRS colleagues. For further understanding of the skills and techniques employed by CRS mediators, I reviewed the online collection of interviews of CRS former mediators that compose the Oral History Project conducted by Richard Salem and Heidi and Guy Burgess.[2] I also interviewed a number of government officials and civil rights leaders to develop my account of the conception and creation of CRS. My second resource was my collection of materials pack-ratted for more than a quarter of a century, including a variety of internal memorandums, informal CRS communications, operations manuals, staff training material, and case evaluation reports, as well as a sampling of CRS publications and relevant publications of other government agencies and national organizations. Third was my collection of CRS Annual Reports, each of which recounts the agency's major concerns and summarizes a good variety of each year's cases. For details of date, local color, and chronology, I most frequently went to the files of the *New York Times* and the *Washington Post*.

That's how I learned about what CRS did and how it did it. I also had the benefit of twenty-four years of professional and personal interaction with my CRS colleagues.

While I share with the reader the obvious question as to whether familiarity may have clouded the author's objectivity, I trust that my many years of studying CRS's performance for shortfalls as well as achievements has resulted in a reasonably balanced report.

Bertram Levine

NOTES

1. In later years, the reporting structure changed with the CRS director reporting to the Associate Attorney General. (note by Lum)

2. Heidi Burgess and Guy Burgess, "The Civil Rights Mediation Oral History Project," Civil Rights Mediation.org, https://perma.cc/74EG-TS2G.

ACKNOWLEDGMENTS

BERTRAM LEVINE

MANY PEOPLE WHO worked for the Community Relations Service between 1964 and 1989 consented to be interviewed by me, and I am grateful for their help and encouragement. While the contributions of only some are identified by name in the text, the work of all is meant to be represented. The picking and choosing was not value-based but opportunistic—a function of what fit with memory and with other sources of information and of a practical need to boil eighteen chapters of original intent down to a doable eleven.

I also enjoyed reading, and benefited from, the interviews of former CRS mediators that appear online as the Civil Rights Mediation Oral History Project.

I am indebted to all I interviewed, as well as to the many other CRS staff members whose experiences and insights during a quarter century enriched my understanding of the matters I have chosen to write about. The CRS staff members I interviewed include: Gonzalo Cano, Leo Cardenas, Jonathan Chace, LeRoy Collins, James Draper, Nancy Ferrell, Harold Fleming, Robert Greenwald, John Griffin, Silke Hansen, Ben Holman, Robert Hughes, Jay Janis, Julian Klugman, Calvin Kytle, Robert Lamb Jr., James Laue, Efrain Martinez, Art Montoya, John Perez, John Perry, Wilbur Reed, Dennis Renault, Victor Risso, Richard Salem, Manuel Salinas, Seymour Samet, A. M. Secrest, Ozell Sutton, Jesse Taylor, Abraham Venable, Martin Walsh, Wallace Warfield, Roger Wilkins.

The story of CRS's creation and first years was greatly illuminated for me as a result of interviews with several participants in, or close observers of, that process. These include Arnold Aronson, Hyman Bookbinder, John Doar, David Filvaroff, Nicholas Katzenbach, Burke Marshall, Harry McPherson, Joseph Rauh, Gerald Siegel, John Siegenthaler, Theodore Sorensen, John Stewart, Lee White.

James Laue enriched his interviews with the gift of relevant CRS papers from his personal collection. His widow, Mariann, later gave me the bulk of his CRS files. Harold Fleming augmented his interviews by later sending me a copy of the CRS chapter of his then work in progress, *The Potomac Chronicle*, which was ultimately completed by his widow, Virginia, and published by the University of Georgia Press.

The program, performance, and ethos of the Community Relations Service described in this book were shaped and influenced by many members of its staff. None had a more significant impact on it than the founding director, LeRoy Collins, who invested it with his reputation for rectitude, fairness, and goodwill; Roger Wilkins, who imbued it with the sense of mission that continued to energize the organization for many years after his incumbency as director; and Gilbert Pompa, whose earlier experience as a CRS conciliator gave a sense of reality to his drive as director to continually elevate the standards of professional performance. Although this narrative focuses on the work of CRS field representatives, the character and quality of that work were enhanced by a leadership cadre that helped to provide guidance and essential "body English." Among those who provided this distinguished service over the years are Jonathan Chace, George Culberson, Harry Martin, Roscoe Nix, Gail Padgett, and Wallace Warfield. Perhaps the most underappreciated heroes of the service were its regional directors, who, because of the small size of the agency, contributed significantly to the formulation of national programs, while they bore responsibility for all conflict resolution in their multistate regions and personally mediated some of the most critical cases. Representative of this group are: Leo Cardenas, Julian Klugman, Robert Lamb Jr., John Perez, Richard Salem, Ozell Sutton, Jesse Taylor, and Martin Walsh. Senior mediators Edward Howden and Lawrence Turner were master trainers who could be counted on for exemplary work in the most demanding of special assignments.

My writing efforts were vastly improved thanks to the critical analyses of Caroline Eisenberg, Daniel Fischell, Gerson Goodman, and Rebecca Salokar. I am indebted to the companionate professional interests of my sons, David and Neil, who provided ever available sounding boards during the full length of an overlong writing journey. The continuing faith of my daughter, Susan Rae, and the encouragement of friends Sandra and Andrew Boots, Marjorie Eiseman, and Maxine Fischell always provided a boost. Elizabeth Lewis was a pillar of support when the going was tough.

GRANDE LUM

I START BY thanking Bertram Levine's children (Neil, David, and Susan Rae) as they have been gracious to me in numerous ways and this book would not have been accomplished but for their openness, encouragement, and support. My hope is that this new edition helps further Bertram Levine's goals for the book of recording a different kind of American adventure: an agency that provided a unique and important service.

Of course, I am indebted to those who worked at the Community Relations Service while I was director as they were the ones who did the hard work each and every day. I am grateful for those who worked at CRS throughout its history and who helped bridge differences in communities across the country. This includes the conciliators and also all the administrative and operational staff, the even-more-unsung heroes who made the CRS service possible. While I name a number of conciliators who worked during this period, I, like Levine, intended this book to be representative of all CRSers who have served the agency.

CRS staffers I interviewed include Thomas Battles, Nancy Ferrell, Edward Howden, Pascual Marquez, Efrain Martinez, Ed McClure, Rosa Melendez, Becky Monroe, Paul Monteiro, Rose Ochi, Werner Petterson, Richard Salem, P. Diane Schneider, Ozell Sutton, Stephen Thom, Martin Walsh, Roger Wilkins, and Ron Wong. Since I interviewed them, Roger Wilkins, Ozell Sutton, Richard Salem, Martin Walsh, and Edward Howden—each a civil rights and conflict resolution icon—have passed on, and I feel privileged and fortunate to have known them.

I am especially grateful to the Ohio State University Law School professor and former dean Nancy Rogers for both enabling me to continue working with communities to transform polarization into collaborative action at the Divided Community Project and to reflect on the Community Relations Service work with more insight. Along with Richard Salem, she also cowrote one of the first law school textbooks on mediation, much of which was based on CRS work. Nancy graciously agreed to write an afterword to help place CRS's work in greater context. Others at the Divided Community Project were incredibly supportive and helped me think more critically about CRS and clarify my writing. These great colleagues included Josh Stulberg, Bill Froehlich, Sarah Cole, and Carl Smallwood. I also had the opportunity to test much in this work with Ohio State students in classes and with those who worked on the Divided Community Project initiatives. They were a joy to work with. In addition, the project's steering committee, which included Andrew Thomas, Susan Carpenter, Sarah Rubin, Craig McEwen, Chris Carlson, RaShall Brackney, and Michael Lewis, were so generous with their time and expertise.

Thanks to the Judicial Arbitration and Mediation Services (JAMS) Foundation, especially David Brandon, Jay Welsh, and Jay Folberg, for their tremendous support including three significant grants to the Divided Community Project. The JAMS Foundation transformed the Divided Community Project from a vision to a reality at a time when the country was in dire need of dispute resolution support.

Writing this book required the agreement of the original publisher, the University of Missouri Press. Clair Willcox and Gary Kass believed in the importance of this project from the get go, and I am appreciative of their work throughout the process.

Deep gratitude goes to Stanford Law School Gould Center director Jan Martinez for providing a research fellowship and an office during the research and writing process, as well as her continuous support of civil rights community conflict resolution work. In addition, she gave me the opportunity to teach at Stanford on resolving this type of community conflict, which helped me develop this new edition as well. Longtime colleague and Stanford lecturer Jonathan Greenberg provided thoughtful critique and introduced me to Clarence Jones, Martin Luther King's personal lawyer and speechwriter. Admittedly I was awestruck to even meet Dr. Jones, let alone to be blessed with the privilege to speak jointly to Stanford students about civil rights and conflict resolution with him. I am also indebted to Clarence Jones for agreeing to write a foreword for this new edition, given his direct involvement in so many crucial 1960s civil rights pioneering events and providing here the moral arc for the CRS story. Both Stanford and Ohio State students' energy and intellect led me to consider how best to form the chapters to bolster the next generation of practitioners working at the intersection of civil rights and conflict resolution.

I would also like to thank former CRS colleagues Paul Monteiro, Daphne Felten-Green, Becky Monroe, Ann Dunn, Kathleen O'Quinn, Marlene Sallo, Sean Barrett, Melody Diegor, Natalia Casella, and Julia White for their support leading into the creation of this second edition. Thanks to my professional home, the Menlo College community, for their support, including President Steven Weiner, the librarians (especially Anne Linvill), faculty, and other staff. It has been a joy to work with undergraduates at Menlo College as they consistently reveal themselves to be beacons of hope for the future of our country.

I was incredibly fortunate to have Elisabeth Andrews play a substantial editing role in shaping and finalizing the manuscript. Elisabeth ensured my new additional chapters connected smoothly with the style of Levine's original book. She did this and more by helping craft a more compelling narrative, pointing out when more analysis was needed, increasing clarity at every turn, and overall strengthening this book many times over. Kathleen Doll assisted Elisabeth and me with additional research, editing, and putting together the index and a wonderful photo section with contribution by Veronica Lempert, which vitalizes the book that much more. Elisabeth and Kathleen ushered this project into reality much more efficiently and quickly than I would have been able to otherwise, especially as I was transitioning into a new job as provost at Menlo College.

Lastly, I want to convey special thanks to my family: my parents, Hampson and Evangeline, my brother, Jordon, and my entire extended family for their unwavering support; my wife, Nan, for her lifetime partnership; and our children, Gianna and Garren, for teaching me how to open up my heart more. The two of them highlight for me the urgency of this work. Sometimes we might despair about the polarization out in the world. But if we make our communities more united through conciliation, we create a better world for all our children.

AMERICA'S PEACEMAKERS

INTRODUCTION

THIS BOOK IS about twenty-five years of racial conflict in America (1964–89),[1] and what was done by federal conciliators to help resolve it. It recounts America's civil rights struggle as seen through the eyes of the federal agency whose observers were almost always at ground zero working with antagonists to find solutions and to avoid or lessen violence.

The book looks at the celebrated breakthroughs that made change possible and the countless follow-throughs that converted possibility to reality. It tells of what happened when "the movement" played out— after bitter and triumphant demonstrations, after great court decisions and the passage of new laws, but somehow things didn't seem to get much better. Through the lens of conflict analysis it looks at the hedge-row warfare that followed the movement's victories—where every change toward a fairer balance of equity had to be defined, demanded, and fought for—issue by issue, institution by institution, city by city. It is about the struggles to consolidate the victories.

The data are drawn largely from the eyewitness experience of the handful of men and women whose job was to be there, at the center of the storm, to help forestall or resolve racial and ethnic disputes. Based in the Community Relations Service (CRS) of the Department of Justice, this multiracial cadre of conciliation and mediation specialists worked behind the scenes in more than twenty thousand confrontations[2] involving racial and ethnic minorities. These have ranged from the disputes that attracted worldwide attention to the everyday affronts, assaults, and upheavals that marked the nation's adjustment to wider power sharing within an increasingly diverse population.

Created by Congress in the Civil Rights Act of 1964 to deal with civil rights disputes, the Community Relations Service dispatched its trouble-shooters to help at the march from Selma to Montgomery; at the urban riots of the sixties, seventies, and eighties; at the siege of

3

Wounded Knee; at the school desegregation battles in the North and the South; and at the Gulf Coast fishing wars between Southeast Asians and Anglos. It helped to lessen the atmosphere of racial violence in every major American city and in many thousands of smaller communities.

CRS was not quite a year old on the night of June 4, 1965, when President Johnson spoke to the nation by radio from Howard University. He concluded by pronouncing a new civil rights goal.

> But freedom is not enough. You do not wipe away the scars of centuries by saying: now you are free to go where you want, do as you desire, and choose the leaders you please . . . it is not enough just to open the gates of opportunity. All our citizens must have the ability to walk through those gates. . . . This is the next and more profound stage of the battle for civil rights. We seek not just freedom but opportunity—not just legal equity but human ability—not just equality as a right and a theory, but equality as a fact and as a result.

The definition of the American condition as set forth by the president that night, and the new civil rights goal he specified, was to forecast the role of the Community Relations Service for the next quarter of a century and more. The battle for equality as a right and a theory had largely been won. The battle for equality as a fact and as a result lay ahead. It would have to be fought in all walks of life, especially on the local scene—in cities, counties, neighborhoods, and individual institutions. CRS would be there to witness the conflict and to help ease its pains.

NOTES

1. Now expanded to fifty-five years, 1964–2019. (note by Lum)
2. Now more than forty thousand. (note by Lum)

PART I

ONE

Lyndon Johnson Sets the Stage

IT WAS JULY 2, 1964. After a decade of racial turmoil, after a year of anguished debate, including a record eighty-three-day filibuster in the Senate, Congress—in the face of still solid southern resistance—had passed the most sweeping civil rights legislation since the post–Civil War period. President Lyndon Johnson was about to sign it, and the White House spared no effort to dramatize the moment.

The Civil Rights Act was rushed to the president within hours of final congressional approval. In the East Room the stage had been set for a full-production signing ceremony at which the president's message would be loud and clear. The media had been alerted so that the word would go forth during prime time. All the leaders of the civil rights movement, the most powerful members of Congress, and the key figures of the Justice Department had been invited to share the moment that would crown their labors and establish the law.

The citizens of a concerned nation were looking on, many with grave doubts and questions. For minorities—particularly Blacks—the question was: would the federal government make sure that the law was obeyed? For southerners, it was: would federal enforcement bring the "police state" that some of their spokesmen had decried? For conservatives, it was: how much federal intrusion would there be in local affairs? For most Americans—and for the president himself—there was one overarching question: would this end the violence, or would defiance of the new law require harsh federal enforcement that would add fuel to the already inflamed passions that had been tearing the country apart?

Chapters 1–10 are reprinted from Bertram Levine, *Resolving Racial Conflict:The Community Relations Service and Civil Rights, 1964–1989* (Columbia: University of Missouri Press, 2005).

TO HELP THE MEDICINE GO DOWN

The Civil Rights Act of 1964 was strong medicine. It reached into the fiber and tissue of American society, creating new channels for redress of racial discrimination. It declared job discrimination unlawful and created the Equal Employment Opportunities Commission. It outlawed segregation in all publicly supported facilities and certain establishments serving the general public. It strengthened protections of equality in voting and in education. It required policies of racial equity in every institution that accepted a dollar of federal assistance.

The president's remarks were a plea for reconciliation. He sounded a call for voluntary compliance. He made little reference to the substance of the new law; he spoke, instead, of how he was going to help the medicine go down. He discussed none of the details of what the legislation contained save for one of its lesser—and little-debated—provisions. This was the establishment in the Department of Commerce of a federal mechanism for the conciliation of racial conflict. The Community Relations Service had been created to help communities voluntarily reduce racial violence and comply with civil rights laws.

The reason for his special emphasis was rooted in his understanding of the times. It also reflected the impact of the previous ten years on Lyndon Johnson the man and Lyndon Johnson the politician.

During this time period, racial conflict born of resistance to the African American thrust for social and economic equity had been searing the American consciousness for a full ten years. It started with the Supreme Court's landmark school desegregation decision in May 1954, which was followed two months later by the formation in Mississippi of the first fortress of opposition, the White Citizens Council. Similar organizations then mushroomed throughout the South. Massive resistance to school desegregation followed. This was marked by violence, intimidation, school closings, and confrontations between Blacks and whites, between federal law enforcement agents and local communities.

The killing of fourteen-year-old Emmett Till in 1955 had been headlined around the world as symbolic of brutally enforced repression of Blacks in America. Ensuing years were marked by a string of dramatic events. There was the Montgomery bus boycott and the consequent birth of the Southern Christian Leadership Conference (SCLC). There were the sit-ins and freedom rides and the birth of the Student Nonviolent Coordinating Committee (SNCC). There were the torchings and bombings of Black churches and the homes of civil rights leaders. There were the murders of civil rights activists. There was the application of federal force: to enforce school desegregation in Little Rock; to face down Governor George Wallace's effort to bar the entry of a Black student at the University of Alabama; to assure safe entry of Blacks at the University of Georgia and the University of Mississippi. There were the assaults by law enforcement agencies on peaceful protesters in Birmingham. And there was the 1963 March on Washington by a quarter-million advocates of civil rights legislation.

In June 1964, at the very time that Congress was bringing the Civil Rights Act to its culminating votes, the nation's headlines reflected a fever of racial violence. Eight hundred whites assaulted a civil rights demonstration in St. Augustine, Florida, hospitalizing nineteen African Americans. The disappearance (and suspected murder) of three civil rights workers in Mississippi alarmed the nation, causing the president to send hundreds of military personnel to help search for the bodies. Thousands of northern college students were recruited and trained for civil rights work in the South that summer. The Justice Department warned that the federal government lacked the jurisdiction and resources to guarantee their safety.[1]

The disproportionate attention given by Johnson at the signing ceremony to the Community Relations Service and to voluntary compliance reflected his reading of the temper of the times. Millions of whites bitterly resented, and many feared, the imposition of federal law that would wipe away a cherished way of life. Millions of Blacks—and whites as well—were determined that the new law, won after ten years of protest in the face of violent resistance, must be obeyed. Many Americans saw the potential for new violence. As a pragmatist, Johnson believed in the value of persuasion and negotiation. As a politician facing nomination and election challenges later in the year, he knew he had to stand four-square behind the nation's now highly popular civil rights goals. At the same time, he must, at all cost, avoid circumstances that might require him to order U.S. troops to take action—at gunpoint if necessary—against a resistant South.

LEGISLATIVE HISTORY

Johnson's advocacy of a federal conflict resolution capability contrasted sharply with the less-than-major priority assigned to that provision by the civil rights bill's staunchest advocates. Most of them looked upon it as a useful adornment but not critical. LBJ, on the other hand, was personally committed to nurturing it and assuring achievement of its full potential. For the next two years he gave it closer personal attention than he did any other federal agency of such relatively microscopic proportions. He gave it higher priority than did any president who followed him.

Johnson had first envisioned a federal agency to mediate racial conflict seven years earlier, during Senate consideration of the Civil Rights Act of 1957. It reflected his conviction that most conflict could be negotiated. "Let us reason together" was a well-worn phrase in his Senate—and later in his White House—vocabulary. Why not create a racial conflict resolution service similar to the Federal Mediation and Conciliation Service, which mediated labor disputes? He took his idea to Arthur Goldberg, a distinguished labor relations lawyer (later to serve as a Supreme Court justice and as U.S. ambassador to the United Nations). At Johnson's request Goldberg and Gerald Siegel, counsel to the Senate Policy Committee (which Johnson chaired as majority leader), worked up proposed legislation. But Johnson did not introduce it. Rowland Evans and Robert Novak reported: "Ben Cohen had told Johnson repeatedly that it would never satisfy the liberals. The proposal never left Johnson's pocket."[2] The civil rights bill that was enacted in 1957 authorized the creation of two other agencies—the independent Civil Rights Commission and the Civil Rights Division of the Department of Justice.

Johnson waited until the next session of Congress to introduce a bill calling for creation of a Community Relations Service. It envisioned a race relations agency with a staff of one hundred working out of regional offices to help local communities when disagreement threatened to disrupt peaceful relations among citizens.

Johnson's speech introducing that bill—considered by the Senate Judiciary Committee, but never acted upon—reflected an acute understanding of the dynamics of community conflict and a vision of the inevitability of civil rights changes. It was years ahead of what the public would hear from any other high-ranking official.

The idea of a federal conciliation effort in the civil rights field caught on in other quarters. The Civil Rights Commission proposed that a conciliation function, to be focused on school desegregation, be added to the commission's own responsibilities. Harris Wofford, counsel of the commission (later to be the civil rights flag bearer of the Kennedy White House and still later a U.S. senator from Pennsylvania), reported in his book *Of Kennedys and Kings*:

> The Commission also recommended that it be authorized "to establish an advisory and conciliation service to assist local school officials in developing plans designed to meet constitutional requirements and local conditions and to mediate and conciliate, upon request, disputes as to proposed plans and their implementation." This was an idea that Lyndon Johnson had been advancing for several years. Civil rights leaders tended to look askance at any such approach that implied mediation instead of enforcement, but the Northern Commissioners joined their Southern colleagues in thinking such a service could be constructive.[3]

In the Eighty-seventh Congress (1961–62), bills calling for a Community Relations Service were submitted by various liberal representatives and senators. None were reported out of committee.

The comprehensive civil rights bill that the Kennedy administration submitted to the Eighty-eighth Congress on June 19, 1963, did provide, in its original Title IV, for the establishment of a Community Relations Service. It was consistent in form and function with the original Johnson proposal of 1959. It had not been included in the White House staff's original conception of the bill but had been added as an afterthought.

Even though Vice President Johnson was chairman of the President's Committee on Equal Employment Opportunity, White House staff had failed to include him in the earliest discussions of the proposed civil rights legislation. Lee White, who served as presidential counsel and civil rights point man under both Kennedy and Johnson, recalls that Johnson brooded about this. "He was a proud and in some ways a sensitive guy. He did not want to insinuate himself. But if President Kennedy asked him to do something, he was delighted."[4] Finally, in the last days before the bill was sent to Congress, President Kennedy directed that LBJ be drawn into the circle, and for the duration of the Kennedy administration he energetically served as a major civil rights strategist.

Theodore C. Sorensen, one of President Kennedy's closest advisers, recalls Johnson proposing the creation of the Community Relations

Service in the course of a long telephone conversation between Sorensen and LBJ on June 3, 1963. Sorensen had called to get the vice president's input for the civil rights bill then reaching its final stages of refinement. In his book *Kennedy*, Sorensen notes that the bill, as finally submitted, "was different in several respects from the bill we had first discussed with Justice the previous month. . . . With the backing of the Vice President, a Community Relations Service had been added to work quietly with local communities in search of progress. (Negro congressmen had urged that the words 'mediation' and 'conciliation' had an 'Uncle Tom' air about them and should be stricken from the title.)"[5]

Burke Marshall, who was Robert Kennedy's assistant attorney general for civil rights, headed the Justice Department's effort to draft a bill that would be both effective and passable. He, too, credits Johnson with primary influence in putting the CRS provision into the legislation.[6]

Johnson's 1958 advocacy of a Community Relations Service is one of the early bits of data that must be considered in the long-running debate of whether LBJ came to be a civil rights partisan as a result of nurture or nature—of politics or commitment. In the late fifties, Johnson was regarded by the civil rights community as "the enemy." Starting as a Texas congressman in 1939, and then as senator, he had voted against every civil rights measure that had been proposed. As majority leader of the Senate, he had orchestrated the fight against all efforts to weaken the filibuster—the parliamentary device by which the southern minority had been able to resist all civil rights proposals.

Then Johnson made a 180-degree turn on civil rights, according to his most bitter foes. Arnold Aronson, who for almost three decades had been the executive secretary of the Leadership Conference on Civil Rights, said:

> Lyndon Johnson was the one who beat us all the time. So from that point of view we regarded him as the enemy. And in '57 it was Lyndon Johnson who engineered the act's passage by removing what we regarded as the most important part, which was Title III, which was injunctive power. So Johnson was the enemy. My own feeling, based on what happened later, was that we were wrong. Lyndon Johnson in the early years really identified primarily with his experience with Hispanics more than with Blacks. And you find in the early period, long before he became prominent, that there

were evidences that he really felt something which as a southern politico he couldn't show. Remember, there were only three southern
members of the Senate who didn't sign the Southern Manifesto.[7]
One of them was Lyndon Johnson. My feeling is that he did what
he could. And as soon as he had the clout of the presidency, he
went all the way. I think it was genuine. There's no question he was
the greatest president so far as civil rights is concerned. Whether
we could have gotten this bill through in the shape that it is with
Kennedy, I doubt very much. Johnson addressed the joint session
five days after the assassination. He said, "This is the Kennedy
legacy and we are going to pass it." It was the first priority that he
took on. We didn't have to pressure the White House the way we
normally did. He was after us. He'd be calling all the time. Have
you done this, have you been in touch with X, have you thought
about Y. He used all of his political pressures and leverage and
know-how.[8]

Joseph Rauh, as counsel for the Leadership Conference on Civil Rights,
had been at the forefront of those lobbying for congressional action.
He saw Johnson as struggling between his dues-paying obligation to
his southern constituency and the requirement of his political ambition
to win acceptance within the broadest spectrum of both the party and
the electorate. To find and focus on "safe" civil rights issues appealed
to him as an acceptable risk. One such safe issue was the Civil Rights
Commission, whose creation he had supported in the Civil Rights Act
of 1957. A second was the Community Relations Service. Both might
be defined as procedural rather than substantive. They did not, by their
creation, change anything. As Rauh put it:

> In '56, or '57, a House bill came over that was very strong on civil
> rights, and Johnson flattened it. He wanted a bill that could be
> called a civil rights bill that wouldn't get him in dutch with Texas.
> So what he did was to say to guys like us—Clarence Mitchell and
> me, primarily—who were the chief lobbyists for the Leadership
> Conference, "I'm giving you these things."
>
> What he "gave" us were largely things for which people couldn't
> hit him too hard: a Civil Rights Commission and an assistant at-
> torney general for civil rights. (Which also meant a Civil Rights

Division.) He had to fight us on the important things like school desegregation.

In '59, when he proposed the Community Relations Service—that, too, was of a character that doesn't get Texas anti–civil rights people up in arms. You've got to have people who try to keep the peace. It was the perfect Johnsonian thing. He needed things to help his national ambition to be president, but as a Texas senator he also needed to make sure the right wing down there wouldn't beat him up politically.

Johnson's role as an advocate of the 1964 legislation first became apparent to the civil rights leaders when a group of them were invited to meet with President Kennedy and his staff for a briefing on the new bill. Rauh remembered:

On the twenty-first of June 1963, President Kennedy called the leaders of the civil rights groups to the White House. He left that meeting after about an hour, and Johnson, the vice president, and Robert Kennedy, the attorney general, remained. I didn't know who was in charge. They hated each other's guts. I knew Bobby Kennedy was not sympathetic to strengthening the bill. I didn't know anything about Johnson. Each of us got a chance to say something. I said, "Mr. Vice-President, will we be able to work together, with us seeking strengthening amendments which you have not put in the bill, the most important of which, of course, would be the Equal Employment Opportunity Commission?"

I held my breath. And Johnson said, "I don't see why that's inconsistent at all. It never hurts for us to have pressure from the left." He gave my dream answer. He was free of all the constraints of Texas politics. He now was going to go to the left of the administration and say that we could work for those additions. And of course we did get them.[9]

Johnson's advocacy was only one of several factors arguing for inclusion of a conflict resolution capability in the Civil Rights Act. There were two others. The first was the example of effective third-party mediation in the recent settlement of conflict in Birmingham. The second was widespread concern that there would be massive resistance to the desegregation of public accommodations, and conciliation teams would be needed in countless communities to limit controversy and reduce violence.

The logic of using federal mediation to resolve community conflict had been demonstrated a number of times in the early sixties, but nowhere more dramatically than in Birmingham, where the Justice Department, at the bidding of the president, went outside its normal responsibilities of law enforcement and prosecution and sought to bring antagonists together to negotiate a settlement.

Birmingham had represented the high-water mark in protest, in anti-Black violence by law enforcement officers as well as by lawless whites, and in worldwide notoriety. Martin Luther King Jr. and six thousand others had been jailed. Public Safety Commissioner Bull Connor had become a world-class bully overnight by unleashing dogs and fire hoses on protesters in the view of television cameras.

At the same time that the protest and violence in Birmingham were reaching a crescendo, Burke Marshall had painstakingly sought to develop a negotiating dialogue. Amid a setting in which passion and posture made true communication between antagonists impossible, he discreetly worked behind the scenes to engineer confidential negotiations between a few of the more conservative African American leaders and influential pillars of the white business community. The resulting peace formula became the basis for the ultimate agreement. Recalling that venture in 1989, Marshall said:

> We had just gone through a period of demonstrations in Birmingham, which showed one thing: that is there was no way legally for the federal government to get at that problem. The demonstrations had to do with employment problems, lunch-counter problems, street problems, a whole array of disparate problems that weren't covered by the existing statutes. I spent a lot of time myself, in Birmingham, doing something that had nothing to do with my job—just to try to bring some kind of racial understanding. So there was a common understanding within the administration that that kind of work needed to be done. The only question was whether it should be institutionalized. I was in favor of institutionalizing it because it was a burden on my own time in addition to all the litigation work.[10]

In his message transmitting the civil rights bill to Congress, President Kennedy specifically cited the effective conciliation work of the Department of Justice in Birmingham. He went on to say that "dialogue and discussion are always better than violence—and this agency [the Community Relations Service], by enabling all concerned to sit down and reason together, can play a major role in achieving peaceful progress in civil rights." He wanted the new agency to "work quietly to improve relations in any community threatened or torn with strife."

In Kennedy's mind and in the minds of congressional leaders, the fear that communities might be "threatened or torn with strife" was rooted primarily in concern that throughout the South there would be widespread resistance to the provision of the new law that barred discrimination in places of public accommodation. These facilities—hotels, restaurants, gas stations, theaters, retail stores—were precisely the ones where denial of racial equality had triggered bitter protest and violent resistance in the past decade.

A confidential survey of opinions in almost six hundred southern communities indicated that while there had been some desegregation of public facilities, one-third of these towns were "dead set against all form of desegregation."[11]

It was certain that access to segregated premises would be tested by America's African American population just as soon as the law was enacted. If there was no compliance, not only would protests be resumed, but it would be incumbent on the federal government to enforce the law.

Burke Marshall could visualize a litigative nightmare. He recalled: "I was very concerned, fortunately without reason, that the bill would be signed and we would have racial discrimination in public places throughout the South made illegal overnight, and that nobody would comply with it. It would be like schools. We would have to bring a hundred thousand lawsuits. I could foresee an enormous law enforcement problem. I wanted to push every button I could find to lead people toward voluntary compliance with Title II."[12]

Negotiation and persuasion seemed to be a far better course for the federal government than legal action. The latter option would require the employment of hundreds of additional Department of Justice personnel: FBI agents to investigate charges, prosecutors to prepare the cases, marshals to enforce court orders, to say nothing of the hundreds of courtroom years.

To political leaders North and South the prospect of federal law enforcement pitted against many southern institutions for many years was one to be avoided at all cost. Also, the idea of first trying to settle conflict by negotiation was seen by many as a spoonful of sugar that might help the bitter medicine of the civil rights law go down a bit more smoothly.

To some political analysts the spoonful of sugar theory was applied even further. Cabell Phillips, writing in the *New York Times* on July 3, 1964, the day after President Johnson signed the bill into law, said:

> The Community Relations Service called for in the bill is intended primarily as a mediator that will compose the intense local feelings certain to arise under application of the public accommodations and fair employment sections of the bill. The new agency is not only to be headed by a Southerner, Governor Collins, but it is to be set up administratively in the Department of Commerce where another Southerner presides, former Governor Luther Hodges of North Carolina. Thus a conspicuous effort has been made at the *outset* to make the mediation agency acceptable to Southern leaders in whose communities its greatest effort will be concentrated.

THE WINNING OF THE CIVIL RIGHTS ACT

The Civil Rights Act of 1964 emerged from Congress with wide bipartisan support, but only after a year of debate marked by bitter conflict, heartening cross-party cooperation, and skillful dealing and manipulation within the legislative process. The proposal for a Community Relations Service, originally known as Title IV of the administration's bill, encountered little serious opposition. Neither friends nor foes of civil rights saw it as a major new protection for minorities. It was regarded merely as a possible cure for the side effects of conflict that the new law might engender. Nevertheless, the proposal almost died before birth—a victim more of neglect than of opposition.

Because of the importance attached to it, the civil rights bill was introduced jointly in Congress by Emanuel Celler, Democrat of Brooklyn, New York, and chairman of the House Judiciary Committee, and William McCulloch, Republican of Ohio and ranking minority member of the committee. Speaker John McCormick assigned it to the Judiciary

Committee, where Chairman Celler assigned it to Subcommittee 5, which he himself chaired. The subcommittee consisted of seven Democrats and four Republicans. Liberals of both parties were clearly in the majority. The overall result of the subcommittee's work was a stronger bill than the administration had proposed.[13] It was so strong that the attorney general requested a hearing before the full committee to ask that it be watered down. The administration feared that too strong a bill might impede its chances of approval by the full House and Senate. In the subcommittee hearings the CRS proposal enjoyed a modest show of support. The only specific opposition came from Representative Armistead I. Selden, an Alabama Democrat. He stated that it was not appropriate for the federal government to be involved in community relations.

The highly organized and effective civil rights lobby had been primarily concerned with preserving and strengthening the more substantive provisions of the bill. The focus of its members was on the achievement of major breakthroughs in voting rights and public accommodations. They wanted to empower the attorney general to bring suit against segregated schools and public facilities. They sought an end to discrimination in all federally assisted programs. Community relations was a far lower priority.

Arnold Aronson recalled: "We were concerned primarily with prohibiting discrimination—whether it was in public accommodations, whether it was in employment, or housing. Our interest was in establishing a body of law—and in overturning existing law—which was segregation. That was tough enough, so that we didn't give CRS any priority."[14]

Thus propelled by no more than mild favor and slight criticism, the provision for a Community Relations Service apparently became lost in the shuffle of highly charged debate. It was not part of the bill that the committee reported to the full House of Representatives. It was restored in a last-minute maneuver that has never been fully explained.

At 6:00 p.m. on February 10, 1964, after nine full days of House debate, and only two hours before the final enactment would occur, Representative Robert T. Ashmore, Democrat of South Carolina, introduced an amendment providing for a Community Relations Service.

Apparently by prearrangement, and to expedite final passage of the bill that night, Cellar and McCulloch both declared the measure to be merely technical, and acceptable to them. It was promptly adopted.

According to Charles and Barbara Whalen, "This ready concurrence was a deliberate move by the two leaders to appease conservative house members by incorporating into the law a mechanism which, if effective, would greatly reduce federal involvement in local civil rights disputes. The new title [Title X] was quickly adopted by voice vote."[15]

The big fight over the Civil Rights Act took place in the Senate, where an eighty-three-day filibuster, the longest on record, was broken by the required two-thirds vote. To weaken the traditional anti–civil rights alliance between southern Democrats and conservative Republicans, careful and convoluted political manipulation was needed. A primary focus of strategy was on winning over the minority leader of the Senate, Everett McKinley Dirksen. He was subjected to the massed persuasive power of Lyndon Johnson, Senate Majority Leader Mike Mansfield, and Senator Hubert Humphrey, the floor manager of the bill. The vehicle for victory was a Mansfield-Dirksen substitute for the House bill. The substitute did little damage to the measure passed by the lower chamber.

The CRS provision was strengthened in the Mansfield-Dirksen substitute. It differed from the House measure in four respects: It eliminated a ceiling of six on the number of regular employees. It specifically added voluntary associations to the state and local public agencies with which CRS was encouraged to cooperate. It imposed penalties of up to a year in prison and a $1,000 fine on employees who failed to hold confidential all information so imparted to them in the course of conciliation. The substitute bill also gave the Community Relations Service an additional role by writing it into Title II, which provided for injunctive relief against discrimination in places of public accommodation. The federal courts were authorized (but not required) to refer such cases to CRS for a period of up to 120 days, for purposes of working out voluntary compliance. The CRS provision received little attention in the ensuing Senate discussion. Initiating formal debate on the House bill on March 30, Senator Humphrey commented on each title. All he had to say about the CRS proposal was: "In many cases mediation and litigation work together effectively. Individual restaurant or hotel owners may be reluctant to admit Negroes unless assured that their competitors will do likewise. Through the good offices of the Community Relations Service, or of comparable state or local organizations, it may be possible to achieve agreement among all or substantially all of the owners."

During the debate, five amendments pertaining to CRS were defeated by large majorities. Senator Sam Ervin of North Carolina proposed elimination of the Community Relations Service because it would be redundant to the Civil Rights Commission and the Civil Rights Division of the Department of Justice. Senator Strom Thurmond of South Carolina offered four CRS amendments. One would have permitted breaches of confidentiality in providing information to Congress. The second would have limited the number of employees to ten. The third would have limited CRS's jurisdiction to cases affecting interstate commerce, rather than to those that *might* affect interstate commerce. The fourth would have barred CRS from entering a case except on invitation of the community.

The CRS amendments offered by Senator Thurmond were among a hundred or so he proposed covering every feature of the act. To his colleagues he was "just going through the motions," since the South had lost its case when cloture had been voted. John Stewart, legislative aide to Hubert Humphrey during both his senatorial and vice presidential years, recalls sitting next to Humphrey and Senator Richard Russell, leader of the southern wing of the Senate, during the consideration of the Thurmond amendments. Russell leaned across to Humphrey and said: "Can't we shut him up somehow?"

EFFORTS TO SOFTEN SOUTHERN RESISTANCE

Even before the congressional battle over the civil rights bill was won, the bill's backers saw the need to build massive public support. This support would be necessary not only to win passage of the law but also to win voluntary compliance with it after it was passed. Strategists in the Justice Department, the White House, and the civil rights community believed that the massive resistance that had followed the Supreme Court's school desegregation decision in 1954 had resulted in part from the silence of the more responsible political and business leaders of southern communities. The false dream that somehow delay and obstruction would prevent the inevitable change had been allowed to blossom so that the leaders themselves became prisoners of the call for resistance. To avoid that scenario when the Civil Rights Act was passed, southern community leaders—and responsible leaders throughout the country—would have to be prepared in advance.

The first step in this strategy had been initiated by the Kennedy White House in the summer of 1963. President Johnson continued and embellished it. It had started with a series of gatherings at the White House at which the president met with the foremost leaders of public opinion in various walks of life. Separate sessions were held with the nation's most prominent lawyers, business leaders, prelates of the religious communities, and educators, as well as with civil rights and civic organization heads. In these meetings the president shared his knowledge and fears as to the potential for violent resistance and sought to persuade his listeners to use their influence to make the inevitable civil rights changes work. A total of eleven White House meetings, with sixteen hundred of America's most influential citizens, were held by both Kennedy and Johnson.

Early in 1964 the administration launched another behind-the-scenes unofficial endeavor. Called Project Compliance, it was designed to persuade government and business leaders throughout the South to use their influence to encourage voluntary compliance with the impending legislation. An informal network of civil rights advocates in the federal government and in the private sector had been consulting together regularly on civil rights strategies. Within that framework Burke Marshall had proposed the idea of Project Compliance to Harold Fleming of the Potomac Institute. The institute thereafter served as the secretariat of the program.

The effort was headed jointly by Fleming and Louis Oberdorfer, then an assistant attorney general and later a federal judge. The project enlisted teams of important businessmen and government leaders and assigned them to visit with their counterparts in selected southern cities. They presented the president's appeal that, as a patriotic duty, they use their influence to prepare their communities for peaceful compliance with the new law.

Special emphasis was placed on appeals to the business community. Discussions with chambers of commerce emphasized two points: first, that the law would be enforced; second, that resistance, with its potential for confrontation and violence, would be bad for business. The community leaders were asked to use their influence with the political leadership to establish a community ethos of peaceful compliance. According to Fleming:

When the Civil Rights Act was pending, the anticipation was that the biggest danger would be massive resistance to Title II—public accommodations. So the thought about controlling the degree of resistance started months before the Act actually passed. We built profiles of many of the southern communities—what the climate of opinion was, the public facilities under siege, what the political leadership and newspapers were like. We had files on possibly one hundred places in the South. An informal steering committee made the decisions as to which places seemed to warrant high priority and who among the business types could wield the most effective personal influence upon the business and official leadership of the targeted city.[16]

Some thought the southern business community did not need a lot of convincing. Lee White recalled that chambers of commerce were already reporting drops in convention business resulting from the civil rights turmoil.

It was apparent that Johnson saw the Community Relations Service as the final link in this strategy for winning voluntary compliance with the law. But before he would let it undertake its duties, he felt it necessary to give his personal direction and support to two additional efforts. The first was to win the cooperation of the southern state governments.

FOCUS ON THE SOUTHERN MODERATE

When he signed the act on July 2, President Johnson announced his intention to appoint LeRoy Collins, a former governor of Florida, as the director of the Community Relations Service. At the same time, he gave Collins his first assignment. He was to form a team with two other former southern governors as the president's personal emissaries to each of the governors of the southern states. Their mission was to enlist their maximum efforts and influence to assure peaceful compliance with the new law. Serving with Collins were Buford Ellington of Tennessee and Luther Hodges of North Carolina. The three were chosen not only because of their records as racial moderates but also because of their personal influence with the state chief executives. Each was a former chairman of the Southern Governors Association.

President Johnson's second effort to win voluntary compliance was to mobilize America's most prominent citizens to be active supporters.

To generate peer influence at the highest levels, he created the National Citizens Committee for Community Relations (NCC) as an adjunct of CRS. For this, he and his aides picked 450 leaders from all walks of life. Some, like Roger Blough, chairman of the U.S. Steel Corporation, and Charles Keller, president of the National Association of General Contractors, were included to note the stamp of approval of American industry. Others, such as Morris B. Abram, president of the American Jewish Committee, and George Meany, president of the AFL-CIO, were included as a link to the committed energies of the liberal community. Also included were the executive officers of Protestant, Catholic, and Jewish religious institutions, in order to harness the nation's moral commitment. Civil rights leaders and other prominent Black and Hispanic individuals were part of the group. The presence of Conrad Hilton of Hilton Hotels, Kemmons Wilson of Holiday Inns, and Julius Manger of Manger Hotels acknowledged the administration's special concern about discrimination in public accommodations.

For chairman of the NCC, Johnson chose a man of towering personal influence in America's corridors of power. He was Arthur Dean, senior partner in the Wall Street law firm of Sullivan and Cromwell. His reputation as a negotiator had long since been acknowledged by his selection in 1953 by President Eisenhower to head America's delegation to the truce negotiations ending the Korean War. The executive vice chairman was Julius Manger. Vice chairman was John Wheeler, one of America's foremost Black bankers.

On August 18, barely seven weeks after signing the Civil Rights Act, Johnson met in the Rose Garden with the 450 members of the NCC. They had assembled at short notice in response to telegrams of invitation from the president. Johnson appealed for their participation in a service of historic significance. He said, "We all know that the Emancipation Proclamation was signed 100 years ago, but emancipation was a proclamation, it was not a fact. So, upon you in your own communities falls the great task of these times, the task of fostering understanding, the task of securing observation and compliance, the task of assuring justice for all Americans."

On this hortatory plea—to achieve fulfillment of the Emancipation Proclamation—the members of the NCC departed the Rose Garden. Exactly how this endeavor was to be pursued was not made clear. Ultimately, as we shall see in the next chapter, members of the NCC were to exercise their influence and "clout" to further a number of activities aimed at advancing racial justice.

As these matters were proceeding, LeRoy Collins was enduring a minor but unanticipated harassment in winning confirmation in the Senate. Johnson had picked Collins, widely respected as a "moderate" southern leader, as the ideal symbol of reconciliation. As governor of Florida from 1954 to 1960, he had been able to make clear his respect for the rights of minorities and their claim for greater equity without losing the support of his white constituency. In 1960, when Tallahassee was threatened with racial violence, he calmed the storm by going on television to state that the issues would not be resolved by mobs, whether they were Black or white. He acknowledged that while store owners might legally refuse service to Blacks if they chose, it was "unfair and morally wrong" to deny service at lunch counters to those whose trade they were willing to accept.

Collins had also shown himself willing to take political risks in the civil rights arena. Thurgood Marshall and Jack Greenberg of the National Association for the Advancement of Colored People (NAACP) had in 1952 unsuccessfully defended a Black man accused of murder before an all-white jury in Orlando. In a community atmosphere of screaming racial invective, the jury, without supporting evidence, had handed down a verdict of death. The Supreme Court twice declined to hear the NAACP's appeal. Finally Collins, as governor, commuted the death sentence.

His influence beyond the borders of Florida had been demonstrated by his election as chairman of the Southern Governors Association. During the same time he also served as chairman of the National Governors Association. He was known to Americans across the nation who had watched on television his skillful and urbane performance as permanent chairman of the 1960 Democratic National Convention, which had nominated Jack Kennedy. Collins was credited with helping to bridge the factional differences between northern and southern delegates.

At his confirmation hearing on July 7 before the Senate Commerce Committee, Collins's nomination was opposed only by Strom Thurmond. In a two-hour interrogation, Thurmond accused Collins of turning his back on the South and also of changing his stand on issues after achieving national prominence. Collins defended his love for the South but conceded some changes in viewpoint. "We all grow and change," he said, "and have to meet new responsibilities. And I will not contend that I have not changed some of my positions as a result of better understanding."[17]

Collins and Thurmond were no strangers to each other. They represented the opposite poles of social viewpoint among southern politicians. The two had faced each other seven months earlier when Thurmond had been in the audience as Collins, then president of the National Association of Broadcasters, addressed the Greater Columbia (South Carolina) Chamber of Commerce. The date was December 3, less than two weeks after President Kennedy's assassination. Collins discussed problems of the South in the context of the violence and extremism abroad in the nation. His speech was studded with phrases that awakened controversy throughout the South:

> We have allowed extremists to speak for the South. . . . Too many of the rest of us have remained cravenly silent or lamely defensive while Dixie battle cries have been employed to incite sick souls to violence. . . . How many Sunday school children have to be dynamited to death? How many Negro leaders have to be shot in the back? How many governors have to be shot in the chest? How many presidents have to be assassinated? . . . Any rational man who looks out at the horizon and sees the South of the future segregated is simply seeing a mirage.

At the first day of a favorable confirmation hearing, the subcommittee's endorsement of Collins was prevented only by Thurmond's calling attention to the absence of a quorum. At the next day's meeting, Thurmond lingered outside the door rather than entering and thus making the nine-member quorum. Senator Ralph Yarborough, of Texas, took him by the arm and urged him to come in. Thurmond then tried to keep Yarborough out. Thurmond twice threw Yarborough to the floor. With his shoulders pinned, Yarborough refused Thurmond's demand that he ask for release. Only when the chairman, Senator Warren Magnuson, rushed from the committee room and demanded that the two sixty-one-year-old senators break it up, did they rise, clap each other on the back, and enter the meeting room. Collins, on learning of the incident, said, "I've been hoping for support from the Senate floor but I was not expecting that kind of support from that kind of floor."[18]

25

The committee thereafter voted 16–1 to recommend Collins's confirmation. The full Senate followed suit with a 53–8 vote.

As further evidence of his concern with the role of the newborn agency, President Johnson personally handpicked Collins's deputy director, Harold Fleming. Fleming was president of the Potomac Institute in Washington, D.C., which had been established in 1961 to provide liaison and access between the civil rights community and federal agencies that were beginning to take on civil rights responsibilities but knew little about the problems, program needs, or players on the civil rights stage. A founder and past president of the National Association of Intergroup Relations Officials (NAIRO), Fleming had been executive director of the Southern Regional Council, an agency respected throughout the South for its research and education about social and economic problems impacting on Blacks and on interracial problems in the region. The administration had previously called on him to serve as coleader of Project Compliance. Fleming was loaned to the Community Relations Service for a six-month period.

Thus launched by a powerful presidential shove, the good ship CRS sailed off on its mission. It had a captain and a first mate. No one knew better than they that despite the ceremonial launching and high expectations, there were no charts in the chart room and no clear star by which to steer.

NOTES

1. Remarks of John Doar, assistant attorney general for civil rights, at a training session in Oxford, Ohio, to prepare two hundred college students for the 1964 summer project.

2. Evans and Novak, *Lyndon B. Johnson*, 126.

3. Wofford, *Of Kennedys and Kings*.

4. Lee White, interview with Bertram Levine.

5. Theodore Sorensen, telephone interview with Bertram Levine; Sorensen, *Kennedy*, 496.

6. Burke Marshall, telephone interview with Bertram Levine.

7. On March 12, 1956, one hundred southern senators and congressmen issued the Southern Manifesto, opposing the Supreme Court's 1954 decision on school desegregation.

8. Arnold Aronson, interview with Bertram Levine.

9. Joseph Rauh, interview with Bertram Levine.

10. Marshall, interview with Levine.

11. Reported by Evans and Novak in the *Washington Post*, May 27, 1964.

12. Marshall, interview with Levine.

13. Whalen and Whalen, *The Longest Debate*.

14. Aronson, interview with Levine.

15. Whalen and Whalen, *The Longest Debate*, 120.

16. Harold Fleming, interview with Bertram Levine.

17. *New York Times*, July 8, 1964.

18. *New York Times*, July 10, 1964.

TWO

Learning Intervention

Intuition, Courage, and Goodwill

WITH RACIAL CONTROVERSY crackling throughout the South, the new conciliation agency found itself with a waiting list of calls for help from the moment of its creation in July 1964. The early conciliators plunged into the peacemaker role armed with little more than goodwill, courage, intuition, and faith in the power of persuasion. Despite a large measure of improvisation, their efforts were, by and large, successful in helping to lessen conflict and violence. But it would take more than a year of learning and testing before the collective experience could be drawn together and take form as a body of professional case practice.

By the end of 1965 assistance had been given to almost two hundred communities. Seventy-eight percent were in fifteen southern and border states. Most of them had populations of less than twenty-five thousand. During that first year and a half, CRS acquired form and function while it intervened in and witnessed events that marked historic social change. The neophyte troubleshooters began to develop a methodology and to hone their skills. While some also began to wonder about how much the role of peacemaker could or should involve the role of change agent, national events would be redefining their priorities and objectives.

PUBLIC ACCOMMODATIONS—
A BETTER OUTCOME THAN EXPECTED

Minority access to public accommodations—the part of the Civil Rights Act that its authors had feared would generate the most violent resistance—took center stage as soon as the law was signed.

The law and its enforcement were quickly challenged. In Atlanta, the Heart of Atlanta Motel sued to have the public accommodations provision declared unconstitutional. In Birmingham, the Justice Department, eager to establish the law's validity before the highest court, sued Ollie's Barbecue for violating the public accommodations clause. The issues in the two cases were slightly different and resulted in opposing decisions as to constitutionality from two different U.S. District Courts. The Heart of Atlanta Motel lost its fight, but Ollie's Barbecue prevailed. Both suits were appealed. They were argued together before the U.S. Supreme Court, which, on December 14, 1964, by unanimous decision, upheld the constitutionality of the law.[1]

At the same time that opponents were trying to get the law overturned, civil rights groups were testing to make sure it would be obeyed and enforced. The Congress of Racial Equality (CORE), long a major generator of social action in behalf of civil rights, was holding its national convention in Kansas City, Missouri, on July 2. One minute after President Johnson signed the act, a teenage delegate from Jackson, Mississippi, asked for a haircut in the Muehlebach Hotel barbershop. When he was refused, CORE members conducted a protest demonstration on the spot. The next morning, following brief negotiations between CORE and the hotel management, the young man returned to the barbershop and was served. Heartened by its success, CORE immediately sent testing instructions to its 114 affiliates around the country.

Within a week of the act's passage, the *New York Times* reported successful testing of public accommodations by Black activists in cities and facilities across the South where there had formerly been unsuccessful protests of segregation. The major hotel chains set the pace for desegregation in city after city. All their chief executives had been taken into the administration's civil rights camp starting with the White House meetings in 1963–64. Local managers had been softened up by the Project Compliance teams. They were particularly sensitive to the suggestion that conflict in the community was bad for business. As former Attorney General Nicholas D. Katzenbach reflected twenty-five years later: "The hotel people said they were all behind it [passage of the Civil Rights Act]. . . . They couldn't get a convention down there. . . . They weren't willing to do much in Congress, but they were willing to guarantee that when the law was passed they would comply from the first day."[2]

In August 1964, CRS surveyed fifty-three southern cities. Most of them reported compliance by about two-thirds of the affected establishments. By January 1965, other surveys showed continuing progress, albeit short of full compliance.[3] Thus, within six months of passage of the law desegregating public accommodations, it was apparent that voluntary compliance would prevail and that the tens of thousands of court cases that Burke Marshall had feared would not eventuate. It also became clear that public accommodations cases would not provide the overwhelming number of the confrontations that federal conciliators would have to defuse.

Despite the failure of public accommodations cases to hit the levels expected, persistent hard-core resistance to the law still overtaxed the government's ability to deal with it. The Justice Department's Civil Rights Division received six hundred complaints in six months. Hundreds of other conflicts that didn't lend themselves to resolution through the courts were also flaring.

THE GROWTH OF THE PROGRAM AND ITS METHODOLOGY

Requests for federal conciliation assistance had begun to roll into the Commerce Department from communities torn by racial confrontation even before the new civil rights law had been signed. Anticipating that the Community Relations Service would be expected to perform from day one, the Commerce Department pulled together an informal task force ready to go into action the moment the ink on the president's signature was dry. Within forty-eight hours—on July 4, 1964—a special command post had been set up to monitor any violent protests that die-hard opponents of the law might generate on Independence Day. Hotlines were set up with the White House, the Justice Department, and other agencies so that all reports of trouble would be routed to one place and response could be coordinated. Jay Janis and Jerry Heilbron staffed the command post. Janis was later to recall: "We arrived at 7:00 a.m. ready for a hectic day but not knowing what to do. Especially me. At least Heilbron had worked for the Justice Department. We waited all day. Finally, about four in the afternoon, one call came in from a lady in the South wanting information about the Civil Rights Act. There were no disruptions, no protests."[4]

This experience was the first of scores that taught CRS two lessons. One was that when it came to forecasting how racial tensions would be acted out, there were no experts. The second was an obvious truth that was to become an article of faith: in the absence of predictability, contingency planning is a must.

Collins and Fleming rushed to recruit and deploy conflict conciliators even before a budget or position descriptions were developed and approved. As a brand-new federal organism, and one known to have the personal blessings of the president, CRS had access to all the strategies and resources that enable the federal government to achieve bureaucratic wonders overnight. The Commerce Department made operational funds immediately available from its own resources until a formal appropriation would be forthcoming. John Macy, chairman of the Civil Service Commission, personally visited with Collins to help plan the staffing and to grease the skids for a quick start. He convinced the new director that his initial personnel request was too modest, as was his request for hard-to-get super-grade positions. He then helped work out special hiring authority to speed recruitment.

While the early cadre was drawn from a variety of vocational backgrounds—law, education, journalism, religion, social service—it was by and large a homogeneous group. This was a consequence of the vision of CRS's role shared by the early managers and the usefulness of personal contacts when time is of the essence in recruiting a team that has to hit the ground running. For the most part, as the following portraits of a few of them show, the first employees were white males, sympathetic to civil rights goals, familiar with community dynamics in the South, and comfortable in dealing with the power structure elite.

Andrew MacDowd (Mac) Secrest, who published a South Carolina county newspaper, had been a Nieman Fellow at Harvard. He was frustrated by the racial inequities about him and believed that his knowledge of the rural South might be useful to the racial conciliation group about to be formed. He wrote to his cousin, Luther Hodges, the secretary of commerce, and asked if he could help. He was the first person named to the CRS task force.

Jay Janis, a Miami builder, was a volunteer civil rights activist for the American Jewish Committee in Miami. Exploring for public service opportunities in Washington brought him to the Commerce Department just as the task force was being formed. He signed on.

Seymour Samet was recruited by Janis. Samet was regional director of the American Jewish Committee in Florida and the first executive director of the Dade County Board of Human Relations. He was the only early worker with professional experience in community conflict resolution.

Jerome Heilbron, an Arkansas attorney, transferred from the Civil Rights Division of the Justice Department, where he had been seen as the leading advocate of negotiation—as opposed to litigation—for winning more rapid compliance with civil rights laws.

John Griffin, who arrived in September, was picked by Collins to be the first director of the conciliation field staff. Griffin, who had experience in labor arbitration, had been vice president of Florida State University at Tallahassee, where he had dealt with civil rights matters.

Abraham Venable, an MBA graduate of Howard University, was working with Undersecretary of Commerce Franklin D. Roosevelt Jr. on a program to enhance business opportunities for Blacks. He was the first, and one of only a few, African American conciliators taken on in the first year and a half.

Their initial approaches were as diverse as the personalities and experiences of each individual. The early cases provided a trial-and-error cram course in the processes and pitfalls of community dispute resolution. Gradually, as seat-of-the-pants intervention became validated by experience, a number of approaches were drawn into frequent use. Among them were establishing a "federal presence"; employing fact-finding and assessment; evoking peer pressure; activating higher authority; energizing civic responsibility; and motivating the power elite.

Immediately, the conciliators learned that outside intervention in a dispute, by its mere appearance, can sometimes alter the relationship and behavior of the antagonists. This was especially true when the intervener was a representative of the federal government. It was that principle that enabled the first conciliators to be at least minimally effective in winning compliance with the law and in lessening conflict. As one of them said, "In the rural south, the minute I step out of the rent-a-car, the scenario changes." It was important to learn where and when to use the federal presence. Local authorities were sometimes antagonized; minorities were sometimes mistrustful.

Even a simple phone call from a federal official signaled to the participants that someone was watching. It sometimes could encourage parties to make sure that their adherents were on good behavior. It often provided an opportunity for improved communication, fresh thinking, or modification of hardened positions. This kind of brief intervention was often necessary when scant resources had to be spread very thin.

A typical example involved an African American family in a rural southern community that was being subjected to abuse and vandalism after moving into a white neighborhood. A CRS phone call to the sheriff inquiring about allegations that he had failed to provide protection resulted in periodic squad car patrols that discouraged the harassment.

A second approach was to trigger the involvement of higher authority. Sometimes an inquiry through the governor's office might result in a more diligent response from the sheriff.

"Onsite assistance" was the buzz phrase denoting the preferred form of intervention, and "improved communication" was an invariable objective. Communication assistance took many forms, as needed. These included: identifying the parties who needed to communicate, carrying messages, clarifying issues, teaching both sides to listen, providing a reality check for participants, moving confrontation from the streets to the conference table, and transforming posturing to good-faith negotiating.

Seymour Samet, who had reservations about overreliance on federal presence, whether provided by telephone or by onsite service, would cite a favorite case to illustrate that more was often required. In late August 1964, CRS was asked to deal with the case of a drive-in movie theater in Fort Lauderdale. The theater segregated the audience by means of separate entrances for Blacks and whites and a fence dividing the viewing area and refreshment stand. CORE had declared its intention to demonstrate in order to desegregate the facility. Samet phoned the owner and advised him of the requirements of the law.[5]

The proprietor remained adamant, so Mac Secrest was assigned to go onsite for face-to-face negotiation. He arrived at the Miami Airport just as Hurricane Cleo was approaching. He met with the protest group that night but could not get to see the theater operator. When he arrived at the drive-in the next morning, he found the owner ruefully surveying the storm damage, including a shattered fence. "I didn't know you fellows had the almighty on your side," he told Secrest. "The fence stays down. The place is integrated."[6]

Use of influential allies was another productive approach, including a number of the "movers and shakers" whom the president had enlisted in the National Citizens Committee for Community Relations. Julius Manger, for one, could always be counted on. On more than one occasion a personal phone call to one of his hotels prompted the manager to take the lead in getting the local chamber of commerce to lean on city hall. A fuller appreciation of how demonstrations were bad for business often contributed to a local government's readiness to negotiate. Similarly, when Dick Gregory was turned away from the Holiday Inn in Selma, where he had gone to encourage the demonstrators, conciliator

Mac Secrest called NCC member Kemmons Wilson, the Holiday Inn board chairman. The Selma Holiday Inn's discrimination policy was reversed in minutes.

Assessment—learning the facts and figuring out what they meant—was an obvious first step in conciliation.[7] It was more than just an information-gathering prelude. It had its own impact on the conflict resolution process. From the outset, conciliators learned that perceptions were often as important as facts. In conflict situations it was how the facts were perceived that moved the parties to action. The search for facts and perceptions forced CRS to cast a wide net in seeking information. The immediate antagonists, generally white authorities and Black complainants, saw the issues from their own highly focused—and sometimes very limited—points of view. Consequently, other factions and observers in both communities also had to be contacted. In the minority community, conciliators reached out beyond the recognized leaders and civil rights activists. They also consulted with informal spokespersons for the disenfranchised as well as with rank-and-file members of the victimized group.

This assessment process often irritated local authorities. They were not accustomed to having their word questioned and were discomfited by having to address long-ignored realities. They resented federal officials dignifying the "disreputable" by seeking their information and treating it with equal respect. But only in this way could the conciliator get a feeling for the phenomenon of multiple truths.

Another early approach was to energize civic responsibility. Members of the business and civic community—church federations, women's groups, chambers of commerce, and the like—were skilled in advocating their own social agendas. Frequently, however, they remained on the sidelines of racial controversy. Discussion with a federal conciliator often helped them to clarify their views and to be more comfortable in playing an active role in resolving the difficulty. Sometimes it worked the other way around; local business interests, valuing a stable community, would call on CRS for assistance.

Such a call came from Hilton Head, South Carolina, which was experiencing racial violence early in 1965 over issues of segregated schools. CRS was asked to intervene by Charles Frazier, a developer who planned to create a major resort community on the island. He saw his investment endangered if the island became the scene of racial violence.

Jay Janis, who worked the case, recalled Frazier telling Collins: "It's bad for business. Besides, I don't want to see the Negroes get beat up."[8]

Janis was teamed up with John Wheeler, the Black vice chairman of the National Citizens Committee. President of the Farmers and Mechanics Bank of Durham, North Carolina, Wheeler agreed to work as a volunteer conciliator as part of his commitment to the NCC. The combination of Wheeler and Janis—a Carolina-raised Black banker and a white builder—struck Collins as a well-balanced team for the case. Janis recalls his first venture into the trenches for CRS as a learning experience:

> After a discussion with Frazier we set out to meet with the Black community. It was eight or nine at night—in a real rural part of Hilton Head. In an old barn. Only one white face in the crowd—me. I was absolutely certain that the Ku Klux Klan was waiting outside to burn the place down. I had done a lot of civil rights work, but I had never been in quite that position before, in the rural South. Then we met with the white group, which was the school board. John's was the only Black face in the room. I guess that John had felt there, and all of his life, like I had felt out there in the barn with the Blacks. It was a great lesson to me how somebody like John had to feel. . . . As to what we accomplished—we got some conversation going between the Blacks and whites. We followed up by telephone. Later, other conciliators went in. The situation was ultimately resolved.[9]

It was not long before the CRS troubleshooters came up against a dilemma the agency was never fully to resolve: what role does the conciliator play when conflict resolution and civil rights progress may be at cross purposes? Jim Draper first faced the problem in Jonesboro, Louisiana, a racial tinderbox at that time. Thirty years of experience as a reporter, advertising executive, and publisher had equipped Draper with hundreds of business and political contacts throughout Mississippi. As the onetime publisher of *Livestock Weekly*, he had personal credibility in rural areas among both Blacks and whites. His strong views in favor of civil rights prompted him to enlist in CRS. Working out of Memphis, he was often the sole federal peacemaker in the back woods of Mississippi and Louisiana. As he remembered Jonesboro a quarter of a century later:

The situation was explosive. There was a railroad that ran diagonally through the town. Whites lived on one side and Blacks on the other. The Negro grievances were everything: no mail delivery, garbage pickup, sewers, or street paving. The Black schools were a travesty. In 1965 there was quite an organization going among the Black people—started by CORE—two or three young people from Grambling. They had a little freedom house.[10] They decided they were going to march from the high school in the Black part of town up over the railroad and meet at the courthouse, where demonstrations were off limits. The Sheriff of Jackson Parish had a mounted posse of about fifty. I learned from a confidential source that they knew about the proposed march and intended to ambush the marchers just as they came over the railroad track. That could have been pretty bloody. I went back to Freedom House and, without telling them what I had learned, I persuaded them to change their route of march to the courthouse.[11]

Later somebody working with CORE berated Draper: "Nothing worthwhile ever happened in Jonesboro after that. Nobody was killed, shot, or put in jail that day. It stopped the movement." Years later, Draper wondered whether intervention that forestalled violence may have made CRS a role player rather than just a dispute resolver. He asked, "Did we slow down the pace of change by not letting events flow as they might have flowed?"[12]

DEALING WITH POLITICAL INFLUENCE

The need for federal conciliators to be insulated from political influence was learned early in the program. The desegregation of the schools in St. Helena Parish, Louisiana, provides an example. During one of Collins's out-of-town trips, Fleming fielded an urgent call from the White House. He was told that the St. Helena Parish school board had been required by the U.S. Court of Appeals to end its ten years of resistance and integrate its school system in September 1964. Violent opposition was certain. Fleming was advised to have CRS discuss the matter with the congressman from that district, Hale Boggs. The White House interest was clear. Boggs, as the majority whip, was a key player in pressing the president's program in Congress. He was currently struggling to maintain his seat in a close race against a white supremacist opponent. In recording his meeting with Boggs many years later, Fleming wrote:

> He made no bones about his political stake in the situation. Yet he wanted Governor Collins to understand that he was concerned about more than his own political fortunes. His position in the House could be vital to the success or failure of the Administration's legislative program. This included the social agenda, which was of even greater significance to blacks than to whites. He wanted the law of the land to prevail, but not at the needless price of his defeat and all that would entail. Besides, he concluded, it was a fact that St. Helena Parish was woefully unprepared for a sudden dismantling of its dual school system. The safety and well being of the black children, as well as the general community, would be served by delaying the effect of the ruling for at least a semester, thus allowing time to prepare the ground for a peaceful transition. . . . Boggs' argument struck me as an eloquent variation on the familiar refrain "the time isn't ripe." Still, I was impressed by the evident sincerity and effectiveness with which he made his case. I responded mildly that blacks might find it difficult to believe that the parish, after all those years of delay and inaction, would put more time to constructive use.[13]

Boggs asked Fleming to convey the situation to Collins and ask him whether CRS would consider appealing to the judge to delay implementation of the integration order for six months in order to reduce the likelihood of violence. He wanted Collins to know he would accept his decision. "You people have your job to do," he said.

Before making a judgment, Collins wanted CRS to conduct its own onsite assessment. In the absence of available staff, a distinguished educational consultant was engaged for the task. His report was grim. Segregationist passions were indeed inflamed. Desegregation in September would likely lead to violence. Black children would certainly be at risk. He recommended that desegregation be delayed and proposed a program for preparing the community for change in the interim.

Collins recognized the high stakes of this judgment call. For CRS to take a "go-slow" posture in its first major case might undercut the credibility of the agency in the civil rights community. On the other hand, consideration had to be given to preventing the violence and psychological trauma that the Black children would face.

In any event, the decision did not rest with CRS. If the federal government was to intervene with the court, it would have to be through the Department of Justice. Fleming was instructed to present Collins's viewpoint to Attorney General Robert Kennedy. Kennedy's conclusion was recounted by Fleming:

> He explained that he had learned from hard experience that blacks were determined to decide for themselves what risks they should take in asserting their rights. This was as it should be. They would deeply resent it, he said, if the government, however well intentioned, should step in at this point and try to undo what they had fought so hard to achieve. All the Justice Department could do, he concluded, was to make every effort to prevent violence and intimidation.

Fleming had no problem with that decision. He thought that Kennedy "now seemed a far cry from the man who had called on the freedom riders to suspend their protest, who had commended the Albany, Georgia, police chief for his gentility in rounding up and jailing black marchers, and who had complained that King's Birmingham demonstrations were ill-timed and ill-advised."[14]

Thus, CRS did not intervene. Desegregation of St. Helena Parish schools was initiated in September without widespread violence. Hale Boggs was reelected to Congress in November.

CRS soon learned that "congressional interest" in a case often went with the territory. It learned, too, that Congress had to be treated with respect but not obeisance. Congressional inquiries were more frequent in the early years. They would often be triggered by local officeholders who did not like to see federal officials conferring with protest leaders— whom they saw as disreputable troublemakers. Fearing, often correctly, that conciliation might lead to change, they called on their congressmen to halt what they saw as an unwarranted federal intrusion.

Sometimes by letter, occasionally by personal briefing, CRS would interpret its responsibility to the inquiring congressman. It pointed out that CRS intervention most likely would prove to be a benefit to his constituency, since unresolved conflicts usually led to greater disruption later. When congressional complaints about CRS went to the secretary of commerce or, later, to the attorney general, CRS would be asked to draft the reply in the name of the cabinet officer. Ultimately, CRS came to understand that in most cases the "congressional interest" was not a veiled threat but simply a form of constituent service, which could be satisfied by a serious response.

FIRE PREVENTION AS WELL AS FIREFIGHTING

Besides fighting the fires of racial conflict in the localities where it occurred, the Community Relations Service developed a fire prevention program. From its earliest days it was apparent to CRS's leaders that the roots of racial animosity lay deep beneath the surface of American society. Turmoil could break forth at any time in any of a thousand localities. The CRS staff could address only the more troublesome threats. It made sense to augment the work of the conciliators by encouraging and assisting other agencies in their efforts to address racial conflicts and the social problems from which they stemmed.

Four support programs were developed to reach out to these other resources. One identified those services within the vast network of federal programs that might help alleviate community conflict. This federal liaison enabled CRS to alert civil rights enforcement officials to neglected violations. It could also encourage grant-giving agencies to direct their resources to specific communities where educational, job training, and employment benefits would help to facilitate the resolution of racial tension.

The second prevention activity reached out to national voluntary organizations. It was designed to assist these groups, whose local constituencies extended into thousands of communities, to maximize their support for civil rights programs. This network also identified local resources that could be brought to bear in specific situations.

A third national program was addressed to the creation and strengthening of local human relations commissions or other local biracial committees that helped communities better utilize their own resources for interracial communication and problem solving. With the help of the Advertising Council, CRS mounted a media campaign to "sell" the idea of human relations commissions to interested local jurisdictions. Then CRS made staff and consultants available to provide onsite assistance with problems of creation or operation of commissions.

The fourth firefighting national program was the NCC. Both President Johnson and LeRoy Collins saw CRS as an educational fountainhead that would reach out to opinion molders and community leaders across the nation to create a climate in which civil rights and racial amity would flourish. The National Citizens Committee for Community Relations was seen as a pillar of this prevention program—450 of America's most influential individuals personally enlisted by the president to give hands-on assistance when called upon. It was CRS's responsibility to provide staff services and program guidance.

In perhaps a score of instances individual NCC members were asked to undertake conflict resolution assignments when staff conciliators were not available. There was no clear consensus on the effectiveness of these performances. Some CRS staff members felt that, without adequate training or supervision by staff, volunteer conciliators presented more trouble and risk than advantage. In any event, for five years the roster of NCC members was to serve as a resource list upon which CRS could call in a variety of cases, large and small. How to use all that NCC horsepower effectively was the challenge. Collins and Harold Fleming both thought that the NCC's size made it unwieldy, but it certainly provided muscle on occasions when CRS was in need of some.[15]

Julius Manger, for example, as chairman of a major hotel chain, designed a program to upgrade the employment status of Blacks throughout his organization. He then sent his design to the heads of five other hotel chains, asking them to consider undertaking similar programs. He received affirmative responses from the Hilton, Statler, Holiday Inn, Carling, and Pick hotel executives. Since these chains also were headed by members of the NCC, it may be assumed that their favorable response was generated not only out of respect for a fellow business leader but also by the force of the president's charge when he had met with them in the Rose Garden.

Donald McGannon, president of Westinghouse Broadcasting Network, headed NCC's Mass Media Committee. He used the good offices of his local stations, and his influence with other broadcasting executives, to help CRS organize the sponsorship of local media conferences on civil rights and race relations. The objective was for local media executives to get together with minority leaders in order to work out better ways to cover minority news and views and to overcome discrimination in the publishing and broadcasting industries. Other NCC members also lent their prestige to the sponsorship of these local conferences, which were held in more than twenty communities in 1965 and 1966. Programs that evolved from these groundbreaking meetings were part of a nationwide effort to drive Jim Crow out of journalism that will be described in chapter 10.

In some instances, individual NCC members, on their own initiative, undertook projects they felt were needed. For example, Norman Cahners, the publisher of a group of trade magazines, established the Business Press Advisory Council in an effort to insinuate civil rights awareness into the consciousness of American business executives. The council functioned as a cost-free syndicate of news and commentary on civil rights themes appealing to the interests of business, which was made available to business publications with a combined circulation of ten million.

Alabama NCC members Winton Blount, Milton Cummings, George LeMaistre, and Arthur Shores were instrumental in getting the power-houses of Alabama industry to issue a pro–civil rights statement calling for change in the state's racial climate. The statement, signed by the State Chamber of Commerce, the Associated Industries of Alabama, and other important business groups, was run in all Alabama dailies, the *Wall Street Journal,* and *U.S. News and World Report.*

The three NCC members in the state of New Mexico persuaded the governor to join them in sponsoring a statewide conference on civil rights, from which emerged recommendations for the state to adopt a fair housing law and to establish a state human relations commission. And the Women's Division of the NCC convened regional seminars for hundreds of the leaders of women's organizations to enlist their support of the nation's civil rights goals.

One of the NCC's most ambitious undertakings was to call attention to the problem of putting the hard-core unemployed into jobs. In the mid-sixties the nation first became aware of the twin specters of structural unemployment and the growth of a permanent underclass of minority nonworkers. Technological advances were eradicating hundreds of thousands of low-paying industrial jobs. The result swelled the ranks of poorly educated Black males who, it would appear, throughout their lives and the lives of their progeny, would never experience sustained and gratifying employment. It was known that they existed by the thousands in America's cities, but their exact number could only be guessed because they were no longer even counted among the unemployed. They were a large component of the social dynamite piling up in poor minority urban communities. Some of these hard-core unemployed, not even ready for skills training, needed help with basic work habits that would enable them to find and to hold even unskilled jobs. A scattering of business organizations and companies were experimenting with special programs for this group, but the unique techniques for effectively working with them were still outside the ken of most American businesses.

To fill this void, CRS organized some of NCC's captains of industry into the Business and Industry Advisory Committee. One of this committee's major objectives was to stimulate the development of, and codify, the state of the art for putting the hard-core unemployed into jobs.

Under the chairmanship of Stanley Marcus, of the Neiman Marcus retailing giant, the advisory committee in June 1967 conducted a conference where industry heads and leading personnel and training specialists shared the sum total of America's extant experience in working with the hard-core unemployed. The book that emerged from the conference was a down-to-earth manual on how to find, understand, motivate, train, and profitably employ them.[16] Unfortunately, the long-term effectiveness of the project was significantly compromised. By the time the book was published, CRS's energies were being expended elsewhere, leaving scant resources for promotion, distribution, or follow-up programming. It would not be the last false start to be made by CRS, which, as a small, ambitious agency, had to guard against letting its reach exceed its grasp.

The National Citizens Committee for Community Relations, which had existed only on the authority of Lyndon Johnson's telegram of invitation to the Rose Garden meeting, expired the moment Johnson departed the White House. The demise of the NCC resulted from a number of causes, perhaps the strongest of which was ambivalence. CRS, never fully comfortable in its marriage with so potentially influential an adjunct, had used the NCC mostly as a roster of volunteers who felt duty bound to help because Lyndon Johnson had asked them to. The task of molding the group into an organization that would genuinely engage the interest of the men of affairs whose priorities lay elsewhere called for a price CRS was unwilling to pay. The small agency could ill afford the resources required. Nor did it dare to risk the independence of action that such an organization would have demanded. CRS made no effort to persuade John Mitchell, the incoming attorney general, to retain or replace the NCC.[17] It was assumed that the Nixon administration, with no legal obligation to continue it, would have no interest in the perpetuation of a group of 450 Johnson appointees. The CRS staff was reluctant to press the case, uncertain about what new problems might arise in relating to a replacement group whose mandate, authority, and selection would come from a new president.

The mixed feelings of the CRS staff also reflected philosophical differences over the balance of resources to be invested in local and national programs. For most of the life of the agency, the prevailing view would emphasize the local effort, which deployed most of the agency's meager staff resources at the points of conflict. In this view, national programs should be used mostly to develop sources of support for local service. Wholesale programming to strengthen the efforts other groups might deliver to the point of conflict was seen as too diffuse to justify more than a minimal staff effort.

THE INTERPLAY OF CONFLICT AND CHANGE IN MISSISSIPPI

The mid-1960s brought dramatic transformations that revolutionized power relationships between whites and Blacks in the South. Rapid, raucous, and violent confrontations in Mississippi over a five-year period produced wrenching changes from a closed, authoritarian system of white dominance to one permitting negotiated change. While precipitating incidents generally focused on the schools, voting rights, or abusive law enforcement, conciliators found that issues were interrelated, and at the heart of most confrontations was the disparity of status and the denial of dignity.

Limited by its mandate and resources, CRS could play no more than a bit part in this sweeping drama. Nevertheless, it did serve as a catalyst that sometimes could reduce the violence and help speed the accommodation to change. Its unique role permitted CRS to witness firsthand the behind-the-scenes interplay of activity at local, state, and federal levels that succeeded in bringing change about.

The rising assertiveness of Black protest and the increase in federal attention set the stage for Black militancy, which forced Mississippi whites to adjust their image of their Black neighbors from punching bag to contender. The nation caught a glimpse of this transition at the Democratic National Convention at Atlantic City in the summer of 1964. There the interracial Mississippi Freedom Democratic Party (MFDP) was partially successful in its effort to unseat and replace the all-white party that had dominated the state since the Civil War. While the MFDP refused a compromise settlement in Atlantic City, it succeeded in permanently breaking the back of lily-white Democratic politics. CRS saw the workings of this kind of political, social, and economic reversal at the grassroots.

For years the great reserves of political strength and purchasing power possessed by Blacks by virtue of their numbers had been rendered useless by a system of political, economic, and law enforcement controls. New federal civil rights laws, federally funded social benefit programs, and more attentive federal law enforcement provided the tools for liberating Blacks' economic and political power. But the tools were meaningless until tested against bitter white resistance.

In the mid-sixties African Americans began to test and to utilize their new strength. Confrontations large and small broke out locally and statewide. One center of anti-Black violence was southwestern Mississippi, where numerous bombings and church burnings marked the answer of the Ku Klux Klan to the African American thrust for change. Natchez provides an example of the problem and of the contribution of federal conciliators toward a solution.

The first city to be built along the Mississippi River, Natchez had been the cultural and economic center of the state of Mississippi before the Civil War. But its development had languished in the ensuing hundred years. In 1964 it was known as a small city of pleasant homes. At the annual Natchez Pilgrimage in March, more than thirty well-preserved antebellum houses were opened to public view, providing a festive and lucrative tourist attraction. The economy was largely based on the surrounding cotton and timber industries and on river commerce. The biggest employer was the Armstrong Tire and Rubber plant. The population of twenty-four thousand was about evenly divided between Blacks and whites. A downtown shopping area employed no Blacks except in menial positions.

Behind the city's public face of gentility was a rough-and-tumble river town, known for years for gambling, prostitution, and the illegal sale and consumption of liquor. The Ku Klux Klan and the Association for the Preservation of the White Race were accepted social institutions.

The local newspaper vigorously supported the Klan, some of whose members were reputed to come from some of the "better families." The Klan exerted significant influence in four surrounding Mississippi counties and enjoyed wide support across the river in neighboring Louisiana.

The acceleration of civil rights activity in the South in 1964, including the Mississippi Freedom Summer program, which drew hundreds of northern college students into the state, brought a quick response from the Klan and other lawless elements. Across the state from Natchez, in eastern Mississippi, this response led to the murders of three civil rights workers—Michael H. Schwerner, Andrew Goodman, and James E. Chaney. In the southwestern corner it launched a wave of bombing and burning centered in Natchez and in McComb, sixty-five miles away.

The civil rights movement first became visible in Adams County when a freedom house was opened in Natchez in June 1964 next to a tavern and grocery operated by an interracial couple. Within two months, three Black churches had been burned and an explosion and fire had destroyed the store and tavern next to the freedom house. In September the home of Mayor John Nosser was bombed at the same time that an explosion fifteen blocks away wrecked the driveway at the home of Willie Washington, a Black contractor. It was the second attempt at Washington's house and the third bombing in eleven days on property owned by Nosser. Nosser attributed the attacks to his role as a peacemaker who had stepped on toes of both sides. He told the *New York Times*, "I don't believe it was done by colored people. I believe it was done by white people. But it could have been either side."[18] By February 1965, a United States Civil Rights Commission staff document reported seventeen acts of violence against Blacks in Adams County in recent months. None of the cases had been solved.

In September 1965, George Metcalfe, president of the Natchez branch of the National Association for the Advancement of Colored People, presented a petition to officials, asking for desegregation of the public schools. A few days later, Metcalfe was seriously injured when his car exploded as he left work at Armstrong Tire.

Black anger first vented itself in a statement of twelve demands that community leaders presented to city officials. Tension peaked when the demands were denied. A mass protest demonstration was planned. Governor Paul B. Johnson Jr., upon receiving reports that people were arming themselves, sent six hundred National Guard troops to police the city, because of "imminent danger of riots, mobs and breach of the peace." Black leaders, fearing violence in the possible use of the troops to suppress their protests, canceled the demonstration. Instead they launched a boycott of downtown businesses.

Charles Evers assumed leadership of the Natchez protest following the attempted murder of Metcalfe. In 1963 Evers had replaced his murdered brother, Medgar, as Mississippi state secretary of the NAACP. Under his guidance the boycott was applied relentlessly for three months. Demonstrations and counterdemonstrations created an atmosphere of impending violence. Describing the emotional climate of the city, the *New York Times* reported: "The attitude expressed to visitors most often by white leaders is bewilderment that 'our Negroes should be acting disagreeably.' They insist that except for a handful of 'extremists on both sides' the white people of Natchez are generous and reasonable and that the Negroes are happy and grateful."[19]

Jim Draper arrived in Natchez in early September, shortly after the troops had been withdrawn and as the boycott was taking hold. He walked into a budding confrontation. The main street was crowded with angry people, Blacks at one end, whites at the other. He was known to the leadership of both groups from previous visits, and they accepted his presence, but, he thought, without visible enthusiasm. Nevertheless the Blacks detailed "a man with a large pistol" as his informal body guard. Late in the day Draper participated in a meeting between Evers and some of the white leaders that resolved the impasse of the moment and enabled both sides to withdraw their forces without injury.[20]

Over the ensuing weeks other impasses and tentative resolutions were to become characteristic. Draper spent much of his time as a message carrier between the groups and as a tester of trial balloons. He developed a respect for Evers as a man "totally without fear." But Draper was frustrated because he was unable to establish the kind of relationship of full and mutual trust that he enjoyed with most of the other civil rights leaders with whom he had worked. Evers conveyed a feeling that he knew where he was going and did not expect much help from the federal government. The city's white population, on the other hand, appeared to welcome anything that would help get the matter settled. To them Draper tried to explain that the Blacks' demands were no more than what federal law required. For that reason, if for no other, those demands inevitably would prevail. Yet he found the whites totally unyielding when it came to making major concessions. With the atmosphere charged by flaring tempers, Draper felt he was making little progress in helping the parties to resolve the substantive issues. He did believe, however, that his role as intermediary helped to avoid misunderstandings that would have led to greater violence, which neither side wanted.

A breakthrough came in mid-October, when Draper "discovered" Ben Callon. A full year of experience as the CRS's agent in Mississippi had taught Draper that there was no more effective way to influence events in the rural South than to find and activate the power elite. Every town seemed to have one—a behind-the-scenes figure (or group) who was generally not visible in the management of local affairs, but who exercised great influence when it came to issues of personal importance. Ben Callon was a planter with extensive interests in industry throughout the area. Although he served as attorney for Adams County, he generally held himself aloof from the clash and clamor of the local arena. A friend of Governor Johnson, he was known as "the governor's man" in southwest Mississippi.

Callon apparently found Draper a man with whom he could talk comfortably, and Draper never visited the city without calling on him. Their conversations were wide-ranging—on one occasion lasting for the better part of a day. Draper urged Callon to exert his potent influence to help in keeping the lid on Klan violence and in persuading the city leaders to accept a settlement that would be consistent with federal civil rights laws. He pointed particularly to the danger of a racial bloodbath, and to the possible federal intervention that might result. He noted the governor's vulnerability to bad press if the Feds found it necessary to move in. While Callon made no promises, Draper observed afterward that he appeared more frequently to be in consultation with the mayor and other city officials, and it also appeared that word had gotten out to the Klan to back off.

In the meantime the Black boycott of downtown merchants continued. Estimates of the loss to some businesses ran as high as 50 percent. Fear and anger were rampant in the business community. In early November a group of white merchants started a movement for a counterboycott. If the Black buying strike was not called off, all employers in the county would be asked to fire all Black employees, and housewives would be asked to fire their domestic help. The movement was derailed when it was presented to the Chamber of Commerce for endorsement. At a meeting attended by 175 members, the president of the chamber and Mayor Nosser successfully argued for delaying the reprisal pending consideration by the chamber's board following a meeting with Black leaders.

A series of agreements was negotiated and as quickly abrogated. With each failure, the Blacks raised the level of their demands. Finally, on December 3, a settlement was achieved. The mayor, the board of aldermen, and the city's business leaders accepted a comprehensive agreement embracing and going beyond the original twelve points that the Blacks had demanded back in August. The agreement covered retail employment, police and other areas of public employment, hospital policies, school desegregation, access to public facilities, appointments to the school board and other public bodies, and street and sewer improvements in Black neighborhoods. Twenty-three of the largest stores had already hired Black clerks and cashiers. Their employees and those of the city were instructed to address Blacks courteously. Demeaning salutations were banned. The stores complying with the agreement comprised only 20 percent of the retail establishments, but they employed the bulk of the workforce. The Blacks would continue a selective buying program, patronizing these stores and picketing others.

In his remarks at the signing ceremony Evers emphasized the triumph of Black economic power. He said that the NAACP had set out to make Natchez a whipping boy, and had won. He expressed the hope that the rest of Mississippi would "take heed."[21]

On the heels of the settlement, James Laue, CRS's research director, made an onsite evaluation of what was done by the federal conciliators—why, how, and to what effect. He concluded that "all whites interviewed had high praise for CRS's role in Natchez, and all but two Negroes had similar feelings. . . . The Negroes who questioned our helpfulness said that CRS 'always wants to talk and bargain us out of our rights—to settle things too soon.'" The evaluation report went on: "Conciliators and Natchez residents agreed that the most effective things CRS did included: (a) constantly keeping communication open between disputants and acting as an honest broker; (b) educating white leaders to the conditions, grievances and settlement terms of the Negro community;

(c) avoiding violence in specific situations; (d) setting a tone of rationality, openness and the need for decision which made it possible for factions to negotiate differences."[22]

Within weeks of the Natchez agreement, Evers and the NAACP started a boycott in Fayette, Mississippi, a town of eighteen hundred people twenty miles from Natchez, in Jefferson County. Four hundred Blacks demonstrated in front of the Confederate monument, where Evers warned a watching group of about fifty whites, with shotguns prominently displayed in their pickup trucks, that violence would be met with violence. The *New York Times* reported his words: "We're tired of your bombings and beatings. We've talked with you and we've prayed for you, and now we're going to sit and wait for you."[23]

Growing more provocative, he said, "The Ku Klux Klan is nothing but a bunch of misfits. You don't have nothing and you ain't going to have nothing." He then launched into a forecast of the political future of the county, which was 75 percent Black. A year before it had no registered Black voters, but since a federal voting registrar had arrived, Black voters had come to outnumber whites by two to one. Evers said, "We're going to replace everybody in the courthouse and everybody in the City Hall that's not right and vote in some decent white folks and some decent Negroes."[24]

It took six months for the boycott to topple white resistance in Fayette, but change, when it came, was as far-reaching as in Natchez. Retail stores were desegregated, as were parks and public buildings. The police force was integrated, the use of courtesy titles was pledged, and street improvements in Black neighborhoods were agreed upon.

Evers's victory statement was more conciliatory than the one he issued in Natchez. He said, "No longer will there be talk of what's best for the Negro or what's best for the white. We'll now discuss what's best for Fayette and Jefferson County. We're going to start working for what's right."[25]

Mississippi continued to command special attention from CRS for the next few years. Local casework continued in the face of ever-present violence. Jim Draper, as the man in the middle, found himself on more than one occasion in the gun sights of desperate men. A Black farmer, protecting his home one night against marauding whites, braced Draper with a shotgun until he could establish his bona fides and his reason for being there. In Grenada one night, two Klansmen, firing an automatic rifle, hunted him through the dark streets near a Black church where he was expected for a meeting.[26]

Mississippi's poverty made the state heavily dependent on federal subsidies to assist agriculture and other programs. Thus, the federal government had been traditionally a passive collaborator in the anti-Black discrimination that characterized the administration of those programs.

When new civil rights laws suddenly required federal programs to be administered with an evenhanded respect for Blacks, and when antipoverty laws required that minorities participate in program management and decision making, the longstanding partnership between white state and federal officials came under heavy strain. African American organizations were eager to participate in the direction and operation of new federally funded education and development programs. State and local officials and politicians were bitterly opposed. In Washington the Mississippi congressional delegation on the one hand and civil rights advocacy groups on the other pulled every string within reach. Special task forces were created whose reports were studied and debated in the Washington headquarters of the federal agencies trying to identify, sort out, and evaluate conflicting claims.

Among the protest groups whose struggles for power in Mississippi drew great attention in Washington were the Delta Ministry of the National Council of Churches and the Child Development Group of Mississippi (CDGM).

The Delta Ministry sought to provide emergency food relief to the poor and also to stimulate community and economic development programs operated by Blacks. In the mid-sixties rapid improvement in farm mechanization was driving Black farm families off the land by the hundreds. Assistance for some was provided in makeshift camps—tent cities—supported by the Delta Ministry. In January 1966, seven hundred representatives of these displaced and homeless families met at Mt. Beulah, Mississippi, to protest "no food, no jobs, no land." Those attending the meeting pondered "dramatic" strategies for drawing attention to their plight. Shortly thereafter, a group from the tent city at Tribbett took over part of a deactivated air force base at Greenville and demanded that it be used as a site for manpower training and other assistance programs. Federal troops were used to oust the "invaders."

Controversy also came to a boil over the funding of the CDGM to run Head Start and other preschool programs—an enterprise that at

51

one time employed as many as two thousand formerly untrained people to serve eight thousand children in more than one hundred centers.

Reliable information from the scene of these and other struggles was a valued commodity to Washington decision makers. Direct access to grassroots data, and a short chain of command, made CRS a key player at subcabinet-level meetings about Mississippi, where the agency won respect for the accuracy and immediacy of its situational reports and its advocacy of rational change.[27]

(ALMOST) READY FOR NEW CHALLENGES

Even as the new federal conciliation workers were molding an organization and learning their craft, new storms of racial conflict were rising. Backlash to African American gains was eroding the climate of civil rights support. The unity of the movement was fractured by the debate over whether integration or Black militancy would yield greater equity for minorities. New opportunities for the poor to participate in developing and running anti-poverty programs set the stage for clashes between minorities and city hall. And civil disorders in northern cities awakened the nation to the intensity of Black rage smoldering in the inner cities.

With more work than it could handle in the South alone, CRS, in its first year, tried to hold itself aloof from major involvement elsewhere. It began to look north in the latter half of 1964, but it would not be until 1965 that, under new leadership and with an experienced staff, it would be poised to provide service on a national basis.[28]

Experience in Mississippi and the other southern states had helped to develop the rudiments of the community conflict resolution process. Not only did conciliators have some sense of what to do and when to do it; they also had a better understanding of their own abilities and limitations.

Late in 1965, following Jim Laue's evaluation of the Natchez case, a staff conference took place in Washington at which the techniques and approaches that CRS had learned to use in problem solving were reviewed. As Laue and his team recounted the process they had observed in dozens of cases and identified the discrete steps that had been taken, patterns began to emerge. The conciliators listened, some with the surprise of the man in the Molière play who discovered he had been speaking prose all his life. Laid out before them was a matrix of what to do and how to do it: how to enter a community, on request or on CRS's own motion; strategies for fact finding; when and how to use or avoid use of the media; how to level the playing field for negotiation between parties of disparate strength; when to involve third parties; when and how to call on other federal resources; tactics for using an "end run" to circumvent an impasse; when, where, and how to engage the power elite; how to move name-calling and harangue to genuine communication, to dialogue, to negotiation.

Yes, they had indeed done those things, not by chance or instinct or common sense alone, but thoughtfully, deliberately, in planned sequence. Whatever intuitive abilities they had originally brought to the job were now buttressed by learned behavior. No, it wasn't hard science; there were no sure prescriptions for every diagnosis, no pills that could guarantee cures. Nevertheless, they had begun to develop a distinct body of professional practice.

Half the communities served during CRS's first year were in just five southern states. Mississippi was the busiest theater of operations, with twenty-two locations receiving service. Alabama was second. While there was a core of similarity in problems and responses throughout the southern states, there were also distinctive differences. At the same time that CRS conciliators were finding their way and earning their spurs in Mississippi, others were dealing with different challenges in Alabama.

NOTES

1. Eighty-one years earlier, in 1883, the Supreme Court had ruled against Congress's authority to enact a public accommodations law, which had been defended then on the basis of the Fourteenth Amendment. In 1964, the Justice Department based its defense on the constitutional right of Congress to regulate interstate commerce. This the court found acceptable.

2. Nicholas Katzenbach, telephone interview with Bertram Levine.

3. As reported in the *New York Times* and *Wall Street Journal*.

4. Jay Janis, telephone interview with Bertram Levine.

5. Seymour Samet, interview with Bertram Levine.

6. Andrew MacDowd Secrest, interview with Bertram Levine.

7. Years later, assessment was to become a formal pillar of CRS's casework, including a written statement of the conciliator's objectives and his plan for achieving them.

8. Janis, interview with Levine.

9. Janis, interview with Levine.

10. A variety of "freedom houses" were set up in the rural South as needed, to serve as headquarters and/or lodgings for civil rights workers and activities.

11. Jim Draper, telephone interview with Bertram Levine. The safeguarding of information given in confidence is an inviolable obligation of the intervener. Any conciliator would be limited in resolving conflicts without the full trust of the contesting parties. For the federal government's racial peacemakers, the obligation was reinforced by law. A year in jail and a $1,000 fine faced the CRS conciliator who revealed information gained in confidence. Congress put the provision into the Civil Rights Act to protect Blacks from intimidation and reprisal as a result of talking to CRS representatives. But the sword cut both ways. To be an effective intermediary, CRS, as an agency, had to maintain a reputation of trustworthiness not only with the minority groups but with their antagonists as well.

12. Draper, interview with Levine.

13. Fleming, *Potomac Chronicle*, 109.

14. Fleming, *Potomac Chronicle*, 112.

15. U.S. Department of Justice, Community Relations Service, Annual Report, 1965.

16. National Citizens Committee for Community Relations, *Putting the Hard-Core Unemployed into Jobs.*

17. In January 1966, President Johnson had issued an executive order transferring CRS from the Department of Commerce to the Department of Justice.

18. *New York Times*, September 26, 1964.

19. *New York Times*, September 5, 1965.

20. Draper, interview with Levine.

21. *New York Times*, December 4, 1965.

22. Staff Report, Community Relations Service, Office of Program Evaluation and Development.

23. *New York Times*, December 25, 1964.

24. Evers's words in launching the boycott were prophetic. He himself was to serve as mayor of Fayette from 1969 to 1989.

25. *New York Times*, June 10, 1966.

26. Draper, interview with Levine.

27. This ability to impart to policy-level discussions data about the nitty-gritty details of daily life on city streets and at county crossroads was a major asset throughout CRS's experience. However, its counsel was sought less after the Johnson years, as other federal agencies became more confident in their own access to the currents of minority life.

28. See chapter 4.

THREE

Selma Blow by Blow

A Dissection of the Community Crisis
That Turned the Tide for Voting Rights

NEWS ABOUT THE civil rights protests in Selma, Alabama, and their brutal suppression blazed across America's front pages and television screens for more than two months in early 1965 and paved the way for passage of the Voting Rights Act of 1965.

Selma's place in civil rights history might have been no more distinguished than that of scores of county seats across the rural south where Black residents were denied their rights, struggled for redress, and were abused for their struggle. The difference resulted from the interlocking roles of a handful of individuals—and the social forces they represented—whose work converged in Selma at propitious times.

Located on a pleasant bluff overlooking the Alabama River, Selma came into being early in the 1820s as a shipping and trading center for the developing cotton plantations. A major munitions manufacturing center during the Civil War, it was captured and burned by Union forces in 1865. A legacy of racial bitterness remained. In 1964 a hooded horseman, depicted on a road sign leading into Selma, welcomed the stranger in the name of the Ku Klux Klan.[1]

Dallas County, of which Selma was the county seat, had been the first county in Alabama to organize a Citizens Council to resist the Supreme Court's school desegregation decision in 1954. Ten years later that council, three thousand strong, was the largest in the state. The county sheriff, James Clark, who maintained a volunteer posse of more than one hundred white men, was noted for his readiness to help police racial demonstrations anywhere in the state.

In the early 1960s, white Selma was peaceful and prosperous, with handsome neighborhoods, stately mansions, eighteen millionaires, a country club, and a growing class of business and industry executives. Black Selma, with as many people, was unpaved and underserved. Race relations were rigidly choreographed according to century-old patterns.

Dominance and subordination were prescribed by color. Black deference to whites was the expected behavior. Segregation was absolute—in church, in school, in social and civic life.

THE CONFLICT OVER VOTING RIGHTS

A small cadre of middle-class Blacks who were not dependent on whites for their livelihood composed the Dallas County Voters League (DVL)—the city's closest approach to a civil rights organization. The DVL worked to enlarge the number of registered Black voters, which stood at about one hundred and fifty out of a total of fifteen thousand of voting age. They encouraged people to register, helped to prepare them for the test, and comforted the many who tried and failed to overcome the obstacle course designed by Alabama law and the Dallas County Board of Registrars that implemented it. Otherwise things were quiet on the civil rights front.

The tempo began to change in late 1962 when SNCC included Selma in its Voter Education Project.[2] Bernard Lafayette, a twenty-two-year-old divinity student, was assigned by SNCC to assist Selma's voter registration effort. Lafayette, like many other civil rights flag bearers, brought to his assignment more than courage and deep commitment. A veteran of the sit-ins and freedom rides, he had been schooled in the theory and practice of nonviolent civil disobedience. He knew the principles and tactics for building a mass movement to bring about peaceful social change.

The civil rights movement in general had been slow to give priority to voting rights. A year earlier, at the height of the turmoil of the lunch counter sit-ins and the freedom rides, Justice Department suggestions that the movement might better invest its energies in voting rights were greeted with suspicion. Militants saw that as a government ploy to quiet things down and slow the thrust for civil rights reform. For its part, the Kennedy administration did indeed wish to dispel the violence in the streets. At the same time it saw the African American vote as the most efficient way to win civil rights progress across the board. The logic was simple: once—and wherever—Blacks gained political clout, they would more easily win other victories.

The Justice Department was winning voting rights cases in the courts, but without a definitive Supreme Court decision progress had to be forged on a case-by-case basis. This tedious process required that Blacks be encouraged, helped, and defended in their efforts to gain registration.

In Selma, Bernard Lafayette immediately reached out to Black school and college students. He helped them to identify and protest their grievances. There gradually developed a program of youth demonstrations, marches, and school boycotts. The authorities clamped down with arrests and suspensions. Fearful of economic and other reprisals, the adult Black community only looked on at first. As law enforcement became more punitive with the use of clubs and cattle prods, adults became more supportive and established a bail fund.

Lafayette was ready for the next step so important to building a mass movement—the large public meeting. It was at the mass meeting that people could take strength from one another, exchange information, and receive inspiration, hope, and a sense of the movement's objectives and strategy. But so intimidating was the racial climate that no Black church would make itself available for that purpose.

The Rubicon was crossed in May 1963 when Sam Boynton, the cofounder of the DVL, died after a debilitating illness. The memorial service in his honor at the Tabernacle Baptist Church was combined with a mass meeting in behalf of the cause to which he had been devoted—voting rights.

The sheriff and his men made a show of recording the license plate numbers of the cars in the parking lot. They next made themselves prominent in the hall. Their presence, meant to be intimidating, had the reverse effect. Somehow the events of the evening brought a sense of militancy and unity to the voting rights movement. Thereafter, the mass meeting became a fixture of community life in Selma.

On June 12, 1963, the night Medgar Evers was murdered in Mississippi, Bernard Lafayette was beaten by two white men who clubbed him with rifles. The rumor that the two events were linked by some anti-Black conspiracy was never validated. Nevertheless, Lafayette insisted on wearing his blood-stained T-shirt for two weeks. It symbolized the outrage and danger that many of Selma's Blacks felt.[3]

The tension continued to escalate. A voting rights demonstration by high school students on September 23 resulted in hundreds of arrests. The sheriff's posse was assisted by fifty state troopers under the personal leadership of state commander Al Lingo. The confrontation made national headlines.

A fact-finding team sent by the National Council of Churches reported on October 1, 1963, that seventy-five demonstrators were still being held under harsh conditions at "Camp Selma," a nearby prison camp. The attitude of the city was expressed by Mayor John Heinz: "Selma does not intend to change its customs or way of life." "Many responsible white citizens," the report said, "are afraid to speak out openly."

When the Civil Rights Act was signed in July 1964, a number of Blacks tried to integrate Selma's movie theater and a few of the white eating places. Gangs of white toughs disputed their passage, and there were some arrests and minor injuries. Demonstrations followed.

To end the demonstrations, Circuit Judge James Hare issued an injunction banning meetings of more than three people, and Sheriff Clark was quick to enforce it.[4] More than four hundred people were jailed for civil rights protests in the fall of 1964. The Justice Department sought to have the injunction overturned in federal court, but it took six months for that to happen.

Selma and Dallas County were no strangers to federal civil rights officials. Since 1961, the Civil Rights Division of the Justice Department had been working a slow, tedious strategy to bring voting rights suits throughout the South. To do this meant finding Blacks who had tried to register and been rejected—and who could withstand intimidation and economic reprisal. John Doar, then assistant chief (later chief) of the Civil Rights Division, personally spent months on the byways of the rural South finding sturdy complainants around whom strong cases might be built. He also made countless court appearances in behalf of Blacks who sought to exercise their right to demonstrate in behalf of voting rights.[5] Selma became a primary focal point for Doar after he encountered Amelia and Sam Boynton, founders of the Dallas County Voters League. On the wall of their real estate office he found an "honor roll" in the form of a plaque with the names of Dallas County Blacks who had tried to register. It was a bonanza of potential plaintiffs.

In late December 1964, John Doar and Burke Marshall suggested to John Griffin, chief of the CRS conciliation staff, that CRS might have a role to play in Selma. SCLC had decided in November to make common cause with SNCC in pushing voter rights in Selma. Martin Luther King Jr. was scheduled to make his first appearance there shortly after New Year's Day. Tension was sure to rise.

Mac Secrest headed a CRS team that arrived in Selma on January 12, 1965. His primary mission was to make an onsite assessment in order to learn for himself what the problems were and whether they might be responsive to conciliation by CRS. The team spent two weeks meeting, listening, and researching. Its members spoke with scores of officials, community leaders, and private individuals—Black and white. These encounters took place at all hours—sometimes in clear view and sometimes in out-of-the-way places to assure confidentiality.

WHEN LEADERS FEAR TO TALK

The CRS assessment found a bitterly divided community, unable to manage true communication between Blacks and whites. Even among whites, the divisions ran deep between extremists and moderates. The inherited wealth and power of Dallas County's first families was being challenged by the urban-focused business community interested in expanding the local industrial base. The business community had recently succeeded in wresting political control from the old guard. Joe Smitherman, the new mayor, was widely assumed to be more tractable on racial issues than his immovable predecessor had been, despite his campaign pledge never to meet with an "outside agitator" or talk to any supporter of Dr. King.

The city police and the sheriff's office contended about how and by whom racial demonstrations were to be policed. J. Wilson Baker, a former police captain, had been enticed by Smitherman from a teaching post at the University of Alabama to fill the newly created city post of public safety director. While the sheriff held sway over the county and the courthouse where the voting registrars did business, Baker insisted on primacy in the city, including the streets around the courthouse where the demonstrations took place.

Although the moderate whites had just won political control, they were fearful of losing favor with a conservative electorate. Worried that racial progress might incite white ruffians to violence, none dared propose interracial dialogue. The chairman of the Selma Ministerial Association, widely respected for moral stature and civic leadership, told CRS that he was part of a group of white men who had been meeting informally in recent weeks to discuss racial problems. But he would not reveal the names of the other members. African American leaders described him as "a good man with a weak stomach."

The Black community had its own divisions—between the older, more timid, don't-rock-the-boat leadership and the more venturesome, younger leaders of the Dallas County Voters League. DVL and SCLC were sometimes at odds over the internal contradictions between local and national agendas. SNCC and SCLC, while pledged to cooperation, were nevertheless rivals as to leadership, organizational prominence, and, sometimes, tactics. Among the local Blacks, Amelia Boynton was regarded as the leader of the militant faction. To whites, she was a stormy petrel. Some felt that because of the vigor of her protest leadership, they could not afford to be in contact with her.

Secrest had first learned of Mrs. Boynton when he had interviewed the owner of the IGA supermarket. The man had said that he once asked Mrs. Boynton to leave his store when she had "demanded" that he employ more Blacks because so many Blacks shopped there. He said he might have treated her differently if she had approached him in a different manner.

Frederick Douglas Reese, a young man who had succeeded Sam Boynton as president of the DVL, was also head of the Negro United Fund. He worked as a science teacher at Hudson High School. While he had the confidence of local Blacks, he also enjoyed the respect of many white leaders and was the primary local contact with SCLC.

Public Safety Commissioner J. Wilson Baker, while a man of contradictions, was clearly the strongest force for racial progress among the white leaders. He had been able to coalesce a majority of white support on the issue of law and order, which he used as a two-edged sword. On the one hand, he required Blacks to conduct their demonstrations in accordance with local law and court decisions. On the other, he sought to protect the integrity of legal demonstrations by keeping Sheriff Clark, as well as white troublemakers, from disrupting the demonstrations. In frequent confrontations with demonstrators he preferred to rely on negotiation and persuasion rather than police force.

Baker's approach was as much a product of power structure strategy as of the commissioner's innate style of law enforcement. The business community wanted to avoid bad publicity at all costs. Selma was on the brink of a major industrial expansion. Several large corporations were considering making major investments in Dallas County. It was hoped that others would follow. These companies, all sensitive to the new federal requirements for equal employment opportunity, might have second thoughts about locating in an area of racial turmoil where they could not be assured of a harmonious workforce.

Many of the business leaders looked on the actions of Sheriff Clark and Judge Hare as an invitation to disaster. They saw Clark as another Bull Connor.[6] Moreover, some believed that SCLC had deliberately come to Selma because it, too, saw Clark as someone who, if aroused, would propel Selma and the voting rights issue onto center stage nationally. Wilson Baker had to succeed in controlling the demonstrators with civility, lest his failure open the gate to Jim Clark's unbridled force.

Wilson Baker, when interviewed by Howell Raines ten years later, said that SCLC's strategy for the State of Alabama had been known by law enforcement agencies since August 1964, when they had obtained a secret planning blueprint.[7] Clark's propensity for offering his posse throughout the state to help suppress civil rights demonstrations had identified him to SCLC as the person to be confronted to assure a response that would attract national media attention.

As was true in so many other towns CRS had assessed, white leaders of Selma said they found it difficult to discern who were the Blacks' true leaders and what were their grievances. Yet Secrest, a stranger in town, already had a copy of a statement of African American concerns, drafted three months earlier. Approved by the leading organizations, it was in the hands of a committee appointed to discuss it with white leaders if and when that became possible.

The Blacks' concerns included: (1) job opportunities and advancement, particularly as policemen, firemen, and retail clerks; (2) improved recreational facilities; (3) improved housing conditions, paved streets, and adequate sewage; (4) equal pay for equal work; (5) an end to mass arrests and police brutality; (6) the opportunity to join the sheriff's posse; (7) freedom to register and vote without fear of reprisal; (8) compliance with public accommodations provisions of the 1964 Civil Rights Act; (9) desegregation of public schools; (10) proper respect in addressing Blacks according to their titles; (11) participation in the decision-making process.

The statement of concerns of Selma's African American community might have been a useful agenda for good-faith negotiation if there had been any response to it at the time it was written. In January, three months later, however, with the community united behind SNCC and SCLC leaders and their almost exclusive focus on the voting rights issue, it had been relegated to a back burner.

The first feeble effort by moderate whites to take a public position occurred after a group of business leaders met with Secrest. They had been considering whether or not to make a public statement favoring law and order, which would be seen as an endorsement of Baker's treatment of demonstrators and a repudiation of Clark's methods. Secrest offered some suggestions and encouraged the statement's prompt issuance. It appeared in the paper the next day.[8]

Secrest had an appointment to meet with Dr. King as soon as the SCLC leader arrived in town on January 17. It had to be canceled because of an incident in the lobby of the newly desegregated Albert Hotel, where King, upon his arrival, was attacked by a member of the National States' Rights Party. Secrest and King did, however, have a lengthy phone conversation. King made it clear that while SCLC had a genuine interest in helping to resolve the grievances of Selma's Blacks, its primary objective was to highlight abuses in Selma in order to support its overall goal of securing voting rights throughout the state of Alabama.

Voting laws in Alabama were designed to look equal in principle but to be anti-Black in application. Each county had a three-person board of registrars appointed by the governor and his designees, thus unaccountable to any local authority. Under state law the county board of registrars met at the county courthouse the first and third Mondays of each month to register voters. Few Blacks surmounted the contrived procedures, particularly the infamous literacy test in which answers to esoteric questions were subjectively graded. In Dallas County, ten to twenty people were processed on each registration day, with most Blacks being rejected. The legitimacy of the literacy test had been called into question by the Civil Rights Act of 1960, but that didn't stop its use in Alabama. In Dallas County, where the DVL had succeeded in two years in doubling the number of Black registrants to three hundred, there were more than fifteen thousand of voting age. At a rate of forty a month, it would take thirty-one years for all of those eligible to be processed. Blacks demanded an increased rate of processing and a fairer application of qualification criteria.

The Civil Rights Act of 1960 provided for the federal courts to appoint voting referees who could register voters if it was established in court that the state maintained a pattern or practice to deny registration to qualified minorities. By seeking registration, even if rejected by the Dallas County Board of Registrars, African American citizens were qualifying themselves to someday apply to the federal registrars.

This ultimately resulted in a fixed choreography on each semimonthly registration day. Hundreds of Blacks would take their places in the prescribed lines, with each applicant accompanied by the registered voter required to vouch for him or her. Those in front would be processed, with most being rejected. The majority of those in line, who were not processed, would return another day. Almost nightly mass meetings at Brown's Chapel Church were designed to encourage more people to seek registration and to cheer the persistence of those who returned to the lines repeatedly to be processed.

January 17 was to be a day of portentous developments in Selma. SCLC, SNCC, and local demonstrators would be out in force to support voter registration and to desegregate restaurants and other public accommodations. Martin Luther King was to address a mass rally that evening. CRS had learned that George Lincoln Rockwell, head of the American Nazi Party, and J. B. Stoner of the National States' Rights Party, as well as representatives of the Klan and other white supremacist groups, were coming to Selma to create disturbances. Selma's civic leaders saw the day as an attempt by King to draw national attention. They decided to respond with deliberate conflict avoidance.

The SCLC agenda, however, was to court conflict as a means of illuminating injustice. That night, at Brown's Chapel Church, King exhorted an audience of eight hundred to mount more and larger street demonstrations. "Continue to plague Dallas County—creatively and non-violently," he said.[9]

The city of Selma, mostly in the form of Wilson Baker and his police force, disposed of the challenge to law and order posed by the white supremacists with reasonable dispatch. The National States' Rights Party member who attacked King in the lobby of the Albert Hotel was jailed promptly and sentenced on the following day. Rockwell was promptly arrested for disturbing the peace when he started a harangue outside the mass meeting that evening. A rabble-rouser in blackface and flamboyant garb who sought to provoke African Americans integrating the restaurants was promptly incarcerated.

The African Americans' public accommodations challenges were not resisted, by and large, although there were isolated attacks by angry whites. Since the start of the year the restaurant owners, anticipating a federal court order requiring them to desegregate under the 1964 Civil Rights Act, were ready for the inevitable. They would accept desegregation calmly, confident that once African Americans had established the principle that they *could* eat where they chose, they would return to their more familiar surroundings. On January 17 the restaurant owners accepted Black diners and distributed to their white patrons a printed note explaining that they were unwillingly complying with federal law.

While conflict avoidance was white Selma's response through most of the city that day, provocation and conflict boiled at the courthouse, where Sheriff Clark held sway. African Americans who marched downtown to register were directed to a rear door and forced to wait outside in a cordoned-off alley. They demanded use of the front door and courthouse corridors, which were accessible to white registrants. Sixty-seven were jailed, including Mrs. Boynton, whom Jim Clark personally seized by the back of the collar and propelled down the street for half a block in clear view of the nation's news cameras.[10]

By the end of January, with the detailed mosaic of his assessment pieced together, Secrest was ready to recommend a sustained CRS commitment to Selma—with the intent of conciliating the immediate crisis and also dealing with the long-range disputes over ongoing inequities. Both issues would require the establishment of genuine communication between Blacks and whites, and so Secrest set that as his first objective. In order to achieve it, the conciliation team would have to help the parties keep the conflict from escalating out of control. They would also try to build bridges of interracial communication in preparation for the time when they could be used for effective conciliation.

At the same time Secrest was troubled by a paradox. There would be times when CRS, in pursuit of its goals, might find itself working at cross-purposes with some of the civil rights agencies. The CRS objectives were to reduce conflict and to help resolve African American grievances in Selma. How would that affect the SCLC objective of dramatizing the injustices in Selma in order to win support for strong federal voting rights legislation?

SCLC's intention to draw national attention to Selma became even more pronounced on February 1. Instead of the usual small-group procession to the courthouse on registration day, King personally led a parade there, in clear violation of the city's parade ordinance. When Baker threatened him with arrest, he calmly continued the march. He and seven hundred demonstrators were arrested that day. In keeping with his plan, King refused to post bond and was kept in jail for five days; from there, he orchestrated continuing demonstrations.

King's arrest and the impact of his published "Letter from a Selma Jail" brought support from across the country. According to Juan Williams, King's letter, published as an ad in the *New York Times*, was drafted before his arrest. The strategy was modeled after his "Letter from a Birmingham Jail," which had achieved resounding public sympathy two years earlier.[11] In the ensuing days Selma was visited by two congressional delegations and a host of civil rights leaders. Malcolm X paid a visit and announced that if Dr. King's doctrine of nonviolence was not successful, others, preaching a different doctrine, might take his place. The arrests brought new life to the Selma campaign, which had begun to show signs of exhaustion and burnout.

Community tension waxed and waned repeatedly through February as new issues passed in and out of focus. On February 4, U.S. District Court Judge Daniel H. Thomas, ruling on a Justice Department suit, decreed that the Dallas County Board of Registrars must process one hundred applications each day that it was open, that it could no longer require a literacy test, and that it must cease rejecting Black applicants on technicalities. Applicants who appeared to register but were not processed would be permitted to enter their names in an appearance book to prove they had made the effort. He further ruled that if all applicants were not processed by July, he would appoint a voting referee to do so.[12]

King immediately called for a respite in the demonstrations while SCLC "evaluated" the court order. The rumor spread that SCLC was rethinking its strategy. Maybe the Selma demonstrations had reached the point of diminishing returns. Could Selma better serve as headquarters for an accelerated campaign throughout the state? The city's white leaders tried to prevail on Sheriff Clark to adopt a low profile. Without provocation by the posse, perhaps the focus of national attention would move elsewhere.

The sheriff did not buy into that strategy. On February 8, the Reverend James Bevel, while leading a protest to the registrars' office, was shoved and repeatedly prodded with Sheriff Clark's billy club before being arrested. Sentenced to five days in jail, he developed a fever and was removed to a hospital, where a doctor later found him guarded and shackled to the bed.

In the midst of the turmoil, King flew to Washington for a long-sought meeting with President Johnson. The president then announced publicly that he would soon send to Congress a proposal for additional voter rights legislation. The announcement appeared to have no impact on developments in Selma.

THE BUILDUP TO BLOODY SUNDAY

On February 10, Sheriff Clark and his posse rounded up 165 children and teenagers who were demonstrating at the courthouse. Under the guise of arrest, he herded them with clubs and cattle prods on a forced half-march/half-run for more than two miles into the countryside. While physical injuries were few and mild, the experience was traumatic for many of the younger children.

After that day, there was no longer any possibility of the protest running out of energy; it emerged that night with a full head of steam. Mass meetings overflowed two churches. New faces swelled the ranks of demonstrators. African American teachers turned out en masse—a certain sign that the conservative segment of the community was moving into the protest ranks. Night marches and round-the-clock vigils at the courthouse were urged. SCLC planned for a demonstration so large as to dwarf all that had been held before. It would take place on the next registration day, Monday, February 15. King canceled a previously scheduled voters march in Birmingham so that civil rights leaders throughout the state would be freed up to rally in Selma.

In the midst of it all, there was a confusing development. On February 11, the day after the mass arrest of children, six hundred students boycotted school and demonstrated again at the courthouse, showing they had not been intimidated by the forced march of the previous day. Clark, whose men had made almost three thousand arrests in the six weeks since SCLC had started its campaign in early January, took no action against the students. People speculated about the sheriff's surprising restraint. That morning the *Selma Times-Journal*, in a front page editorial, had called Clark to task for his excesses in marching the children. Observers wondered if city officials had at last been successful in reining him in.

On Monday, February 15, almost three thousand African Americans demonstrated for voting rights in Dallas County and two nearby counties. With a parade permit issued by Baker, King personally led a march to the courthouse in Selma, where twelve hundred people lined up single file to sign the appearance book, attesting to their intentions to register. By the end of the day 570 had signed, and 120 had actually been registered, 20 more than the minimum required by Judge Thomas's latest order.

On Tuesday, the sixteenth, an additional five hundred Blacks lined up to sign the appearance book. When the Reverend C. T. Vivian led a small group into the courthouse through a side door to take shelter from the rain, Clark's men sought to remove them with the usual prods of their billy clubs. Vivian confronted Clark, calling him a brute and comparing him to Hitler. Clark punched Vivian in the mouth, drawing blood. He then had him arrested.

Clark's abuse of Vivian had an incendiary effect on the Blacks of Selma, already enraged by the shooting of Jimmie Lee Jackson the night before in nearby Marion. There state troopers and white ruffians had attacked Blacks who were leaving a protest rally at a church. Jackson had been mortally wounded. (He died a few days later.)

At the mass meeting the next night King reported SCLC's decision to intensify the effort until voter registration could take place without a single hindrance and until Sheriff Clark was removed. King said that until the power structure saw to it that these things were done, there would be broader forms of civil disobedience. A consumer boycott of downtown merchants would be launched, and nighttime demonstrations were being considered.

Aided by the rising sense of crisis, Mac Secrest found himself finally able, in early February, to move forward in bringing about direct discussions between Blacks and whites. On February 6 he arranged for a small group of white moderate leaders to meet in private with a biracial leadership team from CRS—Deputy Director Calvin Kytle and Assistant Director Roger Wilkins. The Washington officials appealed to pragmatism. Since the Black vote would inevitably result from federal legislation, why not end the turmoil by speeding the registration process? Could the board of registrars be persuaded to seek an increase in the number of registration days per month and quicken the process of registration from one hundred per day? (Montgomery was now doing one hundred per hour.) They suggested other measures that whites might take. One was to build public sentiment for "law and order" to assure the security of peaceful demonstrations. Another was to continue to press for interracial negotiation at the earliest feasible time.

Building on the momentum of the meeting with Kytle and Wilkins, Secrest was able, a week later, to convene the first meeting of Black and white leaders of Selma. For two and a half hours there was a full and frank exchange of views. Secrest felt that each group learned a lot about the motivation and goodwill of the other. He called it a good beginning toward *real* confrontation and *real* communication. But it was slow going; he was unable to get them to agree on a specific date for a second meeting. It would be up to CRS to continue to stoke that fire.[13]

As the tempo of the demonstrations rose, so did resentment in the white community. Smitherman and Baker grew more agitated. They informed Secrest that the threatened night marches were sure to bring violence. Adequate police protection for demonstrators from unruly whites was doubtful; the city budget was already stressed because of police overtime. Baker began to show signs of combat fatigue. He revealed his feelings to Secrest in a late-night conversation on February 18. Continuation of the demonstrations was an act of bad faith. He cited his behind-the-scenes efforts with the registrars and the court to improve registration procedures. He said that the African American leaders knew that these moves reflected the mood and intention of the new city administration to be responsive to Black demands. Moreover, Judge Thomas had promised to appoint federal registrars in July. That meant that by August 1 all who signed the registration book would be registered.

Baker warned of a developing mood of white backlash. After-dark protests would bring it to a head. Night marches were likely to result in bloodshed and death. He was unwilling to subject himself to further twenty-hour days or expose his men to bricks, bottles, Molotov cocktails, and stray bullets in order to protect people who were inciting to riot. He felt that African Americans should recognize that they had won a big victory in Selma. A cooling-off period was needed to enable local whites and Blacks to repair relationships and then move forward.

In his deep despair Baker complained that even the white moderates who had supported his efforts were turning away. He felt isolated. As a result, he had begun to have thoughts of resigning as public safety commissioner.

Baker's fears of growing white bitterness were confirmed the next day in a front-page editorial in the *Selma Times-Journal*. It offered veiled warnings about the consequences of what it saw as SCLC's provocative behavior.

This newspaper regards with mounting alarm . . . the failure of local Negro leadership to assert itself in demanding an immediate departure of outside forces which are now deliberately provoking the understanding and sympathy of all sound thinking citizens perilously near to the breaking point. For almost a month of the most difficult adjustment since Reconstruction Days, Selma citizens have displayed a degree of restraint which has awed and confounded everyone who has sought to exploit our proud city. That our people are temperate and law abiding and can swallow with dignity any dose regardless of how bitter its taste is no longer a matter of speculation but an established fact.

But how long Selmians and their elected officials are expected to endure continuing jabs at the sore spots of their injured sense of justice is already a point of serious consideration.

On Friday, February 19, Governor George C. Wallace ordered the state police to ban night marches in Marion and Selma, blaming the trouble on outside communist-inspired agitators.

SCLC conducted its first night march in Selma that night. Three hundred African Americans moved out, led by Reverend Hosea Williams. Wilson Baker, acting promptly in order to preempt action by the state police, halted the march. Williams was arrested but released once the marchers were dispersed.

Jim Laue joined the federal conciliation team in Selma on February 20. He was a sociologist whose Harvard doctoral dissertation was based on research he had conducted while serving as a volunteer field-worker for SCLC. He had strong personal ties to King and to many of the SCLC leaders. On his way to Selma he stopped off at Atlanta to speak with a trusted friend, SCLC's executive director, the Reverend Andrew

Young. Young confirmed that SCLC would continue its efforts in Selma until the white community did something about African American grievances, which, it would now be made clear, encompassed more than voting rights. From then on, the demands of the demonstrators would also include such local issues as the hiring of Black police and firemen, the paving of streets and improving of other facilities in Black neighborhoods, and the establishment of lines of communication between Selma's Black and white leaders.[14]

On the twenty-first, Laue met with Baker, who reviewed the Blacks' new list of demands. The public safety director explained why there was nothing to negotiate. Street paving in the Black neighborhood would require an assessment on the property owners. Black owners wouldn't want that. Hiring Black firemen was impossible because integrated living in such tight quarters would not be accepted. As to hiring Black police officers, he had told African American leaders he would accept applications but had received none. While the city had no money now for new positions, he hoped he might be able to hire both Black and white officers soon. As for voting, that was controlled by court order and the city could do nothing about it.

On Sunday evening, February 21, more than a thousand people crowded into Brown's Chapel to cheer the announcement that the proposed boycott of Selma merchants was on. Governor Wallace's name was booed for his ban on night marches. Speakers noted that night marches were never banned when the Klan used them.

On Monday morning, the twenty-second, the air was heavy with tension. King and Young spoke at a mass meeting. Then two hundred and fifty Blacks, proceeding in the legally allowed groups of five, lined up at the courthouse—fifty who wanted to sign the appearance book at the courthouse door, the others farther back. Many whites gathered around. The town was buzzing with word of an earlier incident when a Black had been beaten by a bat-wielding white. The state troopers and the sheriff's posse were present in force, but Wilson Baker was in control, directing the procession with a loudspeaker from his car. The crowd disbanded by the time the applicants had signed the book.

Fred Miller, a federal conciliator whose accent and manner permitted him to move easily in hostile white crowds, picked up a rumor of a possible attempt on King's life. Laue passed the word to Baker and Andrew Young.

That night King addressed a rally at Brown's Chapel. Enlarged protests were discussed. The Selma boycott would be extended to the buses. Plans were going forward for a major march from Selma to Montgomery to voice outrage at the shooting of Jimmie Lee Jackson and to protest Alabama's voting laws directly to Governor Wallace. Twilight marches were to begin the following evening. Scheduled to take place between 6:00 and 7:00 p.m., they would be timed to include schoolchildren and workers and yet not breach the ban against night marches.

There was talk of the danger. Dr. King told of a message he had received from a "high government official" warning him of an assassination plot. Young, referring to the whites lining the street outside, said, "It's going to be hell out there." He asked the crowd if any of them had ever been hit by a baseball bat when they were young. Many answered yes. Young responded: "That scar heals in six weeks, but scars of segregation never heal, so you be ready to march."

As King left the church at the end of the meeting, the street was filled with bystanders, most of the whites having come from a meeting of the Citizens Council, where Governor Ross Barnett of Mississippi had been the guest speaker. The city police were on hand. A detachment of Colonel Lingo's state troopers drove up and started questioning Dr. King. Wilson Baker, fearing that they might arrest King, and knowing the consequences of such a move, directed the troopers to move on. There was a verbal confrontation, and then the state forces withdrew.

The next morning Baker complained to Lane about Lingo. "If this goes on I'll probably be leading the night march myself next week." He said that he and Mayor Smitherman would be meeting with Governor Wallace that afternoon to personally protest the colonel's move and seek some restraint.[15] Baker then revealed the city's plan for dealing with the twilight marches so as to shield the marchers from confrontations with county and state law enforcement officers. The city police would arrest the marchers immediately, detain them without charges for a couple of hours, and then release them in small groups after all others had dispersed.

On Wednesday afternoon, about a hundred and fifty Black teenagers started a march from the church to city hall. They were stopped by Baker two blocks short of their destination. They prayed, sang, and went back to the church. Baker felt that the meeting with Governor Wallace probably helped in keeping Clark and Lingo out of the way.

Meanwhile, behind the scenes, the federal effort to encourage nego-tiations between Blacks and whites in Selma continued. On Tuesday morning, February 23, LeRoy Collins, the director of CRS, was sched-uled to attend a meeting in Birmingham. Secrest and Laue saw this as another opportunity to further interracial dialogue. Collins invited Wilson Baker and Carl Morgan, president of the Selma City Council, to join him that evening for a meeting with Andrew Young of SCLC and F. D. Reese of the Dallas County Voters League.

The government representatives thought the discussion provided for a full and frank delineation of SCLC objectives and what might be expected of the city administration and influential whites in response. While no formal agreement emerged, there was an understanding on three specific points: (1) Effort would be made to persuade Judge Thomas to amend his order to require the board of registrars to process a minimum of three hundred to three hundred and fifty applications on each of the two days per month that the board was in session. (2) White leaders would make continuing efforts to support greater fairness in law enforcement and voting. (3) Biracial discussions would be undertaken on a regular basis.

While Young and Reese were unable to offer any guarantee of the cooling-off period requested by the whites, they indicated that a de facto truce might develop in the next two weeks. The movement and its leaders were exhausted, and several were in the hospital. Besides, energy had to be conserved for planning the march on Montgomery. Young said that plans for night marches were temporarily on hold.

The de facto cooling-off period Young had predicted did, indeed, begin almost immediately. While King announced at one mass meeting, "We will win a voting bill on the streets of Selma," demonstrations were uneventful.

During the first week in March, protest activity was at low tide. SCLC made its plans for the march to Montgomery. SNCC tried to discourage the action, questioning whether the objective justified the danger. On March 6, the SNCC Executive Committee met in Atlanta and decided that it would not participate officially. However, individual SNCC members were free to do as they chose. John Lewis, SNCC's chairman, told the group, "I've been to Selma many, many times. I've been arrested there. I've been jailed there. . . . You decide what you want to do, but I'm going to march." Reflecting on that decision, Lewis wrote: "I couldn't imagine living with myself if the people of Selma had marched and I had not been with them."[16]

That day Governor Wallace declared that the march to Montgomery would not be allowed. Plans were made for a joint law enforcement operation to stop it. Sheriff Clark's posse and Colonel Lingo's state troopers would take their positions outside Selma on the far side of the Edmund Pettus Bridge. Wilson Baker threatened to resign rather than permit the Selma police to join them.

On Sunday, March 7, six hundred participants left the housing project playground near Brown's Chapel, walked six blocks through the streets of Selma, and crossed over the Edmund Pettus Bridge on their way to Montgomery. The leaders were John Lewis of SNCC and Hosea Williams of SCLC.[17]

As the demonstrators crested the bridge, they could see waiting for them a solid line of fifty state highway patrolmen about three hundred yards beyond the end of the span. The troopers stood shoulder to shoulder, with their hands in front of them gripping their batons. Dozens of posse members, many of them mounted, were grouped behind. More than a hundred white Alabamans had gathered to witness the action.

As the head of the column approached, Major John Cloud ordered the leaders to halt. They did so.

Hosea Williams called out: "May we have a word with the major?"

"There is no word to be had," came the reply.

Cloud then commanded the marchers to disperse within two minutes. When they failed to do so, came the further command: "Troopers, advance!"

With gas masks on and batons at the ready, the troopers formed a wedge that split the marchers to either side. There quickly followed a barrage of gas canisters, and then the charging posse using ropes and billy clubs. Eighty-four people were injured, seventeen requiring hospitalization. John Lewis suffered a fractured skull.[18]

Fred Miller, the CRS conciliator on the bridge at the time, later remembered it as the bloodiest event he had witnessed in nine years of trying to stave off racial conflict in the rural South. "I saw women beaten to the ground with billy clubs and then the state troopers and deputies would come up and threw [*sic*] tear gas canisters underneath them. They were out to beat heads, not keep order."[19]

Despite an agreement with Baker that state and county law enforcement would not pursue the demonstrators once they returned to Selma, the mounted posse followed the fleeing hundreds through the town to the doors of Brown's Chapel and to the stoops of the housing project. Blacks started to respond to the swinging clubs with bricks and bottles. Some emerged from their homes with firearms. Andrew Young moved through the angry Blacks, appealing to them to forgo the use of force. According to Baker:

> And Congressman Young, he played such an important part of saving a bloodbath. He was just running wild up and down to these apartment units: "Get back into the house with this weapon. . . . We're not going to have any weapons out." Because I was there with him helping him, but I finally found out that that would not do it, so I went to Jim Clark, the sheriff, and told him, "Now, you get your cowboys, and you get 'em out of here, and you get 'em out of here *now*." . . . I finally told him in such a stern way that he did go get his men and get back out of there. I said, "Now, you are fixin' to cause a bloodbath, and there's gonna be a lot of us killed, too, and I mean get 'em out of here and get 'em out of here now." . . . We knew things were really fixing to pop.[20]

THE SECOND CROSSING

The following morning, SCLC headquarters in Atlanta advised Jim Laue that the organization was enraged at the federal government's slowness in responding to Sunday's carnage. It was insulting that the FBI said it was going to investigate to determine whether there was an excessive use of force by the posse and the state police; everyone had seen the brutality on television. There would be a second march the next day—this time to be led by King. Religious, civil rights, and civic leaders from all over the country were being asked to join. Already the response was massive. CRS got word to the Justice Department and the White House of the Black determination to push on regardless of the consequences.

SCLC appealed to U.S. District Court Judge Frank Johnson for an order enjoining Governor Wallace from interfering with a march from

Selma to Montgomery. The judge, on Tuesday morning, set a hearing on this motion for the following Thursday. But, fearing another bloody confrontation, he issued a temporary restraining order barring King and his followers from conducting a march until their petition could be heard in court. The civil rights forces called the judge's response an unconstitutional infringement of their First Amendment rights.

While the judge did not issue his restraining order until the morning of the second march, the leaders of the march expected it. It was a source of agonizing debate deep into Monday night. The federal courts had been a sturdy ally and protector in the fight for civil rights. The movement had never set itself against the federal courts. Could it afford to do so now? That night, at Brown's Chapel, Dr. King told the crowd, "We've gone too far to turn back now. We must let them know that nothing can stop us—not even death itself. We must be ready for a season of suffering."

Governor Wallace responded to these developments by stating that there would be no march on Tuesday. He dispatched one hundred state patrol cars to Selma to reinforce the troopers already there and indicated that there would be no change in police tactics.

On Monday and Tuesday a steady stream of vehicles passed over the Pettus Bridge into town, bearing four hundred and fifty dignitaries and other visitors from throughout the country. They were responding to King's invitation to join him in the second march. Troopers stopped every vehicle to inquire where people were coming from and going to and why.

On Monday evening, March 8, President Johnson summoned LeRoy Collins to the White House to tell him that Sunday's tragic bloodshed shamed the nation. His concern was compounded by the prospect that it might be repeated on Tuesday with even greater ferocity. He instructed Collins to go to Selma and make sure that didn't occur.

On Tuesday morning, Collins and Secrest boarded a White House Jetstar plane at Andrews Air Force Base outside Washington, arriving at Craig Air Force Base, near Selma, at 10:30 a.m. Fred Miller greeted them at the airport. The march was scheduled to step off in three hours.

The government's representatives met with Dr. King and other civil rights leaders at the home of Dr. Sullivan Jackson, a Selma dentist with whom King was staying. Collins told King of the president's concerns and asked him to consider what the consequences of the march might be. King replied that he had already wrestled with his conscience, but he must go forward, even if it meant that he would die on the streets of Alabama. Besides, the movement was determined. Not even Judge Johnson's order would hold the marchers back, and he would lose control if he refused to lead them. Further appeals by Collins were fruitless.[21]

CRS then raised the question of whether, after the march started, a way might be found to avoid violence. Secrest and Young stepped out of the room to consider options. Secrest asked what if the troopers physically barred the roadway? Would the nonviolent marchers seek to march over or through them? Young replied that they would not. What if Collins could get assurances from Clark and Lingo that the marchers would not be attacked if they halted when stopped, conducted their protest on the spot, and returned to the church? Would they do it? Young didn't answer. Instead the two returned to the other room to discuss with King and Collins the realistic options that would face the marchers once they had been stopped. After hearing the Young/Secrest formulation, King said that he would consider it but could not commit himself in advance to turning back after a successful crossing. "He wound up by saying he would do the best he could."[22] That was all the federal mediators needed.

Secrest and Collins excused themselves. Back in Miller's car they raced to Brown's Chapel Church, where they were sure to find Sheriff Clark monitoring the preparations for the march. Collins explained that he had reason to believe that Dr. King, a man committed to nonviolence, would stop when halted. He wanted assurance from Clark and Colonel Lingo that under those circumstances there would be no repetition of the use of force. Clark replied by inviting Collins and Secrest into his squad car. They drove over the Pettus Bridge on Highway 80 east to Colonel Lingo's command post in an automobile dealership down the road.

Lingo was hesitant and noncommittal. Collins repeated his message. The president of the United States personally wanted assurance that there would be no bloodshed. Finally Lingo stated that it was not his intention—unless it should prove necessary—to use force to halt the march or to break up a meeting or interfere with the protesters' right of assembly, petition, and prayer. CRS insisted that no time limit be placed on the highway assembly, and Lingo agreed.

Lingo interrupted the discussion several times to use the phone in another room. Secrest and Collins had no doubt he was talking to Governor Wallace and getting his approval.

They returned to Miller's car to find King. In the playground near the church, where the march was about to start, they advised him of Lingo's stated intentions. King made no commitment as to what he would do when stopped.

Fifteen hundred marchers, fearful but determined, set out on their trek to Montgomery, fifty miles away. The column, four abreast and more than a half-mile long, wound its way out of the Black neighborhood and through downtown Selma—Black citizens of Dallas County of all ages, and dignitaries of all colors from across the United States.

As they approached the bridge a Black man, Stanley Fountain, chief deputy U.S. marshal for the Southern District of Alabama, advised Dr. King and the other march leaders that if they continued their march to Montgomery they would be in violation of a federal court order. The procession moved on.

The federal conciliators headed for the appointed place of confrontation. Lingo had said that he would position his men two or three miles beyond the point of Sunday's face-off so that the demonstrators could march that far. At the last minute he had changed his mind and placed the troopers exactly where they had been on Sunday.

Collins took a position where he could observe the developments and be clearly visible to both Lingo and King. He was still uncertain about how they would perform. The whole arrangement had been based on supposition. No formal agreement had been reached.

As the marchers approached, Major Cloud, as he had done on Sunday, announced over the bullhorn that the group would not be permitted to go further. Dr. King declared that they had the right to march to Montgomery to present their grievances to the governor.

Cloud replied: "We are here to see that this march will not continue. It would not be conducive to the safety of this group or the motoring public."

King then asked for and received permission for the group to pray. After the singing of "We Shall Overcome," four of the march leaders took turns in leading the group in prayer. The leaders then turned and started the column back across the bridge to Selma.

Just before the marchers turned back, Lingo made a surprise move. He ordered his troopers off the highway. The route to Montgomery was unobstructed. Unmindful of this development, the marchers turned around and headed back across the bridge. When Secrest later asked Lingo why he had withdrawn the troopers, the colonel told him that if the demonstrators wanted to go ahead and violate the federal court order, he didn't think it was his place to stop them.

At 6:00 p.m. Collins and his team met with King and other movement leaders at Dr. Jackson's house. The mood was one of relief and cordiality. The talk was of the plight of the Black in Alabama and SCLC's future plans. It was obvious that it would soon be time to move on from Selma. Collins departed from Craig Air Force Base on an Air Force jet at 7:30 p.m., having fulfilled the president's assignment—to assure that there would be no bloodshed in Selma that day.

At 9:00 p.m. Secrest and Miller attended the session at Brown's Chapel Church. Dr. King declared to the crowd that their mass meeting on U.S. Highway 80 across the bridge from Selma was a great victory. He said he fully expected a favorable court decision voiding Governor Wallace's ban on a march to Montgomery. The march would be completed at that time.

Most of his listeners seemed both relieved and gratified by the developments. They had braved the storm fully prepared to be bloodied. They accepted King's view that the day had moved America a step closer to the ultimate victory. However, to others in the audience who felt that King had permitted himself to be turned back, the claim of victory had a hollow sound. Indeed, among militant Blacks it was to remain a smear on King's reputation for years, and in some measure it reduced his influence upon them. In later years the event was to be cited in militant circles as reason to be guarded in working with CRS, which, they said, was sometimes more interested in compromise than in the assertion of principle.

In his notes summing up the contribution of CRS to the conflict avoidance that took place on March 9, Secrest acknowledged the importance of timing and the readiness of antagonists to find a way out. In Selma that Tuesday both the state of Alabama and SCLC wanted to avoid a repetition of "Bloody Sunday," but they were committed to a collision course. CRS provided them with a means of avoidance. March 9 was the time for CRS to play its crisis response role. It was clearly not a time for advancing the long-range conciliation effort started in January. That would have to be resumed later on.

A CRISIS THAT DIDN'T HAVE TO HAPPEN

Selma's torment did not end with the crossing of the bridge. That same evening, Tuesday, March 9, three of the white ministers who had come to Selma to support the march were set upon by four whites, all with police records. James Reeb, a Unitarian minister from Boston, died of his injuries the next morning. That event refueled the fires of protest. Many of the visiting marchers stayed on. From around the country additional clerics and church members of all faiths converged on Selma to express their outrage.

On Wednesday the Selma City Council decreed that there would be no more marches or demonstrations. That afternoon a group set out from Brown's Chapel for the courthouse to lay a wreath in honor of Reeb. They had barely started when they were stopped by the city police led by Baker. Still seeking to avoid arrests, Baker had a rope drawn across the street, beyond which the demonstrators were forbidden to pass. Instead they congregated in the street in front of the church and there commenced an all-night vigil—which was to last for five days and bring Selma to the brink of another catastrophic explosion.

The white population of Selma, particularly its rowdy element, so long held in check by the city police, became increasingly contentious. Growing numbers gathered around the area of the vigil, which was now cordoned off by city, county, and state law enforcement authorities. The area along Sylvan Street between Brown's Chapel and the First Baptist Church became known as "the compound" and the boundary rope set up by Baker as "the Berlin Wall." People could leave individually, but not in groups.

The new developments rekindled President Johnson's concerns. He ordered LeRoy Collins back to Selma. John Perry, then serving as Collins's special assistant, made the trip with him. Years later he was to recall their late-night arrival at the compound:

It had been raining; it was muddy and awful there, and the church which was the headquarters for the civil rights groups was there.

Alabama and local county cops had circled this place, this church. And there they were facing inward—toward the vigil. And this nasty group of people were behind them, yelling taunts and racial epithets at us. I thought, "Why are you looking at us? We don't intend to harm anybody. The trouble is on the other side. Why don't you point your guns that way?" . . . A little later I went back out and stood with a few Blacks and a few whites from New England, holding hands and singing. This Black woman standing next to me cried out. It must have been a pellet gun, because a rifle bullet would have killed her. But it knocked out her bottom front two or three teeth and went under the tongue. She crumpled down, with blood pouring all over her. So I helped carry her in. There was this Black doctor inside the church. He seemed exhausted. They stretched her out on a horsehair sofa, and the doctor started working on her.[23]

Tension mounted all day Thursday. The number of visiting protesters arriving in the compound grew larger, and the hostile crowds continued to gather on the perimeter. At 10:00 p.m. Collins, Secrest, Miller, and Perry met with James Orange, the SCLC staff worker heading the vigil, and some of the SNCC staff. CRS asked whether, in view of the volatility that could turn to violence at any time, they should consider terminating the vigil. The civil rights workers replied that they wanted nothing more than their constitutional rights, and that it was the job of law enforcement not to contain them but to protect them in the exercise of those rights.

The federal conciliators then presented that view to Baker. They pointed out that the parade restraint was self-defeating, since it served to continue the confrontation and focus national attention on Selma. Why risk another outbreak of violence, when relief in the form of a court decision permitting the march to Montgomery was only days away? Baker said that the city council would be unrelenting in its parade ban. Secrest then raised a proposal already discussed with Orange. Would groups of five be permitted to move to the courthouse—as had been previously allowed for voter registration?

Baker said yes; although the mayor would probably be against such a move, he thought he could convince him to allow it. Thus, at 1:00 a.m., the government representatives left the compound with a feeling of progress. A demonstration would be allowed at the courthouse Friday, and the vigil would be disbanded.

On Friday morning Mayor Smitherman rejected Baker's agreement to permit the march to the courthouse. Tension on both sides of the "Berlin Wall" mounted further. The corps of dignitaries was growing in status as well as in size. It now included prelates, labor leaders, and congressmen. On Saturday the ministers decided that they would no longer submit to the parade ban. More than a thousand confronted the police line. Unable to pass, they redeployed into smaller groups; they tried breaking out through the housing project; they tested other routes out of the compound—all to no avail.

On Monday morning, as King presided over what was expected to be a crucial mass meeting, Secrest and Baker entered into desperate council in Baker's squad car. They agreed to ask Justice Department attorneys to call Judge Thomas in Mobile to see if he would persuade Sheriff Clark and Mayor Smitherman to allow the march to the courthouse. The call resulted in a proposal that the march would be permitted, but only two abreast on the sidewalk. Demonstration leaders rejected the idea, insisting that they would march in the street. A second proposal was offered—three abreast on the sidewalk, five minutes of singing at the courthouse, a short prayer service, and a return to the church. This was also rejected.

Minutes before another unauthorized march was to start, Secrest himself called Judge Thomas, and again the judge called Sheriff Clark. Clark talked to Hosea Williams. The deal was struck. The formation would be three abreast, two on the sidewalk, one in the street.

The barriers were removed. At 5:00 p.m. a crowd now swollen to two thousand started out on the brief but solemn procession from the compound to the courthouse. A wreath was placed in memory of Reverend Reeb. Prayers were recited. There was one song. The group returned to the church. The entire event had taken less than an hour. The long vigil and confrontation were over.

That same evening, Monday, March 15, President Johnson addressed a joint session of Congress to seek enactment of the 1965 voting rights bill he was about to submit. It was the first time in nineteen years that a president had addressed a joint session to request domestic legislation.[24]

In one of the most stirring appeals of his presidency, Johnson said:

At times history and fate meet at a single time in a single place to shape a turning point in man's unending search for freedom. So it was at Lexington and Concord. . . . So it was last week in Selma, Alabama. . . . What happened at Selma is part of a far larger movement which reaches into every state and section of America. It is the effort of American Negroes to secure for themselves the full blessings of American life. . . . Their cause must be our cause, too. Because it is not just Negroes, but really all of us who must overcome the crippling legacy of bigotry and injustice.

And we shall—overcome![25]

LeRoy Collins and his wife were guests of the president and Mrs. Johnson at dinner that evening and in the president's box in the House gallery when Johnson spoke. Dr. King had also been invited to sit with the presidential party but went to Selma instead to speak at funeral services for the Reverend Reeb.

THE MARCH TO MONTGOMERY

On Wednesday, March 17, Judge Johnson ruled that the march to Montgomery could go forward, enjoining any effort by the state to restrain it. On Sunday, March 21, thirty-two hundred marchers left their Selma staging area, on the way to Montgomery at last. With that third and final crossing of the bridge, Selma passed from the limelight of national attention. Remaining behind were the still unresolved problems of prejudice, discrimination, and racial inequity.

President Johnson invited Governor Wallace to the White House to make a personal, and what he thought was persuasive, plea that the governor assure the safety of the march. Wallace waited until he was back in Alabama to advise Johnson that the state could not afford to provide protection for the marchers. An enraged Johnson immediately invoked a contingency plan federalizing the Alabama National Guard and also sending troops from the Second Infantry Division at Fort Benning, Georgia.

Johnson was not content to end his personal intervention there. Seeing the success of his voting rights program now intertwined with the behavior and success of civil rights forces, he left no stone unturned in his efforts to guarantee a successful march.

The judge had ordered that only three hundred could continue the march after the first night because the highway narrowed to two lanes. How, the president asked, were the others to return safely to Selma? It turned out that there weren't enough buses; a special train had to be ordered.

Johnson's belt-and-suspenders style of guarding against problems came into full play. John Doar, as assistant attorney general for civil rights, had overall responsibility for security and law enforcement. But the provost marshal of the U.S. Army, a major general, was sent down to provide oversight of the major general in charge of the guard. The president also sent down Ramsey Clark, then deputy attorney general, to look over Doar's shoulder. LBJ also called Burke Marshall out of retirement for a few days and sent him to Selma, too, just to assure that everything went well.

Johnson instructed LeRoy Collins to use his conciliators to facilitate logistical arrangements and liaison with local authorities. CRS staff members made advance contact with mayors, sheriffs, and police chiefs along the route, advising them of the federal government's interest in a trouble-free operation and helping to plan for contingencies.[26]

The most intricate work was in Montgomery itself, where unrelenting local demonstrations over the previous two weeks had already rubbed Black/white relationships raw. NCC member Winton Blount, one of the most influential men in the state, was asked to convene the leaders of the power structure of Montgomery in his own home, to meet with the federal officials.[27] To an audience that tendered only grudging cooperation, Collins, Doar, and Ramsey Clark gave evidence of the high priority the White House attached to the success of the march. Laue recalls Blount muttering about how none of this would be necessary "if not for the little Napoleon [Governor Wallace] up there on the hill."[28] Following a two-hour discussion of Collins's appeal to reason and to regional pride, the leaders present agreed to do what was asked of them.

For all of the complexities, security arrangements proved to be adequate. Laue recalled:

The Montgomery police department asked if I would get the march leaders to move King back in the line of march at a particular point going through a Black area of Montgomery where there were three-to-five-story, old apartments on either side of a narrow street. They felt it would be awfully hard to secure that area against an assassination attempt. And so I proposed that to Andy Young and he took it back to the march leaders and they said, "No." They would not be intimidated by white racism and threats. Instead they decided to keep King in the front line of the march but ask all the Black preachers from Montgomery to wear dark suits like King. Andy laughed, "They can't tell us apart anyway."[29]

Collins later was to pay a price for his role in facilitating the march. Truck-mounted news cameras were constantly focused on the head of the march column. One day they caught Collins and King walking along in earnest discussion. The next morning that picture was front-page news throughout Florida: "Ex-Governor leads civil rights march with King." Years later, when Collins was running for U.S. senator in Florida's Democratic primary, the picture was circulated across the state. Collins was convinced that it was responsible for his defeat.

By mid-April, CRS was back in Selma seeking to encourage the conciliatory efforts it had sought to nurture since early January. The boycott was still in place, but for the most part the days of mass meetings and protest demonstrations had passed. A three-judge federal court had found Sheriff Clark guilty of contempt, and the effectiveness of the posse had been reduced, strengthening Wilson Baker's authority for law enforcement in the city. White moderates were beginning to move a little more boldly.

By June a number of interracial dialogues had begun, although no major reforms had taken place. The mayor and city council began a series of weekly meetings with African American leaders. The Selma Chamber of Commerce endorsed a statement on racial fairness drafted by the state chamber, which it had previously rejected. It persuaded the city council to do likewise. The statement was then reprinted in the *Times-Journal*, along with signatures of endorsement of eleven hundred white Selma citizens.

Two powerful outside forces were offering financial incentives for interracial cooperation: the federal government and industry.

In the past, federal assistance programs for the poor had not been welcome. Blacks were denied help from the federal government's surplus food program because the city and county had refused to provide the necessary start-up funds. It remained for CRS, working with the Department of Agriculture and the Alabama Council on Human Relations, to arrange for an alternate means of channeling surplus food to Selma's poor. Now there was a change. Many of the new antipoverty programs, which required interracial dialogue in planning and execution, offered funding that white Selma found difficult to reject.

Selma's thrust to bring new industry to the area was encountering difficulty because many of the major firms being courted were troubled about making multi-million-dollar investments in unstable communities plagued by racial turmoil. CRS, with the support of some of its NCC members, helped to instill into these discussions an insistence on the part of the companies that the city resolve its problems and offer a climate that would be congenial to equal employment policies.

To clear the way for federal programs, CRS also facilitated contact between Selma's leadership and the Washington officials who made the funding decisions. Mac Secrest recalled, in 1990, his arrangement for an interracial delegation from Selma to visit with several federal agencies in Washington about pending and possible programs. He personally greeted the members of the delegation when they arrived at Washington's National Airport and volunteered to drive them to their hotel. His station wagon proved to be a little small for the size of the group. The solution was found by having Mrs. Boynton sit on Mayor Smitherman's lap. Secrest thought that the interracial communication in the station wagon was just fine.

NOTES

1. Potomac Institute summary, July 21, 1964.

2. With the encouragement and influence of the Justice Department, an informal consortium of church groups and private foundations had put up $500,000 to create and support the Voter Education Project (VEP). VEP then became a vehicle through which SNCC, SCLC, CORE, and the NAACP would coordinate their distinctive efforts to educate and register potential voters.

3. Chestnut and Cass, *Black in Selma*.

4. According to J. L. Chestnut Jr., while Sheriff Clark served as the front man imposing uncompromising, brutal, and racist law enforcement, the power and direction behind the scenes came from Judge Hare.

5. Branch, *Parting the Waters*.

6. Eugene Connor, a native of Selma, was police commissioner of Birmingham when the civil rights demonstrations took place there in 1963. Police use of clubs, cattle prods, fire hoses, and dogs to restrain demonstrators was widely reported through the nation's news and television cameras. The resulting national

outrage helped to build the necessary support for passage of the Civil Rights Act of 1964.

7. Raines, *My Soul Is Rested*, 197.

8. Secrest wondered whether his words had been a decisive influence behind the final decision to go public with the statement. Such second-guessing about the impact of CRS counsel on critical behavior would often bedevil the federal peacemakers.

9. *New York Times*, January 22, 1965.

10. Five days later Clark was again pictured in the nation's newspapers, this time bringing his club down on the head of a woman struggling on the ground in the grip of three deputies. The incident occurred when Dr. King approached the registration line to converse with reporters. The sheriff took King by the arm and ordered him back to the curb. The woman, whom the authorities later said outweighed the 220-pound Clark, had left the line and punched the sheriff in the face.

11. Williams, *Eyes on the Prize*, 261.

12. *New York Times*, February 4, 1965.

13. Andrew MacDowd Secrest, interview with Bertram Levine.

14. James Laue, interview with Bertram Levine.

15. Laue, interview with Levine.

16. Lewis, *Walking with the Wind*, 320.

17. Lewis, *Walking with the Wind*, 323–27. Dr. King felt committed to deliver the sermon at Ebenezer Baptist Church in Atlanta, from whose pulpit he had too long been absent. He entrusted guidance of the march to senior SCLC leaders Hosea Williams, Andrew Young, and James Bevel, who tossed coins to see which one would lead the march with Lewis.

18. Lewis, *Walking with the Wind*, 340.

19. *Atlanta Journal and Constitution Magazine*, May 12, 1974.

20. Raines, *My Soul Is Rested*, 203.

21. Secrest, interview with Levine.

22. LeRoy Collins, telephone interview with Bertram Levine. Secrest's March 23, 1965, report of the events of that week describes the meeting between King and Collins as ending in an agreement that King would turn back if stopped and allowed a prayer ceremony.

23. John Perry, telephone interview with Bertram Levine.

24. President Truman had appeared before a joint session in 1946 to seek authorization to seize the railroads in order to settle a labor dispute.

25. *New York Times*, March 16, 1965.

26. This employment of federal conciliation teams to forestall problems on civil rights marches was to become standard operating procedure in ensuing years. It was used, for example, on the Poor People's Campaign in 1967; to escort "the longest walk" of Native Americans from Sacramento to Washington, D.C., in 1978; and on farm worker marches in California and Texas.

27. Blount was later appointed postmaster general by President Jimmy Carter.

28. Wallace later renounced his racist past publicly, asked for forgiveness from

African American leaders, ran for governor in 1982, received 90 percent of the Black vote, and appointed a record number of Blacks to Alabama state government positions. Wallace's daughter Peggy Wallace Kennedy has been active in racial reconciliation work. Jonathan Capehart, "How Segregationist George Wallace Became a Model for Racial Reconciliation," May 6, 2019, *Voices of the Movement* (podcast), https://perma.cc/QLE9-TFGB. (note by Lum)

29. Laue, interview with Levine.

FOUR

Equality of Results

The Revised Civil Rights Agenda

BY 1965, THE Supreme Court and Congress had affirmed racial equality as a matter of law. But their efforts fell far short of building human equality into the American way of life. A second phase of the battle for civil rights was still to come. Lyndon Johnson identified this second phase as the battle for equality of results. The objectives of this battle would be harder to clarify, and even harder to attain. The struggle would lead the federal government's racial troubleshooters to take on assignments not previously conceived of either by them or by those who had brought the Community Relations Service into being.

MORE THAN ONE KIND OF JUSTICE

The achievement of equal rights under law had created a false expectation among many that somehow a more equal distribution of America's bounty would soon follow. As the realization dawned that the newly won right to dine where they pleased changed little for minority families struggling to put the daily meal on the table, the emphasis of the civil rights struggle changed from a fight for theoretical justice to a struggle for distributive justice. As minorities began to realize that the achievement of equality would have to be further deferred until new economic and social battles were won, new conflicts emerged.

In the second half of the sixties, the struggle to convert equal opportunities to equal outcomes became a crucial factor in shaping the nature of racial conflict. It sharpened the frustration that led to urban riots; it fractured the civil rights movement, bitterly dividing Black power strategists from integrationists; it diluted white support for evolving civil rights objectives. It also explains, in part, the failure of the movement to catch hold in the North as it did in the South.

The thrust for equality of outcomes helped to shape the CRS program in the North and undergirded CRS's enlargement of its mandate beyond the conception of its creators—except, perhaps, for Lyndon

Johnson, who had sounded the most persuasive articulation of the need for distributive justice. In his 1965 speech at Howard University he called for a second part to the battle for civil rights. The challenge, he said, was to move Blacks through "gateless poverty" compounded of the need for employment, education, housing, and health care. He indicated that only a comprehensive program addressed to all these inequities would do: "They are a seamless web. They cause each other. They result from each other. They reinforce each other. Much of the African American community is buried under a blanket of history and circumstance. It is not a lasting solution to lift just one corner of that blanket. We must stand on all sides and raise the entire cover if we are to liberate our fellow citizens." He then pronounced a new civil rights goal: "This is the next and more profound stage of the battle for civil rights. We seek . . . not just equality as a right and a theory, but equality as a fact and as a result."

In redirecting the focus of national concern from legal equity to equality as a result, the president, for the first time, included the problems of northern communities in the federal government's civil rights agenda. The Black urban areas of America's northern cities graphically illustrated the absence of distributive justice. Despite laws in many states that had guaranteed the full measure of civil rights, minority neighborhoods in the core of big cities were islands of desperate poverty, marked by poor income, education, health, and housing and high rates of crime. The new civil rights laws did not change anything in the inner cities. Long-suppressed feelings of deprivation crystallized into outbreaks of free-floating rage. This rage took visible form in 1964, when rioting in New York City, Rochester, New York, Philadelphia, and elsewhere started a spate of "long hot summers."

"RIOT PREVENTION" IN THE SUMMER OF 1965

In the spring of 1965, CRS, still less than a year old, and with a staff that had not yet reached fifty, was designated to spearhead a massive federal effort to reduce the risk of America's most vulnerable cities going up in flames. It required a quick turnabout for an agency whose focus had been southern and rural to gear up for conflict resolution and prevention in the urban North.

In 1965 the programs embraced within President Johnson's War on Poverty, which promised to produce better housing, jobs, and education for the poor, were just beginning to function. Federal administrators saw themselves as in a race against time. How could the new programs have an impact before the heat of another summer triggered a new wave of violence?

The problem was placed in the hands of the President's Council on Equal Opportunity, the cabinet-level committee established to coordinate the federal government's civil rights work. The chairman of the council was Vice President Hubert Humphrey. As the council struggled with the question of how to deal with its implicit assignment to keep the cities "cool," it found its answer in a proposal by CRS, which that agency had drafted in an effort to get the federal government to address civil rights problems in the North.

The CRS plan had been born out of the frustration of a few staff members who were troubled by the agency's preoccupation with civil rights problems in the South. Its adoption by the President's Council on Equal Opportunity resulted in Humphrey creating the Vice President's Summer Task Force on Urban Problems. Task force members included the secretaries of Labor and HEW (Health, Education and Welfare), the attorney general, the director of the Office of Economic Opportunity, the administrator of the Housing and Home Finance Agency,[1] the chairman of the Civil Rights Commission, and the director of the Office of Emergency Planning. LeRoy Collins was named executive director of the task force, and CRS the coordinating agency. Day-to-day management was delegated to the thirty-three-year-old Black assistant director of CRS, Roger Wilkins.[2]

Wilkins, who later succeeded Collins as director of CRS and who imparted to it much of the operating style and sense of mission that characterized it for many years, was at that time something of a reluctant dragon, not quite sure of the CRS mission or his own role in it. He had been practicing law in New York when he was recruited by Fowler Hamilton, the director of the U.S. Agency for International Development, to join him as special assistant. In that capacity, he was one of the highest ranking African Americans in the federal civil service. While not widely known on the national stage of civil rights, he had long since cut his eyeteeth in grassroots activity. He had been born and raised in an atmosphere of familiarity with racial and social issues. His father, who died when Roger was nine, had been a reporter and then business manager for a leading Black newspaper, the *Kansas City Call*.

His mother, a national board member of the YWCA, was prominent in that organization's civil rights efforts. His uncle was Roy Wilkins, the national executive secretary of the NAACP. So it was not surprising that the younger Wilkins would have worked in the NAACP youth movement in high school, or that he would have been president of the NAACP branch at the University of Michigan. While in law school in 1955, he interned with the NAACP Legal Defense and Education Fund, which was then wrapping up its winning efforts in the *Brown v. Board of Education* case. As a practicing lawyer in New York, he had volunteered as a tester to help in the enforcement of open housing, and he had begun to make his voice heard on the need to oppose civil rights abuses in the North.

When asked to be an assistant director of CRS, Wilkins had misgivings. As he later recalled: "I thought that the concept of a group of people in Washington who would fly around the country was not workable. But I thought about it. My final view was that, whatever you think of the legislation, when Congress gives you people and money to do something about civil rights, you damn well better go out and try to do something."

His first impressions of the agency brought him no reassurance. "I remember a staff meeting just about when I got there. September or October 1964. All these white guys were sitting there. And they were talking about how we, CRS, were going to fix Mississippi. And I went home and told my wife, 'What kind of crazy people have I gotten myself involved with?'"

Misgivings turned to resentment as Wilkins found himself without significant influence in the agency's inner council and uninvolved in the conciliation program in the South—in which he had little confidence. Wilkins recalled: "I never opposed the agency doing things in the South. I just didn't think the entire program should be involved hopping from one southern hot spot to another, and my view, which I expressed often, was that we really had to work on the big cities— mainly in the north—because more Black people lived in one block in Harlem than there were in all of McComb, Mississippi."[3]

In response to his demands, Wilkins was given a specific, although vaguely defined, portfolio as head of a newly created Division of Community Action. He recruited Seymour Samet and Jay Janis as his earliest staff, and the three began to lay plans for a federal civil rights effort in the North.

What ultimately emerged was a rough design for a crash program to expedite the movement of the new federal antipoverty programs and resources to America's inner cities. The financial assistance would be coupled with community relations expertise to help local communities be more responsive to the civil rights needs of minorities.

Too new to the Washington scene to shrink from audacity, they proposed that tiny CRS spearhead a major coordination of the full phalanx of federal social benefit programs. The three then sought to trumpet their idea within the federal civil rights community. It was quickly seen as a possible response to the anxieties of the President's Council on Equal Opportunity about the prospects of a long, hot summer, and the Vice President's Summer Task Force on Urban Problems was created, with CRS at the tiller.

From a list of cities where racial tensions were high, eleven were selected to receive task force assistance. Mayors were invited by the vice president to come to Washington with their key lieutenants who would administer the various new and improved federal programs. The invitations were issued without publicity to avoid the possibility that Washington's concern about riots would be construed as criticism of the mayors or serve as a self-fulfilling prophecy. The city officials met directly with the federal decision makers who had sign-off authority on the big funding programs. They then and there debated and negotiated program proposals and modifications, thereby cutting many months from the program-approval process and expediting the flow of federal funds.

At the same time that it was coordinating these meetings, CRS scouted the nation for community relations specialists who could take on summer assignments as CRS conciliators resident in each of the target cities.

Two of the mayors, Samuel Yorty of Los Angeles and Richard Daley of Chicago, refused to participate in the project. The program went forward in New York, Newark, Rochester, Philadelphia, Detroit, Gary, San Francisco, Miami, and Oakland. Each of the participating cities went through the summer unscathed by outbreaks of racial violence. Riots did take place in Chicago and Los Angeles, the two cities that had refused the program. CRS and the members of the Summer Task Force savored the results with discreet silence. They knew that the emergency infusion of federal dollars and community relations sensitivity may have been a good first step, but it was far from being the answer to urban unrest.

CRS MOVES NORTH

The Summer Task Force experience convinced CRS that conciliators should not be concentrated in Washington but instead located closer to the action. It also demonstrated that CRS, working as program facilitator as well as conflict resolver, could do a better job in helping cities to address underlying problems. What happened in Rochester helped lead to that conclusion.

Rochester had been the second city to "blow" in the summer of 1964. It happened in late July, and CRS, still less than a month old, was totally consumed with problems in the South. Rochester was ignored. By October, however, the agency had had second thoughts, and Collins told the staff that CRS should move toward trouble rather than away from it. As a result, Mac Secrest was assigned to assess the situation in Rochester to determine what role, if any, CRS might play.

His recommendations were to put a consultant in Rochester for two months to help the city design a community relations plan and structure and to act as a liaison between Rochester and Washington to expedite the movement of federal programs to the city.[4] However, nothing was done about the report until Rochester was named a candidate city for the 1965 summer project.

My first field assignment, within weeks of joining the CRS staff in the early spring of 1965, was to check out Rochester, as well as Detroit, to help validate their inclusion in the final selection for the Summer Task Force project.[5]

On the plane to Rochester, I studied the report of Mac Secrest's earlier visit and a sheaf of newspaper clippings detailing the city's racial conflicts over the past year. It provided me with an overlarge list of people I ought to see, with some of whom I had already made appointments.

A key name on my list, and a new player at the table since Secrest's visit, was the Reverend Franklin Florence. He was the leader of a new and highly vociferous Black protest organization that had put the old-line Black organizations temporarily into the shadows. Following the latest trend in choosing an acronym to use as a name for a new social protest group, with the full name to be determined later, it was known as FIGHT, which would stand for Freedom, Integration, God, Honor, Today. FIGHT's militant posture, its protest demonstrations, and its provocative language appeared to have Rochester's establishment on edge. Clearly, it had helped to keep the question of racial disparities, and programs to remedy them, on the front page. I had been unable to reach the Reverend Florence by phone to set up an appointment in advance. Seeing him was high on my agenda.

It was standard operating procedure for CRS, on entering any city for the first time, to make an early call on the protest leaders. This approach was sometimes disconcerting to the city's power brokers, who often spoke of those leaders as "agitators" or, worse still, "outside agitators" or "rabble-rousers" and often "communists." CRS was to learn that a surprising number of public officials truly believed that the agitator rather than the grievance was the root of the protest. Only sometimes was CRS able to convince them that the unprotested grievance festers, while protest, by opening the wound, can lead to faster healing.

Getting to see the Reverend Florence was not easy. Telephone calls to possible contact people were fielded gingerly: they might or might not be able to reach him; he might or might not be able to call me back. Inquiries of other Black leaders and at other agencies in the poor urban areas were equally frustrating. In midafternoon, at a neighborhood settlement house, a tall white man in his mid-twenties pulled me aside and said, "Why do you want to see the Reverend Florence?" We spoke briefly and made a tentative appointment for my hotel room at midnight.

Shortly after twelve the young man appeared with the Reverend Florence. The minister did not respond to my greeting, nor did he remove his hat and coat or take the proffered chair. Offers of refreshment were declined. I was interviewed for a half hour by the younger man; at first I could induce no more than monosyllabic participation from Florence. When he finally spoke, Florence treated me to a variety of opinions about the possibility of my being a spy for the FBI, my choice of hotel, and my room on an upper floor, which permitted me to look down on the poor Blacks below. He then wanted my guarantee that Rochester would be included in the summer program. When I told him I could only make a recommendation, he asked me to pick up the phone at that moment and call my boss so that he could hear my recommendation. When I said that I would not report in that manner, at that time, he announced that he would call his good friend Congressman Adam Clayton Powell in the morning, who would jolly well make sure that Rochester got the program. Before leaving, he sat down and shared, in a limited way, some of the perceptions of Rochester's Black leadership. When we parted he assured me that he either might or might not cooperate with the CRS summer representative. I was later to learn that there was nothing personal in Florence's in-your-face conversational style. The persona was part of his job description.[6]

The movement of FIGHT and the Reverend Florence to center stage was not a totally spontaneous phenomenon that emerged by chance from the riot of the previous summer. In fact, it was the enactment of a protest formula taking place in other cities as well. The master script had been written by the Industrial Areas Foundation (IAF). The foundation was the creation of a sociologist and self-styled "radical" turned community organizer named Saul Alinsky. The tall young man who brought Florence to my hotel room was on the IAF staff. He was assigned to Rochester because the Rochester Council of Ministers had contracted with Alinsky to build a militant protest movement that would help impel city leaders to initiate meaningful social change.

The Alinsky technique was to organize a power base around the community's most deeply felt grievances through methods that "rubbed salt into the wounds." Dramatization of the injustice through innovative and outrageous forms of protest built cohesion among the protesters at the same time that it created intolerable consternation within the community at large. With long-ignored injustices suddenly spotlighted, and then made difficult to preserve, it became easier for the city to introduce social change.[7] Church groups that sought Alinsky's assistance in the late sixties in order to create an imperative for social change may also have been moved by another theory. By channeling suppressed anger into organized protest, groups like FIGHT provided a safety valve for the inchoate rage that might otherwise break out into violence as it had the previous summer.

Sam Convissor was recruited to serve as the CRS field representative in Rochester for the summer of 1965. As a former press aide for mayor Hugh Addonizio of Newark, he understood the workings of city government and its nexus with the urban communities. His assignment was broad: to use his ingenuity to help implement the two purposes of the task force. Those objectives were to speed the flow of federal funds coming from the new antipoverty programs and to help the city improve the climate of race relations. Convissor worked as a troubleshooter, mediating between federal and local officials, between public agencies and advocates of the poor people they served, between minority leaders and city hall. When red tape was the problem, he and his CRS counterparts in the other cities participating in the project learned that a phone call to task force headquarters could generate priority attention. When necessary, even the weight of the vice president's office was available to help break a logjam.

At the same time, Convissor worked to improve communication across racial lines and to draw attention to problems of intergroup friction that needed to be resolved. Working unobtrusively, he made contacts throughout the city, offering assistance where need and opportunity suggested. In many ways the job was made easier because Rochester was a city justifiably proud of its civic virtue. Its colleges, parks, and libraries were prized institutions. Eastman Kodak, Xerox, and other major corporations demanded and contributed to the city's problem-solving approach. To help school desegregation work, Rochester instituted the first magnet schools in the country. When it recognized, and decided to come to grips with, the problem of antagonism between its police and its minority community, it recruited Laplois (Lakey) Ashford, national youth director of the NAACP, as deputy public safety director.

An unanticipated dividend of Convissor's summer labors was the urban communities' support activity his presence had catalyzed. In September, I attended a farewell luncheon for Convissor tendered by about fifty city and civic officials with whom he had worked. People rose, one by one, to testify how the federal government's demonstration of interest had energized them to direct their own programs more sharply to the unaddressed needs of the poor and minorities. Some indicated that thanks to Convissor they had begun, for the first time, to work with minority leaders, community aides, and public officials with whom they should have been collaborating in the past. Others said they were impressed that a federal agency working at the street level could get the immediate attention of decision makers in Washington.

CRS JOINS THE DEPARTMENT OF JUSTICE

Even as CRS's activity in southern hot spots and its leadership on the Summer Task Force on Urban Problems were embellishing its reputation within the federal government, other forces were at work to bring about what Collins would see as a clipping of the agency's wings. Following passage of the Voting Rights Act of 1965, discussions were initiated to bring about tighter coordination of the widely scattered responsibilities for federal civil rights activity. The coordinating efforts of the President's Council on Equal Opportunity, under Vice President Humphrey, were seen as inadequate. To many, the attorney general's office was the logical command post. A variety of options were proposed for CRS, ranging from making it an independent agency, to attaching it to the soon-to-be-formed Department of Housing and Urban Development, to attaching it directly to the White House, to making it a part of the Department of Justice.

Collins favored keeping CRS in Commerce, in the belief that it would continue to be most effective by energizing the business community to support civil rights compliance. Besides, Commerce, under Secretary Hodges, allowed CRS the full freedom of an independent agency in determining its own policies and programs. Humphrey was supportive. Burke Marshall, though out of government by the time the issue was joined, had always believed that CRS's freedom to negotiate might be dampened if the agency was placed within the Justice Department, which was seen as a coercive force.

Attorney General Nicholas Katzenbach and Assistant Attorney General John Doar, as well as key presidential aides such as Joe Califano, saw a need to make the attorney general the dominant figure overseeing the government's full civil rights effort. They mistrusted conciliated solutions that weren't bound to verdicts and court orders.[8] They questioned how the government could be conciliatory with respect to those things the Constitution required. They feared that CRS might pursue peace rather than justice.

Collins, Fleming, and Calvin Kytle, who served as acting director of CRS after Collins was elevated to undersecretary of commerce, saw the Katzenbach view as too legalistic. They felt he had no vision of the vast arena of controversy in which CRS operated—the arena that lay between a court decision on a specific case and the final achievement of social change consistent with the law. Wilkins called this the place "where the restructuring of society becomes a personal reality."[9]

Members of the civil rights community, still vaguely untrusting of the Justice Department, lobbied to keep CRS out of its control. But their own unresolved ambivalence about CRS robbed their efforts of vigor.

The determination of the Department of Justice to gain a measure of control over CRS was probably strengthened by its experience in Selma, where it had been disconcerted, at times, by CRS's independent role and informal problem-solving techniques. Katzenbach could still vaguely recall difficulties at Selma, when asked about it twenty-five years later: "One of the difficulties that at least John Doar felt was that Governor Collins would be heading down one track while he was heading down another. This did cause confusion. I remember during the demonstrations at Selma that was certainly John's view. He would say one thing and somebody from the Community Relations Service would say another. And he thought it was very confusing." Burke Marshall's recollection confirmed: "I guess that the Department of Justice thought that it should have control of the Community Relations Service in order to avoid whatever kind of confusion they had at Selma and other places."[10]

In January, Johnson submitted to Congress an executive resolution transferring CRS to the Justice Department, with the agency's director given the rank of an assistant attorney general. Whatever its motivation, the move, approved by Congress in April 1966, turned out to be the right one. Justice Department credentials commanded more respect and attention from local authorities than had those from Commerce, and the direct line to the attorney general amplified CRS's voice within the federal civil rights community. The fear that CRS might be subordinated to the Civil Rights Division was never borne out—perhaps because Ramsey Clark, as attorney general during the early years of the change, understood the importance of CRS's nonlawyerly role and established a pattern of according full respect to its equal status with the litigative divisions. The affiliation with Justice sometimes made it more difficult to explain the intermediary role to both sides, but the conciliators soon became adept at surmounting the problem.

President Johnson appointed Roger Wilkins to be director of CRS in January 1966. That event inaugurated a change in the direction of the agency that no one, including Wilkins himself, would have foreseen. By the end of Wilkins's term in January 1969, program emphases had shifted from South to North, from rural to urban, from firefighting to fire prevention. Recruitment of Black staff members was accelerated; Hispanic recruitment was initiated. Most significant, the balance of program goals that had teetered between mere compliance with the law and wider objectives of social justice moved perceptibly toward justice.

These changes came about not only because Wilkins was adventurous and well connected. He offered a charismatic leadership that infused much of the staff with an almost arrogant sense of mission. But he also had the political savvy not to overstep the bounds of bureaucratic prudence.

USING THE SHADOW AND SUBSTANCE OF POLITICAL INFLUENCE

Wilkins saw the director's influence within government as an important tool for advancing the CRS program, which needed all the support it could get from other federal agencies. He saw the exploitation of the prestige of his position of director as a deliberate strategy for leveraging the strength of a small agency. A close personal friendship with Ramsey Clark, who was confirmed as attorney general in March 1967, gave Wilkins and the CRS running room to test some innovative approaches.

The two men first came together in the aftermath of the Watts riot in Los Angeles, when Clark, as deputy attorney general, headed the federal team looking into the disorders and planning the scope of Washington's relief effort. Wilkins and Collins had gone onsite as Lyndon Johnson's first representatives while the fires were still burning, and Wilkins stayed on with Clark and provided valuable liaison with the Black community.

Later, after Clark had succeeded Katzenbach as attorney general, his understanding of the social dynamite that had led to the Watts explosion helped him to see the good sense in the CRS analysis that without evidence of the government's pursuit of justice for minorities, racial conflict would remain endemic in poor urban communities. Writing in 1970, Clark enlarged on this precept, observing, "There will be no social stability if major segments of society are excluded from the mainstream and millions go on living in poverty." He concluded that "the long history of mankind says you will have neither order nor justice unless you have both."[11]

CRS's influence among other agencies of government was also enhanced by the close relationship between Clark and Wilkins. In Wilkins's words: "If we couldn't get the cooperation we needed from the Department of Labor, I'd call Ramsey and ask him to call [Secretary of Labor Willard] Wirtz. And it would get done."[12]

The respect for Wilkins within the government was also enhanced by the fact that the president had personally presided at the White House ceremony at which he was sworn in as director of CRS—an honor rarely accorded to one of subcabinet rank. Johnson's selection of Wilkins, with Clark's vigorous support, was not hurt by the fact that Wilkins was the nephew of Roy Wilkins, who was reputed to have ready access to the Oval Office and for whom Johnson had a warm regard. Johnson may also have had a more pragmatic reason for the appointment. In later years Wilkins speculated: "Johnson needed to have visible Black executives in his administration. He felt he needed it politically, and he needed it in his heart. He, as a human being, needed to feel—needed to know—that he had given significant responsibility to Black people. So that in the beginning gave me access to a lot."

Nor did Wilkins have any problems—or illusions—in accepting the luster that rubbed off from his uncle's good name. As he later recalled, "The fact that I was Roy's nephew was not unhelpful. Two guys named Wilkins—one's a prominent guy, so be nice to the kid. That's the way a lot of people viewed it."

He also made use of the small network of Blacks within the federal government's leadership ranks. Lacking access to the "old boys' network," they developed a "new boys' network." Wilkins remembered that this group included Lisle Carter, an assistant secretary of HEW; Ed Sylvester, head of the Office of Contract Compliance in the Department of Labor; and Carl Holman, deputy staff director of the U.S. Commission on Civil Rights. To that select group Wilkins added "a person who was outside that group only because she was not in the government, Marian Wright Edelman." Reflecting on the effectiveness of networking, Wilkins said, "Those contacts just magnified the reach and the impact of CRS. Lisle and Carl and Ed and I magnified each other. One of us would go to a meeting at the White House; we'd all know about it. That was enormously helpful."[13]

RESPONDING TO RACIAL CONFLICT IN THE NORTH

As CRS conciliators hurtled from crisis to crisis, priorities were often determined by the volatility and visibility of the confrontations. Minority protest and white resistance set the stage for some of the most visible and most volatile. In many localities, it was the NAACP, or the local ministerial association, that organized the outcry for change. The Urban League, SNCC, and CORE also generated activity that would determine where CRS would go. In the South, the major advocate for change in the most publicized protests had been SCLC. For a time that group also served as a lightning rod in the North—although the outcomes were different.

CRS mediated between Dr. Martin Luther King Jr. and Chicago's Mayor Richard Daley when King first tested SCLC's wings in the North. CRS tried to supply a conciliating presence in Memphis, where SCLC was supporting the sanitation workers' strike, and CRS was with Dr. King at his death on the balcony of the Lorraine Motel. CRS worked in cities around the country to help repair the ruptured fabric of race relations following the riots that marked King's death, and they accompanied the mule trains when his inheritors brought the Poor People's Campaign to its summer encampment at Resurrection City on the Mall in Washington, D.C.

The voting rights victory won on the streets of Selma was the high-water mark of the SCLC's politics of provocation through peaceful protest. The Voting Rights Act of 1965 toppled the last great barrier to full achievement of theoretical justice in the South. But the achievement of distributive justice—attaining the power and the wherewithal to enjoy the full benefit of the rights they had won—still lay beyond the reach of the minority poor in many parts of the country. For this fight the battlefield would have to include the North, where prejudice and discrimination were deeply entrenched in practice, if not in law.

When SCLC turned north, it deliberately looked for the toughest target so that a victory would open the way for significant change and sensitize the nation to the need to do battle against racial discrimination and poverty in the North. The target was housing discrimination in Chicago. The strategy was the same as in Selma—to provoke a brutal response that would outrage the nation. In place of Sheriff Jim Clark and his posse, the foil would be the residents of the lily-white working-class neighborhoods of Chicago and the adjacent city of Cicero.

A coalition of Chicago civil rights organizations had already initiated vigorous protests, focused mainly on discrimination in the schools. CRS had been helpful in brokering a meeting between the protest leaders and the city's powerful mayor, Richard Daley. The mayor was totally resistant to the coalition's demands. Its alliance with King galvanized the movement and brought additional thousands to the protest marches, which now focused on desegregated housing in Chicago and its suburbs. Angry white residents responded with a level of rage and verbal violence that the veteran civil rights workers found as frightening as any they had encountered in the South. Only the massed strength of Chicago's police department prevented the bloodbath many feared.

The Chicago real estate industry was not about to make any moves toward open housing, and the city's power structure, including the mayor, while discommoded, was not about to apply the pressure required for change.

CRS conciliators Sam Dennis and Phil Mason, who had been monitoring the situation from the start, were joined by Jim Laue when SCLC entered the fray. The three endeavored to work with all parties to keep open the channels for negotiation.

Despite the attention the marches had received, SCLC leaders felt they had not been able to generate the overwhelming outpouring they had expected from the Black urban areas. The response of the national media had been less than spectacular. Fund-raising and participation from around the country were not encouraging. King and his strategists considered escalating their gamble by calling for a national infusion of protesters to lay siege to the city. In the face of serious doubt as to the possible success of such an effort, it was never tried. Jim Laue saw in this and other signs evidence that an exhausted SCLC leadership was looking for a strategy to enable it to declare a victory and go home.

At length SCLC decided to play a trump card. It planned for a major march in the neighboring city of Cicero, a lily-white working-class community with a reputation for violent resistance to any Black incursion. The threat brought the desired result. With the mayor's support, the Chicago power structure convened a summit conference at which the leaders of the real estate industry met face-to-face with the protest leaders in the presence of the mayor and the kingpins of the city's business, religious, and civic institutions. Within two weeks, an agreement was worked out. The housing industry and relevant city agencies offered to improve compliance with open-housing laws and regulations, and religious and civic leaders undertook to develop education programs in support of open occupancy policies. While the agreement lacked the guarantees and performance deadlines that the protesters would have liked, pledges were made for a good-faith effort, in exchange for which SCLC and the civil rights coalition suspended the marches for an unspecified period.

While the settlement was hailed by many as a victory, the Chicago adventure had fallen far short of the hopes of King and his associates. Despite SCLC's best efforts, it had failed to galvanize either significant outrage among Chicago's Blacks or an outpouring of support from around the nation. As a pilot program to chart the way for cracking racial poverty and injustice in the North, it had shown them that this was not the way to go.

The importance of the settlement lay less in Chicago than in its confirmation of the expectation of many that segregation in the North was not likely to yield to the methods of the movement that had prevailed in the South. To those who had come to expect that SCLC would produce blockbuster breakthroughs for social justice, it was a disappointing venture.

Jim Laue, reflecting years later on what turned King back from Chicago, pinpointed three contributing factors. One was the disciplined control of the city by an old-fashioned political boss strongly allied both to the ethnic neighborhoods as well as to much of the leadership of African American political and civic organizations. The second factor was the reduced financial support coming from the liberal sources that had passionately put their money into the civil rights struggle in the South. The third was the difference in the immediacy of the issues. As Laue explained:

> Gandhi used to say that 'soul force' is used most effectively when there is a direct correspondence between means and ends. When you're sitting in on a lunch counter stool, the means are the ends; the behavior of your protest is precisely the behavior you wish to be guaranteed by law. When you want open housing, on the other

hand, there's no direct connection between picketing and marching and living in peace in a non-segregated neighborhood.[14]

THE POOR PEOPLE'S CAMPAIGN

By 1967 the civil rights movement's mighty engine for waging war on
injustice through the power of peaceful mass protest lay idle. The legislative victories required to assure equal rights under law had been won.
But the triumph offered no satisfaction without follow-on progress
toward distributive justice. The fact that SCLC's effort to crank up the
war machine to battle for equal housing in Chicago had an ambiguous
outcome did not deter King and his associates from seeing the future
of the civil rights movement as tied to the struggle for a better life for
America's impoverished millions.

The new objective would be to mobilize a mass protest of the poor
in order to awaken the American conscience to economic injustice.
SCLC's leaders envisioned a rough parallel to the successful strategy
of the past: consciousness-raising to ready the nation for legislative
change. To dramatize the issue there would be a great convergence of
the nation's poor upon Washington and a continuing encampment on
the Mall—at the center of the seat of government. The purpose would
be to provide a background drumbeat for an intensive lobbying effort
with Congress and the Executive Branch agencies.

CRS was not alone in seeing this as a high-risk venture. The federal
government at its highest levels had serious concerns. Officials understood that in order for SCLC to find the encampment useful, the
encampment would have to be visible, provocative—even abrasive. The
potential for disorder seemed monumental. Violence, whether stem-
ming from aroused whites, from undisciplined minority members swept
up in the campaign, or from overstressed agents of law enforcement,
could result in a bloodbath. Fear of riots on the streets of Washington
or police violence might shame the nation and be a major setback in
progress toward social change. There could easily be spillover to other
cities.[15]

The fact that Martin Luther King Jr. would be the presiding figure
of this mass lobbying effort offered some reassurance that it would not
get out of hand. Nevertheless, chaos and disaster could result from
any failure in planning or administering the logistics of the envisioned

gigantic tent city. Food, water, housing, public safety, and health services would need to be provided and maintained without breakdown. CRS advocated full support and close coordination by all relevant city and federal agencies.

Under the attentive eye of the attorney general—and the less apparent but no less attentive eye of the White House—the federal apparatus answered the call. With the city government of Washington carrying the burden of responsibility, more than twenty local and federal agencies formed a coordinating mechanism to provide SCLC with logistical assistance and to keep the effort of building and managing a new city in the heart of the nation's capital from going awry. CRS was given the job of "coordinating community relations." This meant monitoring the interface between SCLC and all of the participating agencies in order to anticipate problems, make sure that little went wrong, and that what did go wrong was promptly remedied. For example, Wilkins flew to Miami in January, and to Atlanta in March, to personally sit down with King to stress the need for advance planning and arrangements, such as obtaining the dozens of permits that would be required to plant a new city in the middle of Washington, D.C. And when unrelenting rain converted the encampment on the Mall to a wallow of mud, CRS called on the U.S. Public Health Service to assure the necessary safeguards against the outbreak of disease.

Planning strategies for the Poor People's Campaign had been well under way by early April 1968, when everything came to a screeching halt with the murder of Dr. Martin Luther King Jr.

In late March, the thirteen hundred sanitation workers of the city of Memphis, mostly Black, were six weeks into a strike for union recognition and economic gains. Mass demonstrations supported by the Black community were encountering stubborn resistance. Tensions were high. Against the advice of his staff, already overwhelmed by preparations for the Poor People's Campaign, King accepted an invitation to speak before a Memphis rally, where his presence seemed to reinvigorate the movement. He returned on April 1 to lead a march of sanitation workers and their supporters. A number of people broke away from the march and started breaking windows and looting. "Many stores along the march route were damaged, 280 people were arrested, 60 people were injured, and a black sixteen-year-old boy was killed by police gunfire."[16]

King was upset that a demonstration under his leadership had erupted in disorder. He and his colleagues immediately understood that it had been a mistake to participate in a display of this size without the careful planning, training, and management of SCLC organizers. King decided he would lead another march—this one with proper SCLC guidance. The date chosen was April 8. He and a cadre of aides returned to Memphis on April 3. He died on April 4.

CRS conciliator Ozell Sutton, who had been in New Orleans and Shreveport, was transferred to Memphis in January 1968 because of the sanitation workers strike. He had been mediating between the union and the city, shuttling back and forth communicating demands and underlying interests on union recognition and pay.[17]

Jim Laue had joined the CRS team that was trying to conciliate the Memphis controversy, in order to be available for planning discussions with SCLC leaders about the Poor People's Campaign, now only weeks away. Laue had a strong personal relationship with King, Andrew Young, and other SCLC leaders. CRS conciliator Fred Miller was also assigned to work with SCLC. When King arrived in Memphis, Sutton had responsibilities for working with police and the Invaders, a more militant Black organization that advocated violence. Laue sensed a return to the early days of the civil rights movement, one with large-scale meetings, numerous reporters, government officials, and law enforcement personnel.[18] Laue, who then led CRS's evaluation, had participated in the early 1960s protests as a student and supporter. He wanted to help CRS construct a strategy given this possible resurgence of the civil rights movement.

In a short document reconstructing those fateful last days, written shortly before Laue himself passed away, he shared how he saw that energy and enthusiasm: "Yesterday, and today, I have rekindled the feeling of old-style Southern movement, mass meetings, sometimes stiff visits to law enforcement and media, sitting in on movement strategy sessions, and keeping Washington selectively posted."[19]

On April 3, King gave his last sermon at the Mason Temple, the World Headquarters of the Church of God in Christ in Memphis, with both Sutton and Laue in the church. He ended with these words: "Like anybody, I would like to live a long life. Longevity has its place. But I'm not concerned about that now. I just want to do God's will. And He's allowed me to go up to the mountain. And I've looked over. And I've seen the Promised Land. I may not get there with you. But I want you to know tonight, that we, as a people, will get to the promised land!"[20]

Immediately after the speech, Andrew Young and James Laue spoke. Laue recalled Young telling him, "I've never heard him speak like that. I've never heard him so pessimistic."[21]

Laue, who had been engaged with the civil rights movement since the early 1960s and always wanted to be in the "nerve center of the movement", stayed in homes and hotels owned or operated by African Americans. On that day his white federal colleagues stayed in white hotels downtown.[22] Laue shared a room at the Lorraine Motel with Andrew Young. The adjacent room was shared by King and Ralph Abernathy. On April 4 Laue was in his room listening to the six o'clock news.

The sound of the fatal shot brought him to the balcony door to see the civil rights leader fallen. Others were calling for aid. He rushed back for towels and blankets, feeling as he did so that it was already too late to provide comfort. Sutton recalled being at the Lorraine Motel and driving his car straight to Saint Joseph's Hospital, where the ambulance took King. A doctor came out of the operating room and shared, "He's dead, Mr. Sutton."

Unable to reach Roger Wilkins in his office or at home, Laue called the attorney general to advise him of King's death. Ramsey Clark made immediate arrangements to fly to Memphis, asking Laue to arrange for him to meet with SCLC leaders to express the federal government's concern and offer its assistance.[23] When Wilkins learned of King's death, he moved to augment the CRS team in Memphis and Atlanta so that it could bolster SCLC in making necessary arrangements with the authorities in both cities and for the funeral.

That night Ozell Sutton traveled to the hall in the Mason Temple, which was packed full with more than three thousand people who knew that King had been shot. Sutton recalled telling the throngs of people, "There's nothing you can do tonight, and I'm sure that your leadership will be getting together tomorrow to decide whatever's to be done. And that will be announced, so I would suggest that you go straight home."

Anticipating the wave of outrage that might engulf America's Black communities, CRS took what it feared might be futile measures to help communities deter the onrushing hurricane and alleviate the consequences. In Memphis, CRS arranged for the attorney general to meet with King's followers and the strikers on the one hand and the mayor and public safety director on the other to help maintain a climate of calm. CRS conciliators throughout the country were kept informed of developments in Memphis so that they might be able to dispel rumors as they met with law enforcement and civil rights officials working to relieve tensions. Their efforts proved to be weak sandbags against the mounting tidal wave of riots that broke out around the country.

Within a month of King's funeral, and with Black inner cities still smoldering, nine caravans bearing representatives of the nation's poor left their various points of origin for a labyrinthine journey to the encampment at Washington, D.C. Accompanying the two caravans that started from Marks, Mississippi, was a symbolic mule train with blue-denimed attendants, which SCLC had made emblematic of Black rural poverty. Each of the nine caravans had a CRS team charged with negotiating the travelers' safe passage through what at times would be unsympathetic-to-hostile country. This meant monitoring SCLC's efforts to obtain campsites, route permits, health care, and provisions all along the line of march and improvising ways to forestall disaster. It meant meeting with city policy makers, peace officers, and news reporters to help them understand that the caravan following half a day behind was a group of determined Americans seeking to peacefully petition their government, and not some ragtag rabble bent on trouble.

It was clear from the outset that the CRS role would be one of clearing minefields. Trouble started immediately in Marks, Mississippi. Seven SCLC organizers were arrested, and students and teachers were suspended for their recruiting activities. Conflict spiraled upward with a school boycott, followed by threats of teachers being fired. CRS helped to negotiate a solution—official closure of schools for a few days until the caravans got started, with classes to be made up at the end of the year.

Fear of police overreaction was heightened after a police official from Virginia started a rumor in advance of the caravan reaching Selma, Alabama, that the marchers were armed and prone to violence. To ease that concern, CRS thereafter arranged for each police jurisdiction to reassure itself by having its own scout join the caravan two stops before the scheduled arrival in each city. The outcome was unanimous praise from all the southern caravans for police cooperation en route.

Near Cincinnati, rival participating youth gangs threatened to disrupt the caravan. CRS's recommendations about giving the youth groups specific responsibilities resolved the problem. In Detroit, CRS met with SCLC leaders and the mayor to conciliate police brutality allegations. In Seattle, police refused to allow caravan buses to park at the scheduled staging area, threatening confusion and possible disorder at the very start of the march. CRS, enlisting the assistance of the U.S. attorney and the U.S. marshal, arranged for the police to cover the parking meters. When ideological and personal differences between leaders of the western caravan seemed likely to split the marchers into two groups proceeding separately across the country, CRS took on a mediation role that enabled the caravan to continue as a united group.

The riots following King's assassination, and the determination of King's successors to carry on with plans for the Poor People's Campaign without the stabilizing power of King's personality, added to the government's anxiety that misfortune might befall the project.

The nine caravans converged on Washington in mid-May, creating Resurrection City, an instant community of tents and plywood shacks that was built to house fifteen hundred but at times sheltered as many as seven thousand.[24] The residents were enrolled for an imprecisely programmed season of petition and protest. With the cooperation of the National Park Service, the city government and the city's churches, and other public and private agencies, SCLC was able to accomplish the logistical miracle of organizing, housing, feeding, and entertaining the residents of the tent city and moving them about the city by the hundreds for demonstrations at the Capitol, the White House, and dozens of federal agencies, all the while maintaining an orderly community.

The lobbying efforts scored few victories. Among the many poverty-related issues that the campaign raised with the leaders of government, the greatest energy came to focus on hunger. New reports of starvation in the rural South added fuel to the effort. Immediate relief in the form of liberalizing the food stamp program was totally rejected by the Agriculture Department. Efforts in Congress got little support. The SCLC push appeared to be a total failure. Behind the scenes, Roger Wilkins and Ramsey Clark tried to generate an end run through the White House. With the support of Sargent Shriver, who headed the administration's anti-poverty program, and Joe Califano, the president's chief aide on domestic programs, the proposal was taken to President

Johnson. He liked it well enough to explore funding possibilities with Wilbur Mills, chairman of the House Ways and Means Committee. Mills advised that in view of the extraordinary efforts required to win the recently adopted emergency appropriation for the war in Vietnam, the proposal would be a nonstarter.

In Resurrection City, enthusiasm was wearing down. As platoons of new residents replaced the old, as boredom set in, as sweltering heat and drenching rains and muddy streets made life difficult to bear, tempers wore thin, group cohesion became less effective, and codes of behavior became less binding. The tendency toward disorder became less responsive to the moral influence of camp leaders and more demanding of police presence.

The CRS job of making sure that nothing bad happened became increasingly difficult. Demands intensified for close liaison with SCLC and camp leaders, for troubleshooting problems with the police, for arranging the quick resolution of logistical breakdowns, and for conciliating and avoiding conflicts on the streets.

As the weeks wore on, and with the lobbying effort showing few results and community control becoming increasingly difficult, there was mounting discord within the SCLC leadership. While the prospect of closing the encampment when its park permit expired on June 23 was not unwelcome, there was fear that it held the danger of dismounting a tiger.

Antagonism was rising between police and residents of the camp. There were rumors of residents secreting firearms, and that a hard-core remnant might refuse to leave. A midnight incident of rock and bottle throwing drew a tear-gas response from the U.S. Park Police. The Justice Department was fearful that the closing of the camp might end in violence. The CRS priority became to encourage SCLC's effort to generate strategies to assure a nonviolent withdrawal and to encourage leaders of law enforcement in their plans to assure restraint in the use of force.

On June 24, Ralph Abernathy led about two hundred and fifty residents to a final appeal for economic justice before their prearranged arrest on the Capitol grounds. A half hour after their departure from Resurrection City, Roger Wilkins and other observers accompanied the police, who made a sweep of the tent city, arresting the fewer than a hundred remaining residents. There were no more than a handful of reports of disorderly resistance and forceable arrests. Disorders in Washington, D.C., that night were suppressed by a curfew order and an overwhelming presence of law enforcement personnel.

The ending of the Poor People's Campaign with hardly a whimper signaled the end of formal efforts within the civil rights movement to devise a grand strategy for winning distributive justice. Equality of results would continue to be the elusive objective of the second phase of the battle for civil rights, but the engagements increasingly would be fought on smaller battlefields and by local troops. CRS would continue to adapt its strategies to match the evolving struggle.

PREEMPTIVE PROBLEM SOLVING—A NEW AGENDA FOR CRS

The volcanic intensity of summer riots in 1965, 1966, and 1967 caused American leaders to recognize the depth of Black rage in the central cities. To CRS's leadership the riots were a reaction to racial inequity and injustice beyond the healing reach of civil rights laws. The persistence of inequity and indignity was the demon that had to be exorcised.

As his term moved toward 1968, its final year, Wilkins still found himself unable to define the CRS program to his own satisfaction. He felt that under LeRoy Collins, CRS had rocketed from crisis to crisis, driven by objectives that were always in flux. For all the hundreds of instances of CRS intervention in local conflicts, despite the scores of settlements negotiated to resolve minority protests of unfairness in the schools, on the job, and in the justice system, the total impact seemed transitory and far short of the fundamental change required to help set America straight. He had a gut feeling that CRS would be more effective in dealing with racial conflict if its primary concern was social justice rather than group relationships. Conflict resolution struck him as too opportunistic, lacking precise goals and objectives. Limited to a peacekeeping role, CRS could only respond to situations of other people's making, never initiating programs of its own. More troubling was the fact that peacekeeping was more likely to focus on symptoms than on root causes. It influenced change only at the margins, not at the core of the American dilemma. To play a role of consequence CRS would have to find a way to make its own direct contribution to speeding minority progress from equal opportunity to equal achievement.

Mounting such a new program faced two formidable obstacles: first, neither the Justice Department, nor the administration's budget watchdogs, nor the congressional appropriations committees would approve enlargement of the CRS program beyond its Title X mandate to prevent and resolve conflict; second, a new CRS program would need to fill a role that did not duplicate what other federal agencies were already doing.

With the aid of CRS Deputy Director George Culberson, Wilkins first set about inventing the new CRS role by launching a program planning process that, for a federal agency, was a unique adventure in participatory democracy. Every member of the professional staff was assigned to a task force for researching issues and developing options. The entire professional staff reviewed proposals in vigorous, often clamorous debate.

George Culberson, who had succeeded John Griffin as CRS associate director for compliance in the summer of 1965 before becoming deputy director in January 1966, was one of the acknowledged deans of the community relations profession. A onetime high school principal in Pittsburgh, he served as the first executive director of that city's pioneering Human Relations Commission. He was a founder and early president of the National Association of Human Relations Officials. In the early sixties he headed the Air Force Office of Contract Compliance, which he then staffed with community relations professionals, some of whom subsequently followed him to CRS.

Wilkins and Culberson complemented each other. Wilkins saw in the older man a pragmatic idealist who had learned to navigate the shoals of political infighting on both the local and the national scene. Culberson was trained to provide administrative and technical oversight to a field staff that was still learning its profession, an area in which Wilkins's interest lay in outcomes rather than in details. Above all, Culberson understood and accepted the critical function of any second in command—to leave to his chief those tasks most suited to the director's skills and predilections and to faithfully perform all others.

The program that emerged was one by which CRS would provide technical assistance at the grassroots level that other federal agencies could not reach, supporting minority self-help endeavors leading to "empowerment" of the minority community. This assistance would be provided in five areas: economic development, education, housing, mass communication, and administration of justice.

With a program design in place, a rationale had to be developed to make it square with the congressional mandate of helping communities to overcome disputes, disagreements, and difficulties. Title X had said nothing about community empowerment, and minority assistance programs were already addressed by the War on Poverty.

The rationale that developed was rooted in what CRS had learned about the causes of urban riots. Its line of reasoning was tailored to exploit the high priority that successive national administrations attached to riot prevention. Consistent with the recently published report of the National Advisory Commission on Civil Disorders, chaired by Governor Otto Kerner of Illinois, the theory held that a basic contribution to civil disorder was not poverty alone but the concurrent alienation of the minority poor. Alienation was a product of the indignity of being discounted: of being ignored in the decision-making processes that govern daily life, and being denied participation in the management of the institutions that shape your community. The best way to overcome alienation would be to give minorities a stake in society by maximizing their participation in, and control of, the institutions that influenced their destiny.

That line of reasoning proved to be persuasive. To Attorney General Ramsey Clark, who approved the program in the waning months of his incumbency, it squared with his own thesis that America could not guarantee either justice or order without having both. To the incoming Nixon administration, as represented by Richard Kleindienst, who as deputy to Attorney General John Mitchell gave oversight to the CRS program, it was a pragmatic approach to urban community problems. As a result, budget increase followed budget increase for four years as CRS retrained its staff, added experts and consultants in each of the five fields of technical assistance, opened offices in forty-four cities, and deployed a staff of 323 (up from about 150 in 1968).

From 1969 to 1973, CRS applied only about a quarter of its resources to conflict resolution. Three-quarters of its capacity was dedicated to the new conflict prevention program. The mission was to help in the creation and strengthening of minority institutions and the strengthening of minority influence in majority enterprises. Some called it minority empowerment. This endeavor was largely catalytic: brokering alliances between Party A and Party B, with Party A being a minority entity familiar with a specific need but short on expertise and financial resources and Party B being a white institution (corporation, foundation, university) capable of supplying both. The objectives of these alliances—some of which were successful and some of which never left the ground—covered a wide range of institutions and activities. These included: minority economic development corporations, inner city credit unions, tenant management associations, housing cooperatives, and public housing security agencies. Some community groups were schooled in federal communications law. They learned how to challenge the licenses of radio and television stations when they came up for periodic renewal required by the Federal Communications Commission and use this as a weapon to influence better minority employment and programming arrangements. Minority consortiums found technical assistance to help them bid on television cable franchises. Minority groups began to challenge and change the nature of police practices. The result was a strengthening of minority police officer associations, community support of police minority recruitment programs, special minority training for police promotional exams, and community challenges to culturally biased civil service examinations.

CRS's role in these empowerment ventures varied from that of a major player at a program's conception and community organization stages to short-term assistance at critical junctures in order to facilitate federal funding, circumvent political roadblocks, and conciliate quarrels within the sponsoring community. A sampling of the outcomes that the preventive program yielded in the half year prior to its sudden termination in 1973 includes:

— The Georgia Association of Police Community Relations Officers was formed to bring police and minority citizens together in training workshops around the state.
— A program in Raleigh to train minority community members to relate more effectively with the education establishment received help in organizing and obtaining funds.
— Minority businessmen in four Alabama cities received a shot in the arm via technical assistance provided by business

development organizations established with federal funds.

— In Birmingham, Huntsville, and Mobile, technical aid was provided in the critical areas of loan packaging, contract procurement, and management skill development.

— An industrial park in Tuskegee, funded by the Economic Development Administration, was expected eventually to provide four thousand jobs.

— Latinos in Chicago, who formed the Latin Communications Junta to press for the employment of Hispanics by the media, began to see the first fruits of their effort.

— The sixty members of Detroit's minority Metropolitan Contractors' Association found new doors open to them when a Small Business Administration set-aside program made it possible for them to bid on $2 million worth of contracts for the rehabilitation of properties repossessed by the Department of Housing and Urban Development.

— Puerto Ricans in Connecticut, troubled by miscarriages of justice resulting from language difficulties, were successful in getting interpreters to work in the courts of Hartford, New Haven, and Bridgeport.

— Hispanics in Rochester, New York, formed the Ibero-American Action League, which received the support necessary to plan the development of a $4 million low- and moderate-income housing project.

— Public housing residents in Buffalo formed the Buffalo Tenants Organization to share some responsibility and decision making with management.

— Third-year law students at Texas Southern University Law School, the second largest minority law school in the country, gained new opportunities to intern in the offices of the U.S. attorney, the city attorney, and the district attorney.

— Youth Service Bureaus were organized in Denver to serve as central referral agencies to assist minority youth beginning to encounter trouble with the law.

— A minority land development corporation in Pittsburgh won initial HUD funding to plan development of a new commercial-residential development.

— A group of ex-prisoners in Philadelphia developed a program to provide postrelease services to newly discharged inmates.

— Eighteen hundred minority neighborhood residents arrested in Pittsburgh benefited from the bail reform activities of the newly developed minority-sponsored Community Release Agency.

— Black and Chicano community groups in Fresno effectively utilized the HEW civil rights compliance process to oppose discriminatory practices of the local school board.

— Minority residents of San Bernardino formed a community development corporation that started to revitalize their neighborhood by rehabilitating sixty-four units of abandoned housing owned by the Veterans Administration.

— Native American organizations in Seattle established a migrant housing facility to supply social services and temporary housing for seasonally unemployed migrant workers.

— Local parent advisory committees, required by law to advise school districts with respect to the use of Title I funds for educationally disadvantaged children, but untrained as to their responsibilities, were helped by a network of state advisory councils to become more effective advocates of their children's interests.[25]

In mid-1973, with the nation's fear of inner city urban violence reduced to a distant memory, and with CRS defenders John Mitchell and Richard Kleindienst occupied with Watergate problems, the Bureau of the Budget prevailed in its long-term opposition to the preventive program and brought it to an end. The budget analysts, always troubled by CRS's inability to quantify its outputs in conventional terms, or to prove that its preventive programs lowered the risks of riots, recommended that CRS reduce its staff by two-thirds, abandon its program of crisis prevention, and limit its work to responding to racial crises after they arose.

The rationale offered by the budget cutters was a simplistic one—that the CRS programs directed toward such things as housing, education, and economic development were already within the purview of other agencies of government. They failed to recognize that only CRS utilized the unique approach of helping individual local groups find the skills, resources, and levers of power to make decisions and keep control within their own communities.

The abandonment of the CRS experiment was probably inevitable. The idea of fostering minority community empowerment as a means of overcoming alienation and alleviating discord may have been well conceived, but the resources available to it were too puny to help achieve major social change. If the intent and drive that motivated the CRS program could have been transferred, along with the components of the program, to the relevant major departments of government, a significant outcome may have resulted. But the nation was a far distance away from accepting the notion of minority empowerment as an appropriate function of the federal government—and Lyndon Johnson, who might have understood it, was long gone.

NOTES

1. This agency was the forerunner to the Department of Housing and Urban Development.

2. Jay Janis and Seymour Samet, interviews with Bertram Levine.

3. Roger Wilkins, interview with Bertram Levine.

4. Memorandum of October 19, 1964, from A. M. Secrest to Dr. John A. Griffin.

5. This was typical CRS on-the-job training for recruits—sink or swim on an assignment always beyond your previous experience. Since no one else had ever had such an assignment, mere survival made you an instant expert. In 1965 I was a veteran within the new and tiny profession of community relations workers, having served the American Jewish Committee for seventeen years. But my race relations experience, devoted largely to writing and research, plus volunteer experience in community organization and coalition building, was hardly the ideal preparation for assessing minority urban tensions or analyzing the inner city–city hall relationships of America's central cities.

6. While I did not know it at the time, I was one of the earliest targets of a process later to be described and named by Tom Wolfe in an essay called "Mau-Mauing the Flak Catchers." He pictured it as the use of uncivil and even abusive conversation to intimidate and destabilize a government functionary, presumably to enhance one's negotiating posture.

7. The technique had originated in Alinsky's work in the Chicago slum known as Back of the Yards. This was the area behind the meatpacking plants inhabited by the plants' workers, largely Polish immigrants. Alinsky's teachings and his organizing skills were credited with getting the heretofore hapless workers to organize, to protest, and to sustain their efforts until change resulted. In the space of a few years the Back of the Yards saw far-reaching changes in social conditions.

8. Katzenbach recalled that he and others had reservations about including the concept of conciliation in the civil rights law when it was being drafted.

9. Wilkins, interview with Levine.

10. Nicholas Katzenbach and Burke Marshall, interviews with Bertram Levine. In a telephone interview on August 23, 1990, Doar could not recall any undue tension between the Civil Rights Division and CRS in Selma, nor any differences with Governor Collins related to the crossing of the Pettus Bridge. He noted that in general differences as to the priority to be given the litigative as opposed to the negotiated approach were not unhealthy, and the various attorneys general under whom he served supported each as circumstances indicated.

11. Clark, *Crime in America*, 345.

12. Wilkins, interview with Levine.

13. Wilkins, interview with Levine.

14. Jim Laue, interview with Bertram Levine.

15. Those with an eye for history remembered the disastrous results of a comparable bivouac of the poor on Washington's Anacostia Flats in 1932. There thousands of unemployed veterans of World War 1 moved in for an indeterminate stay in order to lobby for the immediate payment of war bonuses. On orders of the president, the veterans were forcibly evicted by army troops led by Chief of Staff Douglas MacArthur. The harsh tactics left a legacy of bitterness around the country for many years.

16. Hampton and Fayer, *Voices of Freedom*.

17. Ozell Sutton's actions in Memphis are added by Grande Lum and are new for this edition. Ozell Sutton interview, Civil Rights Mediation Oral History Project, https://perma.cc/3ML3-BY2Y.

18. These additional details of CRS involvement in Memphis are added by Grande Lum and are new for this addition. James Laue, "25 Years Ago: A Personal Report from Memphis," April 2, 1993, 1–2, National Civil Rights Museum, Memphis, Tenn.

19. Laue, "25 Years Ago," 2.

20. Nikita Stewart, "'I've Been to the Mountaintop,' Dr. King's Last Sermon Annotated," *New York Times,* April 2, 2018, https://perma.cc/UH4S-7RBE; Laue, "25 Years Ago," 2–3.

21. Laue, "25 Years Ago," 3.

22. Laue, "25 Years Ago," 1.

23. Laue, interview with Levine.

24. Young, *An Easy Burden*, 483.

25. Drawn from U.S. Department of Justice, Community Relations Service, Annual Report, 1973.

FIVE

When Cities Erupt

PRECEDING CHAPTERS HAVE looked chronologically at many of the issues and events that shaped the first decade of the Community Relations Service. The next six chapters, taking a longitudinal approach, will trace specific aspects of racial conflict in America, as seen through the eyes of the Community Relations Service. This chapter will focus on the climate of rage and violence that influenced the events of that time, concentrating on the inner-city riots—how they came about, what happened, how they were controlled, and what their consequences were in terms of America's struggle for a more equal society.

THE CHANGING CHARACTERISTICS OF
BLACK-WHITE RELATIONS

By 1964, civil rights advocates and scholars were increasingly aware that the passage of civil rights laws was no more than a first step toward the achievement of equal status for Blacks. To many, equality under the law would be a hoax if it did not lead to changes in the second-class status that Blacks experienced in their daily lives. Without major changes in policies and massive investment in programs for education, employment, housing, and intergroup understanding, the civil rights revolution would prove to have been a ship with no cargo. While President Johnson's new War on Poverty was seen by whites as a generous commitment to improving the lives of disadvantaged people, Black leaders saw no evidence that the government had either an understanding of the size of the investment required or the will to make the effort. Many sensed, too, that white supporters of the movement did not have the heart for the long and greater struggle ahead. Already these ideas were being translated into social action by so-called extremists who advocated that Blacks go it alone. Black separatism, Black nationalism, Black power became symbols around which many would rally in the years ahead. The issue of whether the struggle for equality should continue

121

on the road to integration or branch off on the path toward Black self-determination would, in the next few years, fracture the civil rights coalition and lessen the vigor of white support for civil rights.

In 1964 Arnold M. Rose, one of America's leading race relations scholars, who had been Gunnar Myrdal's collaborator in writing *An American Dilemma*, sounded a warning:

> It is not certain yet that the conflict has been won. All vigorous protest movements generate new forces that hamper the achievement of the movement's goals. One is the reaction, or "backlash." Social changes and efforts to achieve social changes run up against both concrete vested interests that are hurt by the changes and a general anxiety that is stimulated by the rapid change itself. The full dimensions of the reaction cannot be assessed yet, but certainly one can expect that the conflict between the African American protest and its reaction will generate more violence.[1]

A nationwide poll in April 1964 showed that 70 percent of Americans favored passage of the Civil Rights Act. But many were anxious and even fearful about the changes that would result. How would a new level of racial equality impact their personal lives? Moreover, millions in the South and many in the North were still uncompromising opponents of civil rights. That same spring, Alabama's governor, George C. Wallace, the leading spokesman for racial segregation, won at least 25 percent of the vote in the Democratic presidential primaries in three *nonsouthern* states. He came within 5 percent of winning a majority in Maryland. In 1963 and 1964 more than half a dozen *nonsouthern* cities and states conducted referendums in which the voters turned back civil rights legislation in housing or public accommodations.

Black activists pointed out that even some civil rights allies were quick to resist new arrangements that called for sharing power and authority. A new breeding ground for racial confrontations came into being in August 1964 with the signing of the new federal antipoverty law. This legislation, which would soon provide new resources and means for attacking the social and economic deprivation of the poor, also provided new avenues for minority residents to challenge traditional approaches to allocating social welfare benefits. One component of the War on Poverty, known as the Community Action Program, was to emphasize "maximum feasible participation of the poor" in planning and administering many of the local programs. Organizing and training impoverished residents to participate in the design and administration of programs would prove to be a source of conflict with local officials and established agencies.

Harris Wofford, a White House adviser on civil rights in the Kennedy years, wrote:

> The principle of the anti-poverty program, and particularly its community action program, to encourage maximum feasible participation of the poor was an open invitation to conflict—between city hall and the advocates of the poor, between local government and privately funded philanthropic agencies, and between competing racial minorities. . . . Johnson had been forewarned by his advisors about the political risk, but he said in his memoirs that such democratic processes—by giving minorities a stake in programs affecting them—were necessary to overcome apathy. He wrote: "I realized that a program as massive as the one we were contemplating might shake up many institutions, but I decided that some shaking up might be needed to get a bold new program moving. I thought that local governments had to be challenged to be awakened."[2]

Some analysts saw the antipoverty program, coming on top of civil rights progress in the South, as contributing to a further rise in Black expectations and a consequent increase in the level of frustration within the inner cities. The lag time between the delivery of programs and the achievement of change brought additional frustration.

THE URBAN RIOTS BEGIN

On July 16, two weeks after the president had signed the Civil Rights Act of 1964, there were riots in New York City. It all started outside a junior high school in summer session when the superintendent of a nearby building sprayed water on three boys. In the escalating disorder, which ultimately became a battle between police and three hundred bottle-throwing youths, an off-duty policeman shot and killed a fifteen-year-old Black boy who allegedly had threatened him with a knife.

The killing enraged the Black community. Two days later, at the end of a Harlem rally protesting anti-Black violence in Mississippi, rioting broke out. The looting, vandalism, and police confrontations lasted several days. Before they ended, a similar disturbance took place in the Bedford-Stuyvesant area, a Black neighborhood in New York's borough of Brooklyn.

A week later an outbreak in Rochester, New York, required the National Guard to restore order. By the end of August there had been widespread disorders in Jersey City, Elizabeth, and Paterson, New Jersey; in Philadelphia; and in the Chicago suburb of Dixmoor.[3] The nation recognized with alarm that the discontent of its inner city communities had begun to erupt with cataclysmic force and the outbreaks threatened to be pandemic.

In answer to the question of why, spokesmen from across the spectrum of social analysis were quick to point out that civil rights progress had not changed anything in the Black urban areas of the big cities where the pain of poverty and the insult of prejudice were a daily assault on Black dignity. The civil rights victories had given false hope of change but were really irrelevant to Black inner city life. During the ten years of favorable court decisions and federal legislation since 1954, the gap between Blacks and whites in income, in employment, and in education had increased. Lack of progress in the face of elevated expectations was certain to heighten frustration.

Many activists and social analysts chose to describe the urban violence of this period as "rebellions" rather than "race riots." They saw it as a thrust for equality and revolt against oppression, akin to the violent protests of the prerevolution American colonists. The criminal connotations of the word "riot" were too dismissive of the true significance of the outbreaks. The words "race riot" historically applied to pitched battles between Blacks and whites, or white assaults upon Blacks. These disorders were different. According to the National Advisory Commission on Civil Disorders, "The civil disorders of 1967 involved Negroes acting against local symbols of white American society, authority and property in Negro neighborhoods—rather than against white persons."[4]

As the "long hot summers" became a feature of American life, the infant Community Relations Service, overwhelmed by its assignment to ease racial violence in the South, wanted no part of them. But it soon became apparent that, ready or not, the nation's designated race relations troubleshooters would have to play a hand.

THE INFERNO CLOSE UP

Often the first CRS view of a riot was from the sky—a conciliator's sighting of the smoke or flames from still burning neighborhoods, depending on whether it was day or night and on how soon he had been able to get a plane from wherever he was when news of the outbreak reached him with his assignment. Sometimes it was sooner, when violence erupted in a city where a conciliator lived or happened to be working on another case. In the summer of 1966, Roger Wilkins was meeting with the CRS executive staff in Washington when an emergency call came in from Christopher Mould, a conciliator on assignment in Chicago. Wilkins switched the call to a speaker phone, so that the group could hear Mould's report from a phone booth at an intersection where mob violence was mounting. The call terminated abruptly as Mould announced his departure, to the sounds of the booth being uprooted around him.

The efforts and effectiveness of the Community Relations Service varied from city to city. Opportunities to be useful depended on unfolding events, relationships, and community dynamics. When it came to CRS helping a city deal with outbreaks of civil disorder, there were three stages for possible assistance—before, during, and after. During those peak years of racial ferment there was little that CRS or anyone could do to prevent a riot [5] Whether CRS assistance in stimulating programs for summer youth employment, for better police-community relations, and for improved communication across the racial divide could make that much of a difference was anybody's guess. During the riot control phase there were limited opportunities for a conciliator to be useful. Mayors or police chiefs were most likely to accept or call upon CRS assistance in situations related to the involvement of the minority community's leadership. Such assistance included consultation as to the wisdom and conditions of a curfew, using minority volunteers to discourage violence, or avoiding harsh conditions of arrest and confinement. Sometimes the opportunity for a CRS contribution while the violence was raging was zero despite days of watchful waiting. Often the most useful assistance came at the end of the disturbance, to help resolve grievances, speed emergency repair programs involving federal assistance, and develop programs to repair fractured relations between racial groups.

In 1966, CRS representative Milton Lewis, tied up with problems in East St. Louis, could not get into Omaha until July 7, just after a three-day period of rioting had ended. There his most significant effort in the short run was to help overcome factionalism among minority organizations, so that they could more coherently negotiate their grievances with city hall. Over the longer term, CRS worked closely with the mayor to help the city gain access to federal funding programs that addressed problems that had contributed to racial tensions.

Typical of CRS's experience with riots was its involvement with the civil disturbance in Buffalo in 1967. Starting early in the year the assigned conciliation specialist made regular visits about twice a month to deal with a number of conflict situations. Staying two or three days each time, he had begun to gain the confidence of a number of Black and white leaders. In early May he reported mounting tension among youth in the urban communities. Problems included gang activity, a lack of recreational facilities, a lack of employment opportunities, and poor police-community relations. Tension was also rising about the organizational activities of BUILD.[6] He tried unsuccessfully to get city officials to meet with minority leaders, especially the militants. He perceived more readiness on the part of the mayor than of members of the city council. He also tried, unsuccessfully, to get the police department and the Human Relations Commission to apply for funds from the federal Office of Law Enforcement Assistance for a police-community relations program. Early in June the conciliator was able to get the mayor and city leaders to sit down with Buffalo's media executives and CRS's media experts to discuss how the media might improve the way they handled stories of racial tension. There were also discussions on improving police-media cooperation.[7]

When civil disorder broke out on June 27, CRS sent in an interracial conciliation team. The African American conciliator met with militant urban community leaders and discussed the demands they would like to place before the city's government and business leaders. The white conciliator, in the meantime, worked on those same public officials and business leaders to interpret inner city perceptions and to prepare them to sit down with minority representatives to negotiate the demands likely to come before them. With the cooperation of the U.S. attorney, CRS also consulted with police officials on tactical approaches for restoring law and order while minimizing provocative moves that would impede their efforts.

In the immediate wake of the disturbance, CRS huddled with state and local officials on the failure of the business community's program to generate summer employment for youth. The resulting change put greater responsibility for job creation and recruitment on the State Employment Office and on local African American organizations. At the same time, CRS staff in Washington met with other agencies on ways to improve the relevant federal programs in Buffalo, particularly those bearing on employment and job training.

Omaha and Buffalo were just two of more than two hundred communities that were reported to have civil disturbances in the summer of 1967. The National Commission on Civil Disorders acknowledged 164, which it grouped in categories of intensity. Eight "major" disorders were marked by many fires and by intensive looting lasting more than two days, with sizable crowds, requiring use of National Guard or federal forces. Thirty-three "serious" disorders were characterized by isolated looting, some fires and rock throwing, between one and two days of violence, and the use of state police. Of those classified as "minor" disturbances, many would not likely have received national attention if occurring singly.[8]

A Senate investigating committee that examined seventy-five disturbances in sixty-seven cities reported a total of eighty-three deaths and 1,897 injuries. All the deaths had occurred in only twelve of the disturbances. The worst of the riots came in July, when first Newark and then Detroit erupted in massive looting, uncontrollable fires, and many deaths. In Newark the carnage claimed twenty-three lives; in Detroit, forty-three. Restoration of order in Newark required the National Guard in addition to the full resources of the city and state police. In Detroit, police and the National Guard proved insufficient, and U.S. Army troops were deployed. Property damage in Detroit amounted to $40 million. About seven thousand people were arrested.

In Detroit the triggering incident was a Saturday night police raid of an after hours bar and social club in the heart of the downtown Black business district, a neighborhood known for high crime, substandard housing, and tensions over alleged police brutality. The United Community Civic League was the last of these five so-called blind pigs targeted by the vice squad that evening.[9] The 3:30 a.m. raid found an unexpectedly large party honoring some recently returned Vietnam veterans, and eighty-two were arrested. The July 22 night was hot, and people were still on the street. In the hour it took to transport those arrested, a group of about two hundred gathered. Rumors spread that police had used excessive force in the raid. At about 5:00 a.m. Sunday morning, as the last of the group was being taken away, a soda bottle broke a police car window. A trash can smashed through a plate-glass storefront. A youth cried out, "We're going to have a riot." Vandalism began to spread. The violence commission reported, "A spirit of care-free nihilism was taking hold."[10] The police response, at first permissive because of insufficient personnel on duty, became increasingly harsh.

Mob violence escalated with arson and assaults on the responding firefighters. Again and again firemen had to abandon a fire scene in a hailstorm of rocks and bottles. Reports of snipers, valid in a few cases, were grossly magnified, leading to overreaction by the police and the National Guard troops with which they were reinforced. Undisciplined gunfire by police and the unseasoned and poorly trained guardsmen against inappropriate targets (including at least two instances of fire from tank-mounted machine guns) caused many of the deaths. Exaggeration and rumor contributed to the fear and rage on both sides.

CRS took on a new role in Detroit as part of the federal team dispatched by the president to advise him on the validity of exercising his constitutional authority to deploy U.S. Army troops in response to a state's request for help in quelling an insurrection beyond its ability to control. Authority for the president to make federal forces available to help states overcome domestic violence is rooted in Article 4, Section 4, of the Constitution, with guidelines for its use governed by an act of Congress passed in 1792. The reluctance of the government to deploy the army against Americans has led to great restraint in its use. Governors have requested such support less than a dozen times, most notably in labor disputes, and requests have been denied in instances where the grounds were deemed to be insufficient.

Just before midnight on July 23, Attorney General Ramsey Clark received at his home the first of several phone calls from Mayor Jerome P. Cavanagh of Detroit and Governor George Romney of Michigan, expressing their concern over rising violence and the possible need for federal assistance. The attorney general promptly alerted the secretary of the army, Stanley Resor. Clark advised President Johnson of the situation at about 3:00 a.m. Calls from the army to the Michigan National

Guard indicated the guard's assessment that it would be able to handle the situation. Two thousand guardsmen were in the area and another three thousand would be there by noon.[11] By 6:00 a.m. the army was prepared to move five thousand paratroopers from Fort Bragg, North Carolina, and Fort Campbell, Kentucky, to reach Selfridge Air Base by noon, whence they could readily be deployed to nearby Detroit.

Several conversations ensued between Romney and Clark, in which the attorney general sought to make clear that federal troops could not be committed without a written request from the governor stating that there was an insurrection that the totally committed law enforcement resources of the state could not control. Shortly before noon, the president received a request for federal troops from the governor. Although the message lacked the specific assurance that state forces were unable to control the disorder, President Johnson authorized the movement of troops to Selfridge and asked Cyrus Vance, the former undersecretary of defense, to take charge of the federal operation in Detroit and to ascertain that the situation on the ground met the constitutional and legislative requirements for the deployment of troops. Vance immediately left for Selfridge on a military plane, with a special Department of Justice team consisting of Warren Christopher, deputy attorney general; John Doar, assistant attorney general for civil rights; and Roger Wilkins, director of the Community Relations Service.

The team met with the governor and mayor, police and military commanders, and leaders of the minority community and toured the riot area. The level of riot incidents had abated since the previous day. The governor said he was reluctant to declare a state of insurrection because of a fear that insurance claims might thereby be invalidated.

Vance recommended the deployment of state police and National Guard units that had not yet been committed to riot duties. He later ordered army troops moved to the city's fairgrounds so as to be instantly available for street duty if needed. The incidents of disorder increased rapidly during the evening despite the full commitment of city and state law enforcement resources. Shortly before 11:30 p.m., Cyrus Vance reported to the president. On the team's recommendation, Johnson then signed the proclamation and executive order authorizing the use of federal troops and federalizing the National Guard.

As the soldiers took over, the violence receded. Analysts attributed the troops' effectiveness to a number of factors. They were deployed in large numbers and moved in with a professional, no-nonsense bearing. At the same time, the army was seen as a not-unfriendly presence, since a significant proportion of the troops were Black (unlike the police and the guard); since many inner city residents had seen service; and because the troops appeared initially with guns unloaded. The soldiers were quick to establish civil relations with the residents, and in some instances lent a hand in the cleanup process.

The Washington team continued to provide federal oversight in the following days during which the massive and disciplined presence of the army helped to bring the disorders under control, and as federal efforts to provide disaster relief and support rebuilding efforts got under way.

For Roger Wilkins, this was his second presidential assignment to the heart of the volcano. He had been sent to Watts to assist first LeRoy Collins and then Ramsey Clark in assessing the federal government's role in damage control and repair following the violence there. One of his major concerns was with police behavior and the over-readiness of law enforcement to use deadly force in time of riot.[12]

In Watts, where police had a reputation for abuse of minorities, he had found himself a near-victim. He and John Perry were returning to their hotel from dinner. Perry, who was driving the rental car, was white. He had been special assistant to Collins when Collins was director of CRS and had gone with him to be associate undersecretary of the Commerce Department when Collins became undersecretary.[13] A police car pulled them over after following them for several blocks. Two white officers approached, one on either side, with guns drawn. Perry was taken to the back of the car; Wilkins was spread-eagled across the hood and patted down to the accompaniment of a stream of anti-Black invective. Only after Perry had established his identity did the police seek Wilkins's credentials. The incident ended with apologies and an explanation that there was a lookout for an interracial pair who had just pulled off a robbery nearby. From inside sources, Wilkins later learned two bits of relevant information: no such robbery had been reported, and the officer who had held the gun to his head had killed a minority resident with a shotgun just a few days before.

Detroit presented Wilkins with a sense of déjà vu. On one occasion, while patrolling the city with Vance and Christopher, Wilkins was seated behind the Black driver. Whenever they were stopped by either police or National Guard personnel, officers approaching from the left did so with guns drawn and, on one occasion, with the muzzle placed at Wilkins's neck. When the approach was from the right side, it was accompanied by, "May I help you, sir?" Wilkins hoped that the lesson was not lost on his companions.

At other times it was even scarier. Familiar with reports as to the overzealousness of the National Guard and the state police, Wilkins ventured forth with some trepidation on his nightly patrols to take a reading of the level of activity in the curfew area. At one time a guard convoy passed him, made a tire-squealing U-turn, raced up beside him, and ordered the car over at gunpoint. They stopped a car behind him, too, screaming, "Out of the car! Out of the car!" Remembering Watts, Wilkins was quick to emerge from the car with hands raised, shouting over and over, "Department of Justice! Department of Justice!" As an uncertain guardsman approached, he told him in which pocket to find his U.S. government credentials.

Under Wilkins's watchful eye the soldiers then queried the terrified Black parents and children of the other car that had been stopped. The man turned out to be a night shift employee of one of the auto companies, with a special pass to be out after curfew. His family had picked him up to drive him home. As he left the scene, Wilkins thought about the growing number of reports of people killed and wounded by the unseasoned and poorly trained National Guard and wondered about the terror felt by the family he had just observed, and all those others stopped by the guard without a federal official looking on.[14]

LEGACY OF THE KERNER COMMISSION

On July 27, even before orders had been given to remove the paratroopers from a calmed but still smoldering Detroit, President Johnson announced the creation of the National Advisory Commission on Civil Disorders, chaired by Otto Kerner. Its assignment was to investigate the recent riots and come up with answers to three questions: What happened? Why? What could be done to keep it from happening again?

The president's demands were both wide-ranging and specific. As to the causes of the riot, he wanted to know, on the one hand, the extent to which they might have been planned and, on the other, the extent to which they might have been generated by economic and social deprivation. He inquired as to the role of the police—their training, equipment, and performance. He wanted to know why some cities "blew" and others didn't, why some people rioted and others did not. He asked for recommendations for better controlling outbreaks of violence and also for eliminating the causes.

The eleven prominent committee members selected by Johnson were criticized by some minority advocates as being too establishment oriented to have a real understanding of the way things were in the poor urban areas. The group was a balanced one, varying in social outlook from the president of the American Federation of Labor to the president of Litton Industries. Nevertheless, even its liberal members, such as Mayor John Lindsay of New York and Roy Wilkins of the NAACP, were seen as too mainstream.

As things turned out, the mainstream reputation of the commission was its greatest strength in gaining acceptance for the bombshell of a report it submitted seven months later. The report was a blunt indictment of American society for the squalor and despair that festered in its slums. It appealed for a range of corrective programs that would, if adopted, tax the nation's resources beyond all previous conceptions.

It was clear that the commission had been shocked by what its studies had brought forth and wanted to sound an alarm loud enough to inspire a national effort to reverse what it saw as a catastrophic trend that was moving the nation "toward two societies, one black, one white—separate and unequal." In its introduction, the commission's report declared: "Segregation and poverty have created in the racial ghetto a destructive environment totally unknown to most white Americans. . . . What white Americans have never fully understood—but what the Negro can never forget—is that white society is deeply implicated in the ghetto. White institutions created it. White institutions maintain it, and white society condones it."[15]

The report documented how the cities shortchanged minorities on the delivery of public services (for example, by providing grossly inadequate teachers) and compromised their dignity and physical security (for example, by providing their police with great discretion but little guidance as to interrogation techniques and the use of deadly force). The documentation of inadequacy and degradation extended to the areas of housing, health, welfare, and employment, among others. The report presented "after-action" accounts of twenty-four of the larger disorders, including the social climate in which they were incubated, the triggering incidents (generally involving the police), tactics and strategies for control, and the training, equipment, supervision, and performance of the law enforcement agencies involved. For years it would be referred to as a baseline from which progress, or the lack thereof, could be measured.

Commenting on the nature of its recommendations, the commission warned: "These programs will require unprecedented levels of funding and performance, but they neither probe deeper nor demand more than the problems which called them forth. There can be no higher priority for national action and no higher claim on the nation's conscience."[16]

For years after, CRS representatives, when consulted by municipal officials on the level of interracial stress in their cities and how to relieve it, would refer to the Kerner report as a possible point of departure for self-examination and program ideas.

CONCERN AS TO THE USE OF FEDERAL TROOPS

The frequency of incidents of civil disorder in the sixties encouraged the various administrations in the Justice Department to do two things. First, they examined the constitutional and legislative provisions by which states could request the help of the army to quell a disorder that the state could not control, and they established a written history of such requests. Second, they developed procedures that would permit a swift response to any future requests. The cooperation and coordination among the White House, the Justice Department, and the Pentagon had been demonstrated in the response to the Detroit blowup. Yet that episode was immediately clouded by political recriminations. Governor Romney, a leading contender for the Republican presidential nomination a year away, charged that President Johnson, against whom he expected to be running in 1968, had deliberately delayed committing federal troops in order to exact from Romney the public admission that he was unable to control an insurrection in his state.

The Nixon administration's Department of Justice set up its own standard operating procedures to assure that if the president should ever have to make such a decision, it would be well-informed, consistent with constitutional and statutory requirements, and permissive of a prompt response. A keystone of the procedures was the creation of a Civil Disturbance Task Force composed of senior officials of the relevant divisions within the Department of Justice to compose teams that would, on an instant's notice, fly to a beleaguered community to perform the functions that the Vance team had undertaken in Detroit. I was assigned to one of five teams that were organized, briefed, given guidance manuals, and instructed to stand by. My team was called upon just once—to monitor and advise on the need for military intervention in New Haven, Connecticut, on the occasion of the massive 1970 May Day rally planned in support of Black Panthers on trial for murder.

A year earlier, fourteen Panthers had been arrested and charged with the murder in New Haven of fellow Panther Alex Rackley. Among them was Bobby Seale, national chairman of the Black Panthers, who was accused of giving the order. Seale was not only well known among Blacks nationwide but was also a celebrated figure among left-wing organizations. His fame had resulted from his participation as a leader of protest demonstrations at the Democratic Convention in 1968 and his subsequent appearance in the highly publicized trial of the "Chicago Eight," at which he had been bound and gagged on the judge's order.

Widespread media attention had been drawn to the overly long and allegedly harsh conditions of pretrial detention for those accused in the New Haven trial. The American Civil Liberties Union had appealed the conditions of detention in federal court. A coalition of fourteen mostly white organizations had been formed to raise funds and public sympathy. The New Haven Panther Defense Committee planned a massive protest rally for May Day 1970. Special efforts were made to draw upon the activist student population along the entire East Coast to protest the unfairness of the trial. Fifty thousand attendees were expected to jam the two-block New Haven Green, an area in the center of the city bounded on one side by the courthouse and on the other by Yale University. There was fear that unlawful acts of protest, police confrontations, and incitement of the local Black community (involved in civil disturbances in 1967 and 1968) might generate a riot beyond the capability of city and state law enforcement to control.

The governor had already responded favorably to the city's request for National Guard support. To save time in case the state should ask the president for federal troops, army units were pre-positioned at an airbase in nearby Massachusetts. The Department of Justice team was on hand to assess the situation and advise the president as to whether the circumstances justified deployment of the army, and whether the legal and constitutional requirements had been met.

The leader of the team was Assistant Attorney General William Ruckelshaus, who carried the task force title of senior civilian representative. The other members included, among others, John Dean, special assistant to the attorney general, and James Turner, senior attorney (and sometimes acting assistant attorney general) for the Civil Rights Division.

My role was to provide liaison with the local Black community and with voluntary civic organizations. Fortunately, Joshua Liburd and Jack Middleton were on hand to help. A conciliation specialist stationed in CRS's New England regional office in Boston, Liburd covered New Haven on a regular basis. He was well informed and highly regarded by both the Black community and city hall. Middleton was the executive of the Office of Urban Affairs of the Archdiocese of Hartford, a service organization that sought to further programs reflecting the common interests of the civil rights community and the New Haven business and civic leaders. A seasoned community relations professional, Middleton had taken CRS training on setting up and running a rumor control center in a time of racial crisis. In collaboration with Phil Runner, executive director of the New Haven Council of Churches, he had set up a community-based rumor control and information center specifically for the upcoming protest demonstration. The rumor control center worked closely with police and other city information sources. It was staffed by volunteers from the Yale Divinity School. It was a textbook example of how a private agency should go about organizing and managing a rumor control center.[17]

From Liburd, I learned that the leaders of New Haven's Black community were a sophisticated group vigorously opposed to efforts to involve community residents in the protest, which they saw as a distracting outside political event unrelated to their own programs of civil rights and social reform. They had made a particular effort to discourage Black youths from participating in protest activities that might unnecessarily involve them in hostile encounters with police. Special events for young people had been planned to keep them within their own community during the May Day weekend. The Black community also had organized its own rumor control center, which was more likely to have the trust of the minority community than would Middleton's. The two centers would be linked.

James Ahern, New Haven's chief of police, had, for a brief time, been a police-community relations consultant for CRS. His presence as chief of police, I knew, gave reasonable assurance that the police response to the demonstrators would be at a high professional level.

As I participated in the task force reconnaissance by mingling in the gathering crowd on its first day of assembly, there was little evidence of the deeply imbedded bitterness that had exploded in the minority inner city riots; nor were there visible signs of the level of political outrage and emotional anger that had been ignited in the riots at the Democratic convention in Chicago in 1968. The climate seemed to be marked more by intellectual rage than emotional stress. Conversations in the crowd were punctuated by references to ideological conflicts that had factionalized left-wing splinter groups of the thirties and forties. There were more white faces than Black.

Actual participation in the demonstration turned out to be closer to fifteen thousand than the estimated fifty thousand. Only at one point, when a police confrontation led to a questionable use of tear gas, did there appear to be an awakening of mass anger. The mood was quickly dispelled, however, thanks to the hospitality of Yale University, whose campus bordering the New Haven Green was open to the crowd as an ample area of refuge. At a later time, when National Guardsmen who had been stationed on the next block became a visible presence, the crowd began to stir with hostility. A cautionary word to police commanders promptly led to the guard being withdrawn from sight. A later disturbance was resolved by the demonstrators' own "self-marshals," Yale students who had volunteered and been trained for the job. That evening, a sound-and-light show on the Yale campus helped further deescalate tensions.

The demonstration ended with the weekend. The pre-positioned federal troops returned to their home station, and the Civil Disturbance Task Force went back to Washington.

BLACK POWER

Black rage, as demonstrated in the urban riots, undoubtedly generated a reciprocal anger on the part of many whites and led to the phenomenon of white backlash in some quarters. But it also had a far greater impact in impressing America's political leaders with the urgency of the need for urban community reform. Some Black leaders, convinced that the persuasion and negotiation of the civil rights coalition could never provide the white power structure with the imperative to invest the enormous resources that would be required to effect meaningful change in the lives of the deeply disadvantaged, believed that playing the violence card would help provide that imperative. They learned to manipulate the symbols of violence to magnify the impact of violence.

The Black Panthers were quick to use the attention-getting value of news photos of Black protesters carrying rifles. The "Black Power" slogan, first made a public battle cry by Stokely Carmichael, proved to have a magical power to alarm, regardless of the varied meanings intended by the thousands of speakers who gave voice to it. H. Rap Brown, who succeeded Carmichael as leader of the Student Nonviolent Coordinating Committee, magnified his notoriety with "Burn, Baby, Burn!" The firestorms that consumed Black neighborhoods did not require the help of Brown to get started. Whether some of the later ones burned hotter because of incendiary slogans is hard to know. But there was no doubt that they were attention getters.

"Black Power" first sounded in the nation's ear in the wake of the wounding of James Meredith. Meredith, who had made history in 1962 by being the first Black to attend the University of Mississippi, set out to do it a second time by demonstrating in 1966 that a single Black man could march for civil rights unarmed and unprotected from one end of Mississippi to the other.[18] It was a solo operation, without the support of any of the organized civil rights community. He was severely wounded by three shotgun blasts in June.

Three civil rights organizations seized the fallen banner, instantly mobilizing marchers to take his place. CORE, SNCC, and SCLC muted their growing institutional and ideological differences in united determination to show that the time had passed when Mississippi roads could be denied to Blacks. The rallies, marches, meetings, and demonstrations along the way drew support from local populations despite the absence of any clear unity of purpose among the leaders, all of which was amply reported by a sizable press entourage.

SNCC, which had evolved since 1964 from an organization that welcomed white volunteers to one that now believed that Blacks needed to rely on their own resources, was deeply involved in efforts to build political power in Mississippi jurisdictions where Blacks were in the majority. The march provided the group with new audiences among which to pursue that program. Stokely Carmichael, the recently elected national president of SNCC and a vigorous speaker, sounded the political control note from every platform along the route of march. In Greenwood, Mississippi, on the evening of June 16, an angry Carmichael, just out on bail from an earlier arrest for helping to erect a tent against police orders, first sounded the words that were to preoccupy and confound the civil rights debate for the next several years—Black power!

To a very responsive audience he said: "We're asking Negroes not to go to Vietnam but to stay in Greenwood and fight. We need Black power. What do we want?" The answer came thundering back: "Black power!"

Carmichael continued: "If they put one more of us in jail, we're not going to pay a bond to get out. We're going up there and get him out ourselves. Black power!"

Came the reverberating echo: "Black power!"

The speaker went on.

> You can't depend on the march here in Greenwood. You must build a power base . . . the power has got to get you a Black sheriff. . . . White people aren't going to do it for you . . . you have to stop being ashamed of being Black and don't try to be white. . . . Now that doesn't mean to be anti-white . . . but get the nappiest-headed Black man with the broadest nose and the thickest lips and make him sheriff!

Following the speech, Paul Good, a writer for the *Nation*, first asked the question that would beguile the country. In his August 8 article he reported: "But what did it all mean exactly? Storm courthouses? Run over whites? After the shouting died, Carmichael and I talked quietly together. 'When I talk about going to the court house,' he said, 'it's an allusion. Negroes understand me. But whites get nervous when we don't keep talking about brotherly love. They need reassurance. But we're not about to divert our energies to give it to them.'"[19]

The "Black power" chorus became the hallmark of all of Carmichael's remaining speeches on the march across Mississippi. The news reporters made sure that it captured the nation's attention.

After the march was done, the words echoed and reechoed—in the mouths of other rally speakers, in the columns of the news analysts, in the manifestos of a wide spectrum of organizations, and from the speeches of the president of the United States. Some sought to explain it—each with his or her own definition. Others left it to the audiences to make their own interpretations.

Black civil rights organizations were among the most concerned—especially the old-line civil rights groups that still saw integration as the only reliable highway to equality. Fearful that the impact of "Black power" on white allies would shatter old coalitions and dry up funding sources, they were quick to allay fears and give assurances that the goal of integration was still intact.

In October, leaders of seven civil rights organizations—including Whitney Young of the National Urban League, Roy Wilkins of the NAACP, and A. Philip Randolph of the Brotherhood of Sleeping Car Porters, felt it necessary to take a full-page ad in the *New York Times* to clarify to the nation that the old civil rights movement was still the real civil rights movement and had nothing to do with Black separatism, urban rioting, or Black power. The ad said, in part:

> There is nothing new about these principles [upon which the civil rights movement rests]. What is new are the conditions which compel us to re-state them—not the least of which is their abandonment by some individuals and groups whose positions are nevertheless frequently interpreted as representing the civil rights movement.
>
> I. We are committed to the attainment of racial justice by the democratic process. . . .
>
> II. We repudiate any strategies of violence, reprisal or vigilantism, and we condemn both rioting and the demagoguery that feeds it. . . .
>
> III. We are committed to integration, by which we mean an end to every barrier which segregation and other forms of discrimination have raised against the enjoyment by Negro Americans of their human and constitutional rights.

The ad then said that "society cannot perpetuate discrimination against Negroes and then blame the victims or their leaders for the outbursts of those who have been made desperate." Pointing to all who did not throw rocks and to the Blacks serving in Vietnam, the ad went on: "It is a cruel and bitter abuse to judge the worth of these larger numbers, the overwhelming preponderance of the Negro population, by the misdeeds of a few."[20]

Absent from the list of signatories were the leaders of SNCC and CORE, whose nonagreement with the statement was assumed, and Martin Luther King, whose reasons were unexplained.

Bayard Rustin, whose advocacy of coalition politics as the only way by which African Americans could make any significant social and economic progress had led him to sign the ad of the old-line civil rights leaders, nevertheless sought to create understanding for the origins and necessity of the cry for Black power. In *Commentary*, he took issue with the president, the vice president, and all others who described Black power as racism in reverse. He wrote:

> There is all the difference in the world between saying, "If you don't want me, I don't want you" (which is what some proponents of "black power" have in effect been saying) and the statement, "Whatever you do, I don't want you" (which is what racism declares). It is, in other words, both absurd and immoral to equate the despairing response of the victim with the contemptuous assertion of the oppressor. It would, moreover, be tragic if white liberals allowed verbal hostility on the part of Negroes to drive them out of the movement or to curtail their support for civil rights. The issue was injustice before "black power" became popular, and the issue is still injustice.[21]

Martin Luther King took a conciliatory tone. He wrote:

> Black Power, in its broad and positive meaning, is a call to black people to amass the political and economic strength to achieve their legitimate goals. No one can deny that the Negro is in dire need of this kind of legitimate power. . . . Power, properly understood, is the ability to achieve purpose. It is the strength required to bring about social, political or economic changes. In this sense power is not only desirable but necessary to bring about the demands of love and justice.[22]

If the interpretations of "Black power" were many and varied, "Burn, Baby, Burn," the signature slogan employed by H. Rap Brown, Carmichael's successor as chairman of SNCC, was far less equivocal. It may have first come into prominence in Cambridge, Maryland, where Brown had spoken and where a civil disturbance had resulted in extensive burning in the Black area of the city. Many observers believed the damage would have been far less extensive if the fire department had not stood idly by, watching the conflagration rage. Units of the Maryland National Guard were deployed to restore order.

The state of Maryland charged Brown with inciting to riot in Cambridge. He was arrested by the FBI on July 26 at National Airport in Washington and taken to the federal courthouse in Alexandria, Virginia, where his lawyer, William Kunstler, got him released at 4:00 p.m. on the basis of a defective federal warrant. He was then rearrested on the steps of the courthouse by the Alexandria police. Following a scuffle with Brown's supporters outraged by the second arrest, he was jailed at the police station, which faced an all-Black public housing project. A crowd of about two hundred gathered, including Blacks and nearby white residents. "The potential for a racial incident was high, fed by general uneasiness about riot rumors, the incendiary nature of Brown's message, the nervous anticipation of the crowd, and the lack of experience of the Alexandria police in handling such situations."[23]

A CRS biracial team consisting of James Laue and John Gibson arrived at the jail in time to learn from Kunstler that an extradition hearing had been set for late August and that Brown would be released on $10,000 bail as soon as the money could be raised—perhaps as late as midnight. For six hours, tensions among the crowd of four hundred rose and fell as the comings and goings of police units and the media generated interest or anxiety. Rumors circulated among Blacks on one side of the jail and whites on the other. Gibson and Laue continually circulated in the Black and white crowds respectively, trying to lighten the atmosphere by providing up-to-date information and carrying messages to the police. Gibson worked with an SNCC representative to encourage the clearing away of the pop bottles that had begun to accumulate. The CRS team was able to satisfy the police that the crowd was not hostile; it just wanted to see Brown released. The revised police strategy based on that understanding was to avoid needlessly provocative activity—such as gunning motorcycle engines as a means of crowd restraint. When

Laue pointed out to the police inspector that whites were permitted to circulate up to the police station steps on their side, while Blacks were cordoned off some distance away, the police changed to a policy of exercising equal restraint against both groups.

Arrangements were endangered when the justice of the peace, whose presence would be necessary at the presentation of the bond, threatened to leave if the bondsman did not appear by midnight. CRS prevailed upon him to wait. CRS discussed with the police and the SNCC representatives the wisdom of a speedy departure when Brown was released, as opposed to holding a press conference on the jail-house steps, as the reporters were demanding. SNCC representatives decided to defer the press conference until the next day. The release was finally worked out at about 1:00 a.m. Following a brief wave to the crowd, Brown was ushered by his associates into a waiting automobile. Gibson assured the crowd that Brown would return the next day to thank them for their support (which he did).

As the crowd started to disperse, slowly but peacefully, the CRS conciliators suggested to the police supervisors that hastening its departure with roaring motorcycles was likely to be a needless irritant. The motorcycles were withdrawn, and the crowd dispersed at its own pace.

Two days later, addressing supporters in a church in Washington, D.C., on July 28, Brown told the cheering crowd that the nation was on the verge of a Black revolution that would "make the Viet Cong look like Sunday school teachers." He was also quoted as saying, "We will take an eye for an eye, a life for a life." He suggested that blacks should "do more shooting than looting" when they riot. He referred to the stomping and shooting death of a policeman in Plainfield, New Jersey, as a beautiful example of Black people controlling their community. Despite Brown's verbal violence, United Press International reported there were no incidents following the rally and that only four uniformed policemen, all Black, were assigned to the event.[24]

In Washington, D.C., in the summer of 1967, in the midst of a national epidemic of urban riots, a bravura performance of the "Burn, Baby, Burn" harangue passed almost without notice. In contrast, Washington did "blow" eight months later when the triggering incident was the murder of Martin Luther King Jr.

The urban riots and the verbal violence that accompanied the riots generated two conflicting reactions among those who influenced public policy within the majority community. On the one hand were those whose response tended toward the encouragement of backlash. In May 1967 the Sunday edition of the *New York Times*, under the headline "Rifle Club Urges Antiriot Posses," reported that the National Rifle Association's magazine had advised its eight hundred thousand readers to form posses as the best defense against urban rioters and suggested that the best weapon for household defense was the twelve-gauge shotgun, although "there is a good deal to be said for a sledge or ax handle." During that period a variety of sheriffs and police chiefs were quoted as promising their constituents that "when the looting starts the shooting starts." During the week of the Detroit riots, California Governor Ronald Reagan called the disturbances "riots of the law breakers and the mad dogs against the people." Former President Eisenhower, in an article in *Reader's Digest*, spoke of rioters attacking the police "with animal ferocity."

Other public leaders, however, while they were attentive to the need to restore and maintain public order and justly prosecute the malefactors, were able to see beyond the crimes of looting and torching to the misery and degradation of minority inner city life that had caused and fueled the uprisings.

President Johnson, in an address to the nation on July 27, 1967, announcing the creation of the Kerner Commission, said, "The only genuine, long range solution for what has happened lies in an attack—mounted at every level—upon the conditions that breed despair and violence. . . . We should attack these conditions—not because we are frightened by conflict, but because we are fired by conscience. We should attack them because there is simply no other way to achieve a decent and orderly society in America."[25]

Eight months later, in its comprehensive report on what happened, why, and what could be done to prevent it from happening again, the Kerner Commission said, "To continue our present course will involve the continuing polarization of the American community and, ultimately, the destruction of basic democratic values. . . . The alternative will require a commitment to national action—compassionate, massive and sustained . . . hard choices must be made, and, if necessary, new taxes enacted."[26] The commission's findings were an educational eye-opener for millions of Americans as to the true nature of the racial divide that was wounding the nation. The commission's recommendations were a blueprint for massive reform of America's economic and social structure, some of which actually took place as a result of the commission's impact.

While those who opposed civil rights were quick to label the riots as part and parcel of the civil rights movement, leaders of the movement took pains to distinguish between the two. Although they identified riots as the consequence of oppression, they disavowed them as a means for achieving equality. But history has affirmed that riots were a powerful attention grabber that demanded a new intensity of response at the highest levels. The impact of the civil disorders was also to heighten the American public's understanding of the depth of the deprivation and degradation in the poor urban communities and to bring greater priority to the need to overcome the deficits in social and economic justice.

Not only President Johnson and his riot commission were moved to actions beyond what the civil rights movement had been able to generate. The role of the riots as an agent for change among a broad segment of the population was illustrated by the reaction of *Newsweek* magazine, which on the cover of its November 20, 1967, issue depicted two powerful Black hands, one open in supplication, the other a clenched fist. The headline for the issue was: "The Negro in America—What Must Be Done."

Introducing a special twenty-two-page section, the magazine's editor, Osborn Elliott, described it as the culmination of the magazine's "most ambitious editorial project," involving editors, writers, and reporters touring the country, interviewing experts, and reporting on the subject for two months. As a result of what they learned, Elliott stated:

Newsweek deliberately departs from its traditional method of covering the news. In the 22-page section that follows there is analysis aplenty—but this time there is advocacy as well. The reason for this marked change of approach is that the editors have come to believe that at this particular time, on this particular subject, they could not limit their journalistic responsibility or their responsibility as citizens by simply reporting. . . . In part we were led to this approach by the events of last summer, when inner city streets exploded in violence . . . and America was brought face to face with its central racial dilemma.[27]

There followed a detailed report of the anguish and anger *Newsweek*'s researchers had found in the poor urban communities, and page after page of recommendations for changes that needed to be made by government and other mainstream institutions in American society. According to Elliott, the editors concluded that the crisis required "a mobilization of the nation's moral, spiritual and physical resources . . . and strong and unflinching political leadership from the top."

How much good resulted in the long run from the increased attention stimulated by the riots is still in question. Certainly the federal government did not generate the enormous monetary investment that the Kerner Commission and civil rights advocates had indicated would be necessary to heal the social and economic sickness of the cities. Nevertheless, advocates of the disadvantaged continued for years to cite the danger of "long, hot summers" in order to resist efforts to trim the budgets of social programs. Some believed that fear of riots may have been an unacknowledged ghost at the conference tables of the decision makers, helping to tip the scales in favor of progress or, at least, to moderate cutbacks.

NOTES

1. Arnold M. Rose, "Foreword," *Annals of the American Academy of Political and Social Science* 357 (January 1965): ix.

2. Wofford, *Of Kennedys and Kings*, 464.

3. Dawidowicz, "Civil Rights and Intergroup Tensions," 186.

4. National Advisory Commission on Civil Disorders (Kerner Commission), *Report*, 110.

5. In later years CRS developed a program of risk analysis that identified those cities where racial tensions were critically high and where a blunder might trigger an outbreak of civil disorder. Conciliators tried to work with mayors and police officials in such cities to lower the risk levels. The extent to which these efforts helped to reduce the number and intensity of urban outbreaks, like any "nonevent," could never be measured.

6. BUILD was similar to the FIGHT organization in Rochester, described in chapter 4.

7. Buffalo was one of only a half-dozen cities where CRS was successful in spreading the practice, originated in Chicago, under which all the media agreed to a thirty- or sixty-minute moratorium on reporting news of disorders, to allow time for verification of information and thus avoid false or misleading statements that would inflame the situation.

8. National Advisory Commission on Civil Disorders, *Report*, 113.

9. Blind pigs, or places selling illegal intoxicants, had existed in Detroit since the end of Prohibition.

10. National Advisory Commission on Civil Disorders, *Report*, 86, 4.

11. Details derived from "Final Report of Cyrus H. Vance, Special Assistant to the Secretary of Defense, Concerning the Detroit Riots July 23 through August 2, 1967."

12. Roger Wilkins, interview with Bertram Levine.

13. John Perry, interview with Bertram Levine.

14. Wilkins, interview with Levine.

15. National Advisory Commission on Civil Disorders, *Report*, 1, 2.

16. National Advisory Commission on Civil Disorders, *Report*, 2.

17. CRS subsequently asked Middleton to convert his design into a manual, which served as a model for rumor control centers across the country for many years. Rumor control centers played a vital role in limiting chaos during civil disorders.

18. Meredith did so with the help of a federal court order, weeks of negotiation by the attorney general and his chief lieutenants, the personal intercession of the president of the United States, and in the face of two thousand raging Mississippians who killed two people, wounded twenty-four U.S. marshals, and were finally held at bay by twenty-two thousand U.S. troops. An army detachment, never smaller than five hundred, remained at Ole Miss for the two full academic years he attended.

19. Good, "A White Look at Black Power," 114.

20. *New York Times*, October 14, 1966.

21. Rustin, "Black Power and Coalition Politics."

22. King, *Where Do We Go from Here*, 42.

23. CRS draft report on conciliation activities.

24. UPI teletype report, July 28, 1967.

25. National Advisory Commission on Civil Disorders, *Report*, xv.

26. National Advisory Commission on Civil Disorders, *Report*, 1.

27. *Newsweek*, November 20, 1967, 32.

SIX

Police-Minority Relations

A Lightning Rod for Racial Conflagration

"IN MOST AMERICAN cities, policemen and poor Negroes live in what can only be described as intermittent warfare. Hostility abounds on both sides," wrote U.S. District Court Judge George Edwards in 1968. The former police commissioner of Detroit went on: "all too often, police tend to act like an army of occupation."[1]

In the period from 1964 to 1989, CRS conciliators helped to resolve thousands of conflicts between minorities and police. While serious problems remained, a sea change of improvement occurred in the relationship Edwards had depicted. An examination of the origins, extent, and amelioration of the violence between police and racial minorities will delineate the unique role of the Community Relations Service among the many social forces that helped to bring about the change.

A TOO FAMILIAR STORY

On New Year's Eve 1974, two large lumberyards in Port Arthur, Texas, went up in flames. The event followed a rally by three hundred Blacks protesting the killing of a twenty-two-year-old unarmed Black man who was shot in the back by a white police officer. The victim was fleeing jail following his arrest for a misdemeanor.

City hall and police headquarters had been immediately targeted for protest. Demands for dismissal of the police chief and four officers were placed before the mayor and city council. The mayor rejected the request pending the action of a grand jury. The grand jury found that the police officers had not violated the Texas criminal code.

Anger mounted on both sides of the color line. A protester's house was set afire; downtown stores suffered $5,000 worth of damage; unoccupied units of a predominately Black housing complex were fire-bombed; seventy-five Blacks and whites engaged in a pitched battle at the local high school.

At the CRS regional headquarters in Dallas, Gustavo Gaynett read about the Port Arthur difficulties in the newspaper, made some phone calls, and packed his bags. It was part of his job as a conciliation specialist to monitor his assigned territory, to identify communities in conflict, to assess the need for CRS help, and to recommend a suitable form of assistance.[2]

Port Arthur's upheaval was a sad but familiar story to Gaynett. Among the thousands of conflicts CRS had encountered in its ten-year history, no scenario was more common than this one: an unarmed young Black man shot in the back by a white officer; a violent response and organized protest from the minority community; rejection of demands by the local authorities; escalation of tension and stalemate.[3]

In the eyes of racial minorities across America, agents of law enforcement exerted unfair and heavy-handed control over their comings and goings, with little respect for their rights as Americans or their dignity as human beings. The crowning indignity—seen as the ultimate act of disdain—was the use of deadly force by the police. The outrage was magnified because the criminal justice system appeared rarely to punish the offending officer. Blacks throughout America saw due process of law as a step-by-step ritual of cover-up. Investigations were cut-and-dried exercises by brother officers. Whether conducted by the killer's commanding officer or by the police department's internal affairs bureau, the examination of the facts almost invariably produced a recommendation for the finding of justifiable homicide. Prosecutors, who worked daily as crime-fighting partners of the police, were unenthusiastic in presenting such matters to a grand jury or in pursuing a jury trial. Members of the juries, for their part, were reluctant to indict or to convict members of "the thin blue line" that stood between them and the predators of the criminal world.

The fragility of relations between minorities and the police became evident to the American people when studies showed that many of the urban riots of the late sixties were triggered by police actions. As the most visible representatives of the white-dominated society that exercised authority in minority neighborhoods, police had to bear the brunt of minority resentment for the failures of other institutions whose ministrations did little to diminish the harshness of life in America's inner cities and barrios. The police, for their part no less prejudiced than the society from which they were drawn, were often less than punctilious in respecting the rights and dignity of the minority poor.

Deep-seated mistrust and antagonism between police and racial minorities were inevitable in a society where century-old norms requiring minorities to be kept in their place were being challenged by newly defined national goals of equal standing before the law. The police were totally unprepared by training or indoctrination to meet America's requirements for its peace officers in the last half of the twentieth century.

In the minds of many Blacks, police attitudes were monstrous. "Why Cops Kill Blacks" was the banner headline, in one-inch type, across the front page of the *New York Amsterdam News*, America's largest weekly Black newspaper, on December 17, 1977. It quoted the views of a foremost African American psychiatrist, Alvin Pouissant, professor at the Harvard University Medical School: "They [the police] see blacks as subhuman and it doesn't take them much to kill. So far as they are concerned they are not killing human beings. . . . Most white cops are angry at blacks, are paranoid and full of hate. . . . These types of killings go on every day because white cops are not convicted. It almost seems like they have license to kill and, of course, they always have an all-white jury." These views had wide believability in the Black community.

POLICE-COMMUNITY RELATIONS

CRS's earliest cases in the South required the agency to work with police in three types of situations: to encourage police protection of minorities against unlawful harassment, to encourage police protection for lawful protest, and to discourage police violence against civil rights protesters.

But it was not long before conciliators encountered cases growing out of the pervasive prejudice and discrimination within police departments themselves. Employment discrimination was rampant in every aspect from recruitment to training, assignment, and promotion. Police behavior was characterized by abusive treatment of minority residents that ranged from second-class service, to calculated discourtesy, to verbal and physical abuse. Complaint systems were inhospitable to minority grievances. In community after community, almost without exception, CRS witnessed deeply embittered minorities who felt degraded by their encounters with the police.

149

Bitterness between police and racial and ethnic minorities predated the civil rights struggle; it was rooted in American history and the sociology of class difference. The immigrant poor who crowded the urban slums produced more than their fair share of street crime and unmannerly behavior, inconveniencing and threatening middle- and upper-class lifestyles. For the police, maintaining the peace also meant keeping the poor "in their place." Not surprisingly, the poor tended to perceive the police as defending the property and physical security of the well-to-do, while being indifferent to the property and security of the poor. For the poor who were Black, the police image was even more harsh. For hundreds of years it was the white peace officer who enforced the subordinated status of Blacks in the South, and the migrations of millions of Blacks to northern cities after the two world wars brought that deeply ingrained fear of police to northern cities. The peaceful protest and civil disobedience of the civil rights era, which often pitted police against minorities, contributed to the historical antagonism.

Discriminatory police practices were not only undemocratic; they were also counterproductive. One of the most critical tools in law enforcement is community cooperation; yet in the areas where the incidence of street crime was the highest, where community self-interest would logically have been expected to produce the highest level of citizen cooperation, police tactics seemed stubbornly designed to alienate the community. As a result, public administration experts trying to modernize police management made common cause with civil rights advocates in pressing for a variety of reforms of police behavior. Their concerns were to become linked under the name *police-community relations*. The movement was to gain energy following the urban riots of the mid-sixties. While the exhaustive studies that had followed these riots tracked the root causes to racial inequities in education, jobs, economics, housing, health, and so forth, they also established that most of the disturbances had been triggered by police encounters with minority residents. That fact served as a powerful attention getter in local and national halls of power and brought greater priority to police programs that impacted on minority relationships.

Organized efforts to reform unprofessional and discriminatory police behavior, and to dispel the mistrust and antagonism between police and racial minorities, were born in the late fifties and early sixties. In 1955 the School of Police Administration and Public Safety at Michigan State

University, in collaboration with the National Conference of Christians and Jews, conducted the first of what was to be an annual National Institute on Police and Community Relations. An avant-garde of police executives met with sociologists and leaders of community and minority organizations to define and debate the problems of police-citizen inter-actions in a time of social ferment and change and to find solutions. A literature began to develop, and a handful of progressive law enforce-ment agencies began to undertake programs.

In 1960 the St. Louis Police Department inaugurated the nation's first police-community relations unit. San Francisco followed in 1961. A scattering of communities experimented with improving communica-tions channels by, for example, creating community advisory groups that met periodically with police either at departmental or precinct levels. Faltering efforts were initiated to recruit more minority officers. Special training programs on police-community relations were developed for the rank and file. By 1965 a full-time national center had been estab-lished at Michigan State to be a fountainhead of research, training, and publication. The International Association of Chiefs of Police (IACP) had begun to provide leadership and training in the area.

The bulk of the police profession, however, was resistant to prog-ress, sometimes concealing from public scrutiny a pattern of practice that differed widely from the idealized standards police statesmen were trying to advance, sometimes merely going through the motions of reform. Patrick V. Murphy, an up-from-the-ranks New York City police commissioner, once recalled a convocation of New York City police where an earlier commissioner was introducing new regulations on police-community relations to his troops. Subordinate commanders seated on the platform behind him openly gestured their contempt for his message. In 1961 *Time* magazine reported a meeting of the Houston Police Department at which Dr. Melvyn Sikes, a Black CRS conciliator called in to help the department with its race relations, was introduced by the chief as "another one of those sob-sister, slobbering sociologists."[4]

The disparity between standards and practice was most visible in the inner city and other impoverished areas where residents lacked the pow-er to demand respect for their constitutional rights. However, as the civil rights movement infused minority communities with the courage to protest, issues of police behavior were joined in a raucous public clamor nationwide. The police, circling the wagons in a classic defensive posture, admitted no wrong, uncritically defended their miscreants, and vilified their detractors. In the minds of the minority community, this hard-shell response only served to confirm every charge against the police.

While a few of CRS's neophyte conciliators had a background in law enforcement, many had to learn on the job. Lack of experience in a technical field, such as education or police work, sometimes placed the early CRS conciliators at a disadvantage. Moreover, they often found that school superintendents or police chiefs whose organizations were in trouble tended to have a built-in resistance to accepting help from an outsider, much more so when the outsider was not a brother professional who understood the problems of the trade. To minimize this disadvantage, CRS early on recruited technical specialists to support the conflict resolution teams.

Dante Andreotti, who joined CRS in 1966 as the agency's first specialist in the administration of justice, trained the conciliators in police-community relations matters and supported their casework either onsite or with daily phone consultations. He provided access to research findings, funding sources, and a wide range of experts, as needed. He was soon joined by Robert Lamb Jr., who later succeeded him as head of that office. Andreotti and Lamb were pioneers who had already made a mark in the shaping of police-community relations practice in America.

Andreotti, as a San Francisco police district commander, had been chosen in 1961 to organize and command the city's police-community relations unit, the second in the nation.[5] A no-nonsense street policeman who had worked himself up the ladder to the highest civil service grade of lieutenant, he wondered why he had been chosen for this job for which he had previously exhibited no special interest. He later thought it might have been because of his reputation as a fair man, who in twenty-one years of service had never found it necessary to draw his gun to effect an arrest. He grew into his new position through on-the-job training. From minority leaders and activists to whom he reached out, he learned about the problems of the inner city and the negative impact of police encounters on minority life. His first move to modify the image of the police as an oppressive force in the minority urban communities was to use his unit as a part-time job-finding agency for ex-convicts. His newly developing awareness made him understand that rehabilitation was a meaningless concept in a system where nothing but a dead end awaited the ex-offender. While Andreotti increasingly became an advocate for the urban poor, he found that his effectiveness in overcoming antagonism between the department and the community was limited. The respect won by his unit among minorities did not automatically rub off on a whole department that was resistant to change. At the same time, in the eyes of Andreotti's detractors, his unit's advocacy of minority issues tended to alienate it from the rest of the force.

Lamb was a police captain commanding Atlantic City's police-community relations unit when recruited by CRS in 1967. Having been raised in a household resistant to the indignities of being Black in America (his father had been a supporter of the Back to Africa movement of Marcus Garvey in the twenties), he had entered into police work aware of the contradictory demands that would be made on him by the police culture on the one hand and his identification with the Black community on the other. The challenge had helped him to develop a capacity for strategic thinking—finding ways to work for productive outcomes in a resistant environment.

With Andreotti and Lamb to coordinate backup, CRS's conflict resolution services could offer more comprehensive solutions to more deeply rooted police-community problems. Program tools and models were compiled as a resource to make available to any troubled department the experience of other police agencies in dealing with similar situations. Funding sources were identified to permit the development of new programs that otherwise might not have been affordable. A panel of outstanding police experts from around the nation was enlisted to be available as case consultants, to provide analysis and recommendations whatever the problem. Lee Brown, later to serve as the top law enforcement officer in Atlanta, Houston, and New York before being appointed coordinator of anti-drug programs in the Clinton White House, served as a CRS consultant for more than twenty years.

A critical word in the lexicon of the first CRS conciliators was "credibility." You couldn't be effective without credibility—credibility with the civil rights community, credibility with the activists, credibility with the police chief, the school board, the business community. For many conciliators, developing effective working relationships with police chiefs was the most difficult, except for the few who were at home in the police environment from previous experience. Among their other contributions, Andreotti and Lamb and their string of police consultants were essential for imparting credibility to the full CRS team with which they worked.

Of course the best credibility builder of all was a successful earlier case. The CRS vision of a successful case—as it would impact on the police chief—followed this sort of scenario: The chief goes home to seven o'clock dinner for the first time in weeks, knowing that the streets are clear of protesters and no one has been hurt. Over dinner he reflects on tomorrow's follow-up activities: (1) breakfast with the leading Black activist (with whom he is now on a first-name basis), who last month was calling for his resignation; (2) a 2:00 p.m. appointment with the consultant who is flying in from Washington to help draft proposals for federal grants for a new minority recruitment program and a cross-cultural sensitivity training program; and (3) an evening meeting with the Black Ministerial Association and the chairman of the city council's finance committee about getting the Black community to support a tax referendum that would give the police the first cost-of-living increase in three years. While somewhat idealized, and certainly not invariable, such outcomes of CRS cases—and even lesser achievements—soon resolved the conciliator's credibility problem with the chief.

By the early seventies, conflicts involving police were the most common problem drawing CRS services. A number of factors contributed to this development. One was CRS's track record. In 1966 two-thirds of CRS cases were "alerted" (brought to the agency's attention) through the scanning of newspapers. By 1970 two-thirds were alerted as a result of previous cases, with requests mostly coming from public officials (police, schools, mayor's offices) and minority organizations.

A second factor was a growing awareness among leaders of local government that minority complaints about offensive treatment at the hands of police were legitimate. This new awareness was supported by the findings of the President's Commission on Law Enforcement and Administration of Justice. The commission had been created by President Johnson in 1965 to conduct a comprehensive study of America's justice system and recommend improvements. Chaired by Nicholas deB. Katzenbach, it enlisted hundreds of the nation's foremost scholars and practicing lawmen to examine current practice, identify and debate the issues, and formulate recommendations. Its report, issued in 1967,[6] documented widespread shortcomings regarding police-minority relationships, pointing out that these relations had a direct effect on police operations: "Poor police-community relations adversely affect the ability of the police to prevent crime and apprehend criminals. People hostile to the police are not so likely to report violations of the law, even when they are the victims. They are even less likely to report suspicious persons or incidents, to testify as witnesses voluntarily, or to come forward and provide information."[7]

Hundreds of illustrations drawn from scores of commission studies recorded an overall pattern of police abuse of the rights of minority citizens. A few examples:

> In one commission study observations were made in several cities of several hundred routine contacts between police and citizens . . . 15 percent of the interrogations began with a brusque or nasty command like "Come 'ere, punk," or "get your *** over here, pork chop." . . . Discriminatory statements, in particular, produce both anger and strong counter-prejudice among minority groups. The use of racial epithets such as "nigger," "coon," "boy" and "pancho" appears to be widespread, even though their use is condemned by responsible police administrators.[8]

"Aggressive preventive patrol" was a term that embraced a variety of police practices, some of doubtful legality, which had become common all over the country as standard methods of crime fighting. The simple "stop" for purposes of field interrogation was a common form of harassment, sometimes but not necessarily accompanied by the "frisk." Frequently used to discourage minorities from being where they were not wanted, stop-and-frisk was often applied without even the pretext of being related to a crime. In 1965, in San Diego, written reports were made of two hundred thousand stops, and it was thought that a similar number were unrecorded.[9]

Another dubious practice was the arrest on suspicion, or "for investigation." In Detroit, in the ten years from 1947 through 1956, more than thirty-three thousand arrests were made for suspicion, of which only sixty-five hundred resulted in criminal charges. Suspects were held an average of three days before release or arraignment.[10] The FBI's Uniform Crime Reports for 1965 recorded more than seventy-six thousand arrests for suspicion. In cities where arrest for suspicion was not permitted, minor crimes such as vagrancy or drunkenness were used instead.

The commission also cited the use of firearms by police as often unnecessary. The report expressed alarm at the small number of police departments that provided adequate instruction on when the weapon should be fired. It cited a Michigan State study of forty-nine police departments in Michigan, of which twenty-seven had no firearms policies.

Another powerful force speeding the transformation of police management in the United States was the creation by Congress of the Law Enforcement Assistance Administration (LEAA) to provide federal funding of programs that would enhance the quality of local law enforcement. Although LEAA was originally accused by community groups of being excessively devoted to hardware, it became a significant source for funding local programs to improve police management and police-community relations. Close cooperation between CRS and LEAA at times proved to be a useful means for effectively allocating funding.

CONFERENCE OF CHIEFS

In the early years of the Johnson administration the Justice Department acknowledged a responsibility to help local police agencies correct the deteriorating relationships between police and the minority communities. One of the first steps was for the attorney general to convene a conference of police chiefs to discuss approaches to the problem. The department saw this as a matter of some delicacy. The term "police-community relations" was already in disrepute in some police circles, where it was seen as a device for tying the hands of law enforcement that had been foisted upon the police by the "do-gooders." To minimize the resistance of chiefs, the subject was cast in terms of current management problems in policing. The IACP was given the contract to design and conduct the conference.

At the 1965 conference the civil rights/community relations content had been minimal. In 1966 a larger, but still cautious, dose of attention to inner-city problems was planned. CRS, newly arrived at the Department of Justice, participated on the periphery of the planning group. However, it made some slight contributions through its direct but informal advisory role to Attorney General Ramsey Clark. From the outset, the planners rejected the CRS proposal to include African American experts among the speakers and resource participants. It was too early, the planners thought, to expect police chiefs to tolerate, much less respect, expertise from that source. It was only after great resistance, and on the attorney general's insistence, that they agreed to one Black speaker, Assistant Attorney General Roger Wilkins, the director of CRS.[11]

At least one brave and innovative step was taken by the 1966 planners. They arranged for half a dozen social scientists, rather than police chiefs, to lead the small group discussions. This would be necessary because the thrust of the conference would be the exploration—in a confidential peer-to-peer setting—of the delicate subject of on-the-job stress and its impact on the chief's role. The intent was to use that discussion as an opening to a subsequent parallel discussion of the impact of urban stress on residents of the inner city.

CRS insisted that without the presence of Blacks to provide a grounding in reality, that discussion, filtered only through the eyes of the chiefs commiserating with each other, might well take on an Alice in Wonderland quality that would rob it of all value. The conference planners would not accept African American participation. They finally agreed to a compromise. The six social scientists, none of whom were familiar with minority urban life, would be turned over to CRS for one day of intense training in the realities of police-minority interactions in urban America before they served as discussion leaders.

As faculty for the training, CRS selected three Washington, D.C., Black activists known to be police irritants. One was Marion Barry, the Washington director of the Student Nonviolent Coordinating Committee (SNCC), who was then leader of a popular motivational movement of urban youth. He frequently ran street dances without permits, thereby exciting police surveillance and arrests on slight pretexts. The second was a woman named Willie Hardy. She was an advocate for the poor with a reputation as a thorn in the side of the district's social service agencies. The third was James Lee, whose inner-city laundromat had become an informal community center and gathering place, and whose back lot had become an uneasy frontier between "hanging out" Black men and patrolling police.[12]

The 1966 conference of chiefs was the last of its type under the direct sponsorship of the attorney general, although the Justice Department was to continue its gentle persuasion of police executives through other means—among them being the carrot of grants from the Law

Enforcement Assistance Administration and the much-less-frequent stick of prosecution by the Civil Rights Division.

A far more insistent and effective engine of change was the angry protests of aggrieved minority groups in towns and cities across the country. CRS played its part by helping the antagonists to settle their differences. As the conciliators became increasingly effective, they were better able to move settlements toward long-range solutions rather than just temporary accommodations. The racial conflagration in Port Arthur, Texas, was a case in point.

PORT ARTHUR

Port Arthur's city manager, George Dibrell, knew his city was badly in need of help but saw no clear path to finding that help until Gus Gaynett called and offered him the assistance of the Community Relations Service. In their first meeting, Dibrell was chary about a program that seemed to be an unlikely activity for the federal government. But after learning of CRS's work in other cases, he was ready to listen further. He was particularly impressed by Gaynett's suggestion, confirming his own findings, that the source of difficulty lay deeper than the current shooting incident. Writing later in the *Police Chief*, Dibrell recalled: "The black man's death turned out to be the tip of the iceberg as black citizens brought into the open a number of other community grievances that had been simmering beneath the surface . . . old prejudices resurfaced."[13]

After meeting with the principal antagonists and others in both the Black and white communities, Gaynett found the conflict to be typical of scores of community crises that had proved to be responsive to CRS assistance. Moreover, he saw the potential for going beyond the mere resolution of the current impasse to seeking long-range solutions of underlying problems. In a recent enlargement of its operations, CRS had begun to offer formal mediation in lieu of conciliation in appropriate cases where the parties were willing to invest the time to get at root causes.[14] After city officials and Black leaders agreed to try mediation, Robert Greenwald, a seasoned CRS mediator, was introduced into the situation.

As with many mediation cases, weeks were consumed in getting the parties to agree on the issues, to develop sufficient confidence in the mediator, and to accept the rules of engagement he set forth, such as pledging to avoid provocative acts during the mediation period, to leave all media contact to the mediator, and to strive to build self-enforcement mechanisms into the agreement.

Four issues were decided upon for negotiation: use of deadly force; arrest and detention procedures; improved minority recruitment; and the development of a police-community relations program. Agreement was reached on all four issues, but it took thirteen negotiating sessions lasting into August, eight months following the precipitating incident.

Problems arose even before the first formal issue could be debated. The mayor would not permit any elected official to represent the city on the negotiating team, a position the minority representatives strongly opposed but ultimately went along with.

At the first session, Greenwald put the negotiators to work learning what American law and police science regarded as the state of the art in guiding police officers as to when to shoot. He had deliberately armed himself with material from sources the negotiators were likely to respect. The IACP, in a joint project with the Texas Criminal Justice Division, was developing a model policy on that subject. It placed more restraint on the police officer than did the Texas criminal code, and no city had yet adopted it. In studying the proposed state policy, the two negotiating teams learned that Port Arthur was typical of most Texas cities with respect to codifying when to shoot, but it was lagging far behind the state of the art.

While most authorities believed that the state law on police use of deadly force provided only a bottom line below which municipalities could not sink, the Port Arthur city attorney, who was a member of the negotiating team, asserted that the city could neither fall below nor rise above the state standard, thus making the issue nonnegotiable. His position, however, proved to be malleable as the negotiations proceeded.

Written instructions for officers with respect to arresting and detaining prisoners were sparse. For example, Port Arthur had no written guidelines whatsoever for when to use the stop-and-frisk policy. The chief of police fought against any such guidance being put down on paper. After he was voted down, the issue moved to whether guidance should be in the form of guidelines, which were not necessarily binding, or regulations, which were inviolable and called for disciplinary action against officers who violated them. The final agreement came to rest on written guidelines.

In launching discussion of the police department's arrest and detention procedures, the minority negotiating team, with Greenwald's guidance, prepared a list of a dozen questions, which were answered and debated in turn. The questions were designed so that recommendations might flow directly from the discussion they engendered. They included: "What provisions are there to minimize the necessity for arrest in favor of other alternatives (warnings, summons to appear in lieu of arrest etc.)?" "What precise policies are now in effect which guide officers in stop and search procedures? Has there been any attempt made to make known these procedures to the community at large, and especially the black community?" "What steps can be taken to reduce the likelihood of provocation or confrontation during interrogation or when arrests are made? Are there special procedures in effect regarding search and/or arrest of female suspects and do they adequately safeguard against violation of reasonable standards?"

The problem of recruiting minority officers was defined early on. The city's civil service director, a member of the city's negotiating team, spoke of the difficulty of persuading Blacks to apply. "We have had very few minorities that would even come in and take the test," he said, attributing disinterest to the monthly salary of $759, which could not compete with the starting wages in local industry. This analysis was challenged by the Reverend Ransom Howard, who headed the delegation from the Black community. Asserting that the issue ran deeper than money, he said, "Blacks have never got any respect." He recalled the words of a black officer who had resigned from the police force because of constant references to "nigger this and nigger that and boy this and boy that."[15]

Negotiators almost tumbled in midstream as they confronted the reality that even if they were to agree on a minority recruitment campaign, and even if it were to be successful, it would do no more than find, persuade, and prepare Blacks to apply. It could not assure their appointment. It was always possible that criteria based on test scores and other factors might fill all vacancies in the training academy with whites who attained higher ratings. Even assuming Black applicants entered the academy, there were no guarantees they would graduate.

The two members of the Civil Service Commission on the negotiating committee differed as to how much creative zeal could be used in bending the rules far enough to bring better racial balance to the police department in view of the fact that the state, not the city, presided over the civil service examination and selection system.[16]

Such problems were not new or unique to Port Arthur. So many communities faced similar complexities that the Law Enforcement Assistance Administration had established a special program at the Marquette University Law School to provide technical assistance to police departments in need. Greenwald had arranged for a team of experts from Marquette to study the minority recruitment problem in Port Arthur and to help the city build a program to overcome the problems. The negotiators decided to go ahead and utilize that technical assistance to develop a program.

To overcome the growing antagonism between police and the minority community, the mediating team had accepted the need for a police-community relations program. To help the negotiators decide what kind of a program was needed, Greenwald again had a team of experts to offer. The National Association of Police Community Relations Officers (NAPCRO) was the professional association for police-community relations practitioners. CRS had helped bring it into being several years earlier, to provide status, support, and increased technical proficiency to members of the budding profession. It included some of the best police-community relations people in the country. NAPCRO also was funded by the Law Enforcement Assistance Administration to help cities needing assistance with their police-community relations. The association currently was funded to offer assistance grants for pilot projects in ten cities. Greenwald served as a catalyst to bring NAPCRO assistance to Port Arthur. The two people whom NAPCRO assigned to Port Arthur were among the most experienced in the field. One was Robert Barton, the civilian head of the St. Louis Police Department's community relations unit, the first in the nation. The other was Major Leroy Swift, the commanding officer of the patrol division of the Kansas City, Missouri, police department. After Barton and Swift had reviewed the situation with the mediation committee, both sides agreed to recommend that the city council make a formal request to be designated a NAPCRO project city. This would entail a study of the attitudes of police and citizens toward one another, design of a community relations program to improve relationships, and technical assistance to the police-community relations unit that the police force would select.

Five months and thirteen negotiating sessions after the mediation process had begun, the city council enacted the four recommendations that composed the negotiated agreement. Two new written policies were adopted: one on the use of deadly force and another on arrest and detention procedures. In addition, two new programs were launched, one on police-community relations, the other on minority recruitment.[17]

Addressing the city council on the day of its historic vote, Greenwald noted that Port Arthur's race relations problems were far from settled by that one agreement. He expressed hope that the process demonstrated that future problems could be negotiated. Privately, he also harbored the hope that the deeper understanding that had been developed over the course of the negotiations would prove to be of even greater value for continuing racial progress.

In his description of the case in the *Police Chief*, Dibrell wrote:

Of the four points on which agreement was reached, the one dealing with firearms and deadly force by the police was most directly related to the original shooting incident. The final agreement provided specific guidelines to be followed in future incidents of this nature. Since for the first time policy was reduced to writing, negotiators felt they had provided a more definitive guide to police officers in the field as well as an aid in assessing the validity of their decisions. The new policy spells out the conditions under which an officer may use deadly force but it also stresses that such force must not be used unnecessarily. And—there should be more understanding on the part of the public as to whether proper guidelines are followed.[18]

Two years later the negotiated changes were still in place. Dibrell was able to tell the *Houston Post* that the police force, which had only six Blacks out of a force of ninety-one before the disorders, had ten out of one hundred two years later. While the number of minority officers increased by only four, that amounted to 44 percent of the total growth in the department.

COMING TO TERMS IN TEXAS

Despite isolated instances of improvements of police performance with respect to minorities, as in Port Arthur, unequal treatment of Blacks and Hispanics persisted in Texas as elsewhere. In some places it got worse.

When police-inflicted killings increased throughout the state in 1976–78, Hispanic anger erupted in a wave of community protests. The Brown Berets and other groups led protest demonstrations of from fifty to a thousand Hispanics in Plainview, Lubbock, Odessa, Houston, Dallas, and Corpus Christi, among other communities, protesting the police killing of sixteen Hispanics in the state in the previous eighteen months.

Mounting acrimony allowed no room for any effort to address the problem. Outraged Hispanics, calling for immediate punitive action against offending police, had no ear for police explanations; in turn, the police knew only one defense when under attack—to circle the wagons, stand by their own, and admit no wrong.

The CRS conciliation staff working out of the southwest regional office in Dallas was wearing itself ragged going from crisis to crisis trying to deescalate tensions. For every city like Port Arthur that learned to manage its differences with civility, there were countless towns where racial bitterness fed on itself. The futility of trying to restore harmony to fractured communities through city-by-city crisis response became apparent. Something was needed to alter the whole atmosphere of mistrust throughout the state.

CRS knew that the prospects for the success of such an effort would be slim without the cooperation of Hispanic and police leaders. The longstanding adversarial relationship between these two communities grew wider with each incident, and true communication had become virtually impossible.

An opportunity to break the impasse appeared in May 1978, when a coalition of Mexican American organizations from across the country was called together in Dallas by the Mexican American Legal Defense and Education Fund to review the issue of police brutality. The outrage that police insensitivity had engendered among Americans of Hispanic descent created an unprecedented sense of unity among the diverse groups. CRS regional director Maurillo (Moe) Ortiz and Bob Greenwald had several discussions with leaders of the coalition, and particularly with Reuben Bonilla Jr., the state director of the League of United Latin American Citizens (LULAC). These conversations led to a decision that CRS would explore the willingness of some of the more prominent Texas police chiefs to meet with Latino leaders on "issues of alleged police abusiveness and ways in which some problems might be moderated."[19]

After receiving informal assurances from leaders in both camps that a constructive, problem-solving discussion, unencumbered by recriminations and review of old wounds, would be welcome, CRS invited six law enforcement executives to meet on September 22, 1978, in the CRS office with an equal number of Hispanic organization leaders. Greenwald later reported that the meeting "produced a sense of achievement beyond anything anticipated. It was evident that both sides were willing to face the issues with a degree of candor and with an inclination to move into uncharted waters."[20]

Encouraged by the level of communication and rapport experienced at the meeting, the twelve participants formed the Steering Committee on Texas Law Enforcement and Community Relations. Headed by Bonilla and Frank Dyson, the chief of police of Austin, they took the bold step of planning to bring police and Hispanic leaders throughout the state together to look unblinkingly into the face of the critical issues that had long been the source of bitter controversy. They decided to start in south Texas, where two hundred selected leaders, one hundred from each group, were invited to the Symposium on Contemporary Issues in Texas Police-Community Relations.

To underscore their seriousness of purpose, the conveners invited only police chiefs and organization presidents, permitting no alternates. They crafted the invitation carefully so as to make sure that the troublesome nature of the subject would be clearly understood in advance. Five topics were identified: use and control of excessive force; selection and training of law enforcement personnel; complaint process and internal investigation; roles of community organizations; and role and responsibility of the media.

In focusing the program on the issues of critical importance to the minorities, the planners knew that they risked discouraging attendance by the police, whose positions on these issues came under public attack with every allegation of police abusive conduct. But they also knew that any ducking of issues would defeat their purpose. To allay police apprehensions, the conveners took pains to offer the following reassurance: "There is no intention at this conference to discuss details of specific police-citizen incidents. There will be no debate regarding the guilt or innocence of any parties alleged to have committed wrongful acts. We want objective evaluation and honest dialogue on the issue, as presented in the program outline. Those persons in charge of the presentations and workshop sessions will be responsible for assuring that we remain on that course."[21]

The meeting not only drew the desired attendance; it appeared to fulfill the hopes of the sponsors as an unprecedented communications breakthrough between groups who could never before hear one another for the shouting.

CRS insisted that the planners look on the conference as a starting point, not a conclusion. Built into the planning of the San Antonio conference were the nuts and bolts that would assure an outcome wedded to action. The steering committee of chiefs and Latino leaders pledged to continue to work together in support of conference recommendations designed to reduce excessive use of force by police. CRS field representatives met with conference delegates back in their hometowns to encourage local programs for better communication and reduction of police-community friction. A notable example occurred in Harris County, which encases Houston. There police and other public agency executives joined with Hispanic leaders to form an association that, for several years, served as a forum for ventilating police-minority concerns and for facilitating the development of collaborative programs.[22]

Within the following year, CRS and the steering committee duplicated the whole process by convening another symposium at Fort Worth, to serve police and minority leaders in west and north-central Texas.

THE IMPACT OF MINORITY POLICE OFFICERS

The evolving role of the minority police officer was a continual focus of CRS attention. The initial concern was with employment discrimination, which aggravated racial tensions in several ways. The all-white police patrols in Black neighborhoods reinforced the image of an army of occupation. The token representation of Blacks in many departments was seen by the Black community as a sign that they were considered inferior. Even more troubling was the lack of officers capable of bridging the communications abyss between the different cultures.

In 1967, at the request of the mayor, CRS conducted an assessment of police-community relationships in Akron, Ohio. In this city with a 30 percent minority population, there were six Black officers on a force of 445, and that had been the number since time out of memory. They were almost all detectives assigned only to cases involving Blacks. The occasional patrol assignment was only in Black neighborhoods.

Special training and assignments and other promotional opportunities were denied them. Regardless of their assignment, for administrative purposes they all reported, in Jim Crow fashion, to the single Black sergeant. African American leaders questioned the good faith of the mayor's appeal for Black police recruits. They recounted that the single Black candidate who had passed the last written examination had been rejected by the all-white examination board because of personal indebtedness, even though leaders of the Black community had offered to make good his debts. They testified that to be young, Black, and in debt in the inner cities was no character flaw and could certainly be overlooked if the city sincerely wanted able Black officers.[23]

As opportunity presented itself, CRS gave support to minority recruitment programs, often helping to work them into conciliation agreements and encouraging minority organizations to undertake training programs to better qualify minority applicants for the civil service examinations. CRS also worked with state and local civil service commissions, encouraging their efforts to eliminate cultural bias that unfairly worked against minorities in civil service testing.

Innovative recruitment approaches were encouraged, such as a 1966 statewide effort in Michigan, in collaboration with the Michigan Association of Chiefs of Police and the Michigan Civil Rights Commission. CRS enlisted the resources of the Advertising Council to create and distribute throughout the state a television commercial designed to attract minority applicants. It featured Robert Culp and Bill Cosby, costars of the popular television show *I Spy* and the only interracial team then appearing on American television. Statewide testing was used to qualify candidates for all of the participating jurisdictions, and individuals failing to meet a special requirement for one department, such as age or height, were referred to other departments where that particular standard was less demanding.

As the number of minority officers grew, CRS worked cooperatively with associations of Black officers that were forming as support groups for minority officers who often found themselves in a hostile environment. Resistance took many forms, including open conflict in some departments. Incidents were reported of anti-Black graffiti in the station house, of interracial fights and weapons being drawn, and of Black officers announcing they would not stand by when they witnessed excessive use of force against Blacks. Despite these problems, over time most departments learned to accommodate racial integration.

Racial equity within police departments came more rapidly as minority officers developed their own organizations, and CRS was able to encourage this movement, at times on an after-hours basis. The presence of a CRS conciliator in a city sometimes provided the occasion for a private meeting of unorganized Black officers to consider the organizational experience of their peers in other cities. The occasional use of Black officers as citizen experts to help CRS in cases outside their own cities also provided opportunities for intercity encouragement for the organization of African American police associations.

As they grew larger, these minority officer associations sometimes served as a counterweight to the political influence of the predominating association of white police officers. While the mainstream police associations concentrated their efforts on officer benefits and other conditions of work, the minority police organizations often allied themselves with community organizations to support certain social issues, as well as to provide themselves with a political base. Often Black police associations would take an active role in minority recruitment, staffing recruitment tables at ball games or conducting training programs to prepare minority applicants for civil service examinations.[24]

In 1975 the Joint Center for Political Studies proposed that a meeting of Black command officers (captains or above) be convened to consider ways of dealing with Black-on-Black crime. The Police Foundation, a nonprofit research organization that had been established by the Ford Foundation in 1970, agreed to support the venture. A major obstacle was the nonexistence of any list of who and where the Black command officers were. Robert Lamb and Lee Brown, who had provided CRS assistance to hundreds of police departments around the country, were able to put together the nucleus of an invitation list and became central to the conference planning process. With other planners, they arranged for an informal meeting following the conference, so that the Black command officers could consider ways of exercising their influence on a continuing basis. The outcome was a decision to form their own professional association, and thus the National Organization of Black Law Enforcement Executives (NOBLE) was born.

POLICE USE OF DEADLY FORCE

"Death by legal intervention" was the bloodless language used to count every time that a law enforcement officer killed a civilian. According to the National Bureau of Health Statistics, it happened on the average of 342 times a year for the nine-year period following 1968.[25] More than half of the victims were minorities—whose rate of death was nine times greater than that of whites.

Thus, in the decade following passage of the most important legislation in America's war for civil rights, the most symbolic evidence of unequal justice was highly visible to residents of the nation's racial urban communities. Scientific studies were later to document this experience.

A 1975 study of the decade 1960–70 showed that 30 percent of civilians killed by police were not involved in criminal activity. Of 1,500 police homicide incidents studied, in only three instances was a police officer convicted of a criminal offense. Black males were killed by police at a rate ten times higher than white males. The study found that between 1960 and 1972, police killed 1,899 Black males and 1,914 white males in a population in which about 10 percent were Black.[26]

Another study found that in 1978 excessive-use-of-force complaints from Hispanics rose 50 percent. Data from the twenty-four-year period from 1950 to 1973 showed an average of 245 persons killed by police in the years prior to 1967. For the seven years after 1967, the yearly average increased to 359. Of these, 50 percent were Black.[27]

Throughout the mid-1970s, CRS saw police violence dominating its total caseload and exacerbating racial tension nationwide. Nothing was more offensive to a minority community than a wrongful death of one of its own at the hands of police and the subsequent failure of anyone to admit or redress the wrong. The ensuing controversies caused elevated levels of bitterness lasting for years.

By 1978 public protest rose to a crescendo. In Philadelphia, where more than four hundred brutality complaints had been filed against the police the previous year, crowds ranging from fifty to three thousand demonstrated repeatedly through the summer. In November a committee of the Pennsylvania legislature reported that police brutality in Philadelphia had, at times, "reached the level of homicidal violence." In August, in St. Petersburg, Florida, two hundred and fifty Black residents took to the streets in a rock-and-bottle-throwing protest of the shooting death of a twenty-year-old Black man at the hands of the police. In July, two thousand participated in a protest march in New York City over police violence.[28]

In 1978, Gilbert Pompa, who had been appointed CRS director by President Carter in 1976, acting on the recommendations of a staff study, elevated police use of deadly force to the agency's top priority.[29] Henceforth, instead of engaging only in case-by-case responses to deadly force controversies, CRS would also initiate programs at the national and regional levels to speed the alteration of police practice. Bob Lamb was the moving force bringing CRS to this initiative. It was his memorandum to Pompa setting forth the criticality of this issue that prompted the director to set up the special staff study group, led first by Ozell Sutton and later by Lamb.

Bits and pieces of his experience had led Lamb, over many years, to his understanding of the centrality of this issue to the quality of police-minority relations in America. He recalled the shock when, as an Atlantic City rookie policeman being trained by the New Jersey State Police, he heard the training officer advise the class always to carry a rusty knife or similar weapon, to be dropped at the scene of the crime, whenever it was necessary to shoot an unarmed person. He later learned that the use of the drop-weapon was not an unfamiliar practice in police work throughout the country. It made the justifiable homicide defense that much easier.[30]

In contributing to the movement to change police behavior with respect to the use of deadly force, CRS worked at both the "retail" and "wholesale" levels. The retail effort was the natural consequence of responding to individual outbreaks of racial conflict. This city-by-city negotiation of change in police practice gradually helped to elevate the national norm. At the same time, at the wholesale level, CRS worked with an array of organizations serving the police, religious, minority, and civil rights communities, to change state and local laws as well as police practice through advocacy and education.

A frequently used tool for starting local programs without waiting for a crisis to develop was the regional conference of public officials and minority leaders to address police problems. In Providence, Rhode Island, in October 1978, two hundred law enforcement officials, mayors, judges, and community leaders searched for solutions to problems of police-civilian violence and inadequate procedures for resolving citizen complaints against police. An area conference in St. Petersburg,

Florida, drew a hundred and fifty participants to focus on problems of excessive police force and unequal employment opportunities in police departments.

In June 1978, CRS was invited to sponsor a workshop on police use of deadly force at the annual conference of NOBLE. This was followed by passage of a resolution by NOBLE calling for use of deadly force only to preserve the life of the officer or other persons. FBI director William Webster was the guest speaker at the conference. He publicly praised NOBLE's position on deadly force and announced that the protection-of-life-only policy had long been the rule in the FBI. Many advocates of change felt that this public announcement of the FBI's restrictive shooting policy was an important contribution to the campaign to reform the practices of local police departments. On the following day, CRS held a meeting for representatives of a dozen national voluntary organizations who had been guests at the NOBLE conference, so that they could share their common concerns about police use of deadly force and seek opportunities for mutual assistance.

Soon other serious efforts were afoot to develop uniform standards on the use of deadly force to guide police jurisdictions throughout the country. NOBLE followed up by drafting and publicizing a model policy on the use of deadly force. The Police Foundation produced a model policy a year later. In 1980 CRS served on a Justice Department task force studying statutes and regulations governing police use of deadly force, preliminary to the development of federal recommendations of uniform standards to be proposed for use throughout the country.

CRS convened the National Consultation on Safety and Force in December 1979, cosponsored by the National Urban League and the League of United Latin American Citizens (LULAC). For three days, police chiefs, city officials, and minority leaders from throughout the country huddled with experts in law, sociology, and research to determine when and under what circumstances the police officer should use a gun. Input was drawn from statisticians, liability insurance specialists, civil rights experts, and police union executives. CRS, the Urban League, and LULAC followed up on the conference by launching joint local programs, in cooperation with the local police, designed to reduce the incidence of police use of deadly force. By the end of the year, nineteen such programs had been initiated. Of the thirty-one recommendations for national, state, and local action produced by the national consultation, the most vigorously favored called for "the Department of Justice to promulgate a model policy requiring that police use deadly force only to defend or protect human life, and that the policy be enforced through civil rights prosecutions."[31]

Using the experts who had appeared at the national consultation and others, CRS staged workshops on the topic at national organization conferences and other meetings around the country.

MUNICIPAL LIABILITY TRAINING

While the number of people killed by police did drop significantly, change would have come more slowly if it had depended on advocacy alone. In the late seventies there suddenly appeared a powerful incentive for municipalities to curb itchy trigger fingers. A court decision increasing municipal liability for employee misconduct provided an imperative to public officials to pay attention to a matter they had earlier found it convenient to neglect.

The U.S. Supreme Court, in 1978, in the case of *Monell v. Department of Social Services of the City of New York*, held that municipalities were no longer immune from civil suits under the post–Civil War civil rights legislation and could be sued directly for monetary, declaratory, and injunctive relief. In other words, the cities themselves could now be held liable for the misconduct of their employees.

Prior to 1978, civil suits charging police with civil rights abuses were discouraged by a formidable array of circumstances. The city itself could not be held liable, so only the police officer could be sued. Police officers are trained to be effective witnesses and to impress jurors. Jurors tend to respect police as protectors of the public. Since police officers have limited financial resources, any judgment against one was likely to be small and difficult to collect, making such cases unappealing to attorneys who would be dependent on contingency fees. Of the small number of lawsuits that were pursued, the overwhelming majority were decided in favor of the officer.

In the *Monell* case the court reversed an earlier ruling and held that a unit of general local government (such as a city, town, or county) did indeed meet the definition of a "person" under the law and thus was not immune from civil suit under the post–Civil War legislation giving bite to the Fourteenth Amendment. The court ruled that under certain conditions the municipality could be sued along with the public employee if the alleged conduct was consistent with the policy or custom of the agency involved.

That change suddenly gave the plaintiff access to the deep pockets of local government. Once the municipality became the defendant, a change occurred in the jury's perspective. Local government is a less sympathetic and less trusted defendant than the individual officer; besides, the city has plenty of money—or so the juries think.

Another factor also came into play that broke new ground for the admission of incriminating evidence that had formerly been banned. In the past, when the individual officer was sued, actions of other officers were deemed irrelevant and inadmissible as evidence. Following *Monell*, however, the pattern of police practice became highly relevant in order to establish whether or not the alleged act was consistent with custom in that department. The alleged misconduct of fellow officers could now be paraded before the jury.

One other new development contributed to the sudden increase in municipal liability litigation. The costs of suing City Hall were no longer a deterrent to plaintiffs. The number of lawyers available to take police misconduct cases on a contingency basis suddenly mushroomed. The Civil Rights Attorney Fees Awards Act of 1976 had decreed that in all civil rights cases, if the plaintiff prevailed, attorneys' fees could be assessed against the defendant local government. Suddenly the increase in lawsuits, and in the size of jury awards and settlements, became a significant drain on the coffers of hard-pressed local governments.

In 1981, more than thirty-five thousand lawsuits were filed under the *Monell* decision. The majority involved allegations of police brutality and excessive use of force. Many cities were badly bruised.[32]

The city of Detroit, with one $12 million judgment against it, had a total of ten cases with judgments over $1 million each. In another major city, more than one hundred lawsuits were filed in 1980–81 against the police department and its officers. Twenty-seven involved the use of force or police brutality. Of twelve cases that went to trial in that period, jury verdicts favored the plaintiffs in nine instances. When Washington, D.C., decided it might be cheaper to settle cases rather than go to trial, it set a limit of $10,000 per case. The city soon had to remove the limit as defendants opted for the far more generous jury awards. In 1982 Washington spent a total of $4.1 million in out-of-court settlements—double the previous year. In that same year San Francisco paid out $6.5 million.

The skyrocketing of claims, awards, and settlements hit municipalities in other ways.[33] Legal costs to defend suits escalated as law departments were enlarged and/or outside counsel had to be engaged. The cost of liability insurance went sky-high. Some jurisdictions could not find coverage, or could not afford it. More cities turned to self-insurance. Others experimented with cooperative insurance pools in which several jurisdictions banded together for self-insurance.[34]

To protect their treasuries from this ravaging attack, cities resorted to two strategies. The first was to reduce the number of suits for misconduct by reducing the instances of officer misconduct. The second was to reduce the losses resulting from the remaining suits by showing documented records of training, policies, and supervision that might convince a jury that inappropriate conduct was not consistent with department policy or custom. Both strategies persuaded many cities to ask CRS to help with training their police. If not for the fiscal consequences of the *Monell* case, CRS assistance would have been far less in demand.

CRS was quick to see the *Monell* decision as the long-sought imperative needed to spur cities to pay attention to problems of excessive use of police force. To mayors, city councils, and police chiefs, CRS presented the pocketbook incentive. In the Dallas regional office John Perez, who had succeeded Moe Ortiz as CRS's southwest regional director, saw an opportunity to spread the gospel of responsible use of police force more rapidly than through crisis assistance to one city at a time.[35] He developed a training format that enabled CRS to carry the message of *Monell* to most police jurisdictions in Texas, and later to other states in the region, including Arkansas, Oklahoma, Louisiana, and New Mexico.

The first step of this approach was to persuade a police chief to accept a CRS-conducted workshop on *Monell* for his top staff and commanders. This would provide the foot in the door for the second and third steps. The second would be a review and, where necessary, a revision of department policies regarding police use of force. The third would be a review and revision of training and supervision practices in order to improve police performance. CRS would then make itself available to assist with follow-up training and policy refinement. Generally, the chief would be encouraged to invite neighboring chiefs to the workshop, thus extending the reach of the CRS message to smaller departments in the area.

The most enthusiastic allies supporting CRS's efforts on municipal liability were district attorneys, who had the hated responsibility of prosecuting police charged with unlawful violence, and city attorneys, who had to defend municipalities against civil suits for officer misconduct. Perez enlisted the city attorneys of six of Texas's largest cities to help make a training video. The six came together as a panel, with CRS general counsel Gail Padgett as moderator, to spend six hours sharing their experiences and concerns about the price cities had to pay because individual officers, and sometimes their supervisors, "screwed up." The videotapes of the seminar, boiled down and edited into five fifteen-minute segments, proved to be persuasive tools inducing police and their commanders to pay more attention to training in an area of police behavior too long ignored.

By 1983 CRS was offering the training to police agencies across the country. In New England, CRS reached out to many departments through areawide meetings convened by local chiefs. In Pennsylvania, the Pennsylvania Association of Chiefs of Police provided the auspices. In Louisiana, the State Police Academy offered the training to the fifty-two local police academy directors who had responsibility for training 90 percent of the state's law enforcement recruits.

MARKERS OF CHANGE

The change in police practice with respect to the use of deadly force against minorities was the single most important factor in the revolutionary transition that took place within the broader field of police-minority relations. CRS was only one of many agents and influences generating this transformation, but this is one of the few areas of broad social change on which the footprints of CRS can be so clearly identified.

Other agents for change included the Law Enforcement Assistance Administration (LEAA) of the Justice Department, and particularly its National Minority Advisory Council on Criminal Justice, which helped to impart direction and substance to LEAA's grants addressed to community relations and problems of inner-city policing in general. Another forceful influence leading to change in police practices was the

Police Foundation. It was originally headed by Patrick V. Murphy, a former director of LEAA.[36]

By 1980 CRS's director, Gilbert Pompa, was able to tell Congress that over a ten-year period, the annual rate at which minorities had died at the hands of law enforcement personnel had been cut by better than 50 percent. From 1970 to 1979, the annual total of all killings by police had gradually come down from 354 to 170. The total number of whites killed had remained constant; the reduction had been mostly among minorities.[37]

While reluctant to claim credit publicly for its contribution to social change that stemmed from a host of inordinately complex interactions of events and circumstance, CRS believed that with respect to patterns in police use of deadly force, it had to be recognized as a major player. Since the early seventies CRS had been the loudest and most insistent drum beater for the cause of ending excessive use of force by police. At the retail level, in hundreds of communities where police abusiveness had triggered community disruptions, CRS's peace efforts not only helped to encourage improved practice; they also fertilized the soil for change by pounding away at the message that modern police management was capable of producing better policies, conducting better training, and providing better supervision of patrol practices, thus reducing the amount of unnecessary force and producing higher levels of police-minority cooperation. At the same time, CRS's technical assistance to minority organizations and other advocate groups at local and national levels led to the demand for higher levels of police performance all over the country.

By 1989, there were signs that progress in lowering fatalities as a result of police encounters was eroding, a victim of the drug-induced increase of inner-city violence. Nevertheless, by that time the nature of community relations problems in the inner city had changed. Police use of deadly force was no longer seen routinely by residents as evidence of brutal disdain of minority life. Although questionable shootings still occurred, and could still trigger community rage, there was a greater willingness to give police the benefit of the doubt. The impact of the view of the police as a brutal oppressor had been downgraded from a hurricane to a tropical storm—or perhaps gale-force winds.

Decreased alienation between police and minorities resulted from many factors, including increased minority political power, the growing numbers of minority elected officials, including mayors, the growing number of minority police officers, including chiefs, and significant reductions in the amount and intensity of police discourtesy and harassing police practices. Other markers of change included the termination of the use of degrading language by police; the diminution of aggressive patrol practices that gave rise to the minority urban perception of police as "an army of occupation"; the advent of more equal opportunity in police employment and the rise of minorities to positions of command; improved delivery of police services to minority neighborhoods; greater accountability for acts of police brutality; increased consultation and collaboration between the police and the minority community on problems of public safety; and new and more restrictive rules governing police use of deadly force.

Mostly the change resulted because minority communities refused to accept unequal treatment and because their insistent protests and demands for fairness focused public attention on the need for police reform. Improvement has come in every aspect of police-minority interaction, and in every case it resulted from community-by-community protest and issue-by-issue negotiation.

CRS bore close witness to how the struggle of minorities for equal treatment helped to bring greater enlightenment to the police profession. While police work in 1989 still fell short of delivering 100 cents on the dollar of equal justice, monumental progress had been made in the quarter century following passage of the Civil Rights Act and the creation of the Community Relations Service in 1964.

NOTE FOR NEW EDITION

The first edition covers to 1989 and more than thirty years have passed. It is quite evident that Levine's positivity at the end of this chapter did not play out in the decades that followed. The riots following the beating of Rodney King by Los Angeles Police is a testament to how little trust existed between law enforcement and minority communities. Numerous tragedies like the ones in Sanford, Florida; Ferguson, Missouri; and Baltimore, as well as the rise of the Black Lives Matter movement, shed light on how much has not yet improved in police-community relations. See chapter 15 for an updated perspective and CRS's work in this area since the first edition.

NOTES

1. Edwards, *The Police* on *the Urban Frontier*, 24, 27.

2. A onetime official with the United Automobile Workers, Gaynett was one of the growing number of Hispanic conciliators who began to bolster the CRS ranks following Ben Holman's appointment as director in 1969. Determined to overcome the CRS shortage of "brown" conciliators, Holman had adopted a time-tested method for breaking new ground in minority recruitment: he gave hiring authority to a Hispanic. With Gilbert Pompa as assistant director for conciliation, a wealth of talented Hispanic applicants were identified over the next few years and hired in all parts of the country.

3. U.S. Department of Justice, Community Relations Service, *Police Use of Deadly Force*, 1.

4. Melvyn Sikes, telephone interview with Bertram Levine.

5. "A Strong Police Command Vital to Avert More City Violence," *Washington Post*, June 30, 1966.

6. President's Commission on Law Enforcement and Administration of Justice, *Commission Report: The Challenge of Crime in a Free Society.* Citations attributed to the Crime Commission are drawn from chapter 6, "The Police and the Community," of President's Commission on Law Enforcement and Administration of Justice, *Task Force Report: The Police.*

7. President's Commission on Law Enforcement and Administration of Justice, *Task Force Report*, 144.

8. President's Commission on Law Enforcement and Administration of Justice, *Task Force Report*, 180.

9. President's Commission on Law Enforcement and Administration of Justice, *Task Force Report*, 184.

10. President's Commission on Law Enforcement and Administration of Justice, *Task Force Report*, 186.

11. The IACP was to come a long way in the acceptance of Blacks, although it took many years to do it. Lee Brown, a Black police consultant for CRS beginning in 1968, served as president of the IACP from 1991 to 1993.

12. With the coming of home rule to the District of Columbia, Barry was to enjoy a long career in elective office, including as president of the board of education, mayor, and member of the city council. Hardy, chagrined that Blacks were barred from the chiefs' conference, presented herself at the Airlie House Conference Center outside Washington, D.C., on the opening night and demanded to be heard. Two husky chiefs, at either elbow, escorted her from the premises. Hardy was subsequently to serve many years as chair of the Public Safety Committee of the D.C. City Council.

13. Dibrell, "Mediation in Civil Rights Issues," 80.

14. In general, CRS construed conciliation as embracing any problem-solving mechanism, or combination of techniques, that enabled the antagonists to work

out their differences so as to lessen discord and increase racial harmony. Mediation, on the other hand, followed the strict choreography of formal across-the-table give-and-take, presided over by a neutral third party, and focused on specific predefined issues, with the intention of reaching a formal signed agreement.

15. *Houston Post*, August 2, 1975.

16. *Houston Post*, August 2, 1975.

17. U.S. Department of Justice, Community Relations Service, Annual Report, 1975, 18–21.

18. Dibrell, "Mediation in Civil Rights Issues," 82.

19. CRS staff document: Background Summary for Case Review, March 19, 1979.

20. Robert Greenwald, telephone interview with Bertram Levine.

21. Letter of invitation to Symposium II on Texas Law Enforcement and Community Relations, from cochairmen Reuben Bonilla and Glen D. King. Included in "A Symposium on Contemporary Issues Police-Community Relations" (public record of symposium documents), 12.

22. U.S. Department of Justice, Community Relations Service, Annual Report, 1980, 8.

23. U.S. Department of Justice, Community Relations Service, "Report to Mayor John S. Ballard on Police Community Relations, Akron, Ohio," March 1967.

24. Robert Lamb Jr., interview with Bertram Levine.

25. Cynthia C. Sulton and Phillip Cooper, "Summary of Research on the Police Use of Deadly Force," in *A Community Concern: Police Use of Deadly Force* (Washington, D.C.: National Institute of Law Enforcement and Criminal Justice, Law Enforcement Assistance Administration, U.S. Department of Justice, 1979), 69.

26. Paul Takagi, "Issues in the Study of Police Use of Deadly Force," paper presented to the annual meeting of the National Black Police Association, Chicago, Illinois, August 25, 1978.

27. Gilbert G. Pompa, at tenth annual conference of the National Association of Police Community Relations Officials, in LEAA *Newsletter* 8, no. 6 (June–July 1979).

28. Gilbert G. Pompa, "A Major and Most Pressing Concern," *Engage/Social Action*, November–December 1976, 10.

29. CRS staff memorandum to Gilbert G. Pompa from Robert Lamb Jr., "Excessive Force Task Force Memorandum," July 5, 1978.

30. Lamb, interview with Levine.

31. U.S. Department of Justice, Community Relations Service, Annual Report, 1980, 11.

32. Bertram Levine, Draft of Remarks on Municipal Liability, prepared for CRS-sponsored symposium of Cape Cod police executives, January 27, 1983.

33. Police brutality was by no means the only offense bringing the city within the reach of *Monell* type cases. The damage resulting from high-speed chases by police also engendered claims against local government, as did the alleged missteps of

municipal departments other than the police. Nevertheless, the cases resulting from police use of deadly force were the most visible and the most costly.

34. "CRS Activity Regarding Consequences of Municipal Civil Liability," staff memorandum to Administration of Justice Team from Howard P. Carrington, national administration of justice specialist, February 17, 1983, 5.

35. Perez, who had come to CRS after serving San Antonio as a police officer and then as a schoolteacher, was a vigorous advocate of police training. But he was wedded to the CRS doctrine that training was only one leg of a three-legged stool; it was useless without the other legs: written policies that insisted on correct performance and supervision that assured faithful implementation.

36. One of America's most distinguished law enforcement executives, Murphy, who rose through the ranks of New York City's police department, also served as chief of police in Syracuse, New York, as public safety commissioner in Washington D.C., and as police commissioner in New York City.

37. A definitive study covering this ground for the fifteen-year period 1970–84, conducted for the Crime Control Institute by Lawrence W. Sherman, Ellen G. Cohn, et al., and published in 1986, reported among its findings: "At least 353 citizens were killed by police in fifty cities in 1971; only 172 were killed in 1984. . . . Citizen killings of police in those cities fell by two-thirds in the same fifteen-year period."

SEVEN

Education Amid Turmoil

ON SEPTEMBER 12, 1974, thousands of angry whites took to the streets of Boston in an effort to terrify and turn back Black students being bused to newly assigned schools. Adults, carrying protest signs of the "nigger-go-home" type, and children, many in Ku Klux Klan outfits, screamed epithets as the yellow buses, some with stone-shattered windows, pulled up to the gates of South Boston High School. Police cordoning off the roadways had difficulty holding back the surging crowds. From the stoops of the row houses lining nearby streets, second-, third-, and fourth-generation homeowners, having been assured by their political leaders for a decade that this day would never come, jeered the passing buses.

OBJECT LESSON IN BOSTON

After ten years of successful resistance to the state law requiring school desegregation, Boston had been sued in federal court by the local NAACP, and now, in the ruling of Judge W. Arthur Garrity, it found a judgment it could no longer refuse, evade, or defer.

On the opening day of school, CRS conciliators, assembled at the last minute from other assignments around the country, were paired with schoolboard employees in radio-equipped cars that sped from one crisis site to another to help defuse the confrontations. Lack of adequate preparation had placed Boston—and CRS—behind the violence curve, requiring a long and costly game of catch-up.

In 1974 CRS was still reeling under the previous year's two-thirds cut in staff. Adjusting to the demands of the budget masters that it cut preventive work and focus on crisis response, the agency had been slow to offer assistance to Boston. Not until the weekend before the buses were to roll did an emergency team of a dozen conciliators arrive to reinforce the small regional staff based in Boston.

So highly charged was the hatred that the emergency team would not be fully disbanded until December; so deeply imbedded were the roots of discord that six years would pass before the return of community stability would permit CRS to close the case. Boston would prove to be America's high-water mark of violent resistance to school busing as a means of desegregation. The nation and the world were scandalized that this cradle of American civilization and culture had fallen victim to the naked hatred and unrestrained passions of the mob. From its efforts to help restore racial harmony in Boston, CRS was able to sharpen the techniques and strategies that, in the succeeding years, it shared with scores of urban school districts throughout the country. For all of them, the watchword would be, "Let's not have another Boston."

COMMUNITY CONFLICT AND SCHOOL DESEGREGATION

Local refusal to implement the Supreme Court's 1954 school desegregation requirements had produced firestorms of community controversy throughout the nation for two decades. Throughout the South, under the banner of "massive resistance," state and local governments, private and religious organizations, newspapers, and broadcast media linked arms in a die-hard defense of racially separate schooling. The region's leading citizens mobilized for resistance through newly formed White Citizens Councils, while many of the hoi polloi rallied behind the banners of a resurgent Ku Klux Klan, which again lighted the fires of terror and intimidation. In many jurisdictions private academies were formed for the education of white children, and some school districts even closed their schools, leaving Black children and some whites with no education whatsoever, while most white families managed some private arrangement. Some states pursued the spurious legal doctrine of interposition in a vain attempt to shield local districts from the reach of federal courts.

Court decisions and federal and state civil rights legislation did not, of themselves, bring Jim Crow schooling to an end. They only established the legal requirements—with which relatively few school jurisdictions voluntarily complied. In most instances change would require some specific act of enforcement. Enforcement mechanisms included the Civil Rights Division of the Justice Department, the U.S. Office of Education, state enforcement bodies, and state and local courts. But many fewer changes would have resulted had it not been for specific demands being made by local African American or other minority groups. These demands—and resistance to them—led not only to additional lawsuits and administrative complaints but also to a plethora of petitions, protests, rancor, rage, confrontations, violence, and negotiations.

From this welter of acrimony arose hundreds of requests for CRS assistance. Seventy-seven desegregation conflicts were presented to CRS in its first year—fifty-two in the South.[1] The number grew steadily. Year after year education cases would make up one-quarter to one-third of the entire workload of the CRS conciliators.

At first the focus was on the rural South, where the major issue was unification of the now illegal dual school systems. Later on, the battle lines moved to northern communities, where the de facto segregation experienced by racial minorities was also being found by the courts to be the result of government support and contrivance and therefore beyond the pale of constitutional requirements. By the time CRS was drawn into the volatile conflicts of desegregation in northern cities in the early seventies, it had the experience of more than a thousand school cases under its belt.

HELPING COMMUNITIES ADJUST TO CHANGE

It was violence and the fear of violence that summoned CRS into most of its early desegregation cases, rather than education issues per se. The search for peaceful resolutions, however, often extended into other matters because the parties in conflict were the same city officials and the same minority community leaders who were also contesting issues of voting rights, fair employment practices, and equal justice. The CRS-negotiated settlements generally focused on solving those issues that would permit the restoration of community stability. A CRS goal in all cases, though not always achieved, was not only to resolve the issues immediately at hand but also to leave the adversaries better disposed to negotiate the many issues remaining between them.

The intensity and effectiveness of CRS intervention varied from school district to school district, depending on the level of tension, the needs of the district, and the opportunities for being useful. Conflict mediation and prevention were only half the job. Serving as a resource for technical proficiency was the other. Experience had shown CRS that conflict feeds on confusion, and a poorly designed desegregation plan or a badly managed school invites disaster. CRS helped local officials find the experts—and the funds to pay them—for designing desegregation plans and training personnel, for helping police improve proficiency in crowd control, for enlisting the support of opinion molders, and for gaining minority input in the planning process. CRS often worked in partnership with the desegregation assistance centers established and funded by the U.S. Office of Education at various universities to provide expertise for local school districts. In this symbiotic relationship, the assistance centers would often give priority to situations identified as critical by CRS and would accept CRS's guidance as to local sources of information that should be consulted to assure that the desegregation planning process did not subordinate minority interests. CRS also helped the centers by identifying qualified minority educators to work as desegregation consultants.

The number of new education cases in the South suddenly accelerated in 1970 when the federal enforcement effort moved into higher gear. The Civil Rights Act of 1964 had empowered two federal agencies to enforce school desegregation. The Justice Department's Civil Rights Division was authorized to accept complaints and sue segregated school systems to compel compliance. The Department of Health, Education, and Welfare (HEW), through its Office of Education, was required to withhold federal funding from segregated school districts. Nevertheless, foot-dragging by resistant school systems had been allowed to slow these enforcement programs to a crawl. According to the Southern Education Reporting Service, the number of Black children in segregated schools in the South in 1966 was greater than it had been at the time of the *Brown* decision in 1954.[2]

On October 29, 1969, a unanimous Supreme Court decision changed the time frame for desegregation from the "with all deliberate speed" of the 1955 decision to a doctrine requiring school districts to end segregation "at once."[3] The effect of that decision, which had been specifically directed at thirty-three school districts in Mississippi, was to impel the Nixon administration to pursue enforcement with greater urgency. The decree was the first major decision handed down by the court under Warren Burger, President Nixon's newly appointed chief justice. The *New York Times* called it a "stinging setback for the administration," whose Justice Department had argued that delays were permissible. The administration immediately pledged to support the decision.[4]

Fearful of the consternation that might result from a highly energized federal push all across the South to terminate segregation "at once," the administration directed CRS to back up the Justice Department and HEW enforcement blitz with a program to reduce the likelihood of violent resistance. CRS was provided with special funding to reinforce its field staff. Aided by the infusion of forty-seven specially trained temporary conciliators, CRS was able to give assistance in 492 communities in nine states between August 1970 and February 1971.

The level of help varied from marginal to critical, depending on an assessment of the need and the chances of making a difference in an individual school district. A record of the program shows that its mediators drew on the full repertoire of CRS approaches and techniques. They worked in the school systems and in the communities. The need to help establish or improve interracial communication was basic. Setting up biracial committees and helping them to communicate and to overcome specific impasses was common. Help was given for the design and operation of rumor control programs and student grievance mechanisms. Schools were helped in improving the fairness of disciplinary systems, student government, and extracurricular programs. Campaigns were launched for the elimination of provocative racial symbols and derogatory language. Help was provided to school systems for the design of in-service training in race relations and conflict management for school personnel and for the drafting of proposals for emergency federal funding for special desegregation-related programs.

In the broader community, efforts were made through special media projects, and in meetings with even the most hostile community groups, to explain the law, the court decisions, and the special programs the federal government was offering to help make desegregation work. Parent associations were given assistance in increasing interracial cooperation. Minority groups received training in how to get their story told more effectively through the media. Police departments were helped with recruiting minorities and establishing police-community relations programs. Civic and business leaders were encouraged to exert their influence so that desegregation would take place without violence. In not a single instance was this special conflict prevention effort marred by a report of significant disorderly resistance.[5]

Three years later, in 1973, CRS was again enlisted for a similar special conflict prevention effort when U.S. District Court Judge John H. Pratt found a number of southern school districts not in compliance and ordered HEW to step up its compliance efforts even further. Within four years of the decision requiring the end to desegregation "at once," 46 percent of Black children in the eleven southern states were attending mostly white schools.

Aided by its experience in helping southern cities to desegregate peacefully, CRS, in the mid-seventies, exerted a major influence on the efforts of northern cities to forestall disruption of their efforts to implement desegregation plans.

CRS AND THE U.S. DISTRICT COURT

When the Supreme Court outlawed school desegregation in 1954–55, no thoughtful observer expected that the necessary alterations would take place without major resistance. The pervasive changes required in school operations and relationships would present difficulties even in the most cooperative school districts. Resistant school systems would be able to find a hundred ways to thwart the court's decision by making sure that desegregation would not work well. Moreover, citizen action also could frustrate a desegregation order if student boycotts, intimidation-induced absences, and rancor inside the schoolhouse destroyed the atmosphere necessary for learning. The Supreme Court expected, therefore, that lower court judges, in ruling on desegregation cases, might have to continue their jurisdiction throughout the implementation process.

Resistance to the courts' decisions could take many forms, including inadequate planning, foot-dragging in implementation, and slipshod supervision, as well as intimidation and street violence. A number of American cities found themselves beset by the intervention of a federal judge not only in the management of their school systems but in the operations of police agencies as well, where disorder in the streets threatened the implementation of court decisions.

Nowhere did the reach of the court appear more assertive or longer lasting than in Boston. According to Martin Walsh, the CRS regional director who worked closely with the judge for many years, the reason was that in no other city was the resistance so great and so persistent. Walsh noted that every time the judge had been charged with being overly intrusive, his position had been confirmed by the Court of

Appeals, and every effort to gain review by the U.S. Supreme Court had been denied.[6]

A special CRS role in a score of cities where the desegregation fight was most troublesome began in the seventies when U.S. district court judges sought CRS assistance to prevent their orders from being vitiated by community resistance. In many of these cities the CRS role was written into the court order. Judge Garrity, in Boston, was the first to invoke this groundbreaking partnership.

Ed McClure, a CRS conciliator covering Boston, called upon the judge in August 1974 to inform him of the availability of CRS to negotiate in situations of community conflict and to assist in solving racial problems from the street level up. Garrity immediately saw an ally for dealing with what he feared might be one of the toughest parts of his case—how to keep violence from escalating, and how to keep interracial animosity from sabotaging the quality of desegregated education.

CRS's director, Ben Holman, while welcoming the opportunity to work with the court, was concerned about the impact such a relationship might have on CRS's independence and on its reputation as an impartial troubleshooter. He had to make sure that the embrace would not develop into a bear hug. He therefore assigned CRS's general counsel, Hayden Gregory, to head the emergency team to be sent to Boston to contend with any disruptions surrounding the opening day of a desegregated school system. Gregory worked with the judge to establish appropriate guidelines to govern a continuing relationship.

Both Garrity and Gregory recognized that a collaborative relationship between CRS and the court would require that they walk a delicate line. CRS recognized that in some ways its effectiveness would be enhanced by evidence of the respect in which the court held its advice, as well as by its ability to informally interpret the court's thinking to the community. At the same time it was important that CRS, as an independent and objective mediator, should not be seen as subservient to, or a creature of, the court. With city hall as well as the school committee coming under the court order, CRS held a level of clout that had to be used with the utmost circumspection lest it destroy the agency's credibility as an objective negotiator of voluntary agreements.

High among Garrity's concerns was a need to encourage the constructive elements among the Boston populace to serve as a counterweight to the wrecking crews. To do this, he would have to understand the views and feelings of key groups and their leaders throughout the city. He hoped that CRS might provide an effective and appropriate channel of communication by which this process could be encouraged. Garrity amended his desegregation order to request CRS's assistance and to require the parties to cooperate with CRS's efforts to harmonize relationships so that desegregation could go forward with a minimum of turmoil.

In the ensuing years U.S. district courts in more than a score of cases were guided by Garrity's lead in reaching out for CRS support. In more than a dozen instances the dictum to cooperate with CRS was written into the court order.

SCHOOL DESEGREGATION IN BOSTON

By 1974 the opposition to desegregation in Boston had been building for ten years. A generation of political leaders had won their spurs by assaulting the 1965 Racial Imbalance Act of the state legislature, which stated that thenceforth all public schools were prohibited from being more than 50 percent Black. But passage of the law did not guarantee its enforcement, and efforts to ignore or repeal the law sparked legal and political battles throughout the state.

In Boston, grassroots opposition organizations had been born and had grown large by using the issue as a litmus test for office seekers for every position on the ballot. Anti-segregation sentiment had provided the springboard for every victorious candidate in Boston's local elections, including those for the school committee. It had propelled into prominence City Councilperson Louise Day Hicks and School Committee Chairman John Kerrigan. Hicks, who had led ROAR (Restore Our Alienated Rights), a citywide resistance group rooted in her South Boston power base, had become the archetype of a new breed of local kingmakers. Political pressure had grown so great that even Governor Francis Sargent, a traditional supporter of desegregation, had recently abandoned his support of the state's Racial Imbalance Act.

In March 1973, the Boston NAACP filed suit in federal court seeking an end to segregated schools. In his June 21, 1974, ruling, Judge W. Arthur Garrity Jr. found that the Boston School Committee had deliberately carried out "a systematic program of segregation affecting the city's students, teachers and school facilities, and intentionally brought about and maintained a dual school system." He ordered it to use all legal means, including busing, to secure the rights of the plaintiffs.[7]

Garrity specified that, as the first phase of its remedy, the city must implement an already ordered state plan for the one-third-Black ninety-six-thousand-student school system. The state plan called for reduction of the number of all-Black schools from sixty-eight to forty-four, with the number of Black students in such schools reduced from twenty-six thousand to less than ten thousand. This change would add six thousand to the number of Black and white students already being bused, bringing the total to thirty thousand. Judge Garrity's order noted that this first phase of the remedy would have to be followed by a second phase, which the school committee would have to prepare for his approval for the following year.[8]

Evidence of the passion that was to fuel violent resistance to the Boston busing plan was revealed throughout the spring and summer. In March, Boston's mayor, Kevin White, was jeered as he led the St. Patrick's Day parade because his opposition to desegregation had been no more than moderate. In April, thousands of parents and schoolchildren marched on the Massachusetts State House to protest a state court order that Boston comply with the state's racial imbalance law, and the legislature began hearings on a proposal to repeal that law. In May, in a politically motivated nonbinding referendum, Boston citizens voted fifteen-to-one against busing to achieve integration. In September, Senator Edward Kennedy was driven from the platform at an antibusing rally under a storm of catcalls, a shower of eggs and tomatoes, and the shattering of plate-glass windows.

As the day of desegregation approached, those who had been stirring the kettle of passion suddenly became fearful of the possible consequences of their activity. They issued public statements appealing for the safety of the schoolchildren. However, Mayor White was alone among Boston's elected officials in calling for compliance with the court's order. As a defendant in the case, and as the city's executive officer directly subject to Judge Garrity's ruling, he could do no less. But his situation was far more complicated. As a young, vigorous, ambitious mayor of a major city, with liberal credentials, he was seen by many as a rising star on the national political stage. He was among those whose names were being mentioned as vice presidential possibilities for the Democratic Party in 1976. He could not oppose desegregation without damaging his national reputation; he could not support it without risking the loss of his political launching pad in Boston. The tightrope he had walked successfully thus far was becoming increasingly precarious.[9]

The city agencies, under the mayor's leadership, had undertaken frenetic measures to keep the city calm. Communication centers had been established to coordinate between the school system and police and fire agencies, youth workers, and rumor-control centers. Church and civic volunteers had been mobilized to serve as safety monitors on streets, buses, and school grounds. The mayor spoke on television, sympathizing with the distress felt by white parents but emphasizing the paramount responsibility of complying with the law.

Even though the police department was prepared to escort buses and to protect bus routes and school areas, spokesmen for the police union questioned the mayor's authority to require officers to arrest protesters. To remove any and all uncertainty as to the city's will to enforce the law, Judge Garrity found it necessary—on the day before schools were to open—to issue an order directing Boston's police to arrest anyone blocking school doorways or interfering with the implementation of the desegregation plan.

The focus of attention was on South Boston High School, the physical and emotional landmark for generations of Boston's largely working-class Irish community. "Southie," everyone knew, would be the hotbed of resistance. Even though its educational credentials left much to be desired, the high school was the crown jewel of a lily-white neighborhood, whose families had attended it for many generations.[10]

Southie had been paired for desegregation purposes with newly established Roxbury High. The two high schools and their respective feeder schools had been merged into a single district, with racial balance in each school to be achieved by busing some Blacks from Roxbury to South Boston and some whites from Southie to Roxbury. Similar cross-racial pairings had been accomplished with other neighborhoods, such as that between white, middle-class Hyde Park and the Black Mattapan neighborhood.

On opening day crowds gathered on the streets of South Boston and along bus routes across the city as early as 7:00 a.m., an hour before school began. Buses were greeted with boos and curses. Anti-Black graffiti had been painted and then only partially obliterated from South Boston High's doors.

Several Black students and a bus monitor were hurt by flying glass from the windows of three of the many buses that had been stoned, and policemen had been hit by bottles. At the end of the day Black students were besieged at Southie, and it took three escorted patrol wagons to remove them safely. Five white youths had been arrested on disorderly conduct charges. Fear of greater violence the next day prompted the mayor to issue orders barring crowds and ordering police to arrest unauthorized gatherings of three or more in the troubled neighborhoods.

The fires of resistance continued to be stoked by political leaders. Having failed to stop the desegregation plan from going into effect, the opponents seemed determined to keep it from working. The school committee appealed the court order; City Councilperson Hicks and State Senator William Bulger issued a public statement criticizing police efforts to control the mobs, which they called a "violent police siege." Other foes of busing pursued a course of provocative protest and a school boycott to prove that desegregation would not produce effective education for Boston's children. Hostile crowds at schools and along bus routes prompted some Black parents to keep their children home. Those who ran the gauntlet arrived at their classrooms fearful and hostile. While many white parents recognized the futility of a boycott, others remained responsive to the continuing protests of resistance leaders.

Interracial fear and loathing blanketed the city. Disruption and reduced attendance were intertwined. Protest and disorder in the streets led to disorder in the schools; violence in one school led to increased absences throughout the city. It took more than three months before most of Boston's classrooms could claim a stable attendance in an environment in which educational progress could take place.

Those who wanted desegregation to work—the minority community, Judge Garrity, the professional leaders of the school system, as well as CRS—found that their immediate objectives were determined, in part, by the tactics of the opposition. Two priorities became uppermost: to restore attendance to normal as soon as possible, and to douse the fires of disruption that led to fear and hostility in the classroom.

Citywide attendance on opening day was one-third less than usual, reflecting the fears of Black parents and calls for a white boycott. At Southie, only 40 of the assigned 940 Blacks appeared and only 25 of the 1,600 whites. While attendance rose gradually, it fell off repeatedly as a succession of disruptive acts by desegregation opponents fueled successive cycles of confrontations, violence, and absenteeism.[11]

SEPTEMBER 17 A massive police presence brings calm to South Boston where four buses bring 150 Black students. Only 60 whites attend. Citywide attendance is 73 percent.

SEPTEMBER 18 An interracial fight breaks out at Roslindale High School.

SEPTEMBER 19 Four students are injured in an interracial fight at Hyde Park High School. School is closed while parents and students attend meetings to resolve problems.

SEPTEMBER 20 Two buses are stoned, there are seven arrests, and attendance is down to 69 percent following a high of 76 percent the day before.

SEPTEMBER 21 Police are called to a housing project near South Boston when three hundred gather in the streets. Crowds try to prevent distribution of the Sunday edition of the *Boston Globe*.

SEPTEMBER 23 Four hundred walk out of Charlestown High, protesting the desegregation plan, which won't affect them until the next September.

SEPTEMBER 30 Pro- and anti-busing rallies take place.

OCTOBER 1 Eighty percent attendance is the highest since school opened.

OCTOBER 2 Repeated scuffles between white and Black students at South Boston High are broken up by police, with nine arrests. Attendance is set back.

OCTOBER 5 Five thousand protesters march through South Boston, behind the banners of the Home and School Association, including members of the school committee, city council, and state legislature. Order is kept by massed police forces. Four young men are treated at local hospitals after a run-in with a police tactical patrol. Judge Garrity's home is picketed. Two hundred and fifty gather in front of Cardinal Humberto Sousa Medeiros's house to protest his statement that parochial

schools will not be a haven for those fleeing desegregation. A thousand people in a four-hundred-car motor-
cade demonstrate at police headquarters demanding the
removal of the tactical patrol force from South Boston
and its replacement with local police.

OCTOBER 7 A Black man is beaten by a crowd in South
Boston.

OCTOBER 8 There is widespread stoning of cars with
white riders by youths in Roxbury. The neighborhood
previously had been quiet.[12]

OCTOBER 9 Judge Garrity refuses Mayor White's request
for U.S. marshals to reinforce police in view of the growing violence. The judge cites local and state responsibility.
White confers with Governor Sargent, who assigns 425
metropolitan and state police to help secure the streets of
South Boston.

Violence waxed and waned through November but crescendoed in
early December with a series of student fights at South Boston High—
mostly between girls. White students had to be sent home early one day
after they marched through the halls shouting anti-Black epithets. After
that, a Black girl was struck in the head with a padlock, requiring six
stitches. The next day Michael Faith, a white student, was stabbed by a
fifteen-year-old Black youth.

CRS conciliator Silke Hansen was on her daily tour of Southie when
the knifing occurred. She witnessed the outrage of white students
mounting to a boil as groups bent on retaliation began to tour the halls.
On more than one occasion she found herself trying to reason with a
white group, giving their intended prey time to take off. Eventually
most of the Blacks took refuge in a few classrooms, where teachers
locked the doors against marauding white students.

Schools in the South Boston–Roxbury cluster were dismissed early,
but 135 Black students were besieged in Southie by a crowd of a thousand angry whites. Buses trying to approach the school to evacuate
the Black students were turned back by the human wall. Mounted and
riot-clad police repeatedly moved to force the crowd back, only to have
it re-form. Seven residents and three policemen were treated in city
hospitals. Two parked police cruisers were demolished and one was

overturned. Finally, the mob was distracted by a diversionary massing of buses and police at the main gate while the Black students were led out a rear door and down back streets to an alternate set of buses.[13]

Fearful that the knifing incident would reawaken the white boycott of South Boston High, school authorities decided on Friday afternoon to reassure parents by installing airport type walk-through metal detectors, and to have them in place at the opening of school Monday morning. CRS was called upon to make the arrangements. A request to Logan Airport revealed that the airlines, not the airport, were responsible for security at the gates and that the equipment was the property of the airlines. No airline at Logan had equipment to spare. The CRS team enlisted the cooperation of the Federal Aviation Administration, which located two available devices at the headquarters of United Airlines in Seattle. Shipped on the first available plane, they were installed at Southie by United technicians Sunday afternoon.

On December 15 civil rights forces staged a counterdemonstration to protest the anti-busing violence, with five thousand participants coming from cities across the country, drawn from civil rights organizations as well as a variety of left-wing activist groups. They clashed briefly with the police tactical patrol, which turned them back with the same impartial rigidity it maintained against the anti-busing mobs. The following day six thousand anti-bussers countered with a march of their own.

On December 19, the U.S. Court of Appeals upheld Judge Garrity's desegregation ruling in a strongly worded decision. School Committee Chair John J. Kerrigan announced that the committee would appeal to the U.S. Supreme Court.

The primary objective of the CRS team during those months of disarray had been to help the city and school system regain stability in the classrooms and on the streets. This required effort at two levels: (1) working with public officials and leaders in the private sector to restore a climate of civility and respect for the law within the city at large; (2) monitoring developments in schools and neighborhoods and consulting with police and school officials on tactics and strategies of conflict management, using direct intervention to conciliate confrontations as they arose.

Day-to-day tasks included advising school and police officials and sometimes mediating between the two; struggling to bring coherence to the scores of civic volunteers representing church groups, youth guidance counselors, social agencies, and civil rights groups who patrolled the streets and schoolyards offering help and counseling restraint to students, parents, and local residents; and emergency intervention in school management problems (such as expediting priority repair of a school intercom system to assist a hapless principal who, strangled in red tape, was struggling to manage a distressed school without basic communications). Conciliators helped to find lost school buses to allay mounting parental panic and suggested revised bus routes and schedules to reduce danger. In one school cafeteria, where a Black girl seized a kitchen knife to hold off her tormentors, a CRS conciliator calmed the girl, persuaded her to surrender her weapon, and dispersed the crowd, permitting order to be restored. In another instance a conciliator negotiated a modus vivendi between a warring principal and his faculty senate, to restore the school's capability for sensible management. Teachers who had abandoned responsibility for order in the halls to the newly recruited community monitors had to be drawn back to that duty. Guidelines for when police should enter and leave school premises had to be negotiated between school and police leaders. School officials were helped to define and execute training programs for school personnel ranging from teachers to cafeteria workers to the secretaries who fielded calls from anxious parents.[14]

In the absence of any significant effort by the school system to establish racial harmony and cooperation in the school community, Judge Garrity took matters into his own hands. Following the stabbing of Michael Faith at South Boston High School, the judge decreed that a monitoring program be established to measure tension levels and identify problems at their early stages. CRS was asked to design the program and train and supervise the volunteer monitors. The judge later extended the monitoring system to other schools. In October he ordered the establishment of interracial parent councils in all schools with a mixed student population. He also required the high schools to establish interracial student councils. At the judge's request, CRS undertook the responsibility of coordinating the organization and operation of these councils.

"The councils created a means of communicating among students, parents, teachers and administrators regarding solutions to racial problems. Judge Garrity made it clear that they should not shoulder the major responsibility for racial harmony and school safety. The intent was that by meeting regularly to talk only about problems, parents and students of one race could come to understand the concerns of the other."[15]

By the second semester of the school year a semblance of learning had returned to Boston schools, but the desegregation process had only begun, and racial harmony was still beyond the city's grasp. CRS remained closely involved in part because of its special relationship as a community relations consultant to the court. In addition, racial tensions in the schools increased the intergroup friction in all facets of community life. The case remained active for the next five years.[16]

DETROIT: PLANNING TO "AVOID ANOTHER BOSTON"

Chastened by the Boston experience, CRS was determined to never again fall behind the violence curve by delaying the offer of preventive assistance to cities facing desegregation. Indeed, events had reversed any predilection on the part of CRS's overseers in the administration and Congress to limit the agency's role to crisis response only.

More than a year before the January 1976 deadline for Detroit to become the largest school district in the country to be desegregated under court order, CRS offered its services to that city. Even then, school and police officials as well as a number of community institutions had begun to examine their readiness to deal with the problems ahead, and they responded readily to the offer.

A framework of civic coalitions concerned about race relations was already in place, sensitized by the disastrous riot of 1967. Business organizations, religious groups, and minority and social action organizations existed in networks of networks. Most prominent was New Detroit, a well-staffed and financed urban coalition of business, civil rights, and community service groups.

In March 1975, New Detroit convened a meeting of twenty leaders of various groups, from which emerged People and Responsible Organizations for Detroit (PRO Detroit), which took as its first responsibility outreach to other organizations to save the city from tumult. It intended to enlist both the advocates and opponents of school desegregation. CRS and PRO Detroit immediately recognized each other as a source of mutual assistance.[17]

The federal judge presiding over the Detroit desegregation case was Robert E. DeMascio. Like Judge Garrity, he was sensitive to the unique aspects of this case, which were intertwined with community attitudes and developments. In his court order of April 30 he formally requested CRS "to provide assistance to the city of Detroit, to the parties to this litigation, and to the court in achieving harmonious implementation of a remedial plan to be ordered by the court and of future long-range plans to eliminate racial segregation to the extent possible in the public schools in the city of Detroit."

CRS's director, Ben Holman, set up a temporary field office in Detroit in May to provide full-time assistance to the city. To head the office the regional director, Richard Salem, chose Ed Cabell, who had extensive experience in the Boston school case. To provide Cabell with an appropriately high-powered assistant with a good knowledge of the territory, Salem persuaded Rita Scott, a Detroit resident, to get a leave of absence from her position as education director of the Michigan Civil Rights Commission.

In order to help the new team get off to a rapid start, a special CRS work group was assembled in Detroit to develop a community relations guidebook and resource library for desegregation without turmoil. Veterans of school desegregation cases in Boston, Louisville, Denver, and elsewhere sat down with Salem, Cabell, and Scott to draft a playbook for helping a city prepare for desegregation without violence. They reviewed their own experiences, institution-by-institution and play-by-play—what had gone wrong and what had gone right. Case records in Washington were drawn upon for resource materials—examples of police and school contingency plans, operational orders, and sample lesson plans to prepare teachers, school security aides, and police officers; examples of media campaigns and guidelines for rumor control centers. The examination went beyond the school system to look at the role of city hall, the police, social agencies, the media, and religious, business, and civic groups. The outcome was a summary of the full range of CRS's experience in school desegregation.

As exhaustive as the briefing was, Cabell and Scott knew better than to count on it for any pat solutions for the problems of Detroit. Solutions would have to be worked out by the residents of Detroit, problem by problem. But the CRS team would be well prepared to assist.

In the eight months leading up to the day of desegregation, the CRS team met with the leaders of 125 city agencies and community groups to discuss ways of minimizing disruption. Cabell and Scott—and Gus

Gaynett, who replaced Cabell in mid-project—took part in more than three hundred community meetings at which the status of the case and various contentious aspects were interpreted and discussed.[18] They called upon community groups to enlist the hundreds of volunteers that would be needed to support desegregation. They helped design the assignment and training programs for volunteers and eased recurrent friction between public officials and the civic associations. In addition, CRS helped community groups to design a rumor control and information center that was adopted by the city. Working with PRO Detroit, CRS arranged for media executives from Boston to meet with news executives in Detroit to discuss what they had done to reduce community antagonism toward the desegregation process.

As the new school term approached, the CRS team worked with school and police officials on plans for preventing disruptions within the schools, on school property, in school neighborhoods, and along the bus routes.

CRS made it a point to meet repeatedly with the neighborhood groups that opposed desegregation. While these meetings were focused on concerns for the safety of children, they were also designed to let these opposition groups know that their feelings were respected, even if their view could not prevail over the court's decision. CRS hoped that inclusion of these groups in the discussion would forestall feelings of isolation that could lead to the extremism that might provoke violence. Nevertheless, in three neighborhoods on the northeast side of the city there were expressions of bitter resistance to the pupil reassignment plan. Three one-day boycotts during the fall semester caused heavy absenteeism in more than a dozen schools. The week before desegregation was to take place, several hundred people picketed the federal building, and several hundred participated in street demonstrations and car caravans.

To assure compliance with his orders, Judge DeMascio counted heavily on a blue-ribbon monitoring commission he had appointed for that purpose, following the experience of his fellow judges in Denver and Boston. He relied on CRS for information about the functioning of the commissions in those other cities, as well as for ongoing assistance to the Detroit commission.[19]

The Detroit situation provided a unique example of CRS cooperation with the court to anticipate and forestall problems that could disrupt orderly compliance with the court's orders. From community groups CRS learned that a bitter bone of contention between the Black community and the school system was allegations of discriminatory handling of discipline problems. The discrimination led to disproportionate rates of suspension and expulsion, as well as to interracial antagonism and violence. To introduce a controversial school busing plan in such a climate would have been an invitation to widespread disruption.

At the request of the court, CRS prepared an analysis of the school system's student code of conduct and of its policies on students' rights and responsibilities. CRS then recommended ways to assure that disciplinary problems would be handled in a more equitable and consistent manner. When a revised code of conduct was drafted by school officials and approved by the court, CRS helped to train the managers who would be responsible for administering the revised program.

Three days before desegregation was to take place, another CRS team assembled in Detroit to help school and police officials with their final preparations and to troubleshoot problems in the schools and on the streets when the buses rolled. They provided a one-day training session for the 150 police officers composing the special desegregation task force that carried the burden for school safety during the opening week.

Once the buses started to roll, CRS mobile teams were in constant radio communication with police and school networks, responding to crisis calls on the streets and in school buildings. Following daily debriefings, CRS's assessments and recommendations were shared with school and police officials in preparation for the next day's problems.

Violent resistance to the student redistribution program turned out to be inconsequential. By the third day, when school attendance, which had been down one-third on opening day, returned to almost the normal 88 percent, Detroit's leaders were ready to acknowledge that their careful preparation had paid off. They had dodged the bullet that had devastated Boston. They had succeeded in desegregating their schools without turmoil.

DAYTON

Following four years of bitter political struggle, court-ordered desegregation took place in Dayton, Ohio, without incident on September 3, 1976. Despite the cold-blooded murder of the court-appointed desegregation expert by a demented opponent of desegregation, the change, which involved the busing of twenty thousand children, white and Black, was planned and executed without widespread violence and with a minimum of rancor.[20]

The successful effort resulted from a determined and sophisticated mobilization of the full community, which, while opposed to desegregation, was resolved, like Detroit, that its city would not be blemished by the violent resistance that had characterized the Boston experience.

Dayton was a thriving industrial city that prided itself on its grace and civility. Its population of two hundred thousand included seventy-five thousand Blacks, reflecting a large migration from the South following World War II. Thirty-five thousand newer white immigrants from Appalachia reinforced a solid core of people opposed to desegregation. Racial issues, heavily focused on segregated schooling, had been in the foreground ever since an outbreak of burning and looting in the North End Black neighborhood in 1967.

Following the riot, a board of education resolution declared that "every reasonable and constructive measure" would be taken to "eliminate racial imbalance." Under a liberal school board a number of changes were made and the school superintendent created a far-reaching desegregation plan. That proved to be too much for the voters, who took their next opportunity to oust the liberals and vote in a conservative school board. When the new board rescinded the plan and fired the superintendent, the NAACP filed suit in U.S. District Court.

In February 1972, Judge Carl B. Rubin found the school board in violation of the U.S. Constitution, and in July he accepted the board of education's voluntary plan for desegregation. That wasn't good enough for the plaintiffs, and on two appeals Judge Rubin's decision was overruled as too lenient. The appeals court ordered that a satisfactory systemwide plan be prepared for implementation in September 1976.

Despite their effective resistance to desegregation, which had been mandated by state law since 1926, and by Supreme Court decision since 1954, Dayton's civic leaders now recognized that forty-four months of opposition through litigation had brought them to the end of the line. The city now determined to mobilize its full resources to assure peaceful implementation of the desegregation plan.

The movement for a community coalition to avoid disorderly resistance to desegregation started in Dayton more than a year before the final court order. The initiative was taken by Metropolitan Churches

United, which brought together thirty community organizations to explore activities and concerns. The business community, long dominated by corporate executives accustomed to working together on projects for civic improvement, also weighed in to make sure that since desegregation was inevitable, Dayton would usher it in gracefully. A public relations campaign, staffed and financed by the business community, developed a speakers bureau, media campaigns, a rumor control center, press releases, brochures, bumper stickers, and posters, all designed to educate the community and make it clear that the law would be respected. CRS offered support and guidance to help develop programs, solve problems, and facilitate cooperation.

Judge Rubin complied with the edict of the appeals court by selecting an outside expert to draft the final desegregation plan. Dr. Charles Glatt, the chosen expert, was at work in his office at the U.S. Courthouse on September 18, 1975, when an intruder burst in and shot him to death. At the time of his death, Dr. Glatt was in conference with Tommie Jones, a Black woman working her first day on the job as a CRS conciliator.

A former chemistry teacher in the Dayton schools, Jones was well known throughout the city as a civil rights activist who had, on a volunteer basis, presented intergroup workshops during previous periods of racial tension. With the guidance of CRS's Chicago-based regional director, Richard Salem, who had captained CRS's desegregation work in Detroit and several other cities, CRS designed a low-key catalytic role tailored to the particular circumstances in Dayton and the unique reliance placed on CRS by the U.S. District Court.

Judge Rubin was concerned not only that his plan be initiated peacefully but also that its intent of equitable education not be thwarted either by community resistance or by inept implementation by the school administration. Yet Rubin knew that the court itself should not have to provide day-by-day oversight; this should come from community resources. Rubin found an answer to his dilemma when he learned from a conversation with Salem of CRS's collaboration with the U.S. District Courts in Boston and Detroit. He studied both those experiences and adapted them to the case at hand. In January 1976, eight months before the scheduled desegregation, he issued an order asking for CRS assistance in the "establishing and functioning of a Citizens Monitoring Commission," which he was about to create, and directing all parties to the case "to cooperate with the Service and to afford it all reasonable assistance." He also indicated that CRS would have ready access to the court "as to all matters which bear upon the speedy and harmonious implementation of the desegregation plan."

Behind the formal language was the clear expectation that CRS would energize, and where necessary provide guidance to, the development of community support, and that the monitoring commission would ensure the quality of the school system's preparation. Further, the judge looked to CRS to work unobtrusively with the monitoring commission and to keep the court informed of whatever it needed to know in order to assure that the desegregation that resulted would be consistent with his intent.

How CRS acquitted itself of that responsibility as well as its other tasks was reported in detail by Graham S. Finney in a study of the Dayton desegregation experience. As an example, Finney cited the addition to the court order of a requirement for the training of school personnel "when it appeared in the spring that school administrators were moving too slowly to equip their staff with the skills needed to make desegregation work in the classroom." He marveled at the energy and resourcefulness with which Jones pursued this delicate task, indicating, however, that while much of the work was done behind the scenes, "some bruised relationships were an almost inevitable consequence." He was particularly impressed with the wide diversity of community elements that CRS brought into the desegregation process. He cited the salutary planning work of the city government; the effective police training supervised by Colonel Tyree Broomfield, the police department's chief of staff, who, as a sometime CRS consultant, was familiar with CRS work in other cases; the active support of the church organizations; the enlisting of the national leadership of the AFL-CIO to bolster local labor organization support. Finney reported: "In all these efforts the hand of Jones and the CRS was in evidence, sometimes so subtly that its imprint was barely detectible. Hers was, in fact, the only presence that managed to touch base with all the various parties. This network capacity proved crucial as events unfolded."[21]

In March 1976, Metropolitan Churches United conducted a community conference that, with CRS assistance, featured veterans of Detroit's successful desegregation as speakers. The conference enlisted two hundred and fifty volunteers to build community support in the final months before desegregation. Area committees were formed throughout the city, and dozens of churches issued endorsements. Many churches conducted all-night prayer vigils the day before school opened.

Dayton's Appalachian community of working-class whites expressed its resistance to desegregation and its support for neighborhood schools largely through a community group called Our Common Heritage (OCH), which was foremost among the groups opposed to desegregation. Tommie Jones met often with such groups, discussing their problems in the context of the federal government's concern with peaceful enforcement of the law. After a meeting with Jones in August, OCH declared publicly that it would support compliance with the court order. According to Graham Finney's evaluation, "The OCH endorsement set the tenor of the city's mood in the weeks remaining until the opening day of school."

DESEGREGATION WITHOUT TURMOIL

The turbulence that the fight over school desegregation brought to American cities would have been much worse in many places if civic volunteers had not rolled up their sleeves to make sure that things worked out peacefully. At national and local levels the outpouring of resources and personnel was tremendous. Detroit and Dayton and Dallas did it one way, organizing at the top, with the power structure mobilizing the community. Elsewhere the rallying cry was first sounded closer to the grassroots, as in Prince George's County, Maryland, where in 1971 CRS, on its arrival on the scene, found the League of Women Voters and the Ministerial Association making the case for rational and planned acceptance of inevitable change. In some cities where joint civic action was no more than rudimentary, many groups were hesitant about taking a stand in support of peaceful desegregation because they were uncertain about how to proceed and how prominent a role to play.

The federal conciliators helped the coalition effort in two ways. The first was as a catalyst for community organization. Civic leaders concerned about an impending desegregation crisis could be readily brought together in small groups to talk about the problem informally—and confidentially, if necessary—with someone from the Department of Justice. Such meetings provided encouragement to enter the fray.

CRS pointed out that school desegregation was a new phenomenon, and history had shown that even the most competent of school systems, police departments, and city halls did not have the requisite motivation, experience, or expertise to navigate the minefield of community turmoil. Moreover, since the forces of discord fed on resistance to unpopular change, the thoughtful sectors of the community needed to assert leadership to assure a peaceful transition.

CRS helped community groups to learn from the successes and failures in other cities. This was done by sharing sample materials from other cases, by arranging direct contact via mail and phone, and by intercity visits. In May 1975, 570 coalition leaders from more than seventy cities came together to share experiences at the Conference on Desegregation without Turmoil. Their how-to-do-it exchanges ranged from ideas for working with the schools, police, and city hall to assure adequate advanced planning to suggestions for enlisting the media to build public support. The local coalition leaders learned how to prepare themselves to consult productively with—and sometimes to challenge—school and public safety officials on the adequacy of preparations to avoid and control violence.

Groups shared tips on how they had successfully dealt with common problems—like the charge that the local desegregation decision was the unconstitutional work of a misguided judge. The suggested solution had three stages. The first was to get the local bar association to issue its analysis of the court's decision. Such a report would generally make it clear that the ruling was not only constitutional but also fully consistent with the findings of the appeals courts. The second was to form a media committee to win support for the bar association's position from newspapers and broadcast outlets. The third was to form a speakers committee to stimulate discussion of the bar association position before community groups.

In the campaign to build and strengthen local coalitions to support peaceful desegregation, CRS found powerful allies among national associations. Religious organizations were interested in furthering social justice; business organizations knew that community violence was bad for business. The International Association of City Managers, the U.S. Conference of Mayors, the National Association of School Superintendents, and the National Association of Secondary School Principals were all concerned with providing their constituents with information and resources to deal with critical problems. Several national organizations were helpful in identifying local constituents who might bc interested in leading local efforts. Among them were the American Jewish Committee, the AFL-CIO, and the various social action arms of the national religious denominations.

The Conference on Desegregation without Turmoil was cosponsored by CRS and the National Center for Quality Integrated Education, a project of the National Conference of Christians and Jews. Assistance was provided by the National Education Association. The U.S. Chamber of Commerce published and circulated to its membership the conference reports on how business associations in Detroit, Dayton, and Dallas took the lead in building coalitions to assure peaceful implementation of school desegregation decisions. The AFL-CIO contributed $10,000 to help fund the conference.

The AFL-CIO played a unique behind-the-scenes role in working for peaceful school desegregation. Even though the national organization was a strong supporter of civil rights, many members of local unions were deeply opposed to school desegregation. George Meany, president of the AFL-CIO, was an uncompromising foe of segregation.[22] He instructed William Pollard, director of the organization's Civil Rights Department, to give top priority to the task of winning local support for peaceful desegregation and for stifling opposition efforts by local labor groups. When alerted through CRS, or his own channels, of the intent of a local central trades and labor council, anywhere in the country, to take a public position against desegregation, Pollard would meet with the leaders of the local council. He would advise them, in no uncertain terms, of how deeply unhappy Meany would be at such a turn of events.

HISTORICAL PERSPECTIVE

Martin Walsh became CRS's regional director for New England in November 1974, shortly after the agency entered the Boston school desegregation case, and he managed that case until its closure six years later. For three decades he presided over CRS efforts to resolve racial conflict throughout the six-state area. In recognition of that work Attorney General John Ashcroft presented him, in 2001, with the Attorney General's Distinguished Service Award. It was the second time Walsh had been so honored.

For almost thirty years, he and the men and women working under him had grappled with literally thousands of racial conflicts, working in settings that ranged from disorder in the streets to negotiation around the conference table. They had worked with governors, mayors, police chiefs, school superintendents, business leaders, and the heads of religious and civic communities, as well as civil rights activists and those who carried forward the banner of every embattled minority group. They had learned to assess the tension level in every community in which they worked. They had studied the dynamics of conflict in the most volatile cities, so that they could counsel local leaders on the best approaches for avoiding outbreaks of racial violence.

Walsh made a specialty of helping communities develop preventive strategies. He worked with the bellwethers among public officials—outstanding mayors, educators, police chiefs, and district attorneys—to convene regional or statewide conferences of their counterparts in other communities. These conferences brought together civil rights leaders and experts within each profession to identify emerging racial problems and consider, in advance of a crisis, methods and resources for dealing with them.

Interviewed in June 2001, Walsh identified Boston's school desegregation ordeal as an exorcism, following which the resolution of other stubborn civil rights problems became possible. He thought the school conflict exposed the city's "racial malaise" and bared problems in the underpinnings of other institutions in Boston. He saw it as a turning point for the people of Boston, "stirring them to redeem themselves from being, what Mayor Kevin White himself was to acknowledge as, 'the most racist city in America.'" He felt that "Judge Garrity's steadfastness, over a period of six years, in requiring the city and the school system to do what was necessary to make desegregation work made it clear that the opposition was not going to win." It set in motion changes in the political system that could accommodate subsequent court-ordered reforms such as those affecting the police, the firefighters, and public housing.

Walsh recalled:

Those who were to lead the reform in the 1980s included some of the leaders of the resistance in the seventies. Kevin White, before leaving office as mayor in 1980, created the Boston Committee, to work for improved human relations. Ray Flynn, who had been among the South Boston politicians opposed to Judge Garrity's order, ran for mayor in 1983, promising to try to bring the city together. When elected, he followed through on his pledge. Since that time, race has never been a negative issue in Boston mayoral elections.

Walsh also stated his belief that the Boston experience with school desegregation had a profound influence beyond Boston. The image of intractable hatred and mob violence in one of America's greatest cities, which Boston had communicated to the entire nation, demonstrated the consequences of failed leadership in a time of crisis. It stirred those responsible for the fate of other cities to make the preparations that would enable them to "avoid another Boston."

In 1979 CRS, in cooperation with the National Urban League and the Anti-Defamation League of B'nai B'rith, created the Greater Boston Civil Rights Coalition, an association working for racial harmony. Walsh pointed out that both that coalition and Kevin White's Boston Committee still exist. "By 2001," he said, "the overtness of discrimination and the negative voices of the demagogues have been shunted aside as aberrations. Improving relationships—that's where the dynamic of race is being played out now."[23]

NOTE FOR NEW EDITION

As of 2020, issues of race and class are very much still in play in American public education. A 2019 EdBuild Report notes that "about half attend school in a district that is more than 75% nonwhite and half are enrolled in districts that are more than 75% white." A novel version of "white flight" has evolved utilizing charter schools and open enrollment policies, which allow students to attend schools not within their districts. Class issues within education, which have always existed, have been spotlighted. The same report notes that "there remains a $23 billion gap between white and nonwhite school districts even though they serve the same number of students." While race dynamics have evolved significantly since the 1970s, the story of public education, race, and class is still filled with disparity and remains unresolved.[24]

NOTES

1. U.S. Department of Justice, Community Relations Service, Annual Report, 1965, 23.
2. U.S. Department of Justice, Community Relations Service, "Activities Related to the Desegregation of Public Schools," August 15, 1970, February 15, 1971.

3. *Alexander v. Holmes*, 396 U.S. 19 (1969).

4. *New York Times*, October 31, 1969.

5. U.S. Department of Justice, Community Relations Service, Annual Report, 1971, 10, 11.

6. Martin Walsh, interview with Bertram Levine.

7. *New York Times*, June 22, 1974.

8. *New York Times*, June 22, 1974.

9. *New York Times*, April 14, 1974.

10. Because the high school population of the South Boston neighborhood was "skimmed" by Boston's three elite "exam schools" and a highly desired parochial school system, Southie qualified few students for college, only three having made the grade in the previous year.

11. *New York Times Index*, 1974, 660–64.

12. Up to that time the Black neighborhoods had been models of physical safety for all—in contrast to the intimidating climate faced by Black children in white neighborhoods. The Black community had mobilized to assure an atmosphere of welcome for the newly transferred white students and to guarantee secure streets in the Black neighborhoods. The October 8 incidents were the lone exception.

Boston's Black community had for twenty years sponsored—either by itself or on an interracial basis—a variety of projects to improve the education of its children, including school boycotts, experimental "freedom schools," a program known as "operation exodus" in which the Black community raised money to pay for buses to take children to white schools under an open enrollment policy, and the Metco program by which Black students were voluntarily bused to suburban schools.

13. Silke Hansen, interview with Bertram Levine.

14. Data drawn partially from author Levine's participation in the CRS Boston task force, including thirty days onsite, from September to December 1974.

15. U.S. Department of Justice, Community Relations Service, Annual Report, 1975, 12.

16. For more on the Boston busing crisis, see Lukas, *Common Ground*. (note by Lum)

17. William H. O'Brien, co-chairperson, People and Responsible Organizations for Detroit, presentation at the workshop on the role of business communities, at the Conference on Desegregation without Turmoil, sponsored by the Community Relations Service, U.S. Department of Justice, and the National Center for Quality Integrated Education, May 19, 1976.

18. Gustavo Gaynett, "Community Relations Service Involvement in Detroit School Desegregation Case," report to Judge Robert DeMascio, February 2, 1976.

19. Lila N. Carol, "Viewpoints and Guidelines on Court-Appointed Monitoring Commissions in School Desegregation," report of a symposium sponsored by the Community Relations Service, U.S. Department of Justice, and College of Education, Ohio State University, May 31, June 1, 1977.

20. Richard Salem, interview with Bertram Levine.

21. Finney, "Desegregating the Schools in Dayton."

22. Meany came out in favor of the Supreme Court's school desegregation decision immediately after it was announced in 1954. He called it an act of "simple justice" and lobbied within the labor movement for its support.

23. Walsh, interview with Levine.

24. "$23 Billion," EdBuild, February 2019, 2, https://perma.cc/7M83-DJ4N.

EIGHT

Mediation

The Road Less Traveled

IN 1972 THE commissioner of corrections for the State of Louisiana made sweeping changes in the living conditions of prisoners throughout the state's penal system. Her objective was to reduce racial discrimination and conflict and to raise the standards of respect for the rights of all prisoners. At the root of the change was a written agreement negotiated by CRS the year before, settling civil rights complaints filed by prisoners in the state's maximum security facility at Angola. This agreement was embodied in a consent decree issued by Judge E. Gordon West, who had asked CRS to mediate civil rights issues between the prison authorities and the complaining prisoners.[1] The form of the court's judgment made it easier for the reform-minded corrections commissioner to extend its benefits throughout the state's entire correctional system.

In the eyes of some judges, Judge West's experience suggested a more satisfactory way of resolving many of the issues involving the civil rights of prisoners that were contributing to the overcrowding of federal court dockets. The case proved to be an eye-opener for CRS as well, as its staff perceived the far-reaching social change that might result when a CRS agreement, reduced to writing, was embodied in a court order.

MEDIATION OR CONCILIATION—WHICH WAY TO GO?

In its early years CRS used only one word to describe its peacemaking process—conciliation. Broadly speaking, the term meant "whatever it takes to resolve the conflict." Conciliation encompassed a broad range of methods, techniques, strategies, and resources to be drawn on in whatever combination would get the job done—including, at times, the use of a written agreement. Sometimes that written agreement required formal mediation, a process with which CRS's conciliators had little experience.

In contrast to the wide-ranging, flexible forms of intervention permitted by conciliation, the activities called for in mediation were prescribed, disciplined, and tightly choreographed. Mediation consisted of formal crosstable negotiations between the conflicting parties, presided over by a trained mediator, following specific rules of procedure and with the intention of producing a binding written agreement for the solution of specific predetermined issues.

In the early seventies, CRS's director, Ben Holman, reviewed the agency's limited but growing experience with mediation cases. In the southwestern region, Robert Greenwald had used mediation in Louisiana prison cases. In the Midwest region, Jesse Taylor had produced impressive agreements in school cases and in conflicts between minority groups and industrial corporations. There had been a few other uses of mediation as well. Holman commissioned a staff study that concluded that, while mediation was not suitable in most of the conflicts CRS dealt with, there were instances where it might achieve lasting solutions not otherwise possible. But there were problems. Often, it was not the immediate conflict but the underlying problems that might be amenable to mediation. Additional casework time would be necessary to determine whether a mediated outcome would be more desirable than the settlement worked out through conciliation alone. Also, the antagonists might have to be persuaded to revise the way they looked at the problem before they would buy into the mediation process.

Holman decided that there was a distinct place for mediation in the CRS program, but its use should not depend on happenstance or upon the propensity of the individual fieldworker. Intensive mediation training was begun, and special rules of engagement were set forth as well as guidelines for "marketing" the use of this new and potent tool. Eventually, the agency developed an impressive track record for mediation of cases involving prisons, schools, police agencies, and industrial conflicts.

Mediation cases presented CRS's management with a cost/benefit dilemma. On the plus side, these cases often involved conflicts that were bitter, stubborn, and important. Such cases were mostly successful, producing binding written agreements that often provided long-range as well as short-range solutions. On the minus side was the cost. Conflicts that might profitably be dealt with by mediation were not always readily apparent. The preliminary process of recasting the conflict into negotiable issues and persuading the parties that a mediated written agreement could be in their best interest often took as much or more time than the mediation itself. On the average, five conciliated settlements could be worked out in the time it took to conclude one mediation agreement. That meant that for every mediation case resolved, five other cases had to be either rejected or added to the backlog of cases waiting to be resolved.

THE DIVIDENDS OF MEDIATION
Prisoner Civil Rights Cases in Louisiana

It had all started the year before when Judge West, in an effort to relieve the swollen calendar of cases before him, noted that thirty of them stemmed from civil rights complaints filed by prisoners (most of whom were Black) in Angola. He asked the prison authorities and the lawyers for the prisoners to try to work out some sort of comprehensive settlement using Robert Greenwald of CRS as a mediator.[2]

Greenwald began an intensive period of preparation, helping in the selection of negotiating teams for the prisoners and the prison, establishing an agreement on procedures and guidelines, and getting consensus among the prisoners on the substance and wording of the specific complaints to be mediated. In three marathon mediation sessions, the negotiating teams were able to reach agreement on twenty-eight of the thirty-some-odd issues that had been raised. The outcome, as reported in the CRS Annual Report for 1972, included:

> closing some notorious isolation cells, ending lockdown abuses, eliminating certain restrictions on correspondence and hairstyles, establishment of a grievance process, creation of a joint committee to prepare revisions to the existing rules and regulations, improvement in medical attention to inmates, and increased access to showers. . . . As a result of CRS mediation, many of the complaints filed in court were declared moot. Moreover, subsequent reports from prison officials and inmates indicated that inmate-staff relations improved, and that disciplinary infractions decreased.[3]

On the heels of the Angola case, a second federal judge, Jack M. Gordon, asked CRS to mediate a similar case at the Jefferson Parish Jail in Louisiana. Judge Gordon, enthused about what he saw as an innovative approach to a sticky problem, included in his opinion a detailed description of the process. As he explained in a letter to Greenwald: "I devoted a substantial portion of the opinion to outlining the mediation efforts and the manner in which they were carried out, as well as commenting upon my views as to their efficacy in such situations. I felt that issuing the opinion in this form would be as good a way as any of acquainting others with the success we met in this case."[4]

The opinion to which the judge referred had also noted: "In addition to the formal agreements, the Court also appreciates certain fringe benefits that resulted from this series of negotiations; among the valuable extras are a higher level of rapport between the authorities and the inmates, and, of no small import, the introduction of mediation to both sides as a potentially viable and permanent alternative to the courts in resolving the complaints of inmates."[5]

Integration of the Cook County Jail

Because the five thousand inmates of the Cook County Jail near Chicago were segregated by race, the Civil Rights Division of the Justice Department sued the county early in 1979. Trial was scheduled for 1980. Seeking to avoid a long trial, Judge Hubert L. Will of the U.S. District Court encouraged the parties to work out a settlement. When, in May 1979, they reported to him their inability to make any progress, he directed them to utilize the mediating services of CRS. Six months later the judge was able to issue a consent decree based on the CRS-produced agreement. As a result of that mediation, the county pledged to desegregate the jail, utilizing a plan that would be worked out by the Justice Department's National Institute of Corrections.

In congratulating mediator Jesse Taylor for achieving a settlement without trial, which others had thought impossible, the judge remarked in court that he had never even heard of CRS until the day before he made his referral. At a workshop of the judges of the Fifth Circuit, he had heard Director Gil Pompa describe the work of the agency. Judge Will later wrote to Attorney General Benjamin R. Civiletti, "The agency's demonstrated ability to mediate complex civil rights cases could result in substantial savings of time and money to both the court and the parties and result in earlier settlements which both the parties and the court view as equitable."[6]

Over the years CRS successfully mediated a number of prison cases that often seemed intractable. Some were court-referred; others were instigated by prison authorities. These cases divided broadly into two categories—discriminatory conditions of confinement, and racial tension and violence. While CRS was often successful in working out far-reaching settlements, the overall number of such cases was few. For one reason, prison officials tended to be reluctant to bring in outsiders to help solve the problems of their closed institutions. Second, CRS found that, compared to other issues, there was little community concern about prison conditions and no significant constituency to invite the agency's attention. Third, settlements were inclined to erode with time because of the turnover of inmates as well as of corrections personnel. Fourth, the CRS regional directors, often hard put to choose among the cases competing for the attention of an already overburdened staff, were reluctant to make commitments to prison cases, which were very time-consuming.

Voting Rights in Cairo, Illinois

The racial history of Cairo, Illinois, had been conditioned in part by its pre–Civil War role as a collection point for captured runaway slaves being shipped back to their owners along the Mississippi River. Despite its population of only six thousand, it had been one of the worst hotbeds of racial violence and civil rights protest in the late 1960s and throughout the 1970s. Recurrent periods of tension were marked by protest demonstrations, boycotts of white merchants, vigilante assaults on a Black housing project, armed confrontations, and shootings. The Black population, amounting to about one-third of the city's residents, was large enough to resist white domination but not large enough to exercise political influence. At-large elections for the city's mayor and council had effectively barred Blacks from elected representation since before 1900.

A class-action suit filed in behalf of fourteen hundred eligible Black voters had been in the U.S. District Court for six years when Judge James Foreman, in October 1979, asked CRS to mediate. A far-reaching settlement was worked out in three months and embodied by the judge in a consent decree ending the protracted litigation.[7] The agreement replaced the five-person mayor and council, which had been elected at large, with a seven-person council, five of whose members would be elected from newly designated wards. The new arrangement guaranteed the election of at least two Blacks.

The judge and attorneys were exuberant to have the matter behind them. They had anticipated a three-week trial followed by a lengthy appellate process replete with costly discovery, possibly lasting three more years. They calculated a possible savings in future legal costs and court expenses of $300,000. Further savings accrued to the U.S. Justice Department, which had been poised to enter the case as amicus had it gone to trial.

To CRS and the people in both the white and the Black communities, the greater value of the settlement was to be seen not in monetary costs but in social benefits. The termination of political disenfranchisement of African Americans was expected to usher in other gains that would result in more equitable sharing in the decision-making process. Several bitter bones of contention that had contributed to past conflicts could now he eliminated. The Blacks, possessing for the first time a share of political power and influence, would undoubtedly find ways to redress other longstanding inequities that had fueled a century of bad feeling.

In this case, as in many other instances where mediation was utilized as an alternative to litigation, a trial would have been rooted in the adjudication of past wrongs. Mediation, on the other hand, could more readily concentrate on future arrangements that the parties felt would work. From the CRS point of view, mediation was clearly preferable to a trial in those community situations where the antagonists would have to continue to relate to each other. A trial, based on the adjudication of who was wrong or right, would produce a winner and a loser and per-petuate bitterness. On the other hand, a negotiated settlement based on give-and-take often left the adversaries on a first-name basis and better prepared for face-to-face resolution of future differences.

Police Rivalry and the
Weakening of Law Enforcement in Atlanta

Atlanta's crime statistics were on the rise through most of the seventies. The erosion of effective law enforcement was attributed by many to bit-ter rivalry between Black and white police officers. It was presumed to date back to 1973 when the Afro-American Patrolmen's League and the Civil Rights Division of the Justice Department brought suit against the mostly white city administration, charging discrimination in hiring and promotion. In 1976, with the by then mostly Black city government on the verge of reaching a settlement with the plaintiffs, the Fraternal

Order of Police became a party to the suit, charging discrimination against white officers.

Pending settlement of the case, Judge Charles A. Moye took control over personnel matters and froze all new hiring and all promotions. As the number of officers decreased, and Black-white antagonism was acted out on the job, crime statistics continued to climb.

Over the years a number of respected third-party institutions were called on to help the antagonists work out an agreement. Fearful of the controversy's negative impact on business, the Atlanta Chamber of Commerce tried to bring the parties together—to no avail. The Atlanta Human Relations Commission was the next to try. Then the city council sought to intervene. Finally, the mayor appointed a blue-ribbon panel to try to end the impasse. Each of these efforts failed.

In September 1979, with the case about to come to trial in what most observers expected to be a long and bitter proceeding that would further fray race relations, the parties were induced to try to mediate their differences with the help of CRS. In view of the high stakes involved, Regional Director Ozell Sutton selected an interracial mediation team that he personally headed. He also arranged to borrow from CRS's San Francisco office mediator Ed Howden, widely acknowledged to be among America's pioneers in racial conflict negotiation.

Two months of mediation activity, climaxing in weekend sessions that lasted well into the night before the trial was to begin, finally yielded an out-of-court settlement.[8]

Presented with agreed-upon detailed plans for recruitment and promotion of both Black and white officers, and formulas for back pay for various categories of complainants, Judge Moye accepted the agreement and lifted the hiring freeze—finally bringing an end to the longtime depletion of the Atlanta police force. The judge agreed to retain oversight of the case for three years to assure its full implementation.

The rapprochement between Black and white police officers could not have come at a more critical time. Early in 1980, just a few months after the mediated agreement, the city began to face its most severe racial crisis since the height of the civil rights movement, when it experienced what became known as the case of the missing and murdered Black children.

Over a period of almost two years, twenty-three Black children and six adults were either murdered or missing. A white predator was suspected, and the Black community became increasingly fearful and bitter at what it felt was police inadequacy and white indifference. CRS spent months working with the city's leaders, both Black and white, to help bring federal law enforcement assistance to the city and to demonstrate that the community was united in its concern. Ultimately, a deranged Black man was found to be the killer. Most qualified observers agreed that if the racial conflicts and personnel shortages within the Bureau of Police Services had not been resolved before the episode of the murdered and missing children occurred, the level of interracial bitterness would have been far more severe.

Atlanta was only one of many cities where class-action suits charging racial discrimination in police employment led to protracted conflicts between Black and white officers and consequent deterioration of the quality of police services. Louisville, Kentucky, lived through a similar scenario that, after many years, was also resolved within a few months via CRS mediation. Within a year of the Atlanta case, neighboring DeKalb County used the same course to settle suits within both its police force and its sheriff's department.

A Win/Win Ending to the
Long Antagonism between Hispanics and Coors

From the mid-1970s to the mid-1980s, the Adolph Coors Company, then a growing industrial giant that dominated the brewing industry in the Mountain States, was the target of widespread protest by the increasingly vocal Hispanic population because of alleged economic and employment discrimination. Public demonstrations against Coors contributed to an atmosphere of racial/ethnic unrest in many communities throughout the region. A Hispanic boycott of Coors products appeared to have little impact in bringing about change. Early efforts by CRS to mediate between local Hispanic groups and Coors management fell apart when labor problems at one of the breweries gave rise to a Coors boycott by organized labor. Subsequently, Black organizations also charged Coors with discriminatory practices.

Bolstered by four generations of pride and profit, the fiercely independent Coors family appeared to stiffen its resistance in the face of outside interference. Behind the scenes, however, a shift was under way. The younger members of the Coors family, then moving into positions of control in the company, were deeply concerned about radical changes in the economics of the industry. A wave of mergers and acquisitions was threatening to reduce the number of major breweries to no more than half a dozen or so supergiants. In order to end up among the major players, Coors would have to intensify its drive for growth. The company knew that if it was going to sell its product on a national scale, it could no longer be indifferent to minority markets.

The situation came to a head in 1984 when the chairman of the Coors board of directors, while addressing a meeting of minority business owners, uttered remarks that many in his audience found to be insulting to Blacks.[9] The resulting outpouring of anger from many minority groups so embarrassed the company that its leaders became more amenable to the idea of negotiating minority grievances so that they might put the problem behind them.

While Coors expressed willingness to resume negotiations with Hispanic groups, it now wanted discussions to be national in scope. CRS helped to play a role in the formation of a coalition of national Hispanic organizations to negotiate on behalf of the Hispanic community. Parallel negotiations were also initiated between Coors and Black organizations. Both Coors and the Hispanics favored using CRS as a mediator. Black leaders, having previous experience in negotiating "fair share" agreements with business organizations, saw no need for third-party assistance.

Leo Cardenas, director of CRS's Rocky Mountain regional office in Denver, was cautious on personal grounds as he sought to assist the Coors/Hispanic arrangements. A former newspaperman and author, he had been active in civil rights circles ever since, as a college student, he had helped to organize the first campus chapter of LULAC (League of United Latin American Citizens) at the University of Texas at Austin. He was a former national vice president of LULAC, and though that organization had opted to stand apart from the Coors negotiations, he was nevertheless well known to the Hispanic leaders who would be meeting with Coors. Cardenas asked himself whether his role as a third-party neutral would be compromised. CRS later learned that, although some among the Coors leadership questioned Cardenas's familiarity with the Hispanics, he was also well known and respected by Coors's own Hispanic advisers. Moreover, CRS's credibility had already been established among the Coors people as a result of the aborted local negotiations a few years earlier. While the parties raised no question about his neutrality, Cardenas nevertheless assigned Silke Hansen, his senior staff mediator, to preside over the negotiations.[10]

The progress of the mediation was impeded by the complexities of some of the issues, and because Coors felt a need for the agreement with the Hispanic representatives to be in the same ballpark as its settlement with the Black negotiators. On the other hand, negotiations were aided by a strong desire on the part of both sides to arrive at an agreement. In addition, the major players on both sides—those who would have to sign off on any settlement—personally participated in the give-and-take of almost all sessions. Peter Coors headed the company team. The leading figure among the Hispanic negotiators was Raul Yzaguirre, head of the National Council of La Raza, a major Hispanic umbrella group.[11]

The critical issues centered on equal employment opportunities at Coors and equal opportunities for economic participation, as well as the company's level of community support. The stakes were high for both sides. Coors knew that the bottom line of a settlement would involve the redirection of hundreds of millions of dollars of their community and economic investment. But it would also lead to expanded access to major markets. The Hispanic representatives knew that they were entrusted with two trump cards. One was their likely ability to bring an end to the still-lingering Hispanic boycott of Coors; the other was the influence they could exert on the buying habits of America's Hispanic population. They did not want to bargain away these cards for a pittance. Awareness of the magnitude of the stakes brought the negotiations to an impasse on several occasions. But it also made it easier for CRS to help the parties draw back from the brink.

The signed agreement was a hard-nosed, quid-pro-quo business arrangement, based on the principles of fairness and self-interest—as made clear by the first paragraph: "This partnership is based on achieving equity and parity for the Hispanic community within Adolph Coors Company. Equity and parity are defined operationally as returning a share of company resources back to the Hispanic community in direct proportion to the percentage of business that Coors enjoys from that community."[12]

The final settlement called for, among other provisions, the hiring of Hispanics in all job categories, at a rate of no less than 12 percent for the next five years. An affirmative action plan would require fair promotions, including opening of the executive ranks. The company also agreed to make outright contributions of no less than $500,000 per year to the Hispanic community, of which at least one-third would be earmarked for education. The greater amount of the settlement was to be spent in rechanneling Coors's resources to create new distributorships among Hispanic entrepreneurs. Significant funds would also be directed to Hispanic banks to assist in community revitalization projects. Similarly, a fair share of Coors business would be channeled to Hispanic lawyers, as well as to media, insurance, and advertising services. To make sure that the agreement would be lived up to, an annual audit would be made by an independent Hispanic auditor, engaged by the company with the approval of the coalition.[13]

From an economic point of view, it appeared to be a win/win agreement. Since the size of the total settlement was to be based on the proportion of sales in Hispanic neighborhoods, the Hispanics saw it as an overdue equitable return to the community. For Coors, it promised increased sales, achieved largely through redistribution of the cost of doing business.

The CRS mediators maintained informal contact with members of the committee that audited the contract. At the end of the first five years, both sides indicated satisfaction. While the increase in the number of Hispanic distributorships had not been as rapid as hoped, Coors nevertheless appeared to be leading the industry in that regard.

Successive five-year agreements had been renewed for decades. The coalition of national Hispanic organizations that CRS helped bring together to negotiate with Coors converted itself to a permanent national organization known as the Hispanic Association on Corporate Responsibility. It seeks to stimulate economic development opportunities for Hispanics and continues to work out partnership agreements, similar to that with Coors, with other major national employers.

MEASURING THE COSTS VERSUS THE BENEFITS
OF COURT-REFERRED MEDIATION

The apparent success of CRS mediation—and especially of those cases referred by the courts—raised serious questions for CRS's management in terms of deployment of resources. Almost all referrals were mediated to the satisfaction of the parties and the court, and with significant cost savings compared to litigation. Moreover, the social benefit of the settlements, in terms of reduced racial friction, often exceeded the scope of the original issues. However, the number of court requests was very few. Most judges had never heard of CRS.

To test whether or not CRS should "market" its services to judges, an experimental program was launched in 1979. With the cooperation of the senior judge of the Seventh Judicial Circuit, arrangement was made to acquaint the judges of the circuit with the service available through CRS's Midwest regional office.

Within a year, twelve judges had referred nineteen cases.[14] An evaluation of the pilot project answered critical questions: if judges knew about the service, they would use it; cases referred by the court were consistent with CRS's congressional mandate; most cases could be mediated successfully; CRS would be able to refuse a referral without fear of offending the judge. The program also got high marks for consistently achieving settlement at a much lower cost and often with a much better result than would have been possible through litigation. The pilot program also showed CRS that cases not only were consistent with the agency's own criteria for case acceptance but also often addressed critical problems that would otherwise have been beyond its reach.[15]

The downside of the program was the increased cost to CRS and the greater number of staff hours required. CRS's repeated requests for more mediators met with little success. Nevertheless, CRS extended the program of outreach to the federal judiciary to all regions, leaving to regional directors the hard choices of case selection. Several years of tight budgets had reduced the number of court-referred mediation cases to no more than a handful a year.[16]

NOTE FOR NEW EDITION

Currently CRS still handles an occasional court-referred mediation. However, given the advancement of court-based mediation programs and the increase in lawyers and judges who serve as mediators, for the most part CRS no longer fulfills the role of mediator for the primary objective of avoidance of litigation. CRS will still occasionally have a court-mandated role in police department consent decrees for facilitating community engagement or play a special master role in litigation to gather community input. But while CRS once served a pioneering role in court-based mediation, that role has largely been taken over by others. CRS conciliators continue to play a mediation role within community conflicts.

NOTES

1. Robert Greenwald, interview with Bertram Levine.

2. For a description of this case and the one discussed following, as well as a comprehensive delineation of the CRS approach to mediation, see Greenwald, "CRS: Dispute Resolution through Mediation."

3. U.S. Department of Justice, Community Relations Service, Annual Report, 1972, 26–27.

4. Judge Jack M. Gordon to Robert F. Greenwald, August 29, 1974.

5. *Frazier v. Donelson*, U.S. District Court, E. D. Louisiana, August 23, 1974.

6. Judge Hubert I. Will to Attorney General Benjamin R. Civiletti, January 14, 1980.

7. *Chicago Defender*, March 15, 1980.

8. *Atlanta Constitution*, November 6, 1979.

9. *New York Times*, November 16, 1984.

10. Leo Cardenas, interview with Bertram Levine.

11. Silke Hansen, interview with Bertram Levine.

12. "National Agreement between Adolph Coors Company and a Coalition of Hispanic Organizations," signed October 29, 1984.

13. U.S. Department of Justice, Community Relations Service, Annual Report, 1984, 15.

14. U.S. Department of Justice, Community Relations Service, Annual Report, 1980, 8.

15. U.S. Department of Justice, Community Relations Service, "Evaluation of the Pilot Project on Court-Referred Mediation."

16. Jonathan Chace, interview with Bertram Levine.

NINE

Not All Black and White

Varieties of Civil Rights Conflict

THE RIVERS OF Idaho, which rise at the Continental Divide, were first seen by white people in 1805, when the men of the Lewis and Clark expedition were welcomed to share the bounty of the mighty Nez Percé tribe, whose ancestors had fished those waters since time out of memory. The Nez Percé befriended and guided President Jefferson's Corps of Discovery through one of the most perilous parts of its journey. Seventy years later, the United States cavalry drove the tribe from its homeland and, after a relentless and bloody pursuit, finally defeated the celebrated Chief Joseph and confined the remnant of the tribe on a reservation along the Rapid River.

It was on the banks of the Rapid River, in 1979, during the first week of the salmon run, that CRS mediator Robert Hughes stepped between opposing groups of men and weapons and called out, "You don't want to do this. There's gotta be another way." The law enforcement officials on one side and the Nez Percé on the other took a deep breath, eased back on the revved-up rage and fear, and let the adrenaline rush subside. Things had gotten out of hand. Both sides wanted a way out.[1]

DIFFERENT DRUMMERS

In 1964 the civil rights revolution was defined by the massive efforts being made to overcome the legacy of slavery. When Congress created CRS to help reduce the social anguish and violence that were likely to accompany the changeover, the only minority group it had in mind was Blacks. But the actual law that set CRS in motion made no distinction among races or ethnic minorities; it described the target as community conflict affecting the rights of all racial and ethnic groups.

· Given the way CRS handled many types of cases, it did not make much difference which minority group was involved. The issues were similar, as were the techniques for helping a community find

225

constructive outcomes. But some issues were unique to Asian Americans, or Hispanics, or Native Americans. While each group suffered and fought against unfair denial of equal justice, education, and economic opportunity, the circumstances often varied—especially with respect to Native Americans. The confrontation on the Rapid River that engaged the efforts of Bob Hughes opens a window on this type of case.

INDIAN TREATY RIGHTS: THE MEANING OF THE NEZ PERCÉ

The confrontation in Idaho between the Nez Percé and state fish and game agents had roots in long-running antagonisms about who could fish where and when. The Idaho Fish and Game Commission was authorized by state law to control all fishing. But for the past decade, a number of decisions in federal courts throughout the Northwest had supported the Indians' claims that their treaty rights gave them authority to control fishing on their reservations. The Supreme Court affirmed this, with the qualification that conservation needs had priority over treaty rights. Competition between white sports fishermen and Indians, fueled at times by a limited supply of salmon, was a source of continuing resentment. Game wardens struggled to keep both groups within the bounds of state law.

Early in May, at the start of the salmon run, the state Fish and Game Commission had ordered a conservation closure on salmon fishing in the river. The Indians, who used the fish not only for subsistence but also for religious ceremonies, were not happy with the ban. The Nez Percé Fisherman's Club, composed of many younger members of the tribe, decided to vindicate tradition and treaty rights by conducting a "fish-in" in defiance of the state's edict. Their target would be the state fish hatchery seventy miles south of the reservation. This was where the salmon run was interrupted until the hatchery had obtained its minimum count. Then, to the extent that the run exceeded conservation needs, fish were released in stages to the upper waters, where the Indians satisfied their ceremonial requirements before permitting subsistence fishing. The Indians did not trust the hatchery count, which provided the basis for the amount of fish released into their waters.

On learning that trouble was brewing, Hughes had flown from CRS's regional headquarters in Seattle to Lewiston, Idaho, and had driven to the Nez Percé reservation some hundred miles away. There the tribal chairman had informed him that a convoy of about thirty young men had left a half-hour earlier to drive to the hatchery some seventy miles south. Hughes followed.

For the first day or two it was cat-and-mouse: Indians surveying the river and testing the water; fish and game agents with binoculars on the cliffs above the banks, keeping the scene under surveillance; and other Indians higher on the cliffside, surveying the agents. When the law enforcement contingent was reinforced by the state police, more Indians came down from the reservation to bolster the Nez Percé.

The Indians had set up a camp of eight large tepees along the river bottom. The agents were bivouacked in trailers in another area along the bank. The situation became more delicate when the Department of Fisheries agents began to conduct sweeps through the Nez Percé campsite searching for fish. The incensed Indians ambushed one of the sweeps, descending on the agents with whoops and invectives and brandishing their ever-present ceremonial war clubs. The agents closed ranks and withdrew up the cliffside path as fast as their dignity would permit, to the area where the vehicles of both sides were parked and where the state police were waiting. Indians and agents raced to their respective vehicles to get their weapons. That was when Bob Hughes made his offer of a better way.

In the tense silence that followed, Hughes arranged for each side to designate three representatives who would meet with him to work out some arrangement to avoid bloodshed. He spent the rest of the day shuttling back and forth between the camps, trying to hold the temporary accord together until he got the rival delegations to agree to meet in his motel room in the town of Riggins, about six miles away. It took until nearly midnight to work out an informal understanding that, while permitting the confrontation to go forward, established safeguards to avoid violence. The Nez Percé agreed to allow the agents to come through the camp, but only with advance notice that would be delivered through Hughes. The agents would be accompanied by Indians, and they would not enter any of the tents. As a step toward a long-range solution, when the salmon were transferred from the trap to the hatchery for counting, the Indians would be allowed to count the salmon jointly with the hatchery personnel, so as to establish the credibility of the count.

The peaceful end of the 1979 standoff on the Rapid River marked the start of a new case for Hughes. To reduce the large number of annual conflicts involving hunting and fishing rights, it would be necessary for all concerned parties throughout the state to work together to plan and enforce preventive strategies.

Working with the governor's office, Hughes set up a meeting between the Nez Percé tribal chairman and the director of the State Fish and Game Commission. This led to the development of an improved formula for tribal harvesting of salmon. CRS also worked with local law enforcement authorities to encourage Indian and white fishermen throughout the state to respect each other's rights. Still, when the next salmon season opened, the situation was touch-and-go and required careful monitoring. Hughes returned for the next two years to survey the scene and conciliate problems.

The Rapid River was typical of hunting and fishing locales throughout the Northwest, as well as in other parts of the country, where the interests and practices of Indians collided with those of white sportsmen and commercial fishers. In other walks of life as well, questions of law and jurisdiction governing white and Indian relationships, often strained, had grown murkier as a result of court decisions. The CRS Northwest regional office, in responding to many such cases over a four-state area, had learned that lack of clarity about the law compounded the conflict.

In 1980 CRS, under Regional Director Robert Lamb, took the lead in recommending, and then cosponsoring, a three-state Institute on Indian Law and Jurisdiction for lawyers and law enforcement personnel from Washington, Oregon, and Idaho.[2] Supported by the three governors, the institute focused on issues of hunting and fishing rights on and off the reservation. It also delved into other problems where the confusion of law was adding fuel to the racial fires CRS was trying to put out. These included criminal justice jurisdiction over Indians and whites and cross-deputization of law enforcement officials on and off Indian reservations, the authority and functioning of tribal courts, and methods of conflict resolution.

The hunting and fishing cases showed CRS that its mandate to help resolve racial conflict could not be limited to civil rights issues alone. If the legacy of slavery had written the CRS agenda with respect to conflicts involving African Americans, the legacy of Indian treaties defined much of the CRS challenge with respect to conflicts involving Native Americans.

Where Blacks struggled for integration and the right to be included in the mainstream of American society, many—but not all—Indians were more concerned with distinctiveness. They saw the well-being of their people as being tied up with land and rights that they felt had been illegally taken away by the government, and for which they wanted restitution. For more than a century they had been fighting a rearguard action to preserve or reclaim their land, their culture, and their source of livelihood from an expansive American society in pursuit of its manifest destiny. Only Indians had their rights to property and their status under law determined by treaties and special acts of Congress. Only Indians had a special trust relationship with the United States, under which a federal agency had authority and responsibility over the governance of their land and resources, and presumably for their well-being. But Indian well-being had been elusive. Poverty and the social disorder it breeds had been the consequence for both those who had remained on the reservations and the many who had been driven from the reservations to the squalor of the cities. Many of the Indians' quarrels with their white neighbors and with local, state, and federal governments had to do with preserving and reclaiming rights and property and a way of life that many believed had been guaranteed by the U.S. government.

They had battled for more than a hundred and fifty years in the courts, often losing, sometimes winning, and when winning seeing victories eviscerated over time by Congress and by unfair manipulation in the administration of the law. Indian historians record duplicities of the U.S. government with respect to law and policy affecting Indians dating back at least to 1832. In the case of *Worcester v. Georgia* the Supreme Court, in a ruling handed down by Chief Justice John Marshall, determined that the laws of Georgia were null and void on Cherokee lands because of the Indians' treaty with the United States. President Andrew Jackson, refusing to act on that decision, said, "John Marshall has made his decision, let him enforce it." He then forced the Cherokees and other tribes to accept new treaties, sending them to Oklahoma. Since then Indians had been forced to accept almost four hundred treaties or agreements by which they surrendered ancestral homelands in exchange for other lands and the guarantee of rights to safeguard their way of life. For a period of a hundred and fifty years Indians saw their land holdings and treaty rights winnowed away by an unrelenting series of acts of

Congress, court battles, and federal administrative decisions. That pattern of giving with one hand and taking with the other, of expropriating by force and false pledges, of negotiating with mental reservations, of consuming the loaf a slice at a time, of the government flouting its own laws, continued in various forms down to modern times.

Many Indian leaders and organizations struggled to improve the lot of Native Americans by playing the hand they had been dealt. Advocacy groups struggled in the courts and legislatures to reverse old wrongs or to gain compensation. But to many Indians nothing seemed to halt the long descent by which the once proud possessors of the continent had evolved to be among the poorest of its poor. And so, one hundred and fifty years after *Worcester*, thousands upon thousands of American Indians, poorly educated but well-schooled about these events by oral history, were ready to be revitalized by the idea that treaty rights might yet be regained.

Reflecting on the emotional underpinnings of Indian activism in the last half of the twentieth century, Indian historian Vine Deloria Jr. wrote: "The Modern Indian movement for national recognition thus had its roots in the tireless resistance of countless Indians who have refused to melt into the homogeneity of American life and accept American citizenship. The idea that Indian problems are some exotic form of domestic disturbance will simply not hold water in view of the persistent attitude of Indians that they have superior rights to national existence which the United States must respect."[3]

INDIAN ACTIVISM AND THE TRAIL OF BROKEN TREATIES

In 1964 a group of Sioux living in the San Francisco Bay area, citing provisions of the 1868 Fort Laramie treaty between the United States and the Sioux tribes, took over Alcatraz Island, the site of an abandoned federal prison. Ousted by U.S. marshals the next day, the Indians brought suit in federal court, laying claim to the property. The suit was dismissed, but the takeover drew nationwide attention to the concept of illegally compromised Indian treaty rights. Edward Lazarus indicates that the display of bravado at Alcatraz sent an inspiring signal to Native Americans everywhere that militant assertion of historic rights might restore to the Indian people the vaunted pride and dignity that had been eroded by decades of second-class social and economic status. A spate of Indian takeovers of all kinds of institutions followed for the next decade.[4]

Native American society was in flux. Under the Indian Reorganization Act of 1934, ostensibly designed to bring greater self-government to the reservations, the governance of the tribes was conferred on democratically elected tribal councils, each headed by an elected tribal chairman. The Bureau of Indian Affairs (BIA) would initially guide the Indians in the details of self-government, and then gradually reduce its role on each reservation to that of a supplier of resources. The speed, effectiveness, and integrity of the changeover had varied from reservation to reservation. At the same time, large numbers of reservation Indians still followed old cultural and spiritual practices, scorning the BIA overlordship. Many traditionalists, railing against inefficiency, corruption, patronage, and injustice, questioned the legitimacy of tribal government and its BIA oversight.

Among younger Indians, advocacy groups were on the increase. Some were focused on legal and legislative remedies. Others, inspired by the physical heroism of Black civil rights activists, chose civil disobedience as the means to call attention to Indian grievances. At the same time, among young, impoverished urban Indians there arose a movement to reclaim their cultural identity by returning to their reservations, where they sought the tutelage of, and made common cause with, the traditional chiefs.

Of the several militant protest organizations that arose from this ferment, the American Indian Movement (AIM) was the most successful, because of the imagination, daring, and success of its symbolic and dramatic protests. AIM first came together in 1968 in Minneapolis, as a group that had been toughened by urban poverty, racism, and, for many, prison experience. Its first and primary focus was on the abuses of the criminal justice system, and it established a reputation for programs that monitored police behavior in Indian neighborhoods. As its activities gained a reputation for reducing arrests and police abusiveness, the group was invited to introduce its approach in other cities.

AIM doctrine coupled resistance to current abuse with demands for strict compliance with treaties of the past century. It took as its gospel the Fort Laramie treaty of 1868, which had ended armed combat between U.S. troops and the Sioux tribes by acknowledging the Indians' right to vast areas of the northern plains. Only after the army permitted and protected white encroachment on the land did the Indians learn that the treaty Congress had ratified was not quite the treaty they thought they had negotiated.

One of AIM's first targets for a "takeover" was Mount Rushmore, the national shrine to four great American presidents located in the heart of the Black Hills of South Dakota. Now administered by the National Park Service, the area had been at the core of the land guaranteed to Indians under the Fort Laramie treaty. AIM sent a caravan of twenty protesters to occupy Mount Rushmore, camping just above the massive heads of the presidents sculpted into the mountainside, in full view of the many tourists below. Park rangers ousted the group after twelve hours, but not before the bold venture had drawn nationwide attention to the grievances the Indians had intended to air. A leading actor in the Mount Rushmore takeover was Russell Means, an Oglala from the Pine Ridge Reservation who had been raised on the West Coast and had first been drawn to the fight for Indian rights as a young man recruited for the Alcatraz takeover of 1964.[5]

The conflict between AIM and the United States government in the early 1970s captured and held the nation's attention and imagination for a year and a half. It was highlighted by the cross-country Indian cavalcade to Washington known as the Trail of Broken Treaties and by the takeover and siege at Wounded Knee. The Community Relations Service, serving behind the scenes in this drama, but directly involved from beginning to end, worked with both sides to help avoid any uncalculated blunder that might have brought on a disastrous outcome neither side wanted.

The starting point for the conflict may have been the violent death of Raymond Yellow Thunder, a Pine Ridge Indian who had been tortured, shamed, and murdered by five whites in Gordon, Nebraska, in early 1972. The developing trial of his assailants took on the appearance of a cover-up, and the accused were charged with no more than second-degree manslaughter and freed on bond. To Indians in the area it appeared to be a familiar scenario, trivializing the killing of Indians by whites. The family asked for AIM's help in getting justice. AIM brought a caravan of a hundred cars with five hundred people to parade through the streets of Gordon. Demonstrations continued for two days and nights while AIM leaders negotiated with the city's representatives. The Indian negotiators extracted pledges for a second autopsy and a vigorous murder prosecution, as well as the resolution of other grievances of local Indian residents. The apparent victory brought a heroes' welcome to AIM on its return to Pine Ridge and national acclaim among Native Americans.[6] AIM responded to other killings of Indians with similar demonstrations. Some resulted in violent confrontations.

AIM helped to stage the Trail of Broken Treaties in collaboration with Indian protest groups from the Northwest and the West Coast. A leading participant in the venture was Hank Adams, an Indian attorney who had led fishing rights demonstrations in the Northwest in the early sixties and who had filed some successful lawsuits regarding Indian treaty rights. The purpose of this cross-country motor caravan was to petition the government for a comprehensive reconsideration of Indian treaties and how they were being administered. A twenty-point document of grievances was to be presented to Congress and to the Nixon White House.[7]

Winding its way through Indian country, recruiting adherents on reservations and in urban centers along its route, the caravan delivered a thousand protesters to the nation's capital, arriving a few days before the 1972 presidential elections. CRS's John Terronez accompanied the caravan to Washington, filling the same role that CRS had taken when escorting the Poor People's Campaign to Resurrection City on the Washington Mall a few years earlier. He visited police chiefs and civic leaders a day in advance of the caravan to advise them of the peaceful intentions of the Indians and the wisdom of assuring their uneventful passage.

Faulty planning and poor coordination with BIA resulted in inadequate housing arrangements in Washington and a consequent unplanned takeover of BIA's headquarters by the demonstrators. During the course of the six-day occupation, discipline broke down, leading to appreciable damage to the building and its contents, as well as the removal of some BIA files. CRS conciliators at the scene provided liaison with the authorities and counseled restraint on the part of the outraged BIA Police and District of Columbia Police ringing the building.

It was the White House itself that resolved the problem. Seeking a rapid and nonviolent termination of the incident, White House negotiators offered three concessions to the Indians. They agreed to consider the twenty-point document on treaty revision;[8] they permitted the occupants to vacate the building without prosecution; and they provided $64,000 to expedite the Indians' return to their homes. A key figure in working out the nonviolent outcome was Leonard Garment, counsel to President Nixon, who was the point man of the administration's efforts to conduct an enlightened approach to Indian affairs.

In January, AIM was called on to protest another Indian murder, this one in Custer, South Dakota. A protest caravan was mounted to insist on justice in the trial of the killers of Wesley Bad Heart Bull. Violence between the caravan Indians and reinforced police forces mounted to riot proportions, ending with widespread damage and twenty-seven protesters jailed.

Other confrontations with authorities occurred in Scottsbluff, Nebraska, and Rapid City, South Dakota. In the wake of the takeover of the BIA building in Washington and AIM's several subsequent standoffs with police, Dick Wilson, the tribal chairman at Pine Ridge, indicated that AIM was not welcome on the reservation and that Russell Means would be barred from all public meetings. The tribal court also issued a warrant for the arrest of AIM leader Dennis Banks. Fear that AIM might attempt to take over the BIA building at Pine Ridge led to re-inforcement of the reservation's BIA Police unit with a detachment of eighty U.S. marshals.

In mid-February, as tensions rose, CRS dispatched three conciliators to Pine Ridge, where their first job was to try to sort out the issues and the players. They immediately found themselves in a cauldron of fear and anger. Established rivalries among the Indian residents had grown more bitter since the election of Dick Wilson as tribal chairman within the previous year. Supporting him were those whose lives were centered around the administration of the reservation, those on the tribal pay-roll, and those most strongly linked to the new federal benefit programs resulting from the War on Poverty. This number also included those employed by the Bureau of Indian Affairs, whose support services but-tressed the tribal operations.

The opposition group included most of the full-blooded Indians, who were influenced by the traditional headmen and spiritual leaders who envisioned a reassertion of treaty rights to foster the restoration of a more Indian way of life. They accused Wilson of corruption, nep-otism, a patronage-laden political tyranny, misuse of the tribal police, and creation of "goon squads" to intimidate his opponents. The op-position, including some members of the tribal council, had organized the Oglala Sioux Civil Rights Organization (OSCRO) in an effort to oust the Wilson forces. An attempt to impeach Wilson had failed, and a second effort was being mounted.

The marshals and the BIA Police saw AIM as an outlaw band that had occupied and trashed the BIA headquarters and had a record of engaging in hand-to-hand battle with local and state law enforcement agencies. They were fully expecting and prepared for the possibility of violent confrontation. The BIA building had been reinforced with bunkers, and machine guns were emplaced on the roof. When CRS conciliator Efrain Martinez consulted with an official of the marshals as to how they saw their role, he said they were there to protect federal property, including the BIA building. When Martinez asked if they planned to intervene if AIM leaders resisted the rumored intention of tribal police to arrest some of them on the basis of an expired court order, the officer replied, "If war is to start, let it start here."[9]

With the failure of a second impeachment effort on February 23, OSCRO and the tribal elders began a series of public meetings to enlist community support. They asked AIM to join with them. The meetings, held in the nearby settlement of Calico, were sometimes fired upon by parties unknown. OSCRO invited CRS to attend the meetings, in the hope that the presence of Department of Justice officials might offer some protection.

In search of a way to moderate or avert the gathering storm, CRS made arrangements for a meeting at which AIM and OSCRO leaders could discuss their problems with the leaders of the marshals. The meeting was to take place on the evening of February 26. The Indians attended, but the marshals did not appear.

At a community meeting on the evening of February 27, the leaders declared that the meeting hall was too small for the crowd and transferred the location to a larger hall in the village of Porcupine, about twenty miles away. En route to Porcupine, a caravan with about fifty cars and two hundred and fifty AIM and OSCRO participants stopped instead at Wounded Knee. They took possession of the hamlet, occupying the trading post and Catholic church and preparing to defend the village. The Catholic priest and the Gildersleeve family, who owned the trading post, were taken hostage but later told that they could leave. They opted to stay in the village.[10]

The traditional tribal leaders, who had asked AIM to support their efforts by some dramatic gesture, had also suggested Wounded Knee as the target. "In directing AIM to Wounded Knee . . . OSCRO and the traditionals had selected the most symbolically rich location in Indian America. There, in 1890, Custer's onetime outfit, the 7th Cavalry, had closed the Indian Wars in a burst of runaway savagery. There, 300 Sioux men, women and children lie buried in a mass grave, marking the spot—indelible in Sioux memory."[11]

CRS conciliators John Terronez and Efrain Martinez, who did not arrive at Wounded Knee until after midnight, found most of its new occupants in the Catholic church. AIM leaders Russell Means and Dennis Banks were preparing a statement of demands, which they asked CRS to deliver to the government. The document, drawn largely from AIM's agenda for the aborted meeting with the marshals the night before, focused equally on the need for changes in tribal government at Pine Ridge and on reconsideration of the processes by which the federal government made treaties with the Indians.

As the CRS team members were leaving, they were warned that AIM warriors were posted in the surrounding hills with orders to shoot at anything that moved. They were given headlight signals to use to guarantee them safe passage. (They later would receive other headlight signals from the U.S. marshals to use for nighttime approaches to the government's positions.)

At the BIA building in Pine Ridge, Terronez and Martinez passed the AIM document to Joseph Trimbach, the FBI's special agent in charge. He told them to wait in the office and then posted an armed guard at the door. Finding themselves under virtual arrest despite the Department of Justice credentials in their pockets, the CRS men phoned Martin Walsh, the headquarters coordinator of CRS's conflict resolution activities, reaching him at his home in Washington, D.C., at 4:00 a.m. Walsh spent the next few hours trying to reach the U.S. attorney whose jurisdiction covered Wounded Knee, to explain the CRS mission and the assignment of its conciliators to the heart of the conflict.[12] When Trimbach appeared in the morning to release Terronez and Martinez, he instructed them not to return to Wounded Knee. They indicated that they worked for the same Justice Department he did, and short of a change in orders from Washington, their duties required them to return without delay. CRS indeed did return to Wounded Knee that day, and for the seventy days thereafter.

Within a day the reservation became an armed camp. Reinforcements were rushed to the three federal law enforcement agencies—the U.S. marshals, the FBI, and the BIA Police. Weapons and supplies poured in from army sources. Armored personnel carriers were used to barricade the three roads leading to Wounded Knee. Wayne Colburn, the chief of the U.S. Marshals Service, flew in from Washington to personally take command of tactical operations. Ralph Erickson, a special assistant to the attorney general, had flown in to be responsible for negotiations.

The AIM forces had sacked the trading post at Wounded Knee for shotguns and hunting rifles to enlarge their arsenal. They used a burned-out pickup truck to set up their roadblock and refused access to all federal agencies except CRS. The visitors whom they approved had to be escorted in and out by CRS. All roadblocks were reinforced with bunkers. Nighttime was punctuated by undefined firefights, and random gunshots were heard during the day. A parked FBI car was struck.

In the first two days the CRS team, now grown to seven, set up several meetings between government and AIM representatives that made no progress toward settlement, although they did achieve tentative agreement as to the rules of engagement. The Indians held generally to their previously stated positions demanding changes in tribal government and consideration of treaty reform at the highest levels. The government representatives refused to negotiate any matters of substance until weapons were surrendered and the town evacuated. They did, however, agree to help AIM make contact with its lawyers. In exchange for the government's agreement not to move its forces any closer to Wounded Knee than five miles, the Indians would not fire any more shots. Ralph Erickson told a press conference, "We are not optimistic at the progress today."

What followed was two months of a war that was not a war and negotiation about the procedures for negotiation. The government announced that its forces were instructed not to fire except to defend themselves and the property they were protecting. Indians repeatedly declared that they only fired when fired upon. Nevertheless, both sides expended tens of thousands of rounds of ammunition before the close of hostilities. Two Indians were killed, a U.S. marshal was paralyzed, and a dozen other men were wounded. Fear and anger and mistrust were everywhere. CRS emissaries, shuttling back and forth between the two armed camps, often found themselves looking into the muzzles of loaded rifles.

It was apparent that the government never intended for its siege to be airtight. Its armed checkpoints across the roads into Wounded Knee were mostly for purposes of controlling access rather than for barring all entry. Contraband such as arms and ammunition would of course be confiscated. The noose would be tightened or loosened according to circumstances. While importation of food and other necessities was limited, government negotiators never threatened to starve the occupants out—although in times of greatest trouble they allowed the media to infer such a possibility. Food and medical supplies brought in by the National Council of Churches were first inspected by the marshals, then escorted in by CRS. Members of the press could come and go, except when they were banned by federal agents. CRS was allowed to bring in certain supplies from the BIA hospital, such as lye for the latrines.[13] The perimeter of the occupied area was quite porous. Overland routes through hills, woods, and prairie, though difficult, were available to Indians who backpacked food and supplies, to venturesome media folk, and to occupants under indictment who chose to come and go that way rather than risk arrest at the roadblocks.

The federal conciliators had to take on a new role, helping both sides to guard against an unplanned escalation of hostilities. Martin Walsh felt that for more than two months at Wounded Knee the possibility of a bloodbath was never far away. As one of the rotating operations chiefs of the CRS detachment at Wounded Knee in the early phase of the occupation, he had been there when a federal law enforcement officer was wounded in an all-night firefight in which thousands of rounds had been fired. At the briefing of federal forces the next morning, the prevailing sentiment among law enforcement personnel was that the standoff had been permitted to go far enough. It was time for an all-out assault. Walsh argued for delay so that a new cease-fire might be negotiated. He was given the go-ahead to try.

Flying a white flag on his rental car, Walsh with conciliators Hector Berioz and Pasqual Marquez drove into Wounded Knee while it was still taking intermittent fire. Getting out of the car, Walsh stood to his full six-foot-six to survey the scene. He was promptly dragged down behind the car by his teammates just seconds before a shot struck the wall behind him. The angle of fire made it clear that the shot had not come from government lines. Nor had it come from within Wounded Knee. Further evidence uncovered during the day by both sides raised strong suspicions that the firefight had been triggered by unidentified troublemakers in the hills. Both AIM and the Feds came to believe that at least some of the nighttime firefights had been deliberately provoked by shots from vigilante sources.[14]

The dangerous game between AIM and the federal forces was made more volatile by the presence of some provocative wildcards. Tribal Chairman Dick Wilson was suspected by some of seeking total warfare. At one time Wilson threatened that he had a force of nine hundred available to assault the AIM position if the government did not do it. He was supported by white ranchers and other residents who made their living on the reservation. The ranchers had their own grievances with AIM, which, in the past, had advocated resistance to outside exploitation of reservation resources.

A cease-fire was ultimately worked out. The Feds withdrew their roadblocks to a distance five miles from Wounded Knee, and the Indians agreed not to fire unless fired upon. Walsh and Dick Salem, who had come in to relieve him as operations chief, decided it was important to maintain a CRS peacekeeping presence in the hamlet twenty-four hours a day to try to investigate outbreaks as soon as they occurred. Salem and Burt Greenspan, standing the first overnight watch in the compound, found themselves warmly welcomed by AIM leaders, who felt that a government assault was less to be feared with two federal representatives in their midst.[15] From then until the end of the siege, CRS provided round-the-clock coverage with twelve-hour shifts by one or more conciliators.

But cease-fires were never for keeps, and peacemaking was an ongoing process. It was not surprising that, as the siege wore on, angry men manning lonely, often freezing outposts, sometimes tired, sometimes fearful, would be quick to fire and slow to ask questions. Nightly firing, at times heavy, sometimes continued for weeks on end. CRS would broker a cease-fire between the parties and then try to monitor the truce. It was sometimes dicey moving back and forth between the rival outposts during a nighttime firefight in order to convey dialogue that, essentially, went like this:

"My guys didn't start it—"

"Well neither did mine—"

"Yes, we'll stop firing if they pull back—"

"Well, okay—"

"Well. Okay."

On one occasion Efrain Martinez was at a government roadblock where marshals were deployed to fire on a large group of armed Indians coming toward them from Wounded Knee. He asked the marshals to hold their fire until he could check it out. He then drove down to the approaching party to learn that it was an AIM honor guard escorting a group of elders of the Iroquois and related tribes for the benefit of television cameras. The New York State Indians had just completed a ceremonial visit to Wounded Knee. Martinez advised them of what lay ahead and suggested that the honor guard bid farewell to the guests before coming into rifle range. He then returned to prepare the marshals to allow the distinguished visitors and their media escort to pass through the roadblock.[16]

As the standoff went on, CRS conciliators adapted to the routine of being stopped at gunpoint at each of the three roadblocks on every trip in or out of the hamlet. About six miles away from Wounded Knee was the checkpoint of the tribal police, an outpost manned by followers of Tribal Chairman Dick Wilson, whom many of his political foes preferred to call Dick Wilson's goons. Five miles out was the federal government checkpoint staffed by men of the U.S. Marshals Service and the FBI, who made no bones about seeing the CRS assignment as being tantamount to consorting with the enemy. Closest to Wounded Knee was the AIM outpost, where the CRS identification credentials always had to be shown. But it was only at the last barrier that the peacemakers felt their presence was welcome.

While the leaders of the government team accepted the CRS conciliators as necessary neutral go-betweens, some of the law enforcement agents on the firing line had mixed feelings. On occasion CRS cars would be stopped at the government roadblock and searched for contraband. Martinez was stopped one day and told by a marshal that he could no longer go into Wounded Knee because the Indians were siphoning gas from cars to make Molotov cocktails. Martinez asked, "How can we settle this? You're out here on this freezing prairie, where you didn't ask to be sent, because the Justice Department told you to be here. The same Justice Department told me to be inside Wounded Knee, so I gotta go. Why don't you send a deputy in with me to guard the car?" The marshal thought for a moment, then replied, "Okay, you can go ahead, but be careful."

CRS had known that AIM was siphoning gas to use in its own cars but thought it to be a useful practice since it helped to make sure that AIM's discipline over its outposted warriors did not suffer from lack of communication and control. For the same reason, CRS also provided batteries for AIM's radios. But the question was soon rendered moot when the tribal police checkpoint refused to pass any CRS vehicle whose gas gauge showed more than one or two gallons. On more than one occasion conciliators had to turn back to drive an extra ten or twenty miles in order to bring the gas gauge down low enough to satisfy Wilson's men.

At one point Wilson ordered CRS off the reservation, until it was made clear to him that the attorney general, not the tribal chairman, determined Department of Justice assignments. His men then denied CRS passage through their roadblock. The CRS absence was immediately taken by AIM's leadership to mean that the government was preparing for an all-out assault, thus destabilizing the cease-fire. CRS then arranged for an armed escort by the U.S. marshals whenever Wilson's people barred its way. On one occasion, Jonathan Chace was at the tribal checkpoint waiting for his escorting marshal, when a car of wannabe AIM supporters blundered onto the scene. They were college students on their way to offer supplies and their services to AIM; they hadn't calculated on roadblocks and armed guards. The guard roughed them up and fired a shotgun into their engine. Chace's escort, who arrived during these proceedings, took stock of the situation. He said to Chace, "This is no place for me to be," and made a rapid departure. Minus his escort, Chace never did get into Wounded Knee that day.[17]

In late April, when it was unclear if a settlement could be reached in the two-month-old conflict, Wilson again demanded that CRS leave the reservation and barred the escorting marshals at gunpoint. The standoff between Wilson's Indians and federal officers did not end until Wayne Colburn, chief of the U.S. Marshals Service, personally led a detachment of deputies armed with M-16 rifles to force the termination of the roadblock.

Fully aware of the deadly circumstances of the siege, AIM nevertheless extracted from it the fullest measure of publicity for its cause. Its leaders also knew that the glare of the limelight was their best defense against an assault. The major news media set up full-scale operations on the scene. Supporters, new and old, rushed to AIM's aid. The National Council of Churches took up collections and provided food and medical supplies. Theatrical celebrities and nationally known civil rights leaders visited the encampment, as did Indians representing more than fifty tribes from around the country. Messages of support came from around the world. Prominent entertainers helped to raise funds. Small planes flew in journalists and supplies.

AIM used pageantry and street theater to underscore the seriousness of its intent. It established a symbolic independent Indian nation to negotiate with the United States as a sovereign entity. It asked the United Nations for membership and support of its human rights claims. When it feared a government assault following a major breakdown in negotiations, it invited the media to a traditional ceremony where warriors donned warpaint as a pledge of death before surrender. It frequently invoked Sioux Chief Crazy Horse's famous war cry of a hundred years before, "Today is a good day to die." AIM's leaders understood that their negotiating position as well as their likelihood of survival lay in the credibility of their readiness to die fighting if necessary, and they reinforced that threat in speech and gesture at all times.

Negotiations about negotiations waxed and waned throughout the standoff. The basic position of the government, from which it never wavered, was that it would not negotiate under threat. But safety required that deals be made about day-to-day relations. CRS was sometimes helpful in brokering the arrangements that permitted discussion to proceed. Early on, the government was uncomfortable about negotiating with AIM. Ed Howden, who had flown in from the CRS San Francisco office right after the takeover, proposed that the traditional chiefs, who were aligned with AIM, take a more prominent role in these conversations. Leonard Crow Dog, who had been designated spiritual leader of the forces occupying Wounded Knee, became a key player at that time.

Two weeks after the takeover, Assistant Attorney General Harlington Wood arrived on the scene, to try to break the negotiations stalemate.[18] AIM leaders insisted that the meeting take place within the village, fearing arrest if they met outside their own lines. Wood, against the advice of law enforcement officials worried about his safety, agreed to meet them inside the hamlet. He was escorted into the compound by CRS's Robert Lamb and the Reverend John P. Adams, who headed the

National Council of Churches' food and medical distribution program at Wounded Knee, and who also tried to use his good offices as a mediating influence.[19]

Wood and the Indian representatives appeared to develop a good-faith relationship. After hearing their complaints in full, he indicated that he would try to develop some negotiable issues. A few days later he returned to Washington for consultation. He came back with a new proposal, which he presented to the Indians, again meeting inside Wounded Knee. They rejected it. The stalemate went on as the essential impasse remained the same. The government would not negotiate on substance until the Indians surrendered. The Indians would not give up their occupation of the village, which was their trump card, without an assurance of meaningful negotiations.

Assistant Attorney General Kent Frizzell replaced Wood as the government's chief negotiator.[20] Finding a neutral location for the peace talks became a stumbling block. It was finally agreed that the Indians would erect a large white ceremonial tepee in what became known as the demilitarized zone. The tepee was located on the top of a rise that was visible to each side's roadblock. On the day of the first meeting, random firing from the hills delayed erection of the tepee until CRS was able to resolve the incident. Dick Salem, who was then the CRS chief of operations, sent Frizzell a message to advise him of the delay and asking him to await Salem's call on walkie-talkie before bringing in the government's delegation. About an hour before arrangements were completed, Frizzell and his party arrived by helicopter, landing about a hundred yards from the site. Salem ran over to explain the situation again and to warn that early arrival might well be interpreted as lack of appropriate ceremonial respect, which could start the discussions on a bad note. The Feds took off, to return following Salem's call.

To get around the sticking point that the government could not negotiate under duress, CRS came up with the formulation of negotiating on two separate tracks, one on security and the other on substance. That way, at least conversations aimed at developing a framework for settlement could go forward, with the timing of its implementation to be worked out later. Under that arrangement a tentative understanding evolved that when the time came for the Indians to surrender they would lay down their arms to CRS, which would then monitor whatever other arrangements were agreed upon to assure their safety.

Within a few days the negotiators worked out what appeared to be a formula for settlement of the siege—the Indians would lay down their arms simultaneously with a meeting at the White House to discuss AIM's proposals. They achieved agreement on the issues that would be discussed and also worked out the conditions for ending the occupation. In order for Russell Means to be a member of the four-man Indian delegation, he would agree to be arrested on charges against him, to be arraigned in federal court in Rapid City, and then to be released on bail. Dennis Banks, remaining in charge at Wounded Knee, would order the end of the occupation when he received a call from Russell Means at the White House.

The Indians arrived in Washington for the April 7 meeting scheduled to take place in the office of Leonard Garment, counsel to the president. The entire arrangement then broke apart over a disagreement as to whether Means would call Banks at the start of the meeting (the government's position) or at the conclusion of the meeting (Means's position).

The difference could not be reconciled. The meeting never took place. At Wounded Knee, it was back to square one—except that the tension had escalated. Two thousand rounds of ammunition were exchanged on a single night.

On April 24, the occupants of Wounded Knee sent a message through CRS that they were prepared to enter into new talks designed to end the takeover. In the negotiations that followed, tribal elders who were supportive of AIM, rather than AIM's acknowledged leaders, acted as spokesmen for the insurgents in working out a new draft agreement. Frank Fool's Crow and Matthew King were the recognized leaders among the elders.

A tentative agreement, which Frizzell worked out with the elders, provided that within two weeks of an evacuation of Wounded Knee, a delegation from the White House would come to the reservation to consult with the elders regarding the grievances that had been presented. Other terms of the agreement provided that the government would undertake "an extensive investigation of the operation and finances of the reservation and would protect all legal rights of individual Indians against unlawful abuses by tribal governing authorities."[21]

The Indians agreed, subject to written confirmation from the White House. A letter to the elders from Leonard Garment, confirming the pledge of a White House delegation, was received by the elders at the home of Frank Fool's Crow on May 6. The letter was immediately taken to Wounded Knee, forty miles away, for final review of the tentative agreement by AIM's leadership. The leaders raised some concerns about the details as to how the surrender would take place and demanded clarification. Leo Cardenas, head of the CRS contingent, immediately phoned the government's chief negotiators, Frizzell and Richard R. Hellstern, deputy assistant attorney general. Catching them at dinner in the nearby town of Rushville, Nebraska, he arranged for a meeting without delay to finalize the agreement.

The leaders of the American Indian Movement then declared that AIM's job at Wounded Knee was finished and they were through with any further negotiations with the government. They asked their lawyer, Ramon Roubideaux, and CRS's Leo Cardenas to work out the final arrangements for closure.

At 7:00 p.m. that evening, at the junction of Route 18 and Big Foot Trail, Hellstern and Frizzell joined Roubideaux and Cardenas in Roubideaux's station wagon, where the terms of surrender were reviewed and clarified. The final agreement was signed later by Hellstern, Frizzell, and Wayne Colburn for the government and eleven of the elders for the Indians.

On the morning of May 8, seventy-one days after the takeover, the marshals and FBI removed all roadblocks. The Indians in Wounded Knee turned over their weapons to the CRS men, who then drove the occupants, a carload at a time, to a U.S. marshals' checkpoint for processing, in the presence of lawyers representing the Indians. Those with charges against them were sent to Rapid City for the agreed-upon speedy bond hearing. None of AIM's principal leaders were present in Wounded Knee for the surrender. Most of the weapons had also been evacuated cross-country in advance.

On May 17, Brad Patterson, adviser to the president on Indian affairs, led a White House delegation to a meeting on the reservation at the home of Frank Fool's Crow. Following the discussion, he promised to return in two weeks with a response. When the response did come, it was in the form of a letter from Leonard Garment saying that "the days of treaty making with American Indians ended in 1871, and that only Congress can rescind or change in any way statutes enacted since 1871."[22]

As leaders of the takeover at Wounded Knee, Dennis Banks and Russell Means were tried on a variety of felony counts. After an eight-month trial in the U.S. District Court in St. Paul, all charges were dismissed by the judge on the grounds of misconduct on the part of the FBI and the federal prosecutors. More than one hundred and fifty other participants at Wounded Knee were brought to trial in several federal courts. In most cases charges were dismissed. The few cases that went to trial resulted in acquittals. Later, Leonard Crow Dog and Carter Camp, as leaders at Wounded Knee, were convicted of being responsible for interfering with the postal inspectors who had entered the hamlet to investigate charges of destruction of post office boxes.[23]

THE TEXAS GULF COAST SHRIMPING WARS

The abundant shrimp in the Gulf of Mexico had been a source of livelihood for generations of Texans whose boats plied the waters adjacent to the Gulf Coast towns where they lived. Ten thousand miles away, generations of Vietnamese residing in the Mekong Delta had made their living in the same way. America's post–Vietnam War program that relocated Vietnamese refugees to American communities where they might thrive included the Texas Gulf Coast. This seemingly logical decision had explosive consequences that posed a new challenge for CRS.

The relocation program started in 1975. By 1976 ten thousand Vietnamese had been resettled in Texas, where their sponsoring agencies believed the familiar climate and opportunities in the fishing industry would help them to make a new start. The numbers grew as the "boat people" who fled Vietnam in later years were brought to America, and as many of those who had been transplanted in other parts of the country sought to reunite with family members in Texas.

Church groups, principally the U.S. Catholic Conference, and other relocation agencies introduced the first of the Vietnamese families to the area. They were greeted with reserved civility by their neighbors, who supplied them with their old boats—available for sale, although some were of doubtful economic viability. But trouble arose as soon as it was noted that the Vietnamese did not fish in the traditional Seadrift, Texas, way, and they were making money with those old boats.

The life of commercial shrimpers in the Gulf of Mexico was growing more difficult even before the arrival of competition from the Vietnamese. The shrimp crop had been diminishing for twenty-five years. In the overfished waters, it now required two hours to fill a net that could have been filled in only a half hour ten years earlier. Heavy rains in the Houston area for the previous two years further had reduced the yield in the Galveston Bay region.

The additional harvest that the newcomers brought to the market sometimes depressed the price to a point that on some days the resident Seadrift shrimpers felt that it didn't pay to fish. But for the recent Vietnamese arrivals there was never a time when it didn't pay to fish. The veteran fishermen were offended by the fact that their profit margin was eclipsed by that of the newcomers. They bitterly attributed the discrepancy to the simplicity of the Vietnamese lifestyle. Many families lived together in tight quarters, dining on the part of their catch that longtime residents threw away as "trash" fish. By scrimping and by buying whatever they could for cash instead of credit, the Vietnamese paid off their boats in record time. They drew on their extended families to finance newer boats.

Some of the veteran shrimpers admitted publicly that they did not want to work as hard as the competition. The Vietnamese boats left their moorings at 3:00 a.m. in order to be in the most fertile waters at the legal starting time, a half-hour before sunup. Efrain Martinez, who covered all of South Texas for CRS from a one-man office in Houston, noted a scene that typified the problem. Surveying a fishing pier around noon, Martinez saw a non-Vietnamese boat come in to unload its cargo. Its skipper had lunch and then proceeded to sort and clean his catch. Then a Vietnamese boat arrived and immediately unloaded, into the arms of the fisherman's waiting family, baskets of shrimp, already cleaned and sorted by size so as to yield the highest price. The Vietnamese boat immediately set out to sea in order to get in one more run before the legal fishing time ended a half-hour after sunset.[24]

Hardest of all for the long-timers to take was the Vietnamese violation of the rules of the road—the matrix of law, regulation, and informal custom that helped to preserve the supply and that patterned conduct so as to respect the rights of all. A basic custom was that a boat that found a fruitful fishing spot had exclusive trawling rights within the immediate area. The Vietnamese custom was just the opposite, encouraging the sharing of good spots. Longtime shrimper shouts and hand signals to wave off the intruders were responded to by smiles and signals of language difficulty. The Vietnamese were also accused of other violations ranging from exceeding legal time limits, to using boats with more than the legal five-ton cargo capacity.

Frustration within the white community, fueled by nativist agitation, lit a slow fuse that hit the powder in the summer of 1979 in Seadrift, Texas, a fishing village near Corpus Christi. A white fisherman was killed in a fight with two Vietnamese brothers. In instant retribution, two Vietnamese boats and one home were firebombed. White extremist groups threatened to drive the immigrants out of town.

Martinez responded to the Seadrift situation without delay. His first priority was to mobilize resources for opening up communications channels. This meant drawing into a concerted effort all groups concerned about the problem, including church and other private assistance agencies; local law enforcement; the Texas Department of Wildlife and Fisheries and the U.S. Coast Guard, which administered federal and state laws and regulations governing fishing; the Governor's Task Force on the Resettlement of Indochinese Refugees; as well as the fishermen of both groups.

The veteran fishermen, particularly the whites, recoiled from Martinez's proposal for the formation of a joint fishermen's committee. He wore down their resistance by persistently pressing them to define their self-interest and then realistically addressing the options by which that self-interest might be served. He finally prevailed with the whites by saying, in some anger, "Look, you didn't bring them here. Neither did I. But they're here. And nothing either of us says or does is going to make them go away. So why don't we try to get them to understand why they've got to give up the Vietnamese rules of the road, and play instead by American rules."[25]

Eventually, he did bring together the Seadrift Fisherman's Committee, which lasted for several years as an arena for airing complaints and resolving some of them.

A local task force of interested support groups also came into being. Eventually a comprehensive program took shape. It included the Seadrift Community Council, which was composed of six local fishermen and four Vietnamese. The task force's main purpose was to serve as a grievance committee and to promote understanding and cooperation among all residents of Seadrift.

Town meetings were held, where community anger could be vented and where authorities would provide answers to the many legitimate questions, as well as refute the misinformation that was circulating about the town. The U.S. Coast Guard and the state fisheries department were encouraged to publish translations of fishing laws and regulations and to offer special classes in Vietnamese. Improved English instruction was initiated in the schools, and special language classes were started for Vietnamese adults. Illustrated brochures in English and Vietnamese were published to acquaint the new residents with American customs.[26]

The Seadrift outbreak alerted the entire Texas coast to potential dangers in other communities, and Martinez worked with the most vulnerable jurisdictions to develop contingency plans and to adapt the Seadrift approach for anticipating and responding to the many interracial tensions that were to plague the Gulf Coast for years to come.

Vietnamese in the small fishing port of Palacios were the next to come under fire. Klan demonstrations and physical intimidation caused the refugees to invite the help of the Southern Poverty Law Center, which was able to get an injunction against harassment by the Klan.

Tensions rose as the refugee population continued to increase, reaching thirty thousand in the Houston area by the end of 1981. Even though some of the Vietnamese, tired of the stress and danger, said they would give up shrimping if they could get a good price for their boats and decent jobs elsewhere, the Vietnamese began to make further inroads into the fishing economy, buying up retail fish stores. It was believed that they would next move into the wholesale shrimp business. White fishermen, facing a declining lifestyle, were beginning to withdraw from the fray.

The situation became so threatening that in 1981 the governor was asked to assign National Guard troops to control interracial violence. The most dangerous arena was Galveston Bay, fifty miles south of Houston. That vast arm of the Gulf of Mexico had long been a site of prolific shrimp beds. One-third of the three-hundred-boat fishing fleet in the bay was Vietnamese.

At a Ku Klux Klan parade in February a mock Vietnamese boat labeled "Viet Cong" had been burned in effigy. Shortly thereafter, two boats were burned at their docks in Seadrift, where the 1979 trouble had taken place. That was followed by three burnings and some false alarms in the Galveston Bay area.

In the twin fishing villages of Seabrook and Kemah, where as many as forty-two Vietnamese boats tied up at a single mooring area in Kemah known as "Hanoi Harbor," Martinez worked unsuccessfully for months to create a joint committee of longtime local and Vietnamese fishermen. The most influential person in the local white fishermen's association was the Grand Dragon of the Knights of the White Camellia. He had predicted that if the Vietnamese were not driven out they would one day control the whole industry. The leader of the Vietnamese community was Colonel Nam Van Nguyen, his title reflecting his former status in the Vietnamese army. Neither leader had any interest in meeting with the other. Martinez finally decided to try to exploit the considerable machismo of both leaders. He proposed an off-the-record one-on-one meeting, while subtly planting the notion that each man doubted the other had the courage to go head-to-head. The meeting finally took place. When the two leaders discovered that they could work with each other to advance their respective interests, the biracial Seabrook/Kemah Fishermen's Coalition came into being.

Other moves were also afoot to relieve the tension. The state legislature considered a bill to declare a two-year moratorium on the issuance of new commercial fishing licenses. Agencies in the Galveston Bay area set up a school for fish processing occupations to equip fishermen and their families with new skills.

The opening of the shrimping season on May 15 was greatly feared for its potential for violence. Three hundred shrimp boats, one hundred of them owned by Vietnamese, dropped their nets in Galveston Bay under the watchful eye of local, state, and federal law enforcement agencies. There were no untoward occurrences that day. Bad weather for the next few days kept all the boats in their harbors. The rest of the season proceeded without further major outbreaks of violence.

After that, the level of discord in the shrimping industry diminished year by year as the prediction of the Grand Dragon that the Vietnamese would one day dominate the business gradually came to fruition.

NOTES

1. Robert Hughes, interview with Bertram Levine.
2. U.S. Department of Justice, Community Relations Service, Annual Report, 1980, 14.
3. Deloria, *Behind the Trail of Broken Treaties*, 20.
4. Lazarus, *Black Hills, White Justice*, 290.
5. Lazarus, *Black Hills, White Justice*, 294.
6. Means and Wolf, *Where White Men Fear to Tread*.

7. Deloria, *Behind the Trail of Broken Treaties*, xi.

8. In January, the White House publicly announced its rejection in toto of the twenty-point petition of the Trail of Broken Treaties Organization.

9. Efrain Martinez, interview with Bertram Levine.

10. Means and Wolf, *Where White Men Fear to Tread*, 267.

11. Lazarus, *Black Hills, White Justice*, 306.

12. Martin Walsh, interview with Bertram Levine.

13. Manuel Salinas, interview with Bertram Levine.

14. Walsh, interview with Levine.

15. Dick Salem, interview with Bertram Levine.

16. Martinez, interview with Levine.

17. Jonathan Chace, interview with Bertram Levine.

18. Wood later served as a U.S. district court judge.

19. Adams, *At the Heart of the Whirlwind*, chap. 11. Reverend Adams served for many years on the staff of the Board of Christian Social Concerns of the United Methodist Church and spearheaded the church's work on conflict resolution. He often played an influential role in the leadership of multidenominational efforts addressed to civil rights. His appearance at the site of many of America's major civil rights conflicts had made him a familiar and trusted figure to CRS conciliators.

20. Frizzell later became solicitor of the Department of the Interior, continuing, in that role, as a principal negotiator at Wounded Knee.

21. *New York Times*, May 7, 1973.

22. Lazarus, *Black Hills, White Justice*, 310.

23. Means and Wolf, *Where White Men Fear to Tread*, 331, 336.

24. Martinez, interview with Levine.

25. Martinez, interview with Levine.

26. U.S. Department of Justice, Community Relations Service, Annual Report, 1980, 14.

TEN

Minorities and the Media

The Conversion of the Image Builders

BEFORE MID-TWENTIETH-CENTURY ACTIONS by the courts and Congress to uproot the barriers to racial justice, white Americans saw their country as if on a split screen. Large, sharp, and bright was the mainstream portrayal of how white people lived. On a small, grainy segment of the screen, of which the viewer was only vaguely aware, was the depiction of racial minorities. Shown mostly as menials, they appeared less educated, less skilled, less well spoken, more violent—clearly inferior. This image was reinforced by the media—the broadcasting, film making, news gathering, and publishing industries that influenced people's vision of what America was and, by inference, how it was supposed to be.

The persistence of this image made it easier for some Americans to fight to keep things the way they were. For other Americans, it made it harder to accept the rightness and inevitability of the changes toward side-by-side equality that the law now required. CRS's mandate to promote change without turmoil caused it to focus special attention on ways of working with the media toward that end.

In the early 1960s, radio and television were practically lily-white, and print media were strictly Jim Crow. Discrimination in the image-building business not only perpetuated invidious racial stereotypes, it also barred minorities from employment and ownership opportunities within a major industry. Since the distorted image of Blacks and the absence of Blacks as journalists helped to reinforce each other, the vision among America's image makers was limited to what could be seen through white eyes.

In its earliest strategic planning CRS recognized that for Americans to understand and accept racial equality, changes within the communications industry were important. Within its first year, CRS initiated a program to encourage early efforts—then barely perceptible within the publishing and broadcasting world—to improve the depth and quality of reporting about minority cultures and to employ minorities as news gatherers and presenters.

CRS began to stake out the ground for a program addressed to the media in 1965. Director LeRoy Collins, as immediate past president of the National Association of Broadcasters, had an insider's credibility with the communications industry. His deputy director, Calvin Kytle (who was to succeed him briefly in the role of acting director), was a journalist and publicist of long standing. Using the platforms offered them by the national associations of media executives, they stimulated the dialogue, then just beginning within the industry, to define the opportunities as well as the obligations of the media, to help America survive the critical period of civil rights transition through which it was passing.

To the media moguls with whom they met, Collins and Kytle held up a mirror to an industry that still perceived only dimly its great opportunity to serve the nation during one of the most critical crises of the century. The more thoughtful in their audience undoubtedly heard, behind their diplomatic language, a bill of particulars that challenged the good newsman to do better.

The nation's leading opinion molders were asked to consider how their failure to depict African Americans as normal human beings reinforced the myth of white superiority, and how the persistence of that myth made peaceful acceptance of new legal standards more difficult.

To the American Society of Newspaper Editors, Collins attributed the level of racial violence of the previous decade to the reluctance of American leaders, including the media, to support compliance with the Supreme Court's 1954 decision on school desegregation: "This condition encouraged the 'rough element' to get rougher in defiance, the devious to resort to ingenious legal maneuvering, opportunists to ride into power on the hot winds of political demagoguery. . . . Thus little or no national effort was made to lead the American people to understand why racial discrimination is unjust and unconstitutional."[1]

Speaking to the editors and publishers of United Press International, Kytle drew attention to the need to report racial news with the same skill and intensity they addressed to other critical issues. He illustrated their failure by pointing to specific departures from good journalism. He cited the practice by many papers of routinely placing civil rights news on the same page as the daily crime roundup; stories about civil rights demonstrations that might report "a list of grievances was presented" without bothering to tell what the specific grievances were; failures to seek out good background stories by independently investigating the validity of alleged grievances; failures to seek the views of minority leaders that might differ with the quoted views of the establishment; reluctance to give appropriate coverage to militant groups because of their inflammatory style rather than to present the substance of their viewpoint.[2]

The bottom line stressed the obvious but suppressed truth that a newspaper cannot expect good reporting from reporters who don't know their beat. Citing the paucity of minority newsmen, CRS asked the media leaders to consider how newsrooms and editorial desks might be enriched by the new insights and access to new news sources that would result from minority recruitment and training programs.

Even as they pressed these exhortations for change at the national level in order to focus the attention of news executives on the critical issues, the CRS leaders understood that far more would be needed to bring about change. Persistent demand by minorities themselves and minority-media cooperation at the local level would be needed to hasten the process. Here, too, CRS had a catalytic role to play.

To head this effort Collins chose Ben Holman, a Black journalist who had already obtained the distinction of being a barrier-breaking "first of his race." He had been the first Black reporter on the *Chicago Daily News* in 1952, when there were no more than five or six Blacks in mainstream journalism throughout the country. Ten years later he was the first Black on-the-air television reporter, with Chicago's CBS affiliate, WBBM-TV. The network later moved him to New York, where he became one of the first Blacks to report the news to a national television network audience.[3]

At CRS, Holman's program was almost blown out of the water before it got started. When the initial draft of a concept paper found its way into the hands of some news-hungry journalists, a cry of concern arose about federal agents planning to exercise undue influence over coverage of the news. Charges of a move to subvert the First Amendment brought agitated inquiries from the White House and Capitol Hill. The teapot tempest was soon resolved, but it put the agency on notice that any effort pertaining to how the news industry did its job would require the delicacy of working in a minefield.

The program that emerged under Holman's leadership, and that endured for many years, ended up as a cooperative effort between media organizations and the minority community, at both the national and the local levels, with CRS being accepted and saluted as the catalyst that brought it into being and nurtured it.

The job was made easier in many communities where the growing tide of civil disorder was engendering friction between police and the press. Anxious and overstressed police departments, concerned about instances of inflammatory reporting, wanted tight control over the news as a means of riot control. The media, citing the people's right to know, wanted full freedom to report when and what they pleased and from where they pleased. CRS offered to help them work out their differences. In city after city, during periods of calm, CRS initiated media-police conferences to develop mutually agreed upon guidelines for the reporting of racial conflict. A third point of view that CRS insisted be present at these talks was that of the minority community. The meetings did more than work out problems between the police and the news organizations. One byproduct was a recognition of the usefulness of these new federal peacemakers. Another was the development of ongoing relationships between minority leaders and the media. These contacts facilitated the convening of many of the formal media-minority conferences that were to follow.

Holman put together a staff of journalists, including Charles Cogen, Willis Selden, and Lawrence Still, who canvassed the nation identifying news organizations and media executives who had already taken the lead in introducing civil rights awareness into their operations. CRS then sought to reinforce networking among these pioneers and to showcase their efforts throughout the industry.

While the landscape that CRS sought to cultivate was almost bare, it was not a total wasteland. Some news organizations had already made initial ventures, as evidenced by Holman's own experience. Willis Selden, who succeeded Holman in running the CRS media program, has noted other early beginnings.[4] The Associated Press Managing Editors (APME) had a Black News Committee, which, in 1970, published a booklet entitled *Help Wanted: More Black Newsmen*. It listed seventeen special programs and twenty scholarship programs for minority students interested in a career in journalism. The American Newspaper Guild, in 1962, had adopted a nondiscrimination clause in its constitution and directed its locals to seek nondiscrimination clauses in collective bargaining agreements. The Newspaper Fund, a foundation supported by Dow Jones and Company, owner of the *Wall Street Journal* and other publications, in 1968 started programs to train minority high school students for careers in journalism. There were other tentative efforts, but the output was microscopic.

To get its own program off the ground, CRS generated minority-media conferences in a score of cities. These brought broadcasting and publishing executives together with minority and civil rights leaders to focus on two problems: how to bring about fuller and fairer reporting of minority life, and how to achieve more employment opportunities for minorities in the news business.

The way it worked out was typical of how CRS, serving as a catalyst, helped to generate a process of change that would otherwise have taken years longer. While minorities were bitterly resentful of their abuse and neglect by the news media, they accepted it as a given, like so much else of inner city life. The energy latent in their resentment had nowhere to go until CRS brought it together with a change-making mixture of other elements. These included: a handful of pacesetting captains of the media industry, knowledge of arcane laws and regulations that could provide leverage toward change, expert consultants eager to enlist in a good cause, and a problem-solving process in which the demanders of change could make their case before those capable of making change.

Having been sensitized to journalists' skittishness about the intrusion of the federal government into their business, CRS was careful to confine its role to that of a catalyst and technical resource. Primary sponsorship of local and national conferences came from media and community institutions. A typical scenario called for CRS conciliators on the local scene to excite interest among media leaders and in the minority community. Then, CRS's media experts would make their experience available to the local planning committee. The sponsors of the first national conference, held in New York in October 1967, included the Columbia University Graduate School of Journalism, the American Jewish Committee, and the American Civil Liberties Union. Attendees, in addition to civil rights and community relations organizations, included executives from the major networks and public television, the two major national news services, New York and Washington, D.C., newspapers, some of the mass-circulation magazines, as well as Black and Hispanic publications.

While originally focused on the relationships of Blacks and the media, these seminars were later enlarged to embrace Hispanic and other minority groups. By 1970 at least twenty-one such events had been conducted in cities across the country. The goal of the local meeting was to create a follow-up program aimed at improved minority employment and improved reporting on minority communities.

A prototype of the CRS-initiated meetings, but organized independently, had taken place in June 1966 in Boston, where basketball great Bill Russell and other Black leaders initiated a series of discussions with some Boston media executives.[5] These meetings ultimately led to the formation in 1968 of the Boston Media-Community Committee. A history of the committee written in August 1968, as recounted by Selden, noted that media executives reported the following progress in minority hiring:

> Channel 4 now has 15 black people (10 in full time, five temporary) as opposed to four in 1967. Channel 5 employs three blacks. Channel 7 has ten full-time, one coming next week, and two summer trainees. . . . Radio reported that eight stations now have 21 black employees compared to a total of five a year ago. . . . The press reported that there are now 110 black employees on four papers, working as columnists, reporters, typesetters, photographers, artists, copy editors and trainees.[6]

Russ Raycroft, a former broadcast executive who worked with the Boston committee, was subsequently used by CRS as a consultant for follow-up programs in other cities. None of these committees, however, lasted as long as the Boston committee, which continued until the 1980s.[7]

The first meeting of the media with a local Hispanic community took place in San Antonio in 1969, following organizational efforts by CRS's first two Mexican American conciliators, Gonzalo Cano and Gilbert Pompa. Subsequent meetings in other cities led a group of Hispanic leaders and journalists to organize a permanent national organization to work for better media coverage of Hispanic life, as well as for recruitment and training of Hispanics for employment in the media. The leader of the effort was Ruben Salazar, an award-winning journalist with the *Los Angeles Times*. With the help of CRS, the group was brought together in June 1970 with the National Urban Coalition's Communications Task Force, a group of the nation's top media leaders. Twenty Hispanics met with a like number of people who were giants in the American communications industry. Some of them, like Katharine Graham of the *Washington Post* and William Randolph Hearst Jr. of Hearst Publications, owned chains of broadcasting outlets as well as major print media.

A direct outgrowth of the meeting was the formation of the National Hispanic Media Coalition, with Ruben Salazar as its chairman. The president of McGraw-Hill Publications offered to provide office space for a headquarters, and financial contributions came from Hearst and other sources.[8]

Two months later, Ruben Salazar, while covering a Chicano demonstration against the Vietnam war, was killed by a tear gas shell fired by a Los Angeles deputy sheriff. Bereft of its leader, the National Hispanic Media Coalition continued to function for more than a year, but its achievement failed to match the high hopes that attended its founding.

CRS's media program took on an additional focus in June 1970 when, at the Denver Hispanic-media conference, a speaker awakened the minority community to the availability of a potent tool: the ability of community groups to challenge the license renewals of radio and television stations. Two of the criteria for license renewal, established by the Federal Communications Commission (FCC), were hidden weapons, just waiting to be seized: a broadcaster seeking license renewal could be called upon to demonstrate a record of fairness in news presentation and a record of community service. Knowledge of these rarely used provisions, when made available to minority groups of growing political sophistication, was to provide strong leverage for negotiation and change.

An outgrowth of the 1970 Denver conference was the formation of the Colorado Committee on Mass Media and the Spanish Surnamed. Denver-based CRS conciliator Manuel Salinas, with the help of Bill Selden, introduced the committee to the Citizens Communication Center in Washington, D.C., a community advocate in matters of license renewal. Two years later the Colorado Committee was ready to initiate challenges to the license renewals of the four major television stations in Denver. In the negotiations that resulted, the media made commitments to hire Hispanics, and each station engaged a Hispanic coordinator to work with a Hispanic advisory committee.[9] Similar negotiations were conducted by Black organizations.

An agreement with more widespread impact, also assisted by the Citizens Communication Center, was negotiated by a group of Hispanic and Black organizations with McGraw-Hill, which was moving to buy five television stations from Time-Life. The upshot of the challenge was an arrangement under which McGraw-Hill agreed to increase minority employment and to work with national and local minority advisory committees on employment and programming.[10] Specific provisions of the May 1972 agreement provided minority employment goals for each station, including the number of Blacks and Hispanics in front of and behind the camera. Provisions about programming specified the number of documentaries to be made each year on aspects of minority life and culture, as well as the number of public affairs programs advocating controversial viewpoints on minority issues. In the early seventies other civil rights and religious groups became active, challenging license renewals before the FCC. Within a few years this movement had opened the doors for minority ownership of broadcast stations.

CRS also teamed up with various professional associations to encourage minority employment and training programs. A notable collaboration was in support of a major effort headed by Ossie Davis Jr. within the National Academy of Television Arts and Sciences.

The CRS media program suffered a sudden demise with the termination of the agency's preventive work by the Nixon administration in 1973. Although the media staff was dismantled, experienced staff members continued to be supportive as appropriate opportunities arose. By the end of the seventies, small but measurable changes were being reported within the communications industry. A 1978 survey found that among professional journalists working on daily newspapers, 4 percent were not white. An article in the *Columbia Journalism Review* by Nick Kotz noted that while "Jim Crow is gone, and the number of lily-white newspapers is declining, . . . there has been progress in integrating the newspaper business. But it has been halting, uneven, and far too modest to celebrate . . . two-thirds of the country's 1,762 dailies still have not hired a single minority news professional."[11]

There was still a long way to go, and progress had been slow, but CRS workers such as Ben Holman and Bill Selden, who had sought to build momentum for change, hoped that their efforts had helped to jump-start such movement as had occurred.

NOTES

1. LeRoy Collins, text of remarks before American Society of Newspaper Editors, Washington, D.C., April 15, 1965.

2. Calvin Kytle, text of remarks before Sixth Annual Conference, United Press International Editors and Publishers, Washington, D.C., October 5, 1965.

3. Ben Holman, interview with Bertram Levine.

4. Selden, "Employment and Retention." Many of the elements of the CRS media program are chronicled in this thesis.

5. Selden, "Employment and Retention," 13.

6. History of the Boston Media-Community Committee, June, 1966–October, 1968, cited in Selden, "Employment and Retention."

7. Selden, "Employment and Retention."

8. Author unknown, paper on "Hispanics and the Media," cites audio tapes by Nick Reyes.

9. Manuel Salinas, interview with Bertram Levine.

10. Francisco J. Lewels Jr., *The Uses of the Media by the Chicano Movement* (New York: Praeger, 1974), cited in Selden, "Employment and Retention."

11. Nick Kotz, "The Minority Struggle for a Place in the Newsroom," cited in Selden, "Employment and Retention."

Figure 1. Lyndon Baines Johnson signs the Civil Rights Act, which created the Community Relations Service, with Martin Luther King, Jr. and others looking on, July 2, 1964. Photograph by Cecil Stoughton. Courtesy of the Lyndon Baines Johnson Presidential Library.

Figure 2. Marchers making the third and final march from Selma to Montgomery, March 21, 1965. From left to right: John Lewis; Andrew Young; LeRoy Collins, the first director of CRS; Martin Luther King, Jr.; Coretta Scott King; and Ralph Abernathy. When Collins ran for the U.S. Senate in 1968, his opponent distributed this photograph, and Collins believed it was responsible for his defeat. Courtesy of the Florida State Archives.

Figure 3. James Laue joined CRS as assistant director of community analysis in 1965 and served as a mediator in the marches from Selma, the Memphis sanitation workers' strike, and housing discrimination in Chicago. Courtesy of George Mason University.

Figure 4. Roger Wilkins introduces his daughter, Amy, to President Johnson after being sworn in as CRS director, February 4, 1966. Left to right: Roger Wilkins, Amy Wilkins, Johnson, and Roy Wilkins, Roger's uncle and NAACP executive director. Bettmann Archive via Getty Images.

Figure 5. Civil rights leaders Ralph Abernathy, Andrew Young, Jesse Jackson, James Laue (kneeling), and others on the Lorraine Motel balcony with the body of Martin Luther King, Jr. following his assassination. Memphis, Tennessee, April 4, 1968. Laue wrote, "His life—and his death—changed my life. He taught me that 'conflict resolution,' a laudable goal on the surface, does not truly occur without struggle refined in love and that justice is not fulfilled without reconciliation." Photograph by Joseph Louw/The LIFE Images Collection via Getty Images/Getty Images.

Figure 6. Richard "Dick" Salem, CRS conciliator and regional director for the Midwest region, mediated the Nazi conflict in Skokie, Illinois, and the American Indian movement takeover at Wounded Knee. Courtesy of Greta Salem.

Figure 7. President Ronald Reagan announcing his intent to nominate Grace Flores-Hughes as the first woman director of CRS, September 1987. Left to right: Vice President George H. W. Bush, President Reagan, U.S. Treasurer Katherine Ortega, Manuel Casanova, Rebecca Runge, Rudy Beserra, and Flores-Hughes. Courtesy of the U.S. Department of Justice.

Figure 8. Ozell Sutton, Southeastern regional director from 1972 to 2003, mediated the Sister Spirit case and led the CRS Church Burning Response Team. Courtesy of Alpha Phi Alpha Inc.

Figure 9. As part of the Church Burning Response Team, Efrain Martinez, center, meets Rev. Charles Stevenson, left, of the Garden of Gethsemane Church on March 19, 1997. Courtesy of the U.S. Department of Justice.

Figure 10. In the mid-1990s, CRS formed a Church Burning Response Team with Martin Walsh as the first national director and Ozell Sutton chairing the task force. First row (left to right): Ernie Stallworth, Patricia Glenn, Sutton, Janet Reno, Rose Ochi, Thomas Battles, George Henderson; second row: CRS intern, Frank Amoroso, Nancy Ferrell, Gwen Whiting, Gus Taylor, Efrain Martinez, Walsh, Art Slater. Courtesy of the U.S. Department of Justice.

Figure 11. Thomas Battles, regional director of the Southeastern region, provided conciliation services in numerous conflicts, including the Elián González case, the 1990s black church burnings, and Sanford, Florida, after the killing of Trayvon Martin. Courtesy of Kappa Alpha Psi Fraternity, Inc.

Figure 12. In 2000, CRS had a headquarters office, ten regional offices, four field offices, and 37 mediators on staff. Courtesy of the U.S. Department of Justice.

Figure 13. Azekah Jennings, a senior conciliator who served at CRS from 2005-2015, providing mediation services at a 2009 march in Memphis, Tennessee. Courtesy of the U.S. Department of Justice.

Figure 14. CRS celebrates its 45th anniversary in the Great Hall at the U.S. Department of Justice, August 25, 2009. Left to right: CRS Legal Counsel George Henderson; CRS Director Sharee Freeman; Attorney General Eric Holder; CRS Director Rose Ochi; CRS Director Roger Wilkins; LeRoy Collins, Jr., son of CRS Director and Governor LeRoy Collins; Hermelinda Pompa, widow of CRS Director Gilbert Pompa; Ms. Lillie Mae Holman, sister of CRS Director Ben Holman; Congressman John Lewis; CRS Director Ondray T. Harris. Courtesy of the U.S. Department of Justice.

Figure 15. President Barack Obama greets Louvon Harris (left) and Betty Byrd Boatner (right), sisters of James Byrd, Jr., and Judy Shepard (center), mother of Matthew Shepard, at a reception following the enactment of the Matthew Shepard and James Byrd, Jr. Hate Crimes Prevention Act, October 28, 2009. Official White House Photo by Pete Souza.

Figure 16. Ron Wakabayashi, regional director for the Western region from 1999 to 2020, provided conciliation services following the killing of Oscar Grant in Oakland, California, and in protests in Phoenix, Arizona, against the signing of SB 1070, the anti-immigration law. Courtesy of the U.S. Department of Justice.

Figure 17. Becky Monroe, CRS Acting Director, appears before Congressional members with Trayvon Martin's parents at a Washington, D.C. forum. Left to Right: Daryl Parks, Benjamin Crump, Sybrina Fulton, Tracy Martin, Becky Monroe. Photograph by Brendan Smialowski. AFP via Getty Images.

Figure 18. On July 14, 2014, the Justice Department honored CRS on its 50th anniversary, as current and former CRS employees gathered in the Great Hall of Justice, Washington, D.C. Courtesy of the U.S. Department of Justice.

Figure 19. Conciliator Linda Ortiz of New York speaking at the 50th anniversary event. The celebration included addresses by Attorney General Eric Holder and others, a roundtable discussion moderated by Charlayne Hunter-Gault, and an interview of civil rights leader and Ambassador Andrew Young. Courtesy of the U.S. Department of Justice.

Figure 20. Eleven days after Michael Brown was shot in Ferguson, Missouri, sparking protests and violence throughout the country, CRS Director Grande Lum facilitated a town hall meeting in St. Louis Community College–Florissant Valley that featured Eric Holder. "I am the attorney general of the United States. But I am also a black man," Holder said. Courtesy of the U.S. Department of Justice.

Figure 21. President Barack Obama speaks with CRS director Grande Lum at his first visit to the Department of Justice, January 17, 2014. Courtesy of the U.S. Department of Justice.

Figure 22. CRS staff at its new Washington, D.C., offices, 2019. First row (left to right): Rita Valenciano, Melody Diego Caprio, Gerri Ratliffe, Antoinette Barksdale, Linda Ortiz, Marquez Equalibria, Natalia Casella, CaJonna Lewis. Second row: Kenith Bergeron, Kim Milstead, Ron Wakabayashi, Rosa Salamanca, Thomas Battles, Daedra MacGhee, DurShawn Seward Robinson, Iyunia Dyer, Stephanie Mott, Synthia Taylor, Mary Gorecki, Alex Chavez, Mildred Duprey de Robles. Third row: Dion Lyons, James Williams III, Justin Lock, Matthew Lattimer, Sean Barrett, Charles Phillips, Walter Atkinson, Darryck Dean, Harpreet Singh Mokha. Courtesy of the U.S. Department of Justice.

Figure 23. Wallace Warfield served as a conciliator, regional director, and acting director during his time at CRS from 1968 to 1988. Courtesy of George Mason University.

Figure 24. Silke Hansen joined CRS in 1972 after being recruited by Warfield. She had a lead role mediating the desegregation at Boston Public Schools in the 1970s and with Korean American groups after the beating of Rodney King by Los Angeles police officers in 1991. Courtesy of the U.S. Department of Justice.

Figure 25. Nancy K. Ferrell, a CRS conciliation specialist from 1985 to 1997, mediated as a member of the CRS's Church Burning Response Team and in a major Southern university conflict concerning Plantation Day, a white fraternity and sorority event. Courtesy of Universal Art, Photographic Services.

PART II

ELEVEN

Nazis, Free Speech, and Hate

Preventing a Bloodbath in Skokie and Beyond

NAZIS AT SKOKIE

MORE THAN THIRTY years after World War II, a violent encounter between Nazis and Jews was brewing on American soil. The setting was the village of Skokie, a suburb fifteen miles north of Chicago. A small group of Nazis planned to stage a demonstration in the predominantly Jewish suburb, which in 1977 was home to the highest concentration of Holocaust survivors in the United States. Tens of thousands of Jewish counterprotesters around the country planned to swarm the small village, some promising to cause the Nazis physical harm. CRS intervention succeeded in relocating the Nazi demonstration, deescalating the extremely charged confrontation, and keeping the peace.

In the late 1970s, Frank Collin was the head of the National Socialist Party of America (NSPA), a neo-Nazi group that adopted the swastika as its primary symbol and espoused white supremacist beliefs. The name of the group deliberately echoed that of Adolf Hitler's National Socialist German Workers' Party. Composed entirely of white males, the NSPA's membership numbers varied but never exceeded twenty-eight. While it might seem easy to dismiss the NSPA as a tiny fringe group, in the 1970s several such U.S. Nazi groups succeeded in broadcasting their hateful and violent philosophy on a substantial scale. They ran for office and appeared on television, including popular talk shows like *The Phil Donahue Show*. The NSPA, including Collin himself, frequently got into yelling matches and fistfights with counterprotesters, a pattern other Nazi groups mimicked throughout the country.

These encounters resulted in a number of violent tragedies. In 1977, a Chicago Nazi used hydrogen cyanide to gas a Jewish victim to death.[1] Some of Collin's group members were indicted for attempted murder

---

Chapters 11–15 are by Grande Lum

after an encounter with the Jewish Defense League (JDL). One Nazi murdered five New Yorkers; another fired gunshots at African American families at a Labor Day picnic in North Carolina. The threat these groups posed was clearly greater than their small numbers would suggest.

Collin's NSPA headquarters was located in Chicago's Marquette Park. The group's main activity was protesting African American families moving into previously all-white neighborhoods. While a significant number of Marquette Park residents wanted the NSPA out of the area, some viewed the Nazis' presence as beneficial, believing that it would prevent Black families from moving in. However, violent clashes with African American groups marching in Marquette Park and with counterprotesters when the NSPA ventured outside the neighborhood led the city of Chicago to seek to curb the rallies. The city's strategy was to create a new policy requiring demonstrators in Marquette Park to pay a $250,000 insurance fee. Outraged, Collin challenged this bond-posting requirement through a lawsuit. In the meantime, he planned to protest in Chicago suburbs that required no such fees.

In the fall of 1976, Collin sent copies of a letter to the trustees of numerous Chicago North Shore suburbs requesting a public meeting in each. Simultaneously, the NSPA distributed thousands of leaflets in the North Shore area with the text, "We Are Coming!" and a picture of a swastika with arms extending to choke a caricature of a Jewish person.[2] In addition, numerous threatening calls were made to homes in the North Shore.[3]

Skokie was the only district to respond, and in doing so the village inadvertently made itself a bullseye. In its October 1976 response, the Skokie Park District required NSPA to provide $350,000 in insurance coverage to gain a park demonstration permit. Collin responded with the intention to protest the permit denial outside the Skokie Village Hall. Initially, the Skokie Village trustees relented and agreed to grant the permit. However, the response from large numbers of local Holocaust survivors persuaded the trustees to change their minds.

Approximately half of Skokie's population was Jewish, and one in six residents was a Holocaust survivor or direct relation.[4] The prospect of the Nazi demonstration was deeply upsetting. One local resident who had survived the Holocaust told the Board of Trustees: "We are a special breed of people, people who went through unbelievable things. History doesn't even know the things that happened to us. . . . This thing should not happen in our village." Another explained, "We never thought in our wildest dreams that it could happen like that again, that [Nazis] would have a right to confront us . . . to say those obscene words without being punished. This realization brought back a terror . . . here we are again, in the same position."[5]

Collin was unmoved by the residents' sentiments. He told the *Chicago Tribune*, "Good. I hope they are terrified. I hope they're shocked. Because we're coming to get them again. I don't care if someone's mother or father or brother died in the gas chambers. The unfortunate thing is not that there were six million Jews who died. The unfortunate thing is that there were so many Jewish survivors."[6] The NSPA planned to protest the trustees' decision wearing Nazi-style uniforms and displaying swastikas. Skokie filed for an emergency injunction. The American Civil Liberties Union (ACLU) took on Collin's case appealing the injunction, arguing that the injunction violated the NSPA's First Amendment right to free speech.

The Skokie Village Board of Trustees passed three ordinances to prevent the Nazi demonstration. The first banned military-style uniforms counter to the tradition of civilian-run government as well as decency and morality standards. The second prohibited distribution of materials that incited racial and ethnic hatred. The last ordinance called for posting an insurance bond. After a series of rulings against the ordinances and ACLU appeals that reached all the way to the U.S. Supreme Court, in early 1978 the federal district court ruled all three local ordinances unconstitutional.

Up until this point Collin had been waiting for the results of two state legislature bills that would prohibit Nazi protests in Illinois before pushing once more for the Skokie demonstration—which was itself intended as a bargaining chip to gain access to the original desired location, Marquette Park.[7] In a letter to the *Chicago Tribune*, Collin stated, "By forcing the 'free speech for National Socialism' issue in Skokie we are fighting for our basic rights everywhere."[8] Meanwhile, the impending clash in Skokie had taken on national significance. Jewish groups around the country were organizing to confront the Nazi group. The rhetoric was becoming violent; in a press release, the JDL promised "blood in the streets." A spokesman for the Warsaw Ghetto Uprising Coalition explained, "The mission of American Jews should not be to look nice and upper-middle-class, and to please the government officials and the media, but to let anti-Semites know it will be an unpleasant experience to march in a Jewish neighborhood."[9] One organizer in Phoenix stated, "We will break legs if we have to" in order to stop the NSPA's march.[10]

Recognizing a losing legal battle and fearing uncontrollable crowds, Skokie officials reached out to CRS.[11] Up until this time, the CRS Chicago office had been monitoring Collin's activities and speaking with various city constituencies but had not been directly involved in any negotiations. Richard Salem was the CRS Midwest regional director, located along with conciliator Werner Petterson in the Chicago office.

At this point Salem had been in charge of the office for ten years. Previously he had been a director in the U.S. Small Business Administration, implementing programs created by President Lyndon Johnson's War on Poverty. While at CRS, Salem had mediated the dispute over construction on the site of the 1970 student shootings at Kent State University. From President Richard Nixon, he received a citation in 1973 for his work in mediating at Wounded Knee in South Dakota. Both Salem and Petterson did conciliation work in law enforcement–community conflicts, school desegregation, and prison race issues as well.

The conciliation team of Salem and Petterson stepped in during February 1978 and contacted Collin's ACLU attorney, David Goldberger.[12] "My initial reaction was that it was a waste of my time by some do-gooders," Goldberger recalled. "When I got the call I thought [CRS's involvement] was the silliest thing I ever heard. I just absolutely said what a waste of my time and everybody's time."[13] Goldberger was unfamiliar with the agency, and he assumed that CRS was inserting itself into the conflict because the situation was becoming well publicized. CRS conciliators often encounter these assumptions, reflecting the double-edged sword of CRS's commitment to confidentiality. By working without publicity, CRS is more able to successfully mediate complex and controversial conflicts. On the other hand, operating behind the scenes without garnering publicity frequently means CRS encounters initial skepticism when first entering a conflict.

Goldberger's perspective on the futility of CRS's participation was shaped by his conversations with his client. Goldberger had urged Collin to find another venue, regarding the Nazi group's physical safety to be at risk in Skokie. With so many people promising violence, he told his client the situation was "a recipe for disaster." Despite these warnings, "Collin was adamant about going forward," Goldberger recalled. Committed to his function as an ACLU attorney to allow the client to "call the shots," Goldberger was prepared to support Collin in proceeding with the Skokie protest.[14]

On March 1, 1978, Salem and Petterson met with Goldberger and Illinois ACLU executive director David Hamlin. Gaining the trust of the ACLU attorneys was a hurdle. Would the ACLU find CRS to be a credible and trustworthy mediator, given that it was a Department of Justice agency and the ACLU had a civil libertarian philosophy? According to Hamlin, the ACLU representatives "took an instant dislike to both men." Hamlin's perspective was that the CRS staff's focus on maintaining neutrality made it seem as if they were "willing to ignore principles of free speech."[15] Despite the ACLU attorneys' skeptical attitude toward CRS, Goldberger felt obliged to inform Collin that the agency had offered its services.

"I said [to myself], I have an ethical duty to reach out to the client and let him decide what to do with it," Goldberger recalled. "My predisposition always in these situations is to do so, whenever anyone wants to sit down and talk about possible settlement, so that no one can accuse the client of stonewalling." When Collin expressed interest in the meeting with CRS, Goldberger initially surmised that it was the Justice Department's prestige that appealed to Collin: "It was another opportunity for him to make clear to the world that he was important," Goldberger recalled. He agreed to talk further with CRS about the possibility of a meeting with Collin, but no meeting was set at that time.[16]

On the CRS side, the initial goal was not to prevent the Skokie demonstration but to establish relationships that would allow the conciliators to aid in keeping the peace during the forthcoming event. Petterson later noted, "We wanted to introduce ourselves so that he would recognize us later at the rally."[17] This approach was in keeping with CRS's established stance of providing assistance that allows for the exercise of First Amendment free speech rights while maintaining the safety of all parties. In an article he wrote about the case, Salem observed, "We rarely asked any group to consider abandoning its right to conduct a lawful demonstration, even when a physical confrontation seemed inevitable, especially in a case where obtaining a permit to demonstrate was a central issue to the dispute."[18]

The CRS team initially viewed mediation as unlikely in the Skokie conflict. The experience of CRS conciliators over the years had led to a general practice of not mediating with extremists such as NSPA, given that not only their means but also their aims tend toward adversarial conflict rather than a mutually satisfactory agreement. However, as the likelihood and magnitude of violence and property damage increased, CRS sought to offer mediation services to broker a compromise regarding the place, time, and manner of the demonstrations.

The estimate of counterdemonstrators continued to rise as the story spread nationwide and worldwide. The JDL stated that 134 buses would bring 1,800 people from the New York area. A travel agent booked flights for two thousand people to fly from Los Angeles to Skokie. Still more participants were expected from Phoenix. Eventually, estimates of the expected crowd of counterdemonstrators would grow to fifty thousand. The Jewish community began to feel more emboldened. "And suddenly," one Skokie resident recalled, "I didn't feel so alone. I realized the whole world was paying attention to Skokie. And thousands of people were behind us."[19]

Recognizing the growing potential for violent conflict, the CRS team met with Skokie Jewish community leaders to propose a large counterdemonstration at a significant distance from the NSPA protest site. A small leadership group would then silently confront Collin's group through a vigil. This strategy, commonly employed by CRS as well as government and law enforcement officials experienced in dealing with protesters and counterprotesters, aimed to keep the opposing crowds as far apart from each other as possible to reduce the likelihood of physical encounters.

Salem and Petterson also deployed CRS expertise by convening a meeting of Eugene DuBow, the regional director of the American Jewish Committee and lead counterprotest planner, with Chicago deputy police superintendent James Riordan at the CRS Chicago office. This ability to facilitate dialogue between parties that may not know each other or commonly work with each other—or may even be at odds with each other—is one of the unique contributions CRS makes. As outside, third parties, CRS conciliators can leverage the credibility of the federal Justice Department to bring together religious groups, protest groups, law enforcement, and other stakeholders. Additionally, by taking on the peacekeeping role and facilitating additional needed resources, CRS can help local law enforcement save face if there is reluctance to ask for help. At CRS's urging, Riordan committed to be on call to work behind the scenes given his extensive experience with street demonstrations. State officials committed up to a thousand National Guard and state trooper personnel to supplement the hundreds of local police. Nonetheless, according to Salem, "Despite the extensive planning, nobody believed that tens of thousands of emotional counterdemonstrators could be restrained, especially if hundreds of JDL members were on hand to arouse the crowd."[20]

Collin's NSPA members appeared to be aware of the growing risks to their own safety. Newspapers indicated that the small Nazi group was beginning to hesitate, faced with the prospect of hordes of irate counterprotesters. Salem and Petterson suspected that the NSPA would welcome the chance to abandon the Skokie demonstration if they could do so without appearing to give in. "We gave credibility to the media report that Collin's supporters were wavering, and we sensed that he needed a face-saving way out," Salem recalled. "Helping to find that way was the only course we could consider in light of the risks of not doing so."[21]

The CRS team knew, however, that there were moral and ethical questions embedded in the prospect of mediating with Nazis. Salem, who was Jewish, wondered, "Was it proper to negotiate with a group that espoused a Nazi philosophy? Was it legitimate to trade off Skokie for an alternate site? Can mediators maintain impartiality when dealing with such a group?"[22] None of the other stakeholders would sit at the table with Collin and his American Nazi group. For many Jewish Americans, it was simply morally wrong to meet with people who advocated for their extermination. "A lot of people saw it as shaking hands with the devil," Petterson recalled.[23] Ultimately, given the stakes involved, the CRS conciliators determined that their own misgivings were "more theoretical than actual," Salem wrote.[24] Preventing violence was the primary objective, and CRS was in a unique position to broker the peace.

As in Selma and Wounded Knee, conciliators utilized shuttle diplomacy to work toward an agreement. Petterson described their efforts as presenting various "what if" scenarios to different parties in order to introduce alternative paths. This approach provides plausible deniability to any party that might not be in a position to disclose they were directly involved in negotiations. Petterson also noted that no one else was talking to all the different parties, that is, Collin, the American

Jewish Committee, legislators, local and federal government agencies, law enforcement, and so on. In less openly adversarial conflicts, and in situations where long-term relationships are necessary or desired, CRS conciliators can bring together parties to talk directly, but the Nazi demonstration in Skokie was not one of those situations. Unlike in Selma or Wounded Knee, the number of groups and individuals among the counterprotesters would dwarf the size of the NSPA, and their primary aim was antagonistic to the Nazi group on principle.

Indeed, no public official or Jewish community leader would go on the record as even being party to negotiation with the Nazis, let alone the agreement. Salem stated that CRS would rely on Collin's attorneys to hold the NSPA accountable. With the politicians and public officials involved, Salem's attitude was that CRS "would take their chances" on people sticking to agreements made off the record. This risk, which conciliators often take, meant that officials might not follow through on their closed-door commitments or could perhaps even blame the conciliators if problems arose.

Before any meeting between CRS and Collin was arranged, on May 22, 1978, the Seventh Circuit Court of Appeals upheld the lower court's finding that all three of the Skokie anti-Nazi ordinances were unconstitutional and ordered the town to issue the permit to Collin. The Skokie attorneys stated that the village would be appealing the ruling to the Supreme Court. In response, the next day the NSPA provided a press release making three demands that, if not met, would lead to a demonstration in Skokie on June 25. The first demand was that the village of Skokie repeal the three demonstration ordinances it had passed. Second, the state of Illinois was to withdraw its anti-NSPA legislative proposal that would prohibit Nazi demonstrations. Finally, the Chicago Park District was to withdraw its insurance bond mandate. The *Chicago Tribune* noted of this public negotiation: "His group will 'consider' cancelling their proposed march in Skokie if the Park District drops its demand for an insurance bond for Nazi rallies in Marquette Park."[25]

Collin's public demands led, predictably, to politically tough positioning. Skokie mayor Albert Smith responded by saying he would not require the Skokie Park District to concede to the demand. The Illinois state senators who had sponsored the anti-Nazi bills pushed back and refused to withdraw them.

The CRS team, however, sensing an opportunity in the increasingly tense atmosphere, met with the Chicago Park District information officer in order to understand his perspective and potential flexibility. The officer said the park district would not permit the Nazi group to protest in Marquette Park unless there was a court order. He did share with the CRS team that there were four other parks in Chicago where a permit was not needed.

While the legislative trend suggested that such a court order might indeed be forthcoming, it would likely take months to be issued, and the planned demonstration was but weeks away. Salem quickly took the insight he had gained from the park district officer into a meeting with one of the planners of the counterdemonstration. He wanted to see if Jewish community leaders would be willing to provide leverage in negotiating with the district and the Chicago mayor to exert political pressure to make up for the legislative lag. "The answer was a clear and irrevocable no," Salem recalled. "Nobody in the Jewish leadership would be involved in making a deal with the Nazis, we were told."[26]

On May 26, Salem and Petterson met again with Hamlin and Goldberger.[27] All four agreed that Skokie would likely lose the Supreme Court case and that the Illinois state legislation was also unlikely to pass. However, Hamlin noted that the remainder of the meeting "was a most frustrating encounter." Hamlin and Goldberger, who had fought so hard in the face of death threats for the NSPA's First Amendment rights, strongly believed that violence would erupt if the Nazis demonstrated. The two ACLU attorneys perceived that Skokie was not assembling adequate security to maintain a safe distance between the Nazis and counterprotesters. In his book *The Nazi/Skokie Conflict: A Civil Liberties Battle*, Hamlin later noted that if two groups could not be kept apart, a bloodbath would result and "the precious [First Amendment] victories would not mean a damn thing, for all of Skokie's fears would be realized and the law would turn to mush."[28]

Given the impending and explosively charged encounter, the fact that a court ruling was likely months away, state politicians' reluctance to intervene, and the refusal of the Jewish community to engage in talks with the Nazi group, Salem and Petterson felt it was critical to speak directly with Collin. Goldberger responded to this request by setting three ground rules: CRS "would make no misrepresentations, [CRS] would do nothing to interfere with the progress of the legal cases or

Collin's civil rights, and no one would mention the meeting to the press unless all parties concurred."[29]

On June 1, Salem and Petterson met with Collin and Goldberger at the ACLU offices. Goldberger had understood up until that point that his client's objective was to go forward with the Skokie demonstration: "I assumed he would sit through the meeting, listen and chat a little bit, and say, 'Thank you but no thank you' and the meeting would be over."[30]

Petterson later recalled that despite Collin's public vitriol, the NSPA leader appeared calm and polite. "He was certainly not an intimidating, hostile presence," Petterson said.[31] Salem opened the meeting with concerns about police ability to protect the NSPA and keep the peace, in spite of the planned presence of over one thousand police officers. According to Salem, Collin knew about the growing size of the counterprotester groups and the JDL's highly publicized threats of violence. Collin said that "he did not want violence and if it occurred, it would not be his fault."[32]

Salem pointed out that Collin's three conditions for halting the protest would likely be met in the course of time. This is where Salem made a move that surprised the ACLU attorneys and likely also Collin. In keeping with the "what if" strategy, Salem asked if Collin would consider some type of compromise that did not meet all three demands. Collin responded that he was open to considering an alternative. According to Hamlin, Collin decided on that day that the NSPA would not protest in Skokie.

"I about fell out of my chair," recalled Goldberger of Collin's openness to working with CRS toward a compromise. "The picture changed dramatically in that single meeting. . . . It completely turned things around."[33]

In a second meeting with Collin the following day, CRS proposed that the agency announce a cancellation of the Skokie protest. The reasoning given was that Collin had won his right to protest in Skokie and that he would eventually gain the right to protest in Marquette Park. These victories would prove that he had won on the First Amendment principle. The NSPA could demonstrate in any of the four Chicago parks that did not require a permit, CRS pointed out. Collin reiterated that the permit-requiring Marquette Park was where he had always desired to demonstrate, but he consented to weigh the offer.

To negotiate effectively with Collin, CRS was determined to address the dilemma of Collin's demand to withdraw the Illinois state-level anti-Nazi legislation. This presented something of a catch-22. The bills had passed the Illinois senate, but support in the house appeared to be contingent on whether the Skokie march was going forward. If the march was happening, then the house was likely to pass the bills. If the march were to be canceled, however, the legislators would likely drop the bills as there was, according to Salem, "considerable sentiment in the State Capitol that the bills were bad legislation—a political necessity for legislators with a Jewish constituency, perhaps, but bad legislation nonetheless."[34] This situation meant Collin could achieve his goal of stopping the legislation—but only by canceling his march first.

On June 4, an Illinois state legislator who had heard of CRS's mediation work summoned Salem to his home. The legislator conveyed that the bill would pass unless there were signals that the Nazi group was not going to protest in Skokie. By this point, however, Salem and Petterson sensed a growing consensus that the proposed bills were unconstitutional. They interpreted the meeting as a measure of desperation: "We sensed that these words were a bluff," Salem observed. He reasoned that legislators with significant Jewish constituencies were feeling pressure to prevent the Skokie demonstration, and the leader was utilizing CRS to try to force a retreat on Collin. "We played our role and took their message back to Collin," he recalled.[35] In this way, CRS served in a shuttle diplomacy role providing a path toward negotiation between parties who refused to communicate directly with one another despite goals that required mutual agreement.

The conciliators suggested to Collin that they could discreetly pass on to the media that an NSPA demonstration at another site besides Skokie was possible. This move, they argued, could achieve three objectives: (1) persuade the Illinois state legislature not to pass the bills, (2) reduce the rush of out-of-town demonstrators coming to Skokie, and (3) most importantly, lessen the mounting tension. Once again, by providing a face-saving option that did not require admission of a weakened position, CRS moved the parties closer to standing down. Rather than Collin having to personally cave in and back down from holding a protest in Skokie, having CRS mediators as a third party presenting a proposal removing Skokie as the protest site allowed Collin to act as the one in seeming control, receiving offers and making demands. Collin agreed, and on June 9 the *Chicago Sun-Times* published the story, which was picked up by news outlets all over the country. Jewish leaders, sensing the Nazi group wavering on Skokie, continued to threaten that appearing in Skokie would have grave consequences for the Nazis.

Salem acknowledged that at this point in the negotiations, "We certainly didn't feel in control of the situation—something a mediator never wants to acknowledge."[36] Although the CRS conciliators perceived that no party actually wanted the Skokie demonstration to take place, the looming event had been headlining newspapers for weeks with consistently escalating bluster from both the NSPA and the counterprotesters. Calling for still more participants in the counterdemonstrations, the chairman of the Public Affairs Committee of the Jewish United Fund stated in the *Chicago Tribune*, "Let Skokie be remembered as the place in which all America rose up to reaffirm the values and ideals on which the nation was founded."[37]

On June 12, the U.S. Supreme Court, by a seven-to-two vote, agreed with the Seventh Circuit and refused to grant a stay of that court's ruling. This was the highest court of the land, and it meant that the courts would not block the Nazis' rally in Skokie. The next day, the two group libel measures were defeated in the Illinois House of Representatives.

At this point, two of Collin's three demands had been satisfied. It appears that on June 12 Collin wrote a letter to the General Services Administration stating that the NSPA would stage a rally in downtown Chicago's Federal Plaza a day before the planned Skokie protest. However, as Salem later observed, "Nothing would come easy in this case."[38] CRS had to intervene to coordinate multiple parties to get through attempts to block the NSPA from appearing in Federal Plaza, even though, up until then, the site had not required a permit.

To demonstrate in Marquette Park, however, Collin was still required to comply with the insurance bond requirement. The Chicago Park District's attorney, Richard Troy, affirmed that the district would not cede the bond requirement.[39] There were at least two ways for NSPA to avoid the requirement, but pride appeared to prevent both. The NSPA had refused to share their finances, which could have allowed a waiver based on lack of funds. Alternatively, the group could demonstrate by applying for a permit for seventy-four people or fewer, which required only a few days' notice. According to Troy, "Collin would not admit . . . that he could not find seventy-five followers."[40]

Salem called David Goldberger and brought up this "rule of seventy-four," which had not come up in any CRS meetings with Collin and the ACLU. Goldberger countered with the observation that counterprotesters were always considered to be part of the crowd for permitting purposes. Salem proposed urging the park district to count only the Nazis, which rarely numbered over two dozen. Troy expressed that if the Nazi group did not hand out leaflets or post notices, then bystanders would not be counted. If CRS drafted such an agreement, Troy said, the park district would support it.

Finally, a solution was in sight. Ideally, this would have been the appropriate time for CRS to bring together Collin, the ACLU, and the Chicago Park District to put together the agreement. However, the emotional volatility was still too high and trust too low to allow for that direct approach, so the CRS mediators continued their shuttle diplomacy. It appeared that while the NSPA might be willing to concede their small numbers, they could not be easily dissuaded from leafleting, a core component of their tactics exhibited earlier in the "We Are Coming!" notices. The urgency of these delicate negotiations increased when a newspaper reporter shared that NSPA members were considering going forward with a rally in Skokie without Collin.

Salem ultimately broke through the stalemate by convincing Troy that the extraordinary media attention made it impossible to determine whether crowds had been drawn by NSPA handouts or the constant newspaper headlines. The lawyer agreed, and a letter granting usage of Marquette Park was signed. This breakthrough provided the path forward. The letter, along with an additional message from the CRS conciliators, was hand-delivered to NSPA headquarters on June 16. At a press conference before cameras, the Nazi group announced they had gained access to Marquette Park, yet they held off on canceling the Skokie demonstration until the district court had officially ruled on the bond requirement.

Meanwhile, Collin continued with his bravado, threatening, "It's only the beginning. If we don't get our rights, they haven't seen anything yet."[41] At last, on June 20, the district court ruled the bond requirement unreasonable and commanded the Chicago Park District to provide the NSPA with a July 9 demonstration permit. On June 21, Collin announced that the NSPA would rally in Marquette Park and Federal Plaza but not in Skokie.

After all the lawsuits, threats, refusals to negotiate, demands, bluffs, and multiparty maneuvering, the fate of the Skokie powder keg all came down to a single man changing his mind. This turn of events could not have been achieved without Collin's attorney David Goldberger, who represented him in a highly professional and effective manner in the face of death threats and constant pressure, and the CRS conciliation team that was able to persuade Collin to shift his stance despite a glaring spotlight. As the only people in communication with all the relevant players, Salem and Petterson provided a crucial means of reaching an alternative agreement.

On Saturday, June 24, 1978, less than a dozen NSPA members rode a police van from their Chicago headquarters to Federal Plaza. They faced several thousand protesters but nothing close to the crowds that had planned to congregate for the Skokie march. Even with the aid of an amplifier, Collin's statement, "These creatures should be gassed!" could scarcely be heard over the roar of counterdemonstrators.[42] After approximately twenty minutes, the Nazi group was escorted by police back to their headquarters.

On Sunday, June 25, not a single Nazi exercised his hard-won First Amendment rights on the steps of the Skokie Village Hall.

The Supreme Court case *National Socialist Party of America v. Village of Skokie* is a landmark one setting the precedent that the Nazi swastika is a symbolic form of free speech entitled to First Amendment protection. This ruling remains controversial. The case is often raised when situations involving offensive speech and symbols arise, such as the 2017 alt-right marches in Charlottesville, Virginia.

What would have happened had the march taken place in Skokie? Even though none of the parties truly wanted the demonstration to happen, with some fifty thousand counterprotesters ready to push back against the Nazi group, a horrible tragedy might have unfolded. Whether law enforcement could have kept the peace is questionable. CRS's key contributions in suggesting and paving the way to alternatives appear to have been critical in diverting this potentially explosive encounter.

Goldberger is clear in his understanding that CRS prevented what appeared to be inevitable violence: "I think had CRS not intervened, it would have gone forward in Skokie. There's no doubt in my mind about that." After sitting down with CRS, he recalls realizing, "'Wow, this is going in a completely different direction than I anticipated,' and I was not unhappy with the direction it was going. . . . I [had] anticipated a bloody confrontation."[43]

NEO-NAZIS IN ARIZONA

On April 23, 2010, emotions were running high in Arizona. The state's governor, Jan Brewer, had just signed Arizona's Support Our Law Enforcement and Safe Neighborhoods Act, popularly known as SB 1070, a highly stringent anti-immigrant law. National and international attention, and over seventy protests nationwide, followed. White nationalist and Ku Klux Klan groups jumped into the fray. As it had done in Skokie and numerous times through its history, CRS played a role in keeping the peace while focused on advancing its jurisdictional mandate from the 1964 Civil Rights Act and the 2009 Matthew Shepard and James Byrd Jr. Hate Crime Prevention Act, which is discussed more in depth in chapter 13.

Context for the SB 1070 controversy stemmed from Arizona's history and changing demographics. Arizona governor Evan Mecham memorably canceled Martin Luther King Jr. Day as a paid holiday for state employees in 1987, garnering national attention and a boycott. It was not until 1992, after the National Football League pulled the Super Bowl from the state, that Arizona made MLK Day a state holiday.

In 2005, Arizona governor Janet Napolitano declared a state of emergency due to illegal immigration. In 2007, after rejecting earlier, more extreme versions, Napolitano, then secretary of the Department of Homeland Security, approved a bill to heavily penalize employers of undocumented immigrants. By most objective measures, Arizona had the most illegal border crossings during those years, due to its location and terrain.

SB 1070 had four primary provisions focused on immigration enforcement: (1) residing in the United States without legal documentation was an Arizona state crime; (2) working in the United States without legal documentation was also a state crime; (3) Arizona law enforcement was required to verify legal status of all those arrested or otherwise detained; and (4) state law enforcement provided for the arrest of individuals based on probable cause of unlawful presence, even without a warrant.[44]

Over the years, CRS has provided service involving neo-Nazi and Ku Klux Klan groups, which could challenge the deep, personally held

279

values of conciliators. This concern applied to James Williams, a CRS conciliator who was African American, and Ron Wakabayashi, a regional director who was Japanese American.

On Saturday, May 29, 2010, one of the largest protests against the signing of SB 1070 occurred in Phoenix, Arizona.[45] It was a prototypical sweltering hot day in Phoenix, but it did not stop more than fifty thousand from gathering. Wakabayashi and Williams had been working with local law enforcement, protest groups, government officials, fire departments, and others to both help prevent violent encounters and allow for the practice of the First Amendment, the right to free speech. The CRS team engaged with local and national immigrant rights groups who had focused on May Day, a traditional workers' day rally, as a peak moment to protest against SB 1070. In fact, seventy protests were taking place all over the country that day.[46]

As CRS had done before and after the Skokie case, it also engaged neo-Nazis and Ku Klux Klan–type groups. For a number of years, such groups would engage local law enforcement and CRS as they often needed more protection from counterprotesters; this time was no different. Unlike in Skokie, though, the neo-Nazis, Ku Klux Klan, and other white nationalists were not the central and primary focus of the protest.

CRS Acting Director Becky Monroe was on the ground with the CRS team in Phoenix for the protest. According to Monroe, she was walking alongside conciliator James Williams when J. T. Ready, the leader of a neo-Nazi group, stopped and spoke to Williams: "Hello! It is great to see you again! I am so glad you are here today." Ready then went on to spew offensive insults at the protesters, targeting immigrants, Jews, Muslims, and African Americans. Williams did his job, positioning himself between the protesters and the neo-Nazi group.[47]

Weeks earlier, Williams and Ready had crossed paths at a protest where Williams used his conciliation skills to help cool down a conflict between Ready's neo-Nazi group and the protesters. Notably, Ready voiced his appreciation to Williams while nearly simultaneously voicing hatred for Blacks.[48] In the years since Skokie, CRS has worked in numerous situations with neo-Nazi, Ku Klux Klan, and other white supremacist groups, often where these groups are outnumbered by counterprotesters. CRS's role is to maintain the safety of these white supremacist group members and counterprotest groups while providing space for free speech.

Regional Director Ron Wakabayashi led the CRS team in Phoenix. Wakabayashi was the child of parents who had been in Topaz and Rowher, two of the Japanese American internment camps during World War II. Born in Reno, Nevada, Wakabayashi grew up in East Los Angeles and began working in nonprofits. He was founder and director of the Asian American Drug Abuse Program. In 1981, he became director of the Japanese American Citizens League and helped lead the fight for redress and reparations for those who were imprisoned in the internment camps. He then served as executive director of the Los Angeles City Human Relations Commission and as director of the Los Angeles County Commission on Human Relations. In 1999, Wakabayashi joined CRS as regional director in its Los Angeles office.

Monroe later wrote that while she was with Wakabayashi at the May 29 protest, he found anti-immigration flyers which contained the words "immigrant hunting license" and "shoot to kill." As Monroe and Wakabayashi further assessed the situation, its potential for violence, and strategies to deescalate tension and reduce the possibility of violence, Wakabayashi shared how his father kept a similar flyer from World War II that contained the words "Japanese Hunting License" and shared how hurtful it was to him to have seen such a thing.[49]

Throughout the protest, the CRS team continued to do the work of resolving conflicts, preventing violence, and increasing peace. Problems began brewing between a protester and a Maricopa County sheriff's deputy. The protester was attempting to block an area entry by using a technique called the "sleeping dragon," using PVC pipe and handcuffs to bind himself to fellow protesters. Wakabayashi talked with both parties and found a way for the protester to remain while providing legal access to the entry.[50]

CRS often provides event marshal training for protests, where individuals are trained to help keep protests safe and learn techniques to prevent peaceful protest groups from being antagonized to physical violence. In Phoenix, religious leaders and young volunteers were trained to be event marshals by the CRS team. One of those trained, a college student, observed armed neo-Nazi groups taunting and egging on a group of peaceful protesters. Monroe recalled the young Latina telling the group, "Don't fall for it. They are trying to provoke you because they are cowards. If you want to truly stand up for our community, go stand with the community. Don't dignify their words with a response."

The protesters heeded her advice and shunned the neo-Nazis, turning their backs. The neo-Nazi group, finding themselves disengaged, packed their gear and departed from Phoenix.[51]

On July 28, a federal judge granted a preliminary injunction preventing the most controversial aspects of SB 1070 from taking effect. The constitutionality of SB 1070 was tested and went all the way to the Supreme Court. In 2012, the Court declared three provisions unconstitutional.[52] Even the one provision held to be constitutional, requiring an immigration status test by local law enforcement if there is reasonable suspicion, has rarely been implemented.

UNITE THE RIGHT IN CHARLOTTESVILLE, VIRGINIA

On August 18, 2017, a Friday night in Charlottesville, Virginia, about one hundred neo-Nazi white supremacists and white nationalists, armed with blazing tiki torches, marched in unison through the University of Virginia's Charlottesville campus. This was part of a Unite the Right rally, the largest public gathering of alt-right groups in decades, to protest the Charlottesville City Council's decision to remove a statue of Robert E. Lee from Emancipation Park. Shouts of "Jews will not replace us" and "you will not replace us" rang out as marchers gave the Nazi salute.

The next day, the white supremacist group came face to face with counterprotesters. These counterprotesters included local civil rights groups like Black Lives Matter, Charlottesville clergy, and national groups like Antifa. Numerous fights and skirmishes broke out. By 11 a.m., the city of Charlottesville had declared a state of emergency and Governor Terry McAuliffe followed up with a similar state declaration an hour later. Three people were arrested and thirty-four people injured.

At approximately 1:45 p.m., a 2010 Dodge Challenger plowed into a group of peaceful protesters. Heather Heyer, a thirty-two-year-old paralegal, was killed, and nineteen people were injured, five critically. Two state troopers who were monitoring the protests also were killed when their helicopter crashed.

While numerous politicians from both sides of the aisle—including Republicans such as Attorney General Jeff Sessions, Senator John McCain, and House Speaker Paul Ryan—condemned the white supremacists, President Donald Trump's comments that day did not point out the alt-right at all. Instead, he denounced the "egregious display of hatred, bigotry, and violence on many sides." Two days later, the president stated that "racism is evil" and that "those who cause violence in its name are criminals and thugs, including the KKK, neo-Nazis, white supremacists, and other hate groups that are repugnant to everything we hold dear as Americans." It was the first time Trump blamed white supremacist groups, though by saying "other hate groups," he still insinuated that the other side had racist haters too. By the following day, the president had reverted to his first comments and pointed out, "You had a group on one side that was bad. You had a group on the other side that was also very violent. Nobody wants to say that. I'll say it right now."[53]

Trump's characterization of the Charlottesville rally made sense given that the Unite the Right rally itself was connected to the president's election, as many if not all white supremacists supported Trump's campaign. Former Ku Klux Klan imperial wizard David Duke noted that white supremacist demonstrators were "going to fulfill the promises of Donald Trump" to "take our country back."[54] The Unite the Right rally can certainly be distinguished from all other CRS work prior to Trump's ascension to the White House, as the alt-right groups were emboldened by the new president, a dynamic not seen before.

CRS was not involved in the runup to the rally. It was involved afterward in dealing with the aftermath, however. This work included CRS conciliators Suzanne Buchanan and Charles Phillips organizing an August 27 town-hall meeting.[55] CRS conciliation specialists were monitoring the rally but not involved in preparation nor did they provide any other services during the rally.[56] This may have been due to orders from Justice Department leadership to CRS. How much CRS could have made a difference here would be purely conjecture. But it could easily be why CRS was sidelined initially and targeted for elimination by the Trump administration.[57]

In many situations working with white hate-based groups, CRS's success has been based on the individual rapport CRS mediators built with the leaders of such groups. In the cases discussed in this book—whether it was Efrain Martinez and the Grand Dragon of the Knights of the White Camellia in the Texas Gulf Shrimping Wars, Dick Salem and the head of a Chicago-based Nazi group, or James Williams and the leader of the Arizona-based neo-Nazi group—the rapport might have been partially based on a utilitarian mindset: the white nationalist group leader wants to achieve an end and sees the CRS conciliator as a means to that end. Yet, the historical record also indicates the benefit of the conciliator being a trustworthy, honest broker.

Williams's experience with J. T. Ready reveals an African American person working toward keeping all parties safe in a protest, including Ready and his followers. None of the CRS conciliators shared the racist or anti-Semitic agenda of the white nationalist group leaders. However, in such highly charged situations, having a third party who is trusted by the other groups helped save lives and prevent injury. Dick Salem always credited his success with Frank Collin in the Skokie situation to a phone call where Salem was attentive and friendly while chatting for nearly thirty minutes about Collin's struggle traveling through a storm. In Salem's view, speaking with the Nazi leader as another human being led to increased rapport and trust. Salem did not compromise his values or principles in accomplishing what he and Werner Petterson did in Skokie.[58]

NOTES

1. James L. Gibson and Richard D. Bingham, *Civil Liberties and Nazis: The Skokie–Free Speech Controversy* (New York: Praeger, 1985), 27.

2. Downs, "Skokie Revisited."

3. *Skokie: Invaded but Not Conquered* (Illinois Holocaust Museum and Education Center, 2014), film, 57 min.

4. Deborah Long, *First Hitler, Then Your Father, and Now You* (Morrisville, N.C.: Lulu.com, 2010), 71.

5. Downs, *Nazis in Skokie*, 2, 53.

6. Downs, *Nazis in Skokie*, 28–29.

7. Downs, "Skokie Revisited," 629.

8. Ron Grossman, "Flashback: 'Swastika War': When the Neo-Nazis Fought in Court to March in Skokie," *Chicago Tribune*, March 10, 2017, https://perma.cc/2SG8-UD3R.

9. Carolyn Toll, "Angry Feelings: Holocaust Victims Want to Face Nazis," *Chicago Tribune*, June 23, 1978, D3.

10. Salem, "Mediating Political and Social Conflicts," 154.

11. Downs, *Nazis in Skokie*, 77; Hamlin, *The Nazi/Skokie Conflict*, 154.

12. Salem, "Mediating Political and Social Conflicts."

13. David Goldberger, interview with Grande Lum, February 24, 2018.

14. Goldberger, interview with Lum. In response to an interview question concerning the ACLU's interest in seeing a high-profile case move forward, Goldberger emphasized that as an ACLU attorney his main goal was pursuing the client's interests.

15. Hamlin, *The Nazi/Skokie Conflict*.

16. Goldberger, interview with Lum.

17. Werner Petterson, interview with Grande Lum, September 24, 2018.

18. Salem, "Mediating Political and Social Conflicts," 152.

19. Anne Keegan, "A Quiet Day in Skokie," *Chicago Tribune*, June 26, 1978, 1.

20. Salem, "Mediating Political and Social Conflicts."

21. Salem, "Mediating Political and Social Conflicts," 155.

22. Salem, "Mediating Political and Social Conflicts," 155.

23. Petterson, interview with Lum.

24. Salem, "Mediating Political and Social Conflicts," 155.

25. Downs, *Nazis in Skokie*, 79.

26. Salem, "Mediating Political and Social Conflicts," 157.

27. Downs's *Nazis in Skokie* places Collin at this meeting, but both Salem and Goldberger recalled that CRS did not meet with Collin until June 1.

28. Hamlin, *The Nazi/Skokie Conflict*.

29. Salem, "Mediating Political and Social Conflicts," 157.

30. Goldberger, interview with Lum.

31. Petterson, interview with Lum

32. Salem, "Mediating Political and Social Conflicts," 157.

33. Goldberger, interview with Lum.

34. Salem, "Mediating Political and Social Conflicts," 158.

35. Salem, "Mediating Political and Social Conflicts," 158.

36. Salem, "Mediating Political and Social Conflicts," 159.

37. Estep, "Jews Plan Anti-Nazi Rally."

38. Salem, "Mediating Political and Social Conflicts," 159.

39. Downs, *Nazis in Skokie*, 81.

40. Salem, "Mediating Political and Social Conflicts," 163.

41. Douglas E. Kneeland, "Nazi Backed on Rally in Chicago; Move Could Avert Skokie March," *New York Times*, June 21, 1978, A1.

42. Downs, *Nazis in Skokie*, 81.

43. Goldberger, interview with Lum.

44. Ariz. Rev. Stat. Ann. §11-1-51 (2012).

45. Stephen Lemons, "Anti–SB 1070 Demonstration Rocks Phoenix, Marchers Number in the Tens of Thousands," *Phoenix New Times*, May 30, 2010, https://perma.cc/B2CA-4U58; Nicholas Riccardi, "Thousands in Phoenix Protest Arizona's Immigration Law," *Los Angeles Times*, May 29, 2010, https://perma.cc/JF5X 5NAY; Stephen Piggott, "Neo-Nazis Antagonize Marchers Protesting SB 1070 in Phoenix," IMAGINE 2050, June 1, 2010, https://perma.cc/VSS3-XBPG.

46. Monroe, "An Attack on America's Peacemakers," 321.

47. Monroe, "An Attack on America's Peacemakers," 301–2.

48. Monroe, "An Attack on America's Peacemakers," 302.

49. Monroe, "An Attack on America's Peacemakers," 322–23.

50. Monroe, "An Attack on America's Peacemakers," 323.

51. Monroe, "An Attack on America's Peacemakers," 323.

52. See *Arizona v. United States*, 567 U.S. 387 (2012).

53. Jenna Johnson and John Wagner, "Trump Condemns Charlottesville but Doesn't Single Out White Nationalists," *Washington Post*, August 12, 2017, https://perma.cc/4BAW-RGJP; "Statement by President Trump," August 14, 2017, WhiteHouse.Gov, https://perma.cc/GN2D-L3XH; "Remarks by President Trump on Infrastructure," August 15, 2017, WhiteHouse.Gov, https://perma.cc/U9LL-SPVG.

54. Julia Manchester, "David Duke: Charlottesville Protests about 'Fulfilling Promises of Donald Trump,'" The Hill, August 12, 2017, https://perma.cc/6JK4-YHKQ.

55. Sarah Rankin, "Pain, Anger, Frustration at Charlottesville Town Hall," AP News, August 28, 2017, https://perma.cc/2W39-S2VT.

56. U.S. Department of Justice, Community Relations Service, Annual Report, 2017.

57. Grande Lum, "Trump Budget Would End Agency That Resolves Differences in a Time of Deep Division," The Hill, February 23, 2018, https://perma.cc/V6U8-H3PX.

58. Peter Salem, interview with Grande Lum, January 30, 2020.

TWELVE

Arabs, Muslims, and Sikhs

Preventing and Responding to Unfounded Violence after 9/11

SEPTEMBER 11, 2001, TERRORIST ATTACKS

ON THE MORNING of September 11, 2001, New York City–based CRS regional director Reinaldo Rivera was at a New Jersey summit on racial profiling. At 8:46 a.m., an American Airlines 767 crashed into the North Tower of New York City's World Trade Center. Because Rivera was with the New Jersey state attorney general, he learned quickly of the attack. Rivera immediately called his staff, who at that moment were traveling to Long Island, New York, for an unrelated case. Getting into Manhattan had already become difficult, so Rivera instructed his conciliators to remain on standby. At 9:03 a.m., another 767, United Airlines Flight 175, flew into the World Trade Center's South Tower.

September 11 initiated a new, fraught-filled era for the United States. For CRS, it was the beginning of a long-term immersion in conflict issues that involve discrimination and violence against those whose appearance led them to be targets of antiterrorist hysteria or misplaced backlash. Appropriately, in the days following 9/11, the federal government, including the FBI, concentrated on ferreting out the culprits for the heinous acts. However, once the discovery was made that Middle Eastern terrorists were responsible for the tragedies, communities around the nation saw a surge of violence against people who appeared to be of Middle Eastern descent, requiring a response to protect those unfairly targeted.

VIOLENCE AGAINST PEOPLE WHO APPEARED TO BE OF MIDDLE EASTERN DESCENT BEGINS, SEPTEMBER 12, 2001

These outbreaks began as soon as September 12. Illinois law enforcement halted three hundred individuals from protesting at a mosque in the Chicago area. In Gary, Indiana, a man fired twenty-one shots at a Yemeni American gas station attendant. In Texas, six bullets struck a mosque.[1] On September 15, Chevron gas station owner Balbir Singh

Sodhi, a Sikh American, was shot by a man an Applebee's waiter had reported as saying he wanted to "shoot some rag heads." The man, Frank Roque, fired through his car window, and five bullets hit Sodhi, killing him instantly. Roque drove to a home he previously owned and had sold to an Afghan American couple and fired on it. He then shot a Lebanese American man. According to a police report, Roque was quoted as saying in referring to the 9/11 tragedy, "I can't take this anymore. They killed my brothers and sisters."[2]

Due to CRS's unique jurisdiction to resolve community tensions relating to discriminatory practices based on race, color, or national origin, it was one of the few federal government agencies in the immediate aftermath of 9/11 reaching out to the nation's Arab, Muslim, and Sikh communities. As Rivera described in an interview in October 2001, "As quickly as [the attack] was linked to Middle Eastern terrorists, we wanted to avoid creating a tremendous backlash against other people who were Middle Eastern or appeared to be Middle Eastern, which included South-Asian and Sikh populations."[3] From 2001 to 2016, CRS addressed a growing number of incidents in first responder fashion, provided preventive measures to reduce hate crimes, and undertook national initiatives to better confront these issues.

CRS mobilized quickly following the terrorist attacks to assess community racial and ethnic tensions in areas of the country with high concentrations of Arab, Muslim, and South Asian populations. Staff were deployed to sites where violence had or would most likely occur. On September 12, 2001, staff in each CRS office were to locate cities with major concentrations of individuals of Middle Eastern or South Asian descent or of Muslim faith.[4] CRS contacted local police personnel, city and state officials, and educators. It also reached out to civil rights leaders—those who were Muslim or Arab American as well as others that could be called on for support. In New York, Rivera and his team worked with state officials, police departments, and state troopers to urge Americans to restrain any urge to act in a retaliatory way against other community members. As Rivera later recalled, CRS conciliators "encouraged that messaging to go into part of what Governor [George] Pataki and Mayor [Rudy] Giuliani were saying in New York, that is, while the primary emphasis was on the rescue and the recovery, [CRS] encouraged messages around maintaining this moderation, restraint, tolerance, and vigorous law enforcement of hate crimes."[5]

Rivera noted, however, that while officials wholly agreed with the need to urge restraint from any retaliatory impulses, "The question was how much air time they could give that particular message in the context of the immediate recovery effort."[6] In the days directly following the tragedy, the tolerance messaging was sometimes "left on the floor of the editing room." Still, there were hopeful signs for protecting vulnerable communities in the wake of the tragedy. In New York, the police department was supportive of preventing misplaced retaliatory violence by securing Arab Muslim neighborhoods along Atlantic Avenue in Brooklyn as well as Bay Ridge's Islamic schools and cultural center.

President George W. Bush crucially and memorably fashioned a statement that not only affirmed the nation's intent to hold the attackers responsible but also sought to discourage unfounded backlash against people of Muslim faith. In his September 20 address to a joint session of the 107th Congress, the president stated,

> I also want to speak tonight directly to Muslims throughout the world. We respect your faith. It's practiced freely by many millions of Americans, and by millions more in countries that America counts as friends. Its teachings are good and peaceful, and those who commit evil in the name of Allah, blaspheme the name of Allah. The terrorists are traitors to their own faith, trying, in effect, to hijack Islam itself. The enemy of America is not our many Muslim friends; it is not our many Arab friends. Our enemy is a radical network of terrorists, and every government that supports them.[7]

Attorney General John Ashcroft went forward with a similar message. He warned, "We must not descend to the level of those who perpetrated Tuesday's violence by targeting individuals based on their race, their religion, or their national origin. Such reports of violence and threats are in direct opposition to the very principles and laws of the United States and will not be tolerated."[8]

To support this message of unity and tolerance, Rivera worked with the New Jersey state attorney general, the New Jersey Association of Chiefs of Police, and the League of Municipalities to cosponsor a series of three seminars on best practices and building bridges for police-community relations in the wake of the tragedy. The goal of the seminars was to reinforce the presidential, FBI, and attorney general's messages of restraint and rigorous enforcement of hate crime laws, as well as to encourage more CRS involvement in the rescue-and-recovery effort, described further on in this chapter.

CRS conciliators in New York and New Jersey (and throughout the country) had already established relationships with local Arab, Muslim, and South Asian groups that could be leveraged in CRS's hate-crime prevention efforts. Given his limited CRS staff of two permanent conciliators, it was critical for Rivera to also work in coordination with federal partners like the U.S. Attorney's Office and the FBI; state partners like the state attorney generals, public safety offices, and their civil rights divisions; and local partners like chiefs of police and municipal officials. Throughout this network, the goal was to deliver consistent messaging on tolerance, community protection, and the vigorous monitoring, investigation, and prosecution of hate crimes.

The stress on New Jersey communities was magnified by terrorism investigations in Paterson and Jersey City, where some related terrorist activities were known to have taken place in 1993. Rivera recalled, "There was a larger premium by the investigative efforts on the Arab-Muslim and South-Asian communities [in New Jersey] than elsewhere in the country initially." People in these communities became understandably fearful of being detained or arrested, jailed without due process, and eventually deported. CRS's goals centered on "developing relationships with institutional partners so that we [could] do two things: reduce the level of community tension, preventing its escalation, and maintain community stability."[9]

Critically, CRS efforts in the New York area and across the nation did not divert law enforcement and other governmental resources away from recovery and investigatory efforts. Because CRS has a distinctive mandate and has the specific function of reducing tension, it complements law enforcement by helping keep peace in communities during chaotic and anxious times. This parallel approach also enables a constructive avenue for conversation between federal law enforcement and community members. New York City region CRS conciliators worked in such a fashion with Muslims and South Asians in cooperation with the Immigration and Naturalization Service (INS) and the New York Immigration Service. Rivera recalled,

290

In our outreach to INS we introduced that there were some individuals who might be victims of hate crimes and have concerns around civil rights and civil liberties in addition to immigration questions. When we framed it with INS we talked to the larger sets of concerns that the community would have and then instead of it simply being a meeting around an individual's concern with INS we were able to raise them as larger questions and respond to them as federal partners. This permitted INS to show that it really did have more leniency in its policy and program work and also provided the community leadership groups with the reassurances they needed that their other concerns around civil rights as well as hate crimes were going to be addressed by INS and the Department of Justice.[10]

CRS's communication efforts were enhanced by the recent technological shifts of the era. Although telephone landlines were down in the New York City area for several weeks after the tragedy, the new phenomenon of widespread usage and availability of cell phones allowed CRS to work in ways it previously could not, accessing individuals at a faster pace and while displaced or in transit. Combining these new abilities with the agency's longstanding and trustful relationships with community-based organizations and advocacy groups allowed CRS to play a facilitating role among the New York Police Department, the FBI, and communities experiencing incidents and receiving complaints about law enforcement treatment or lack of hate crime enforcement.

Because CRS does not have an investigative mandate, it is able to gain trust in communities that are otherwise reluctant to engage with state and federal authorities. In this case, deep mistrust hampered relationships between New York law enforcement and communities racially profiled as potential terrorists. CRS conciliators' ongoing relationships with these communities and the law enforcement agencies put them in a position to clarify miscommunications, convene both sides peacefully, and broker agreements. For example, organizations such as the Arab American Institute and the National Merchants Association heard complaints about law enforcement profiling and harassing individuals or failing to follow up on alleged hate crime incidents. In Paterson and Jersey City, New Jersey, CRS conciliators brought together clerics, mayors, chiefs of police, and city councils to develop strategies for reducing tension through a series of community meetings. Positive dialogue resulted in the deployment of handpicked officers who were inclined to a community policing approach to work with Muslim and other minority communities. A brief training for law enforcement on handling community tensions and responses in the World Trade Center disaster effort was also provided.

As part of its commitment to reducing tensions and facilitating communication, CRS took on a first responder role. Throughout its history, CRS has worked in disasters where community conflict exists not only when individuals are targeted for violence because of their race but also when racial tensions occur with respect to a lack of adequate support. In response to these issues post-9/11, CRS became involved in helping those affected by the tragedy access needed services. For example, the proximity of New York City's Chinatown to Ground Zero made Chinatown inaccessible to trucks for an extended period of time. Police barricades for rescue and recovery efforts further isolated the community. During the recovery period, the merchants in the area, who comprised 95 percent of Chinatown business, were experiencing a 70 percent revenue loss. As a result, many businesses were being forced to close.

CRS conciliators worked with merchants and other community leaders to alleviate some of the initial concerns regarding lack of phone communication, lack of road access into Chinatown, and loss of business. In concert with the Federal Emergency Management Agency (FEMA), CRS helped to provide technical assistance and consultation services in Chinatown by connecting those in need with organizations that could provide the services. Part of this assistance involved bringing in CRS conciliator Ben Lieu, who was then working out of CRS's Philadelphia office and could provide access to nearby resource networks.

New York's Chinatown also served as a hub for distributing products to Asian groceries in cities along the East Coast. Conciliator Lieu worked with Verizon to bring in a truck with working phone lines so that Chinatown businesses could communicate with their East Coast customers.[11] Rivera recalled, "We were able to work along with NYPD in Manhattan South and also their emergency command center to allow some access for vehicles for food distribution businesses and others during certain hours of the day. That's something CRS can do, but FEMA cannot. It's just not part of their mission."[12] CRS also helped convene town meetings with FEMA and the Small Business Administration for financial support.[13] This example illustrates how CRS can play a problem-solving role that is outside the purview of other federal agencies, utilizing its knowledge of how to navigate federal and other governmental bureaucracies; its cultural competency; its relationships with specific communities; and the ability to convene stakeholder experience, expertise, and resources.

Beyond Chinatown, community conflict based on race, color, and national origin over access to recovery services was a major concern, especially for low-income areas with a significant concentration of minorities and recent immigrants, some of whom had limited English proficiency. This dynamic is often seen in large-scale disasters. Those with resources, networks, English fluency, and knowledge of how to access support systems can more readily get their needs met than those who do not have the same advantages. Conflicts arise, particularly when local leaders and representatives advocate for their communities and criticize politicians and agencies for not doing enough. Early on after the 9/11 attacks, CRS engaged the United Way of New York and New York Community Trust, which created the September 11 Fund. The fund provided for urgent and longer term needs of those affected by 9/11. Its grants addressed needs such as cash assistance, employment assistance, health care, and mental health services.

Prior to CRS's involvement, these organizations determined they would use Safe Horizons, which was at the time the nation's biggest victim-services organization, to provide social services to crime and abuse victims throughout the city of New York. Numerous local, state, and federal agencies were involved in providing relief services through Safe Horizons and other community- and faith-based organizations. These organizations decided to provide relief services in the wake of the attack regardless of immigration status, which was critical because most governmental assistance required citizenship or legal immigrant status. Rivera further noted that "individuals, between language difficulty and immigration questions, even if they are legally here, have not always been able to get what they need from FEMA." CRS coordinated and facilitated communication concerning accessing these services. "That was an important entrée for people across the board," Rivera noted, "particularly in the lower income areas in New York, and those who might have immigration status questions, to actually be able to get some relief."[14]

CRS's engagement was not bounded by the New York city or state area. Rivera noted, "I think taking the approach of working with high-level officials at the state level, then replicating it at the national level, was very important in maintaining a degree of restraint in the local community settings in New York, New Jersey, Puerto Rico, and the Virgin Islands."[15]

In addition to conducting outreach throughout the country immediately after the tragedy, CRS senior leaders, led by Director Sharee Freeman, worked with officials from national Muslim, Arab, and Sikh organizations from September to November 2001 to guide CRS's conflict resolution and violence prevention activities in the aftermath of potential and real backlash against such communities. Specifically, in the months following September 11, CRS under Freeman's leadership conducted a number of activities to prevent violence and reduce tension. The actions taken were:

- To conduct hate crimes training for police departments and school administrators with major Muslim and Arab-American populations.
- To help and to encourage State Attorneys General and U.S. Attorneys to establish working groups to focus on September 11 backlash issues.
- To encourage municipalities, police departments, schools, and colleges and universities with major Muslim and Arab-American populations to plan and organize racial dialogues.
- To assist local Human Rights Commissions and similar organizations to develop work plans that focus on outreach to the Arab and Muslim communities and strategies to bring about better relations between these communities and the broader community.
- To convene leading superintendents of schools and principals to discuss "best practices" and other measures to address backlash issues affecting Muslim and Arab-American students in their school systems.[16]

CRS conciliators worked not only with Arab and Muslim communities but also with South Asian and particularly Sikh communities, which have origins in India. Although the Sikh religion is not affiliated with Islam, the visually distinct cultural practices of observant Sikhs—especially the men, who wear turbans and sport full facial hair—have attracted attention from people attempting to target Muslims. While anti–Middle Eastern prejudice and discrimination in the United States predates 2001 and had previous spikes (for example during the Iran hostage crisis in the late 1970s), the shock, horror, and tragedy of September 11 was unprecedented. For Arab, Muslim, South Asian, Sikh, and other residents whose appearance could recall Middle Eastern characteristics, the fear of prejudice, discrimination, and even violent hate crime increased exponentially.

For example, a cabdriver from Bangladesh recounted to the *New York Times* how his vehicle was pelted with rocks following the attacks.[17] A spokesman for the mission of Afghanistan to the United Nations said his voicemail hit capacity each hour with reports from people receiving death threats.[18] "Our turbans have turned us into targets," explained one California Sikh. "It's made it incredibly difficult for Sikhs to walk down the street safely."[19] The director of the National Muslim Merchant Association described a "double blow" of first suffering a terrorist attack and then enduring misplaced retaliatory violence. "Hundreds of Arabs worked in the World Trade Center," he pointed out, "and many are missing. I myself know of 20 and their families are devastated."[20]

SHOOTING AT SIKH GURDWARA IN OAK CREEK, WISCONSIN

These issues were not quick to resolve. Even more than a decade later, they continued to plague the nation. On August 5, 2012, six worshippers at a gurdwara were shot and killed by a white extremist in Oak Creek, Wisconsin.

Immediately after the shootings, CRS was in communication with local and national Sikh officials, the local U.S. attorney, and local and federal law and governmental officials. The next day, CRS senior leadership and White House staff participated in a conference call with more than eighty community organizations, as well as an Incident Community Coordination Team conference call organized by the Department of Homeland Security. The objective of these calls was to provide timely assistance and support as well as to solicit feedback from community leaders. On the same day, in response to a reporter's question, President Barack Obama stated,

> If it turns out, as some early reports indicate, that it may have been motivated in some way by the ethnicity of those who were

attending the temple, I think the American people immediately recoil against those kinds of attitudes, and I think it will be very important for us to reaffirm once again that, in this country, regardless of what we look like, where we come from, who we worship, we are all one people, and we look after one another and we respect one another.[21]

U.S. Attorney James Santelle of the Eastern District of Wisconsin and CRS organized a community meeting to focus on hate crimes, share fears over the shooting, coordinate law enforcement, and facilitate funerals needs. CRS and local and federal entities prepared and facilitated a broad community meeting at Oak Creek High School, attended by more than 250 individuals.[22] As one of the members of the local Sikh community noted in the *Milwaukee Journal Sentinel,* recalling having previously been the target of "soft attacks" like verbal insults and being told to leave the country, the massacre brought the tension and fear to a new level: "This was a heart attack. This was a cardiac arrest. This was a watershed moment for our culture."[23]

CRS participated in many community and national conference calls to find resources, provide consultation, and deal directly with issues. CRS conciliators also reached out to Sikh and Muslim leaders throughout the country due to concerns over possible copycat crimes and safety at their houses of worship. Across the country, conciliators began convening meetings and providing cultural competency trainings. On August 10, Attorney General Eric Holder spoke to comfort and praise the victims and their families. He acknowledged the reality of racially profiled hate crimes and pledged action: "Unfortunately, for the Sikh community, this sort of violence has become all too common in recent years. . . . This is wrong. It is unacceptable. And it will not be tolerated."[24]

Given CRS's expertise in Sikh culture and its relationships with Sikh organizational leadership throughout the country, myself and CRS regional director Harpreet Mokha Singh met with First Lady Michelle Obama's team to prepare for her visit to Oak Creek. On August 23, Obama privately visited with victims and families to offer her support and condolences. Before a meeting in the Oak Creek High School, she told Mayor Stephen Scaffidi and temple secretary Kulwant Dhaliwal, "I am anxious to meet with the families and lend whatever support I can."[25]

CRS stayed involved in the Oak Creek community, conducting a follow-up conference six months later. In attendance were local community members; U.S. Attorney Santelle; Oak Creek's mayor, police chief, and school superintendent; and representatives of the Milwaukee County District Attorney's Office, the FBI, and the Bureau of Alcohol, Tobacco, Firearms, and Explosives. The attendees discussed (1) government funding used to increase Oak Creek Gurdwara security measures, (2) Justice Department victim compensation funding that distributed medical and other compensation to tragedy victims, and (3) Sikh cultural awareness training that had been conducted in the area. The Oak Creek police chief noted at the event, "It is not their temple. It is now our temple."[26]

In response to the tragedy, CRS took a lead role—along with the Department of Justice Civil Rights Division—in working with the FBI to add anti-Sikh, anti-Hindu, and anti-Arab categories to the hate crimes being tracked in the Uniform Crime Reporting Program's hate crimes data collection. Law enforcement workers use this form to track hate crimes throughout the country. Without a specific anti-Sikh category, it was not possible to disaggregate data to determine how many incidents were targeting Sikhs rather than Muslim individuals, so it was difficult to determine the problem's extent or trends.[27] Hate crimes, which often succeed in their intent to intimidate and terrify communities of those who look like, speak like, or worship like the crime's individual victims, can further worsen tensions and embolden copycat incidents, particularly if they are not recognized as having this intent. Because reporting by law enforcement is voluntary, hate crimes are tremendously underreported in the United States. Having more specific categories like crimes against Sikhs and Arabs increases trending data on who is being targeted for hate crimes and allows for more systemic prevention.

In September 2012, CRS, under my leadership, launched a newly revised Sikh cultural awareness training program to inform and educate communities experiencing tension, serve as a resource to prevent hate crimes, and train people to assist their communities in preventing and responding to hate crimes against Sikhs.[28] At that event, Deputy Attorney General James Cole announced that the Justice Department supported the addition of these newest categories. Shortly thereafter, the U.S. Senate Subcommittee on the Constitution, Civil Rights, and Human Rights received the testimony of Harpreet Singh Saini, who lost his mother in the Oak Creek tragedy. Saini emphasized the importance of the categories: "The FBI does not track hate crimes against Sikhs. My mother and those shot that day will not even count on a federal form. We cannot solve a problem we refuse to recognize."[29]

The Civil Rights Division and CRS hosted a community roundtable meeting to discuss the issue with faith organization officials. Firm advocacy came from the groups in attendance for requesting the addition of anti-Sikh and anti-Hindu categories to the hate crime data. The suggestion was also made to provide for an anti-Arab bias category as well.

On August 18, 2013, in one of his final acts before leaving the office, FBI Director Robert Mueller included this statistical reporting in the bureau's Uniform Crime Reporting Program. The final categories to be included were hate crime offenses committed against Sikh, Hindu, Arab, Buddhist, Mormon, Jehovah's Witness, and Orthodox Christian individuals.[30] The FBI worked with members of the Hate Crime Coalition, a task force of civil rights groups, to develop new definitions and training scenarios based on the new religion and Arab bias motivations. The collection of new categories began on January 1, 2015, and has been reported in the annual *Hate Crime Statistics* reports ever since.

GOING FORWARD

Former transportation secretary Norman Mineta, reflecting ten years later on the hate crimes that followed the attack on the World Trade Center, said, "The tragedy of September 11th should be remembered in the sense of making sure that we don't let our emotions run away in terms of trying to show our commitment and conviction about patriotism [and] loyalty."[31] The events created a new chapter in American race relations, one in which racial tensions and fear were the highest they had ever been for Arabs, Muslims, South Asians, Sikhs, and others who could be targeted in anti-Islamic hysteria because of their physical appearance or dress. In 2011, a CBS/*New York Times* poll found that most Americans—78 percent—agreed "that Muslims, Arab-Americans, and immigrants from the Middle East are singled out unfairly by people in this country." Shortly after the September 11 attacks, this number stood at 90 percent. The same poll also "found that one in three Americans think Muslim-Americans are more sympathetic to terrorists than other Americans."[32]

To address these misconceptions, in the years following 9/11, CRS has done a significant amount of outreach, dispute resolution, and training to deal with unfounded backlash against Arabs, Muslims, and Sikhs. Under CRS Director Freeman, the agency produced Sikh and Muslim cultural competency trainings and two training videos: *On Common Ground*, which provides background on Sikhism and concerns about safety held by Sikhs in America, and *The First Three to Five Seconds*, which provides background on Muslims and information on their interactions with law enforcement. When I became CRS director in 2012, following the continued incidents of unfounded violence and prejudice against those perceived as sharing heritage with Middle East terrorists, I directed the agency to update the trainings and launched an initiative for regional offices to conduct these Sikh and Muslim cultural competency trainings.

In the months and years after 2001, controversy has continued over racial profiling of Arab, Muslim, and Sikh individuals. Owing to the nature of the attack, one particular area of ongoing concern has been access to airplane flights. Mineta recalled how the racial profiling he witnessed as Secretary of Transportation echoed his own experience as a Japanese American citizen: "There were a lot of people saying, 'We're not gonna let Middle Easterners or Muslims on the planes.' And I thought about my own experience [during World War II] because people couldn't make the distinction between the people who were flying the airplanes that attacked Pearl Harbor and the people who were living in Washington, Oregon, and California, who looked like the people flying the airplanes."[33] In response to this problem, CRS has trained thousands of law enforcement and Transportation Security Association employees on cultural professionalism in working with Arab, Muslim, and Sikh individuals. The work of addressing profiling or mistreatment of Arab Americans, Muslims, and Sikhs also spiked after the 2013 bombing of the Boston Marathon, when CRS conciliators again reached out to leaders throughout the country at mosques and gurdwaras to confront safety and security issues regarding houses of worship and concerns about backlash violence based on faith, nationality, and race.

Since 9/11, the work CRS has done in this area of racial profiling continues to respond to increasing conflicts and tensions both within the United States and around the globe. CRS as a whole adjusted its priorities and reallocated resources in the wake of the September 11 tragedy to address the needs of targeted communities and further intercultural understanding. This trend has led to a fundamental shift in CRS's work in terms of increasing religious awareness training provided to law enforcement and other agencies and committing resources to working with Muslim and Sikh faith and advocacy organizations and people. The 1964 Civil Rights Act that created CRS did not originally envision this work. Nonetheless, this new focus reflects how the model of the African American civil rights movement has inspired other efforts to attain equality and justice for U.S. minority groups.

Much as the tragedy in Selma helped lead to the passage of the 1965 Voting Rights Act, the Oak Creek tragedy helped lead the FBI to update its hate crime categories and, as former FBI director James Comey stated, "do a better job of tracking and reporting hate crime to fully understand what is happening in our communities and how to stop it."[34]

NOTES

1. Chris Wragge, "Tenn. Church, Islamic Center Embrace Post 9/11," CBS News, September 8, 2011, https://perma.cc/YDE5-QX44.

2. Simran Jeet Singh, "A Unique Perspective on Hate-Crimes: The Story of a Convicted Killer," HuffPost, July 20, 2012, https://perma.cc/H533-VC5D.

3. "Re[i]naldo Rivera," Civil Rights Mediation.org, October 29, 2001, https://perma.cc/9CCQ-L2JZ.

4. U.S. Department of Justice, Community Relations Service, Annual Report, 2001.

5. "Re[i]naldo Rivera."

6. "Re[i]naldo Rivera."

7. George W. Bush, "Address to the Joint Session of the 107th Congress," September 20, 2001, in Selected Speeches of President George W. Bush, 2001–2008, 68, https://perma.cc/89TB-VXKE.

8. However, over time, the Bush administration did run programs that targeted Muslims, such as the Special Registration Program overseen by Ashcroft, which began in June 2002 and required Muslim men from specific countries to join a federal register and submit to fingerprinting. Attorney General John Ashcroft, "Prepared Remarks," U.S. Department of Justice, September 13, 2001, https://perma.cc/2G7D-LSDL

9. "Re[i]naldo Rivera."

10. "Re[i]naldo Rivera."

11. Ben Lieu, interview, March 2013.

12. "Re[i]naldo Rivera."

13. Lieu, interview.

14. "Re[i]naldo Rivera."

15. Reinaldo Rivera, interview, March 19, 2013.

16. U.S. Department of Justice, Community Relations Service, Annual Report, 2001, 23.

17. Randy Kennedy, "Cabbies: Drivers Say They Risk Violence by Working, and May Even Lose Money," *New York Times*, September 24, 2001, B8.

18. Laurie Goodstein and Gustav Niebuhr, "Retaliation: Attacks and Harassment of Arab-Americans Increase," *New York Times*, September 14, 2001, A14.

19. Tamar Lewin and Gustav Niebuhr, "Violence: Attacks and Harassment Continue on Middle Eastern People and Mosques," *New York Times*, September 18, 2001, B1.

20. Robert Worth, "For Arab-Americans, a Time of Disquiet," *New York Times*, September 30, 2001, WC14.

21. Gautam Raghavan and Paul Monteiro, "Honoring the Victims of the Oak Creek Tragedy," The White House, August 14, 2012, https://perma.cc/8BY7-DHU4.

22. U.S. Department of Justice, Community Relations Service, Annual Report, 2012, v.

23. Meg Jones and Annysa Johnson, "Temple Cleaned, Forum Held: Conditions of Two Injured Upgraded," *Milwaukee Journal Sentinel*, August 10, 2012, B1.

24. "Attorney General Eric Holder Speaks at the Oak Creek Memorial Service," Justice News, U.S. Department of Justice, Office of Public Affairs, August 10, 2012, https://perma.cc/4NR3-LF8K.

25. Annysa Johnson, "Michelle Obama Meets with Sikh Shooting Victims, Families," *Milwaukee Journal Sentinel*, August 23, 2012, https://perma.cc/VZ5H-VXFZ.

26. "Sikh Coalition Attends Six-Month Follow-Up Conference in Oak Creek," Sikh Coalition, February 4, 2013, https://perma.cc/RY7Y-CQ6W.

27. Ronald L. Davis and Patrice O'Neill, "How Low Hate Crime Numbers Keep Tensions High," *Not in Our Town*, June 6, 2016, https://perma.cc/P4DD-BJPH.

28. U.S. Department of Justice, Community Relations Service, Annual Report, 2012.

29. Harpreet Singh Saini, testimony at "Hate Crimes and the Threat of Domestic Terrorism: Hearing before the Subcommittee on the Constitution, Civil Rights, and Human Rights of the Committee on the Judiciary," 112th Congress, 2012, 62–64.

30. "Crimes against Minorities to Be Considered Hate Crimes in US," FirstPost, August 3, 2013, https://perma.cc/5QSA-9LUM.

31. Jennie L. Ilustre, "Mineta Urges Vigilance vs. Post-9-11 Racial Profiling," *Asian Fortune News*, August 28, 2011, https://perma.cc/D276-HDXP.

32. Brian Montopoli, "Poll: Most Say Muslims Are Singled Out Unfairly," CBS News, September 8, 2011, https://perma.cc/EKM2-YHGT.

33. Ilustre, "Mineta Urges Vigilance vs. Post-9-11 Racial Profiling."

34. James B. Comey, "The FBI and the ADL: Working Toward a World without Hate," Federal Bureau of Investigation, April 28, 2014, https://perma.cc/4RS2-HQEE.

THIRTEEN

Not Only Race

Confronting Other Types of Hate

AT THE FOUNDING of CRS in 1964, its mission focused solely on resolving disputes, disagreements, and differences based on race, color, and national origin. Throughout the country's history, the United States has also grappled with other social differences, such as issues of gender, sexual orientation, gender identity, religion, and disability. As a result of the 1964 Civil Rights Act, other civil rights organizations followed the example of African Americans and advocated for their rights via legislation, litigation, and negotiation.

For years, CRS worked in cases that involved not only race but also other issues. Victims of racism were sometimes targeted for sexual orientation, gender identity, religion, or disability. As this chapter explores, Attorney General Janet Reno directed CRS to work in Ovett, Mississippi, after local residents harassed occupants at Camp Sister Spirit, a lesbian retreat center. CRS also played a lead role in helping to protect African American churches from arson following President Bill Clinton's signing of the 1996 Church Arson Prevention Act.

Hate crimes were another broad area of CRS involvement. For years, civil rights groups worked on federal hate crimes legislation. Finally, in 2009, President Barack Obama signed the Matthew Shepard and James Byrd Jr. Hate Crimes Prevention Act. For the first time, CRS jurisdiction expanded beyond race to include gender, gender identity, sexual orientation, religion, and disability in the response to and prevention of hate crimes. The legislation reflected American society's evolution on issues that called for the tools of community conflict resolution. This expansion helped reenergize and revitalize the Community Relations Service and led to innovative work, for instance in addressing transgender issues.

CAMP SISTER SPIRIT

In August 1993, Brenda and Wanda Henson, along with approximately twenty other women, opened Camp Sister Spirit, a feminist retreat and self-described "folk school" on a 120-acre hog farm near Ovett, Mississippi. The Hensons were a lesbian couple from Gulfport, Mississippi, who had also founded Sister Spirit Incorporated, a nonprofit volunteer organization that ran a clothes closet providing work-appropriate attire for those in need, a food pantry, and a flea market. Camp Sister Spirit was intended to serve as a getaway center for lesbians and others with an interest in positive social change, as well as a site for the Gulf Coast Womyn's Festival, a music and arts event for women.

In choosing a location that would contrast with the city life of their visitors, the Hensons found themselves surrounded by hostility. Ovett is a poor, rural community in southeastern Mississippi with 250 residents at the time—primarily farmers and small business owners. The vast majority were Christian, and many were fundamentalists. The threat to the camp became apparent on November 8, 1993, when a female puppy was shot and draped over the camp's mailbox with sanitary napkins underneath it. A new gunshot hole also appeared in the mailbox itself.

This gory incident was only the first in what became a constant stream of harassment. Local males, young and old, were on the Hensons' property in the middle of the night, drunk and armed. Brenda Henson spoke of "drunk rednecks calling from bars, calling us 'lesbuns' and saying things like, do we sell women, and 'Can we watch?'" Helicopters would also fly low and buzz the ranch.[1] A dead skunk was dumped at their gate. An adult bus driver came to a halt at the gate and encouraged school children to scream "faggot" at the individuals inside. Numerous rounds of gunfire were shot right at the boundary of the retreat. Eventually there would be several death threats against those at Camp Sister Spirit.[2]

As the conflict escalated, the situation captured national media attention, with reporters descending on Ovett. In an extraordinary, high-profile move, the Hensons met for the first time face to face with self-proclaimed "Ovett Citizens Group" leaders on *The Oprah Winfrey Show*, which aired nationally on television on December 21, 1993. The Ovett leaders on the show were J. D. Henry, who published an anti-lesbian column in the local newspaper; John Allen, a local Baptist minister; and Paul Walley, a lawyer representing the group.

As the controversy grew, members of the First Baptist Church in Richton, a town ten miles from Ovett, organized a meeting of the Ovett Citizens Group on January 3, 1994, with four hundred people attending, representing a greater turnout than the total population of Ovett. They raised $852 for the cause of ridding Camp Sister Spirit from the area. During the meeting, attendees watched a videotape of the *Oprah Winfrey* episode, and some laughed when Brenda Henson cried as she conveyed to Oprah Winfrey her fears.[3]

Also in attendance was the National Gay and Lesbian Task Force (NGLTF) spokesperson, Robin Kane. She was in Mississippi for three days, seeking to gain information to persuade the Justice Department to get involved. Kane remarked, "We've hit a dead end in certain areas because sexual orientation isn't covered in federal civil rights law."[4]

This same governmental dead end, however, prevented CRS from assisting. Its mandate was explicitly limited to race, color, and national origin. Although CRS had assured the Hensons it would monitor their situation and notify the FBI, it could not become directly involved without violating its jurisdictional mandate.[5]

As media attention grew, so did the harassment and threats. On Christmas night of 1993, a death threat was phoned into Camp Sister Spirit. Women from the group alleged they were shot at on December 30, 1993. In January 1994, callers to a local radio show violently threatened the women. In the same month, the driveway was spiked and tires punctured. A bomb threat came through the mail on January 13.[6]

NGLTF staff members were determined to pursue Justice Department assistance. They met in January 1994 with representatives of CRS, the Civil Rights Division, and the associate attorney general's office, to which both agencies reported. Although Justice Department officials stated in the meeting that federal civil rights laws did not cover sexual orientation, Kane insisted that "NGLTF continues to stress the need for the Attorney General to direct the Community Relations Service to mediate."[7]

These advocacy efforts paid off, as Attorney General Reno signed an order the following month that transferred the Civil Rights Division's legal authority to advise on civil rights matters to CRS.[8] In doing so, she created legal authority for CRS to work outside of the jurisdiction mandated by the 1964 Civil Rights Act. It would be the first time CRS worked on a case explicitly involving sexual orientation, yet this authority was limited to the specific case at hand.

Reno's actions reflected the concurrent actions of the Clinton White House to address discrimination against homosexual people as a civil rights matter. Earlier the same week, the White House had issued a letter from Clinton opposing state and local referendums designed to block gay civil rights. President Clinton had also appointed the first openly gay federal administration official confirmed by the Senate, Roberta Achtenberg, the previous year. (By contrast, however, he signed the controversial "Don't Ask, Don't Tell" bill that would allow gay service members in the military as long as the individuals did not disclose their sexual orientation. Many gay civil rights groups opposed the watering down of the original bill, which would have outlawed discrimination against openly gay service members.)

CRS's Ozell Sutton and Susan Brown were assigned to the case. Upon hearing of Reno's decision to transfer advising authority to the CRS, Brenda Henson told the *New York Times*, "I'm just overwhelmed and thrilled. We've been forced to build fences instead of bridges. Now the Justice Department will try to find some common ground between us and the idiots."[9] On *Larry King Live*, Henson provided a less inflammatory perspective on mediation: "We asked for the mediators to come in . . . because we want to sit down at a table together, where we can dispel myths and rumors and lies about us."[10]

The Ovett Citizens Group's lawyer, Paul Walley, on the other hand, stated of Reno's order, "It's a waste and shows that the Administration is out of focus and allowing its bias to overcome its rationality. The area is a conservative religious community that has a standard based on biblical morality. Residents at Camp Sister Spirit reject that standard and have a radical agenda that would seek to change our way of life." With respect to mediation, Walley told the *Times*, "I don't know where there is room to compromise. Our position has no compromise."[11]

Mississippi sympathizers with the group voiced similar arguments. Christian Action Commission executive director Paul Jones expressed that mediation was not possible as Christians cannot compromise their values.[12] Others in the Ovett area commented that they were unwilling to participate in mediation because they did not want to validate what Reno was doing: setting a precedent for negotiation with those whose views they found intolerable.[13] CRS conciliator Sue Brown noted in a phone interview that one reason local members did not come to the mediation table was because they felt doing so would show support for the lesbian lifestyle and Camp Sister Spirit's mission.[14]

Sutton and Brown met with both the Hensons and local leaders to assess the situation.[15] Although Jones County sheriff Maurice Hooks said after meeting with CRS, "I'm for whatever will bring a peaceful solution," the Ovett Citizens Group representatives refused to meet jointly with the Hensons.[16]

To further assert its disapproval of the mediation process, the Ovett group renamed itself Mississippi for Family Values (MFV) and sued Attorney General Reno on March 5, 1994. They claimed that Reno's authorization was unconstitutional and ran counter to the Ninth and Tenth Amendments limiting federal interference and federal powers. The plaintiffs noted in the suit that Reno's statement that "the intolerance and bigotry demonstrated by some of the people of Ovett has no place in this country" was, in the plaintiffs' words, "contradictory of a genuine desire to mediate." The attorney representing the group, Michael Barefield, argued that the problem with the Hensons "should not be settled behind closed doors. It is a hot issue in America today and arguments for both sides should be public."[17]

Department of Justice spokesperson Carl Stern defended CRS involvement, noting its successes in defusing conflicts ranging from tax disputes to nuclear power.[18] District Court Judge for the Southern District of Mississippi Charles Pickering threw out the MFV case. He found that "the power of this Court to second guess actions of any governmental agency is limited" and added that authorizing CRS involvement could not be construed as interference because "the Attorney General has no authority to compel mediation." The 1964 Civil Rights Act Title X clearly states CRS's work is provided strictly on a voluntary basis.[19]

The issue brought greater attention to gay rights in the U.S. House of Representatives, which chose to host its House Judiciary Subcommittee on Civil and Constitutional Rights that summer in Jackson, Mississippi. The subcommittee was chaired by openly gay Massachusetts congressman Barney Frank and New York congressman and gay rights advocate Jerrold Nadler. The subcommittee called CRS Regional Director Sutton as a witness; he noted how communication breakdowns are magnified by the public aspects of conflicts, which can lead to theatrical tactics.

Direct communication in such situations can fall apart entirely and occur exclusively through the media. Sutton explained the CRS role as one of reopening the lines of communication to reduce hostilities, rebuild trust and relationships, and generate options to resolve conflicts.

The nuisance case brought by MFV against Camp Sister Spirit finally went to trial on May 19, 1995. In July of that year, a local chancery court judge, Frank McKenzie, decided in favor of Camp Sister Spirit and held that they were free to use the land for retreat purposes.

In this community conflict, the communication broke down before it started. Parties met for the first time on a national television show and communicated through the media. Reno's offer of mediation was a workaround to enable the Justice Department to take action despite the Civil Rights Division's being hamstrung due to the limitations of federal civil rights laws. At the time there were no federal laws on the books that would enable the division's attorneys to take action in the case.

However, a lasting outcome of CRS's involvement in the high-visibility Camp Sister Spirit conflict was identification of the need to expand CRS's jurisdiction beyond race. It became clear that CRS needed to be available for conflicts concerning other civil rights legislation related to individuals' identities, such as sexual orientation. Illinois senator Paul Simon, in a 1994 Department of Justice oversight hearing before the U.S. Senate Judiciary Committee, noted that the Camp Sister Spirit conflict marked the first time CRS was involved in a sexual orientation case. Attorney General Reno remarked on "continued interest by both House and Senate members about the parameters of the CRS' jurisdiction." Reno, in responding to a question from Simon, stated, "If the goal is to routinely involve CRS in sexual orientation and religious disputes, then I believe the best strategy for officially involving CRS in these issues is to expand its mandate through legislation. I would be willing to support such legislation if it did not result in a reduction in the services that CRS provides under current law."[20]

The hearing opened the door for advocates, such as NGLTF, to push for such an expansion.[21] A *Los Angeles Times* op-ed cited CRS's involvement at Ovett as a reminder for "the pressing need for a national gay civil rights bill."[22] However, it would be another fifteen years before the passage of the Matthew Shepard and James Byrd Jr. Hate Crimes Prevention Act. Reno's dispatching of CRS to Camp Sister Spirit motivated not only gay rights organizations on the left but also conservative organizations on the right. These organizations characterized Reno as a lawbreaker for acting beyond the bounds of CRS's official jurisdiction.

Looking back on the Camp Sister Spirit case, one can see why MFV refused to come to the mediation table. Both sides used the high-profile case to try to win hearts and minds through the media, whereas CRS mediation would by definition be held confidentially. Clearly, for the Hensons, the desire to mediate an outcome that would allow them to run Camp Sister Spirit peacefully in the community was their primary goal. Although some individuals in Ovett were comfortable with the camp's presence, the MFV had the explicit goal of driving the camp out, which was unlikely to result from mediation.

Perhaps if the mediation offer had been framed differently, not as a means of overcoming local resistance to the camp but as a way of creating civility and safety without any party having to compromise their beliefs or values, local representatives would have been more receptive. However, it is possible that the MFV would have pursued litigation no matter how the mediation offer was presented.

Despite these hostile encounters, for more than a decade, the Hensons and others at Camp Sister Spirit succeeded in building a positive and constructive relationship with many residents of Ovett. This high-profile case has sometimes been called the southern "Stonewall," likening its impact to the protests that followed police raids on the Stonewall Inn, a gay-friendly bar in New York City. As other identity-based issues have joined race at the forefront of national consciousness, federal agencies have sought to expand civil rights protections using approaches that were successful in addressing racial discrimination. Before she passed away, at the end of a letter to the *Advocate* magazine, Brenda Henson noted with great pride, "it was the first time in history sexual orientation was addressed by [the] Community Relations Service!"[23]

FREEDOM OF RELIGION

As with sexual orientation, religion was not originally included within CRS's directive. Nevertheless, CRS worked with religion in a significant way through intersectionality with race issues. The United States has experienced a long history of arson, bombings, and shootings of African American churches, from the bombing of the Sixteenth Street Church in Birmingham, Alabama, that killed four girls in 1963 to the shooting in the Emanuel African Methodist Episcopal Church in Charleston,

South Carolina, that killed nine parishioners in 2015. Such attacks were particularly prevalent in the mid-1990s, when an arson occurred approximately every five days at an African American church. An attack on a church can be extraordinarily hurtful to its congregation and its community, as the action strikes at a spiritual core for that group. A racially motivated arson can be particularly devastating, as the church is so central to the lives of African Americans in the South, especially when the violent act itself removes the place where worshippers normally go to grieve loss.[24]

At the 1996 Congressional Hearing on Church Arsons, CRS Southeast regional director Ozell Sutton testified,

> The attack on African American churches is more than just an act of terrorism against a place of worship. A black church to the African American community is far more than a place of worship. It is an attack on the very soul of the African American community. It is the source of their humanity, their sense of self-worth, their fight for dignity and equality, their leader and their trainer in the struggle for freedom and justice.[25]

Concern about these attacks led Congress to unanimously pass the Church Arson Prevention Act, which President Bill Clinton signed into law in 1996. In addition to increasing the prison sentence for house of worship arson to a twenty-year maximum, the law contained an "Authorization for Additional Personnel to Assist State and Local Law Enforcement." This provision provided for the appropriation of additional monies to the Departments of Treasury and Justice, including CRS, in fiscal year 1996–97 to increase "the number of personnel, investigators, and technical support personnel" as needed in order to "investigate, prevent, and respond" to potential church arsons or terrorist acts.[26]

The act formed the interagency National Church Arson Task Force, which included the Departments of Justice, the Department of Treasury; the Bureau of Alcohol, Tobacco, and Firearms (ATF); and the FBI. The Departments of Justice and Treasury were to investigate and prosecute the arsons. The Community Relations Service's primary role was to dispatch conflict resolution experts to help ease community tensions.

The Federal Emergency Management Agency conducted a comprehensive prevention initiative, and the Department of Housing and Urban Development partnered with the National Council of Churches, the National Congress of Black Churches, and other community agencies to rebuild burned houses of worship across the country.

Attorney General Janet Reno asked then-CRS director Rose Ochi to put together a task force, the CRS Church Burning Response Team (CBRT), to work with the FBI on the church burnings. The FBI provided CRS with a $1 million budget to do so. Martin Walsh, who was the CRS regional director in the Boston office, became the first national CBRT director. Ozell Sutton chaired the task force. Walsh brought together approximately twenty individuals for the CBRT, twelve of whom had recently been transferred from CRS to other federal departments. Additional members were existing CRS personnel, retired CRS staffers from the Atlanta office, and consultants.

The CRS staff members were then placed into teams of two with responsibilities for specific southern states. Teams were deployed when church burnings occurred in their assigned states. The CBRT pair would go to the community, make contact with the FBI and ATF special agents in charge for that location, and reach out to a variety of people including local police, the mayor, the pastor of that particular church, and any faith leader alliance in the community. Whereas the FBI and ATF had investigatory responsibilities, CBRT would take great pains to ensure communities understood its role as conciliatory and healing rather than investigatory or prosecutorial.

The church burnings became a figurative lightning rod for community tensions. In addition to targeted congregations, members of the larger Black community experienced both anger and heightened anxiety in anticipation that other churches would be targeted. Meanwhile, white community members expressed fear of retaliation. CRS conciliator Frank Amoroso noted, "Our role was to get both Black and white communities to come together, sit down and work things out. In the process, we would also help bring together communities to help rebuild the church."[27]

Amoroso recalled that he typically observed a high level of hostility toward the FBI and ATF as law enforcement entities. "The FBI agent would initially polygraph the pastor, and community [members] saw this as an accusation," he explained.[28] White community members displayed different suspicions with respect to the federal officials present, echoing deep-rooted resentments of federal agencies viewed as attempting to supersede the authority of state and local officials. Local mayors, Amoroso said, believed they could handle these situations themselves, and the presence of the federal government only brought more unnecessary media attention.

The CBRT members spent significant time working with FBI and ATF agents on how to approach these communities and overcome barriers to trust. Interestingly, in addition to the need to bring Black and white community representatives together, CRS conciliators discovered that a major problem was bringing together clergy and members from different churches or denominations, such as Methodists and Presbyterians. One solution was for CRS to facilitate clergy exchanges, in which one church facility would host a church service from another congregation. However, Black churches were often more receptive to this idea than white ones.

In most cases, the course of CBRT work involved first facilitating dialogue among different elements of the community and then rallying all these residents to help the people who had lost their church. In one case in South Carolina, three white teenagers were arrested for burning a rural Black church. When the teenagers were asked why they had done it, they responded that they were inspired by the movie *Mississippi Burning*, which depicted a town's hostile response to the investigation of the murders of civil rights workers. Recognizing the need to counteract such impulses, the town's white sheriff—a self-described "redneck"—spearheaded a community-wide effort to rebuild the church.

In addition to bringing the credibility of the federal government to the task of rebuilding community trust, the alignment of different federal agencies within National Church Arson Task Force ensured that the facts of the case were made clear in order to reduce rumors and speculation. Moreover, the task force report captured best practices to help communities reconcile, which CRS used to shape into a best-practices community outreach activities guide. The report provides four points for effectively responding to church burnings with a racial component:

First, assembling a group of seasoned professionals knowledgeable in a variety of subject areas is key to CRS's ability to assist communities in the aftermath of church burnings. Second, extensive information-sharing and expeditious pooling of resources among various agencies involved has been essential to the Task Force's success. Third, developing local mechanisms to continue dialogue in the aftermath of a church burning helps ensure that problems will be addressed in the community before they lead to another crisis. Fourth, a well-designed conference format at the state-wide level can provide a constructive forum in which members of affected communities can discuss their points of frustration.[29]

The Church Arson Task Force was active from June 1996 to August 2000. During this time, its members opened 945 investigations, made 431 arrests, and obtained 305 convictions. The most prominent was the conviction of Jay Scott Ballinger, who pleaded guilty to twenty-six church burnings in eight states. The larger Church Arson Task Force along with CRS's Church Burning Response Team was disbanded in 2000. In its final report, the task force shared that there had been a 53 percent reduction in church burning incidents between 1996 and 1999.[30]

CRS's contribution to this success came from taking the lead in outreach efforts, which included cosponsoring six statewide arson prevention conferences. CRS worked with law enforcement to create Church Watch programs to facilitate collaboration in seventeen states among community members, fire department personnel, and law enforcement officials in the prevention of and response to church fires.

In 2015, studies from the Pew Research Center revealed that over a twenty-year period (1996–2015), the number of church fires declined, though the percentage of intentional fires (as opposed to those that were accidental or caused by nature) continued to be high. Compared to an average of 191 intentional fires reported each year between 1996 and 2000, the incidence of church fires dropped to an average of 74 per year between 2010 and 2014. However, the percentage of all church fires intentionally set did not drop substantially, decreasing only from 52 to 48 percent.[31]

For the Community Relations Service, the church arson response initiative was a unique opportunity to be given significant resources to address a civil rights issue of widespread concern. CRS was able to help over 250 localities in seventeen states heal after a devastating event, ease community tensions, and rebuild community trust. Conciliators reported that it was rewarding to see how many of those communities, after being so adversely impacted by attacks on their churches, were able to come together and emerge from this crucible as more resilient and trusting communities.

MATTHEW SHEPARD AND THE HATE CRIMES PREVENTION ACT

The role of CRS in improving community relations around issues of sexual orientation again gained relevance following the brutal murder of Matthew Shepard. On October 6, 1998, the twenty-one-year-old University of Wyoming student, who was majoring in politics and minoring in foreign languages, talked with two other young men at the Fireside Lounge in Laramie, Wyoming. The men, Aaron McKinney and Russell Henderson, offered to give Shepard a ride to his home. The three of them left the bar in a pickup truck.

Eighteen hours later a cyclist discovered Shepard and first thought he was a scarecrow. The young man was tied to a fence with his face covered almost entirely in blood. By the time help reached him, he was in a coma, having suffered extreme brain damage from being beaten and set on fire.

On October 12, Shepard died. By this time, news of the gruesome act had traveled around the country and world. Its motivation appeared clear: Matthew Shepard was openly gay.[32] Writer and gay rights advocate Andrew Sullivan wrote, "I think a lot of gay people, when they first heard of that horrifying event, felt sort of punched in the stomach. I mean it kind of encapsulated all our fears of being victimized."[33]

The murder focused attention on the need for federal hate crimes legislation, which had been introduced in Congress the previous year. Over the ensuing decade, Congress had passed versions of the Hate Crimes Prevention Act (HCPA), but it never came to President Clinton or President George W. Bush for a signature. The HCPA ultimately did become law in 2009, signed by President Barack Obama, and the conferees honored the victims by naming the bill after both Shepard and James Byrd Jr. Byrd was a Black man who had been dragged to a brutal death in Jasper, Texas, also in 1998, in another case that drew national attention for its savagery.

The HCPA specifically authorizes funding for CRS not only to respond to but also to prevent hate crimes, defined as attacks committed because of a person's race, color, religion, national origin, gender, sexual orientation, gender identity, or disability. On October 28, 2009, at the signing of the HCPA, President Obama stated,

> We have for centuries strived to live up to our founding ideal of a nation where all are free and equal and able to pursue their own version of happiness. Through conflict and tumult, through the morass of hatred and prejudice, through periods of division and discord we have endured and grown stronger and fairer and freer. And at every turn, we've made progress not only by changing laws but by changing hearts, by our willingness to walk in another's shoes, by our capacity to love and accept even in the face of rage and bigotry.[34]

President Obama's words capture the space in which CRS has always operated: that arena in which the light of legislation shines on interrelations within communities. He recognized that it is not just the changing of laws that results in progress but also what individuals do in terms of understanding a person different from themselves emotionally and intellectually.

EXPANSION OF CRS'S PURVIEW

For the forty-five years leading up to that point, CRS conciliators had been working to enhance that understanding in terms of racial conflicts as a result of the 1964 Civil Rights Act. Although they had neither the power of litigation nor the tools of investigation, CRS conciliators worked to voluntarily resolve disputes, differences, and disagreements where issues of race, color, or national origin arose. With this new legislation, CRS would now be able to add to its purview gender, gender identity, sexual orientation, religion, and disability.

With significant support from the Department of Justice's leadership offices, including Deputy Associate Attorney General Karol Mason, CRS Senior Counsel Becky Monroe led CRS's preparation for implementation of the HCPA. This effort included working with regional directors from across the country to develop policies and practices necessary to identify and respond to conflicts in the new jurisdictional areas, namely preventing and responding to violent hate crimes on the basis of gender, gender identity, religion, sexual orientation, and disability. CRS also developed the public-facing materials to describe how CRS would fulfill its mandate under the HCPA, providing state and local government, law enforcement, and community leaders with plain-language explanations of how CRS could help communities prevent and respond more effectively to hate crimes.

To ensure that CRS was sufficiently prepared to implement the HCPA, Monroe directed and convened an all-staff training and engaged experts from all of the newly articulated areas in late February 2010. The Leadership Conference on Civil and Human Rights, an umbrella organization of the nation's leading civil rights entities, brought together groups representing communities that could be targeted for violent hate crimes committed on the basis of race, color, or national origin. As noted in CRS's 2010 annual report, some of the groups included representatives from the NAACP, the National Council of La Raza, the Asian American Justice Center, and the American-Arab Anti-Discrimination Committee.[35]

To help CRS work well with communities that may be targeted for hate crimes on the basis of gender, gender identity, or sexual orientation, representatives also participated from the Human Rights Campaign, the Transgender Civil Rights Project, the National Center for Transgender Equality, and the National Gay and Lesbian Task Force. CRS convened panelists from organizations representing communities that could be targeted for violent hate crimes on the basis of their religion. The Anti-Defamation League (ADL) facilitated "a panel including representatives of the ADL, the Interfaith Alliance, the Baptist Joint Committee on Religious Liberty, the Unitarian Universalist Association of Congregations, Muslim Advocates, Third Way, and the Sikh Coalition."[36]

The National Disability Rights Network assembled a dialogue panel on disability communities that could be targeted for violent hate crimes as well. Among the speakers were representatives from the Brain Injury Association of America, the Protection and Advocacy for Individuals with Mental Illness Project, Western New England Law School, the Smith College School of Social Work, and the National Council on Disability. Professor Nancy Chi Cantalupo from Georgetown University and the American Association for University Women spoke about hate crimes targeting people on the basis of gender.[37]

When Monroe became acting director of CRS, the agency conducted outreach throughout the country around HCPA-related issues, partnering with the Civil Rights Division, U.S. Attorneys' Offices, and the FBI's headquarters and field offices to conduct trainings for law enforcement and community members about the provisions of the HCPA. CRS also partnered with these same offices to conduct more basic outreach and informational sessions. In 2010, CRS made 130 community outreach presentations, building on its long history of working with community members from diverse backgrounds to re solve conflict and address tensions that come about from differences of race, color, and national origin to help ensure communities across the country understood the new ways in which CRS could work with them under the HCPA. Federal, state, and local government leaders as well as school administrators and faith and community leaders requested support to address hate crimes and related issues. Just as CRS had done for decades in response to requests regarding crimes associated with race, color, and national origin, conciliators began to mediate disputes, facilitate dialogues, provide technical assistance, conduct trainings, and utilize other conciliation services to respond to all types of hate crimes defined under the HCPA.[38]

SEXUAL ORIENTATION AND GENDER IDENTITY

To date, more civil rights progress has been made on sexual orientation than gender identity, although overall progress has been made for both domains through the work of umbrella lesbian, gay, bisexual, transgender, questioning (LGBTQ) organizations. In 1973, the same year that Lambda Legal (a legal organization advocating for equal rights for gay and lesbian individuals) was established, homosexuality was removed from the American Psychiatric Association list of mental disorders. In the 1990s, openly gay candidates began to win political office in several areas around the country and openly gay characters appeared on television. As mentioned earlier in this chapter, gay service members were allowed to serve in the military (provided they did not disclose their sexual orientation). States began to legally recognize same-sex civil unions.

After the HCPA passed in 2009, same-sex marriage was supported by both President Obama and the Democratic Party, which included this stance as part of its national platform at the 2012 Democratic National Convention. The Supreme Court in *United States v. Windsor* ruled against section 3 of the Defense of Marriage Act, stating in 2013 that legally married same-sex couples are entitled to federal benefits. In 2014, the Supreme Court allowed several lower court rulings to stand, opening the door for states to allow same-sex marriage.

Transgender rights have not progressed as quickly. In 2011, the National Center for Transgender Equality found that "individuals who expressed a transgender identity or gender non-conforming while in grades K-12 reported alarming rates of harassment (78%), physical assault (35%) and sexual violence (22%)." Such factors lead to high marginalization and increased rates of suicide attempts and suicides. The survey found that 41 percent of transgender respondents had attempted suicide. Additionally, a 2012 survey by the National Coalition of Anti-Violence Programs revealed that transgender individuals are more than three times as likely to experience police violence as cisgender people.[39]

CRS responded to a number of high-profile transgender hate crimes in 2010 and 2011. One of the most extensive interventions occurred after a series of murders committed over an eighteen-month period in Puerto Rico took the lives of eighteen LGBTQ individuals, most of whom were transgender. CRS worked to both address the rising tensions in the local community and provide technical assistance to build collaboration between local criminal justice officials and LGBTQ communities. Earlier Department of Justice investigations into the police department in Puerto Rico had uncovered biased policing of individuals who were transgender. This included the targeting and profiling of transgender women of color and harassment and violence toward transgender victims of violence.

CRS regional director Reinaldo Rivera led a team of conciliators who collaborated with law enforcement officers, prosecutors, and members of the LGBTQ community to reduce tension by providing hate crimes prevention training. The CRS team also worked with the Puerto Rico Police Department and the New York Police Department Hate Crimes Task Force to deliver a hate crimes train-the-trainer program in San Juan. CRS conciliators convened dialogues between local community members and law enforcement and helped create structured working groups in the thirteen Puerto Rico police regions. The regional chapters then developed action plans to strengthen police-community relations.[40]

Because the HCPA enabled CRS to work with issues of gender identity, and because transgender communities faced specific, often overlooked challenges, in 2012 as CRS director, I initiated the creation of the Law Enforcement and Transgender Community cultural professionalism training. To begin, CRS convened a series of meetings with leaders from transgender advocacy organizations including the National Center for Transgender Equality; Parents, Families and Friends of Lesbians and Gays; the Human Rights Campaign; and the Transgender Community of Police and Sheriffs International.

Most of these representatives remarked that this was the first meeting they were aware of at any federal agency focused solely and specifically on transgender issues. I was both surprised and touched that so many individuals commented on the pioneering nature of the effort. I did not realize at the time that the effort was without precedent. Their remarks, and their profound appreciation for CRS's commitment to preventing hate crimes and improving community relations with respect to gender identity issues, made me realize the importance of every step toward equality, especially for marginalized minority groups whose rights have not progressed as far as others. It made me even prouder of the work CRS has done and continues to do.

Our meetings with transgender advocacy leaders were followed by an in-person meeting of law enforcement leaders to discuss these issues, many of whom had implemented progressive approaches to working with transgender individuals. They shared best practices in terms of policies and training, provided feedback on training requirements, and offered different scenarios to include in CRS's training video for public safety officers.

In total, more than sixty individuals were involved in shaping CRS's training materials including law enforcement executives, transgender community policy experts, LGBTQ police liaisons, antiviolence program members, and transgender police officers. Numerous meetings and discussions were necessary to ensure a highly professional, relevant, and helpful set of training materials.[41]

CRS Chief of Staff Daphne Felten-Green and Hate Crimes Analyst Kelly Collins-McMurry, who was CRS's first openly gay staff member, initially pushed for CRS to meet separately with community members and law enforcement officials, because they felt those representing transgender or broader LGBTQ advocacy organizations would feel more comfortable without the presence of law enforcement and would more easily build trust with CRS. Ultimately, three main topics percolated from the many meetings: relevant terminology for understanding gender identity, misconceptions that impact prevention and response to hate crimes, and resources and strategies for effective collaboration.

In March 2014, the first federal video specifically focused on law enforcement interactions with transgender individuals was launched with an audience of two hundred people, including top Justice Department officials, transgender community leaders, law enforcement executives, and media. Deputy Attorney General James M. Cole stated,

> CRS's new training helps ensure that we in law enforcement proactively protect the civil rights of all persons, including those who suffer from acts of hate violence or discrimination on the basis of his or her actual or perceived gender identity. . . . At its most basic level, the new training will provide tools to enhance an officer's ability to build partnerships with community members and to work with fellow citizens, who share a commitment to public safety.[42]

Since March 2014, CRS has used a unique cofacilitation model with law enforcement officers and transgender community organization representatives to provide the training. To date, 37 individual trainings have been conducted and 1,400 law enforcement officers have been trained. More than 87,000 people have watched the CRS transgender–law enforcement relations video, which is publicly available on the Department of Justice website and YouTube.

As Attorney General Janet Reno noted in 1995, she supported expanding CRS's jurisdiction as long as doing so did not constrain work in the original jurisdiction of race, color, and national origin. Unfortunately, CRS did not receive additional funds for the HCPA-related work. As a result, the staff time and financial resources that were devoted to CRS's new jurisdictional areas were carved from preexisting staff time and budget. Despite these constraints, CRS undertook numerous initiatives and devoted significant employee time and budget toward learning from experts, creating trainings, convening and facilitating dialogues, and mediating disputes related to the new areas of coverage. The transgender initiative is one example that illustrates a step-by-step approach to supporting previously marginalized groups in increasing their voices and working toward their empowerment.

Throughout its history, CRS has worked with different groups as they move toward greater civil rights. As laws are passed aiding groups that have not previously received those legal protections, CRS plays a critical role of showing up in communities to witness, to reduce tension, and to help groups be engaged in problem-solving to manifest equality in fact, not just law. In 1964, the initial goal of creating CRS was to desegregate public accommodations like hotels, theaters, and restaurants. President Lyndon Johnson and the U.S. Congress recognized the critical role that conflict resolution practitioners could play in helping to make fundamental legal change happen with respect to race in a less adversarial manner. In 2009, the Hate Crimes Prevention Act was passed to respond to and prevent hate crimes based not only on race but also on gender, gender identity, sexual orientation, religion, and disability. President Obama and the Congress recognized the essential role of conflict resolution practitioners to help implement this law in a more collaborative fashion.

NOTES

1. William Booth, "For Lesbian Couple, Mississippi Retreat Is Hardly a Haven," *Washington Post*, December 12, 1993, https://perma.cc/FH8X-CTWM.

2. Katie Green, "Fear and Loathing in Mississippi: The Attack on Camp Sister Spirit," *Journal of Lesbian Studies* 7, no. 2 (2003): 89–95.

3. "Mississippi Town Roiled by Lesbians' Plan for Women's Camp," *New York Times*, January 9, 1994, https://perma.cc/J3U7-X9DF.

4. "Mississippi Town Roiled by Lesbians' Plan for Women's Camp."

5. Booth, "For Lesbian Couple."

6. Green, "Fear and Loathing in Mississippi," 90.

7. J. Epperly, "FBI Steps into Miss. Situation," *Bay Windows*, January 27, 1994, 4.

8. "Reno Sends Mediators to Mississippi as Lesbian-Run Camp Divides Town," *Washington Post*, February 19, 1994, https://perma.cc/ZLT9-7FNB.

9. Stephen Labaton, "Reno Orders U.S. Mediation in Lesbian Harassment Case," *New York Times*, February 19, 1994, https://perma.cc/D9QN-LW9V.

10. Lynch, "Camp Sister Spirit," 155.

11. Labaton, "Reno Orders U.S. Mediation in Lesbian Harassment Case."

12. R. Mullins and J. Dilmore, "Ovett Residents Confused by Sister Spirit's Agenda," *Student Printz*, January 11, 1994, 1.

13. Lynch, "Camp Sister Spirit."

14. Lynch, "Camp Sister Spirit," 156.

15. Peter Applebome, "Mediators Taking Role in Dispute on Lesbians," *New York Times*, February 21, 1994, https://perma.cc/A32M-UBGL.

16. Labaton, "Reno Orders U.S. Mediation in Lesbian Harassment Case."

17. "Suit Rips Reno in Dispute at Ovett," *Memphis Commercial Appeal*, March 8, 1994, B1.

18. "Camp Sister Spirit," Associated Press, March 7, 1994, https://apnews.com/604da8028b02234329a497f45518ba5e.

19. Lynch, "Camp Sister Spirit," 157.

20. *Department of Justice Oversight: Hearing before the Committee on the Judiciary*, 103rd Cong., 2nd sess. (July 28, 1994), 112, https://perma.cc/L2X8-GXZ6.

21. National Gay and Lesbian Task Force, "Expand CRS Mandate," Alert, April 1994, https://perma.cc/C99L-TS5P.

22. Robert Dawidoff, "The Feds, Civil Rights and Camp Sister Spirit: Gay Rights: The Mississippi Case Shows the Need for a Law," *Los Angeles Times*, February 25, 1994, https://perma.cc/GU2E-SU6A.

23. Brenda Henson, "A Friend Indeed," *The Advocate*, August 30, 2005, 16.

24. Tom W. Smith, Michael Davern, Jeremy Freese, and Michael Hout, *General Social Surveys, 1972–2016* [machine-readable data file], sponsored by National Science Foundation; produced by National Opinion Research Center at the University of Chicago; distributed by the Roper Center for Public Opinion Research, University of Connecticut, 2014, https://gss.norc.org.

25. National Church Arson Task Force, *Fourth Year Report for the President*, U.S. Department of the Treasury, U.S. Department of Justice, Bureau of Alcohol, Tobacco, and Firearms, Federal Bureau of Investigation (September 2000), 3.

26. H.R.3525, "Church Arson Prevention Act of 1996," 104th Congress, 1995–96, 110, https://perma.cc/PU5S-5M8S.

27. Frank Amoroso, interview with Grande Lum, October 2018.

28. Amoroso, interview with Lum.

29. National Church Arson Task Force Report, *Second Year Report for the President*, October 1998, https://perma.cc/VA27-HBWS.

30. National Church Arson Task Force, *Fourth Year Report for the President*.

31. Aleksandra Sandstrom, "Half of All Church Fires in Past 20 Years Were Arsons," Pew Research Center, Fact Tank, July 24, 2015, updated October 26, 2015, https://perma.cc/47DN-U26S.

32. This explanation has been challenged by the investigative reporting of Stephen Jimenez, who concludes in *The Book of Matt: Hidden Truths about the Murder of Matthew Shepard* (Hanover, NH: Steerforth Press, 2013) that Shepard's murder was not a hate crime but was instead connected to drug-dealing.

33. "New Details Emerge in Matthew Shepard Murder," ABC News, January 5, 2006, https://perma.cc/FZE8-7CFV.

34. Barack Obama, "Remarks by the President at Reception Commemorating the Enactment of the Matthew Shepard and James Byrd Jr. Hate Crimes Prevention Act," October 28, 2009, https://perma.cc/VT7Z-SEHW.

35. U.S. Department of Justice, Community Relations Service, Annual Report, 2010.

36. U.S. Department of Justice, Community Relations Service, Annual Report, 2010.

37. U.S. Department of Justice, Community Relations Service, Annual Report, 2010.

38. U.S. Department of Justice, Community Relations Service, Annual Report, 2010.

39. Jaime M. Grant et al., *Injustice at Every Turn: A Report of the National Transgender Discrimination Survey* (Washington, D.C.: National Center for Transgender Equality and National Gay and Lesbian Task Force, 2011); National Coalition of Anti-Violence Programs, "Lesbian, Gay, Bisexual, Transgender, Queer and HIV-Affected Hate Violence in 2012," 2013, https://avp.org/wp-content/uploads/2017/04/ncavp_2012_hvreport_final.pdf.

40. U.S. Department of Justice, Community Relations Service, Annual Report, 2011.

41. Christopher "Kit" Chalberg and Kelly Collins-McMurry, "Department of Justice Agency Facilitates Improved Transgender Community-Police Relations," *LGBTQ Policy Journal at the Harvard Kennedy School* 6 (2015–16): 7–21.

42. "Deputy Attorney General James M. Cole Delivers Remarks at the Community Relations Service Transgender Law Enforcement Training Launch," U.S. Department of Justice, March 27, 2014, https://perma.cc/VR4H-GX6B.

FOURTEEN

Crossing Borders

The Elián Gonzáles Custody Dispute

ON NOVEMBER 21, 1999, five-year-old Elián González; his mother, Elizabeth Brotons Rodríguez; and several other Cuban nationals departed Cuba in a tiny aluminum raft seeking asylum in the United States. Four days later, on Thanksgiving Day, Elián was alone, hanging onto an inner tube three miles off the Florida coast. He and two other survivors were rescued at sea by fishermen who escorted them over to the U.S. Coast Guard. Elián's mother and the other passengers died in the crossing.

The U.S. Immigration and Naturalization Service (INS) did not follow normal protocol for dealing with unaccompanied Cuban migrants found at sea. Elián should have been placed with the Community Relations Service, which at the time ran the Alien Unaccompanied Minors Shelter Care Programs. However, because it was Thanksgiving weekend, and because Elián was so young, the INS officials made the decision to give temporary custody to Elián González's paternal great-uncle Lazaro González, who was waiting at the dock in Miami when Elián arrived.[1] After Elián was released from the hospital on November 26, INS immediately placed him with González and his adult daughter Marisleysis González, who were living in Miami. Little did they know that this fateful choice would lead to a full-blown international crisis.

Elián's father, Juan Miguel González, did not know that his ex-wife had left Cuba with their son. After hearing rumors, he called relatives in Miami. Discovering Elián was with them, Juan Miguel told his uncle to take care of Elián until he could arrange to bring him home. Marisleysis, who by all accounts had already bonded with Elián, later said, "In the beginning of everything I always had a picture in my mind that [Juan Miguel] was going to come and stay and it was like wow, my whole family is going to be reunited."[2]

Juan Miguel petitioned Cuban government officials for help in repatriating his son. That same day, the Cuban government sent a message to the U.S. mission in Havana asking for Elián's return to Cuba on the grounds that he had taken the journey without his father's knowledge. The next week, Elián's father filed a complaint with the United Nations to draw focus to his custody plight. The State Department recused itself from determining custody, leaving the question to the Florida courts. Elián's Miami relatives, backed by leaders and politicians in the Cuban exile community, indicated they would not return the boy. They believed that Elián would not be safe in Cuba but rather would become a puppet of Fidel Castro's communist regime. The Cuban American National Foundation, the most powerful Cuban exile organization, began publicizing the incident to media outlets across the country. This national publicity in turn led to a strong response by Castro and Cuban officials, who began a campaign to bring Elián back to Cuba.

On December 10, the Miami relatives filed a request for Elián's political asylum. An acrimonious and highly politicized custody fight ensued, causing turmoil within the Miami community. The case became a battleground for community leaders, politicians, the archdioceses, and local exiles to powerfully express their anti-Castro sentiments. In essence, as CRS conciliator Thomas Battles, who became closely involved with the case, recalled, Elián "became a symbol of the fight between the exile community and Fidel."[3] The young boy's plight served as a mobilizing force for each side. Thousands of demonstrators would turn up for rallies in both Cuba and Miami.

The case highlighted already tense relations between Cuba and the United States, which have been strained since the Cuban Revolution ended in 1959 and the communist regime of Fidel Castro took power. Many Cubans fled Castro's regime and sought asylum in the United States, making immigration from Cuba to the United States a particularly fraught issue. In an attempt to normalize migration between the two countries, in 1995 the Clinton administration made several changes to U.S. immigration policy regarding Cuban immigrants. Through various mechanisms, Cubans were allowed to legally migrate. Programs included the diversity lottery, refugee admission, immigrant visa issuance, and the Special Cuban Migration Program. These generous immigration policies led to a massive influx; by the 1990s, the U.S. Cuban exile community had grown into a politically vibrant and economically powerful force in Miami.

This community was prolific in its protests and media appearances as Elián's case was pending. Conciliator Battles, based in Miami, was involved in the case from the beginning. The INS International Affairs Division requested he arrange communication between community leaders and INS officials in an effort to prevent outbreaks of violence. CRS was well positioned for this role as it was already deeply involved with the Cuban immigrant community through its work helping to administer the federal Cuban-Haitian Entrant Program. Several Spanish-speaking conciliators were brought in from around the country, such as Rosa Salamanca, Carol Russo, and Efrain Martinez. These conciliators gained the trust of the Miami Cuban community and convened on a regular basis with its leaders to better understand its interests and assure peaceful protests. The CRS team gave the INS and the U.S. Attorney's Office continuous assessments of the racial tensions in Miami and of the Cuban American community's responses to INS positions.[4]

In addition to this community-level work, CRS was involved in facilitating communication among the parties in the custody dispute. Battles's established relationship with the INS in Miami and close community ties gave him the resources to play a pivotal role in keeping the custody dialogue moving forward under adverse conditions. Battles was a protégé of civil rights and CRS icon Ozell Sutton. Both men became regional directors of the Southeast Regional Office, overseeing an area that had had a historically high volume of difficult race relation cases since Selma. Both were prominent members of African American fraternities and both had a huge network of relationships they often leveraged to successfully conciliate situations.

Notably, this work has been lost to history. Even a leader in the dispute resolution field, Bernard Mayer, wondered in his 2004 book *Beyond Neutrality* "why there was no serious attempt to mediate [Elián's custody] situation."[5] This chapter attempts to provide that missing piece of history and illustrate how much CRS work went into the mediation attempt.

INTERNATIONAL CUSTODY BATTLE

On January 5, 2000, INS commissioner Doris Meissner announced that Elián would be returned to his father in Cuba by January 14. While this could have been the end of the story under normal circumstances,

Elián's relatives in Miami refused to relinquish custody. They filed suit in state family court to have his great-uncle named the child's guardian. On January 10, a circuit court judge granted emergency custody of the child to Lazaro González. Attorney General Janet Reno rejected the family court jurisdiction, informing the González clan that they had to file in federal court.[6] She did, however, lift the January 14 deadline to return Elián to his father. The Cuban American National Foundation assisted Elián's Miami relatives in these legal efforts.

Although Reno represented the federal government, she was also a Miami native whose parents were both reporters for Miami newspapers. After graduating (as one of sixteen women in a class of five hundred) from Harvard Law School in 1963, she had spent most of her professional legal career in Florida. In 1978, Reno became the first woman to serve as a Florida state's attorney, positioned within Dade County, now Miami-Dade County. She was familiar with cases involving children's well-being: Reno's office prosecuted high-profile child abuse cases, using a controversial approach that involved interviewing young victims and obtaining graphic details. Her work inspired the passage of legislation that allowed these children to provide testimony via closed-circuit television.

Nominated by President Bill Clinton, Reno was the first woman to serve as U.S. attorney general. It is easy to imagine how her prior experiences might have colored her response to the Elián González case: in 1993, she authorized the FBI to use force to take over the Waco compound of the Branch Davidian religious group led by David Koresh. Seventy-six people died that day. Reno apologized for that decision and took responsibility for the deaths. This experience must likely have weighed heavily in Reno's thoughts as she considered whether to use force to remove Elián from his Miami relatives' home.[7]

In her time as attorney general, Reno championed mediation arguably as much as any attorney general in history. She created and funded the Office of Dispute Resolution in the Department of Justice and brought in CRS to play a central role in high-profile cases including that of Elián González, the Camp Sister Spirit situation, and various African American church burning cases. Reno directed her senior Department of Justice team and included herself in after-hours mediation training that was conducted by Georgetown law professor and mediator Carrie Menkel-Meadow and D.C. mediator John Bickerman.[8]

While the González case was proceeding through the courts, CRS endeavored to broker talks and define a workable agreement between family members, the U.S. Attorney's Office, and INS. Battles met regularly with the Miami family and their representatives in their home. The Miami family demanded that Juan Miguel come to Miami to pick up his son to prove Elián's return was Juan Miguel's will and not Castro's. It was unclear why Juan Miguel had not made the journey, though some speculated he was prevented from doing so by the Cuban government, either from fear that he would defect (and choose to remain on U.S. soil) or because Castro preferred that the high-profile conflict continue.

In an attempt to find a compromise, Reverend Joan Brown Campbell, general secretary of the National Council of Churches, became involved in the dispute. Campbell asked Castro for permission to bring Elián's grandmothers to the United States so that they could petition for his return. This request was granted, and the two women, Mariela Quintana and Raquel Rodríguez, came to Miami in January 2000. Battles facilitated a meeting between Elián, his Miami relatives, and his grandmothers at the Miami Beach home of Barry University president Sister Jeanne O'Laughlin, a close friend of Reno. Battles recalled that the women were offered asylum in the United States but refused.[9] No compromise was reached. Marisleysis later stated that Elián ran out of the room saying, "Run, run! They are going to take us," which she interpreted as Elián fearing that his grandmothers would take him away despite his desire to stay in the United States.[10] Both women traveled to Washington, D.C., after the meeting and spoke with members of Congress and the attorney general. After nine days of nonstop media coverage, the two grandmothers returned to Cuba. Elián did not attend any future meetings.

Throughout January and February, Juan Miguel continued to publish open letters to the U.S. government restating his demand for his son to be returned while refusing to personally retrieve him. Meanwhile, CRS conciliator Ben Lieu responded, at Battles's request, to activity brewing at the Cuban Interests Section (similar to an embassy) in Washington, D.C. A group of Cuban exiles were planning to gather outside the building to protest and deliver their own open letter to the Cuban government. There was concern that the situation might escalate if the protesters attempted to enter the property, which is considered Cuban soil. Conciliator Lieu successfully negotiated with the Cuban government representatives and the protesters for the letter to be accepted without trespassing. The protesters were able to voice their concerns without a major incident.

On January 28, the U.S. government asked the judge to throw out the Miami family's federal lawsuit, and on March 9, a U.S. district judge did so. Adding to tensions, several prominent elected officials weighed in on the case. In a speech in Miami's downtown, Miami-Dade County mayor Alex Penelas stated that the municipality would not cooperate or assist with Elián's repatriation. Presidential politics also leveraged the situation to try to win votes in Florida, a swing state divided almost evenly between Republican and Democratic voters. The Democratic presidential nominee, Vice President Al Gore, announced that he supported legislation that would provide Elián the ability to stay in the country while the lawsuit was settled in family court.

However, there was also Democratic support in Congress for helping Elián's father regain custody. Democratic senator Patrick Leahy arranged for Washington, D.C., lawyer Gregory Craig to represent Juan Miguel. Craig flew to Havana to meet directly with Castro. Craig recalled Castro shaking his finger and saying, "Why do you think an American court would rule in favor of a Cuban national? There's never been a case where a Cuban national has won." Craig's response was, "I don't know of any time when the government of the United States has been on the same side of the case as the Cuban national, which in turn [would] be on the same side as the government of Cuba. That's never happened in history. So maybe the results will be different."[11] Upon his return, Craig announced that Juan Miguel González would be coming to the United States.

Tensions grew further as it became clear to the Miami family and Cuban exile community that negotiations were not progressing in their favor: Attorney General Reno was moving toward returning the boy to his father. On April 3, the U.S. State Department approved a visa for Juan Miguel to come to the United States. He arrived in Washington that same week and met with Reno, who insisted on speaking with him privately so she could ask him if he wanted to stay in the United States. According to INS Commissioner Meissner, "He cut off the conversation almost when it started, saying, 'I stand by my word. I have a family in Cuba. I have a life in Cuba. My son is going to grow up as a Cuban, and I am not going to be claiming asylum.'"[12] Following this conversation, Reno stated that U.S. officials would take steps to transfer Elián to his father by April 13.

Jorge Mas Santos, a prominent Cuban American business leader, called for "a neutral third party" to mediate between the Miami relatives and the U.S. government and sought out the Catholic Church. Pope John Paul II allowed the use of the Vatican Embassy in Washington, D.C. Elián was to stay at Santos's home, be flown to Washington at 4 a.m., and then taken to the embassy, where dialogue would proceed to return Elián to his father. At the last minute, the Miami relatives decided not to go through with the plan and refused to allow Elián to be brought to D.C. The González family released a videotape of Elián telling his father that he did not want to go back to Cuba.

PLANNING FOR TRANSITION

During the week of April 9–16, CRS held multiple meetings to discuss a peaceful transition of custody. These discussions focused on identifying community leaders to assist in moving the situation toward resolution. Battles participated in another meeting at the home of Sister Jeanne O'Laughlin in Miami Beach. This time, the meeting was between Attorney General Reno, Elián's Miami family members, and their attorney. The meeting was held to discuss the process of transferring Elián to his father, but still the Miami relatives opposed any such action.

When no agreement had been reached by the April 13 deadline, in a separate meeting in Miami, Reno met with Battles and the CRS team to seek their assessment of potential conflicts if the Department of Justice initiated efforts to obtain Elián by force. To respond fully to Reno's concerns, CRS regional director Ozell Sutton flew to Miami to conduct an onsite assessment of staffing needs and discuss with Reno the latest activities related to CRS involvement. Reno, Battles, the U.S. Attorney's Office, and INS continued their negotiations with the family during this time.

On the evening of April 16, the CRS team met with community leaders who were in direct communication with the Miami family. They indicated that a plausible agreement negotiated by CRS, Reverend Jesse Jackson, and Florida senator Robert Menendez could include four major points: (1) Elián would be able to travel back and forth from Cuba to visit his Miami family, (2) a monitoring commission composed of exile leaders and clergy would assess Elián's well-being in Cuba, (3) the

Miami family would be able to visit the child in Cuba on negotiated agreement with the secretary of state, and (4) Castro would guarantee that no harm would come to Elián in Cuba. These terms were not accepted by the Miami family.

A COMMUNITY REACHING ITS BOILING POINT

CRS team members were monitoring round-the-clock protest demonstrations, the largest of which drew more than fifteen thousand people. These demonstrations were held in the Little Havana neighborhood near the home where Elián was living with his Miami family. As the name suggests, many Cuban exiles had settled in this neighborhood, which functioned as the social center of the Miami Cuban community. Drama was high, and a media circus ensued. Local radio and television stations broadcast live around the clock, prayer vigils were being held, tires were burned, and cars were caravanning, honking their horns, and waving Cuban flags. A stage was set up where leaders and Catholic clergy periodically spoke to the crowd. During the day, there was often a party atmosphere that turned to a more serious tone at night.

Miami police had a large and ongoing presence at the demonstrations, which may have deterred violence but also heightened tensions. On one occasion, community distrust of the police presence rose to a near flashpoint when officers arrived in riot gear carrying gas masks and other combat paraphernalia. Meanwhile, the police force itself was being pushed near its breaking point by the extensive overtime required to maintain a constant presence. Officers on the rotation were weary and irritable. CRS was able to diffuse the situation by working with law enforcement to meet their needs for preparedness without inciting protesters at the scene. For example, measures included assigning police with Spanish language skills to the rotation. Ensuring a shared language helped to facilitate a more amicable relationship between police and protesters.

Another situation CRS helped manage concerned the spread of out-of-control rumors about the federal government's plan to remove Elián on the one hand and community plans to retaliate or block the government's efforts on the other. Expectations of extreme actions from both parties were creating high levels of stress for the police officers onsite in Little Havana. Police requested CRS assistance in setting up a rumor control center. The resulting initiative tracked rumors as they emerged and leveraged communication with trusted community leaders to dispel false stories.

Battles was also involved in facilitating communication between local Cuban American and African American leaders. The Miami exile community expressed frustration that they were not receiving more support from the African American community. However, the position of the local African American leadership was that Elián should be brought back to his father on the grounds that if a willing parent is available, he should be responsible for his child. There were also political tensions underlying this stance, as Miami Cuban leaders had previously blocked South African president Nelson Mandela from receiving the keys to the city due to Mandela's gratitude toward Fidel Castro for assistance with his antiapartheid work. Through Battles's position of trust within both communities, he was able to help ensure these tensions did not escalate.

On April 19, the Eleventh U.S. Circuit Court of Appeals agreed to a request by Elián González's Miami family to prevent his return to Cuba. The ruling stated that Elián must remain in the nation until his Miami family could appeal for an asylum hearing in May. Lazaro lost temporary custody when a local family court judge revoked it. At that point, Elián's father had rightful custody in the eyes of the United States, though the asylum hearing decision would not come until May.

The situation appeared to be edging toward resolution as Elián's father was able to have a twenty-five-minute phone conversation with Elián, and Reno was working with numerous intermediaries, including the Miami González family's lawyer and a local negotiator, to form an agreement for transfer of custody. They proposed a plan for the four Gonzálezes—Elián, Juan, Lazaro, and Marisleysis—to travel to either Wye Plantation on Maryland's Eastern Shore, where Middle East peace conferences had taken place, or Airlie House, a hotel near Warrenton, Virginia. Battles met again with Lazaro and Marisleysis to discuss the proposal. But because the offer by this new group still did not involve immediate transfer, the government officials perceived it as a delaying tactic by the Miami family to extend the negotiation clock without committing to a final resolution.

With negotiations stalled again, Justice Department spokesperson Carole Florman stated that Reno was "looking to our law enforcement officials to determine the best timing and methods" for federal law enforcement to enter Lazaro González's home and forcibly take Elián from the premises.[13] Seeking Battles's advice but careful to avoid involving him in the actual planning of a raid so as to preserve his position of trust with the community, Reno presented Battles with several different hypothetical situations in which federal officials entered the premises. One idea was for Reno and Battles to enter the home, which Battles said the family would allow them to do. However, he believed the family would not turn Elián over to Reno. This approach was abandoned due to the likely political cost of a failed raid. Another suggestion was for someone from the Unaccompanied Minors Program to collect the boy, but Battles cautioned against putting someone who lived in Miami in such a position, as there would likely be a severe backlash. This guidance led to the decision to identify an INS agent from outside the area to retrieve Elián.[14]

On April 21, a crowd gathered in front of Lazaro González's home. Many Cuban exiles had promised to form a human blockade to prevent federal authorities from removing Elián. At the house were a number of attorneys and Miami civic leaders who came in as last-minute mediators, including the University of Miami's president, Edward T. Foote, and two of its trustees, Carlos Saladrigas and Carlos De la Cruz, as well as lawyer Aaron Podhurst.[15] A fax machine was brought to the González house to convey documents to the Justice Department. At 11 p.m., Ramon Saul Sanchez, head of the anti-Castro Democracy Movement, told the crowd there "had been progress in the talks but urged the demonstrators to stay in case they need to reform a human chain to prevent the government from forcibly removing Elián."[16]

Attorney General Reno, Immigration Commissioner Doris Meissner, Deputy Attorney General Eric Holder, and others waited in the attorney general's D.C. office to see whether the Miami relatives would accept the counteroffer. Reno was on an open line with Podhurst, while Meissner was speaking with the INS team that would lead the raid. Holder was the liaison to Greg Craig, Juan Miguel González's attorney, who was with Juan Miguel. Battles, who had been told by Reno that afternoon to cease his negotiations, was not involved in this stage of proceedings and unaware of the impending raid.

Midnight was the original internal deadline Reno had set for an agreement. If no agreement was made, the plan was to initiate removal of the boy at 4 a.m. While many at the Justice Department were concerned about the dangers of a nighttime raid to remove a small child, law enforcement's analysis was that there would be fewer people present at that hour, and those who were present would be less alert. Numerous law enforcement agencies including the U.S. marshals, local police, and the INS were involved in the plan. Despite fears that the plan would be leaked, word did not get out to the Miami relatives that the date and time had been set.

Utilizing telephones and fax machines, offers and counteroffers were proposed into the small hours of the night involving the length of Elián's continued stay, the site and conditions of transfer, Miami relatives' visitation time in Cuba, and the use of mental health practitioners to evaluate Elián's well-being. Still, no agreement could be reached. At 4 a.m., Reno provided the order to go forward with the raid. White House chief of staff John Podesta notified President Clinton. At 4:45 a.m., Meissner noted, "We actually held the operation for five minutes to see whether there was perhaps a final last-ditch possibility of agreeing, but it was not there."[17]

THE RAID AND REUNION

At 5:10 a.m., in the predawn of April 22, armed U.S. federal agents began their raid. Chaos broke out in the surrounding vicinity. Mace and pepper spray were utilized on protesters outside the home who were trying to get in the way. The agents had to force their way into the house when family members inside would not open the door. They searched the house, eventually finding Elián, who was hidden in a closet. Associated Press photographer Alan Diaz captured the photograph that went around the world of an INS agent pointing his rifle at Elián and Donato Dalrymple, the man who saved Elián at sea. Cornered, Dalrymple handed over Elián to the INS agent.

Despite all the attempts at mediation and negotiation, it had come to forcible withdrawal. As hard as Attorney General Reno, CRS conciliators, and others tried, they were not able to prevent the armed confrontation. The Justice Department came under heavy criticism for forced removal, yet the evidence indicates there had been arduous and extensive efforts to end the situation peacefully. The case intermingled the personal and the political so tightly, the mediators and negotiators could not come to a resolution within the timeframe. Battles later recalled of the Miami family's willingness to negotiate the return of Elián to his father, "At one point in time I thought that there was a possibility that they would give [Elián] up. But I think the politics of Fidel and the exile community overshadowed that."[18] Perhaps a peaceful resolution would still have been possible with more time, but after nearly five months of failed proposals, such an outcome did not appear likely.

Elián and his father were finally reunited a few hours later at Andrews Air Force Base. Later on the day of the raid, those involved in the last-minute mediation gathered in the office of *Miami Herald* publisher Alberto Ibargüen. The mediation team—Aaron Podhurst, Edward Foote, Carlos Saladrigas, and Carlos De la Cruz—gathered there to recollect the mediation talks before more time passed, so they could capture it more accurately. They chose Ibargüen's office because two of the four were attending a Miami Heat playoff game.[19]

By the time the four arrived, Podhurst had received a message to phone Attorney General Reno. Ibargüen offered to leave his office during the conversation. The four mediators stated Ibargüen would be able to remain as long as the dialogue was treated as confidential. In an interview with a *Herald* reporter, Ibargüen shared, "I could have walked out, gone into the newsroom and said, 'These people are talking to the attorney general. As soon as they open the door, grill them.' That would have been completely unproductive. I would not have known what happened. They wouldn't have said anything."[20]

The conversation might have stayed unknown but for the fact that Elián's Miami relatives included dialogue from the *Miami Herald* office meeting to support a request for an appointed guardian for Elián. Saladrigas queried Reno on whether the child was with his family "outside the control of Cuban agents." According to reports, the mediators thought that if they had more time they could have arrived at a peaceful solution, while Reno stated that Elián's relatives lacked good faith in their negotiation approach.[21]

Notably, Ibargüen cited a book he had read ten years ago, *Getting to Yes* by Roger Fisher, William Ury, and Bruce Patton to explain why the mediation attempt failed.[22] He attributed the misunderstanding to the team of mediators being involved for only three days. In that time period, the four mediators felt they had accomplished a great deal, including the family agreeing to give up Elián and community groups accepting that. However, Reno's team had been at this for months, and the courts had already ordered Elián to be reunited with his father. The

Department of Justice officials likely viewed the family and community as enacting more stalling tactics. Ibargüen sensed that from the Justice Department's perspective, there had not been much progress and there were too many issues to be negotiated out.

It is important to note that Reno was personally close to the four mediators, and they had a reservoir of goodwill. Ibargüen commented that even though the negotiation failed to deliver a peaceful transfer, Reno called the same day to go over what had happened. He observed that even though the mediators had known Reno for years, they misinterpreted her saying "you have five minutes, not six" as a negotiation tactic rather than as the literal amount of time before she would call for the raid.

The four viewed Reno as the ultimate decision-maker. They were surprised to hear that she saw herself as the mediator. The attorney general had told them that "there would be no deal unless she said there was a deal." The four had interpreted that as meaning she would be the decision-maker. According to Ibargüen, she "meant that they should not get [their] hopes up too high until she confirmed with the other side that they agreed." Whether that would have changed the ultimate outcome is unclear, but the miscommunication certainly could not have helped.[23]

Although Juan Miguel legally had Elián in his custody, they stayed in the United States as the Miami family explored all their legal avenues. It would be two months of court procedures, demonstrations, and counterdemonstrations before Elián and his father returned to Cuba. On June 1, the Eleventh U.S. Circuit Court of Appeals determined that Elián was not old enough to file for asylum on his own, and because his Miami relatives lacked legal standing, only his father could speak for him. On June 28, the U.S. Supreme Court refused to review the case. Hours afterward, Elián and his Cuban relatives departed for their homeland.

THE AFTERMATH

Although Battles learned of the raid when everyone else did—from Channel 10 news, he recalled—he became a target for retaliation. The threats were dire: "You're going to go to your grave."[24] Battles was forced to relocate to an undisclosed location for several months. Later, when tempers calmed, he was able to return to Miami, restore his relationships with leaders in the Cuban immigrant community, and continue his CRS work in a city still reeling.

Public sentiment about the custody battle and raid on the González's Miami home was extremely divided. Many people outside the Cuban community in Miami, especially the African American community, felt that the Cuban exile community was given preferential treatment. Haitians who flee their country for the United States do not benefit from the same kind of generous immigration policy that Cubans receive. Representatives of the large, primarily black Haitian immigrant community in Miami stated that this disparity was due to racism. Additionally, many Americans in Miami and across the United States saw the custody battle as a waste of resources and an inappropriate proxy war against Castro. They believed the boy should have been returned to his father immediately.

In this highly sensitive case, CRS was critical to the ongoing communication among INS and other federal officials, local law enforcement, and Cuban community leaders. Although no agreement was reached between the parties, in the time before the April 22 raid, CRS played a significant role in reducing the amount and volume of the violence, providing mediation, technical assistance, training, and facilitation on the streets and in convenings. For weeks after Elián's removal, CRS provided reconciliation services to support the normalizing of relations between law enforcement and the community. CRS continued to work with the community to build bridges between different racial groups and neighborhoods.[25]

Former Cuban American National Council president Guarione Diaz, who worked with Battles to reduce tensions after Elián González was extracted, reflected on the peacekeeping impact of Battles's work throughout the tense months leading up to and following the raid. Diaz stated, "During the Elián case, Thomas was a steady person, working hard to see different sides of the issue and getting everyone to the table. There was great respect for him in the Cuban-American community. We were having a lot of community conversations about how to keep violence from erupting."[26]

Throughout the entire saga, Battles worked in his CRS conciliator role to bring the heart-wrenching dilemma to resolution by convening and facilitating meetings including talks with Elián's grandmothers, by constructing a four-point plan to return Elián to his father, and by providing consulting to Attorney General Reno as she personally tried to broker an agreement. Other CRS officials played a significant role in preventing round-the-clock demonstrations from escalating into violence. Even though the peaceful handover preferred by most stakeholders was not achieved, CRS conciliators created as many opportunities as they could to allow for a voluntarily negotiated outcome.

In complicated, highly politicized, and publicized conflicts, polarization can easily overwhelm the force of reason and lead to stalemate and violence. For peacemakers like CRS mediators, there are times when the headwinds blow at hurricane-force speed. CRS team members work in situations where the likelihood of success is minimal and the odds are stacked against them, but that is the nature of the job. Success should be measured by increasing the possibility of resolution through bringing people together, proposing solutions, and reducing tension. Although it could not be grasped, peace was so tantalizingly close in Miami in 2000.

NOTES

1. Thomas Battles, interview with Grande Lum, November 20, 2018.

2. *Elián*, directed by Tim Golden and Ross McDonnell (CNN Films and Gravitas Ventures, 2017), film, 108 min.

3. Battles, interview with Lum.

4. U.S. Department of Justice, Community Relations Service, Annual Report, 2000.

5. Mayer, *Beyond Neutrality*, 102.

6. Andrew Kennis, "Double Standards? An Evaluation of the Propaganda Model and the Indexing Hypothesis on Immigration Coverage," conference paper, National Communication Association, January 2008, 1–43, esp. 32.

7. For more on the Waco negotiation, see Jane Seminare Doherty, *Learning Lessons from Waco: When the Parties Bring Their Gods to the Negotiating Table* (Syracuse, NY: Syracuse University Press, 2001).

8. Carrie Menkel-Meadow, interview with Grande Lum, February 10, 2020.

9. Battles, interview with Lum.

10. *Elián*.

11. *Elián*.

12. *Elián*.

13. Michael J. Sniffen, "Move On to Reunite Elian, Dad," *Record* (Troy, NY), April 22, 2000, https://perma.cc/25Q5-GCQ2.

14. Battles, interview with Lum.

15. Lizette Alvarez, "The Elian Gonzalez Case: The Overview," *New York Times*, April 24, 2000, https://perma.cc/8KYH-5A2X.

16. Michael J. Sniffen, "Reno Tries to Arrange Elian Deal," Associated Press, April 22, 2000, https://perma.cc/5WBF-2CSF.

17. Karen DeYoung, "Raid Reunites Elian and Father," *Washington Post*, April 23, 2000, https://perma.cc/YV3H-3UCU.

18. Battles, interview with Lum.

19. "Publisher in Miami Sat In on Talks with Reno," Associated Press, April 27, 2000, https://perma.cc/VVQ6-BQCW.

20. "Publisher in Miami Sat In on Talks with Reno."

21. "Publisher in Miami Sat In on Talks with Reno."

22. Alberto Ibargüen, "The Elian Negotiators: Ships Passing in the Night," *Miami Herald*, April 27, 2000, https://perma.cc/HDW3-BFPZ.

23. Ibargüen, "The Elian Negotiators."

24. Battles, interview with Lum.

25. Community Relations Service, "Unifying America by Responding to Conflicts and Violence and Building Local Capacities for Local Solutions," in U.S. Department of Justice, Community Relations Service, Annual Report, 2000.

26. Audra D. S. Burch, "Federal Mediator Thomas Battles Serves as Peacemaker in Sanford," *Miami Herald*, July 4, 2013, https://perma.cc/R3TS-7SA9.

FIFTEEN

Back to the Future

Law Enforcement and Race
Takes Center Stage in Sanford, Florida

CHAPTER 6, "POLICE-MINORITY Relations," covers CRS work prior to 1990, addressing conflicts between law enforcement and minority communities. Since that time, conflicts between African American communities and law enforcement have remained center stage. From 1991, when a videotape surfaced of Los Angeles Police Department officers beating Rodney King during his arrest, to 2015, when Freddie Gray died in Baltimore Police custody, the death or injury of unarmed African American men at the hands of law enforcement has repeatedly presented itself as emblematic of the racial inequalities that persist today.

This chapter looks closely at CRS's work following one particular tragedy: the death of teenager Trayvon Martin in 2012. This incident, in which the seventeen-year-old Martin was killed by neighborhood watch volunteer George Zimmerman in Sanford, Florida, broke through the American consciousness as it became the most reported story in the country and led to the creation of the Black Lives Matter movement. CRS played a crucial but mostly unknown role in Sanford during this time.

This discussion examines the role of the Community Relations Service in a new and significant chapter in America's struggle for equality and justice, as well as the misinformation campaign that targeted CRS and attempted to undermine its work.

RACIAL HISTORY IN SANFORD, FLORIDA

To understand the Trayvon Martin case and its aftermath, it is important to consider the city's racial history. Henry Shelton Sanford, a wealthy businessman whom President Abraham Lincoln appointed minister to Belgium, bought the land that is now Sanford to build a new "Gate City of South Florida" in the late 1870s.[1] African American families came to the area in the aftermath of the Civil War as it grew into a regional business hub. These families purchased lots directly from Sanford.

From the start, white residents in the area shot, killed, and tried to drive away these Black families. Lynching was commonplace in the South post–Civil War, and well into the first half of the twentieth century Florida had the highest per-capita lynching rate of any state.[2] According to Sanford, he provided these families with housing and protection against those who would do them harm.[3]

However, the city of Sanford later forcibly annexed nearby Goldsborough, a town that had been built and was run by African American community leaders. The annexation led to a number of lost jobs for Black residents of Goldsborough, including the mayor, marshals, and jailers.[4] White mob threats persisted in 1946, when Jackie Robinson, who had just been signed to a Major League Baseball contract, came to Sanford for training camp. The baseball star left Sanford twice in response to threats of violence.[5]

Racial tensions continued into the twenty-first century. Prior to the Trayvon Martin tragedy, mistrust between Sanford's African American residents and its police department festered as a result of two incidents. In 2005, a white police officer was rehired by the Sanford city manager despite having been fired by the police chief for punching an African American man who was already handcuffed and on the ground.[6] In 2010, a Sanford police officer's son sucker-punched a homeless African American man. The boy's father sent another officer to the scene, who overruled the two patrol officers who wanted to arrest the boy. Video footage of the boy's battery of the homeless man went viral, and the subsequent outrage led to Sanford police chief's early retirement.[7]

STAND YOUR GROUND LAWS

Another important context in Trayvon's death is Florida's Stand Your Ground legislation. The concept that individuals have particular rights within their homes dates back to Roman law. In the seventeenth century, English common law created the principle that a person's home is that person's castle, that is, the area over which they have sovereign power. In establishing its own legal system, America looked to England and imported the common-law system. Over time, homeowners came to have the legal right to use deadly force in their homes, regardless of whether they could have safely retreated without use of deadly force. Homeowners did not have to prove they were in danger to fire a gun, for example.

Florida historically has had permissive policies when it comes to owning and openly carrying a gun. In 2005, Florida became the first state to permit individuals to use deadly force when they felt they were faced with imminent danger of serious bodily harm in any place and at any time.[8] This permission extended the legal right to use deadly force in response to a perceived imminent threat beyond one's domicile to essentially everywhere else. Gun rights advocates lobbied for this law in Florida and numerous other states. At the time of its passage, law enforcement officials shared their concern that this expansion would lead to increased shootings and deaths, as claims of self-defense increased. Their concerns proved prescient as these incidents, dubbed "justifiable homicides," nearly doubled between 2000 and 2010.[9]

THE RETREAT AT TWIN LAKES

Trayvon Martin's father was engaged to a woman who lived in the Retreat at Twin Lakes, a Sanford gated community. It was built in 2004 during the state's building boom as Florida developers were attracted to the quiet, small community; reputable school district; outlet malls; and proximity to Disney World amusement parks. The gated townhouse community had 263 units, with touches to give it a middle-class appeal like granite countertops, walk-in closets, and master bedrooms. The original cost of these townhomes was approximately $250,000 apiece.[10]

In 2008, the global mortgage crisis destroyed property values. By 2012, the price of a townhome at Twin Lakes had fallen below $100,000, 40 of the homes were without residents, and more than 50 percent of the occupants were renters. The racial demographics also changed as more Black and Hispanic renters moved into the community. A former neighborhood watch captain noted that serious issues in the gated community began during the economic downturn; he claimed that foreclosures led purchasers to rent the townhomes to "low-lifes and gangsters."[11] In the twelve months prior to the Trayvon Martin tragedy, there had been a number of burglaries, thefts, and break-ins reported in the community.[12]

Sanford police helped the gated community start its neighborhood watch program. Such programs are intended to empower neighbors to actively monitor their neighborhood and convene to get to know each other better. A twenty-eight-year-old renter, George Zimmerman, who self-identified as Hispanic and had a white father and a Peruvian mother, volunteered to be a neighborhood watch captain. Records show that Zimmerman contacted local Sanford police nearly fifty times in the year prior to Trayvon's death to report numerous issues.[13]

TRAYVON MARTIN

Trayvon Martin was an African American seventeen-year-old from Miami Gardens, Florida. He had no criminal record (although he had been suspended from high school for cutting class).[14] His father, Tracy, decided to bring him to Sanford to spend a few days at his fiancée's house. On February 26, 2012, Trayvon walked to the nearby 7-Eleven convenience store, where he bought a bag of Skittles candy and an Arizona Watermelon Fruit Juice Cocktail drink. As Martin walked home in the rain, the hood of his sweatshirt covering his head, Zimmerman, who was on a personal errand, observed the teenager and contacted the police.

Zimmerman had a gun, for which he had a license. According to Martin's friend who was on the phone with him when Zimmerman called the police, Martin became concerned that a stranger was following him. Zimmerman told the police operator that Martin was running. The operator warned Zimmerman not to pursue the boy. After the call ended, an encounter ensued between Zimmerman and Martin. Tragically, Zimmerman pulled the trigger at point blank range, and Martin died as a result, about seventy yards from the house at which he was staying.

IMMEDIATE AFTERMATH

Sanford police officers arrived soon after the shooting. Zimmerman, after being treated by paramedics for injuries to his face and back, was brought to the police precinct for questioning.[15] He was released after five hours. The officers wanted to arrest Zimmerman initially but were told to wait by the local prosecutor.[16] Later, Sanford police chief Bill Lee stated that there was a lack of evidence to counter Zimmerman's assertion of self-defense. Because of Florida's Stand Your Ground law, the police were prohibited from making an arrest.

The grieving father, Tracy Martin, was outraged that the person who killed his son was not arrested or charged with any crime. On February 28, he was connected with prominent Florida civil rights attorney

Benjamin Crump. Martin retained Crump's firm's services and they quickly began publicizing the case through the media.

Norton Bonaparte, the city manager of Sanford, was concerned about relations throughout the city given the area's history of discrimination against African Americans, recent events that exacerbated law enforcement–community relations, and the added fuel of the nation viewing the event constantly via internet, television, and other media. Bonaparte, who had received mediation training, spoke several times with Andrew Thomas, a Sanford employee with a deep background in conflict resolution. For more than twenty-five years, Thomas had led the Rochester, New York, Center for Dispute Settlement. At the time, his job at Sanford was as a community development block grants coordinator. He had initially come to Sanford as a consultant to assess the state of the relationship between Sanford law enforcement and its African American community.[17]

SANFORD REACHES OUT TO CRS

Both Bonaparte and Thomas were concerned about national media and protesters coming to Sanford, which would put great pressure on the employees and citizens of the small city. Thomas encouraged officials to talk to other communities who had experienced similar issues. A week after the shooting, Bonaparte had a growing sense of impending community unrest. Given that many African American residents did not view local Sanford employees positively, Bonaparte and Thomas agreed that contacting CRS would be helpful.

Prior to coming to Sanford, Bonaparte had been the city manager of Topeka, Kansas, and had worked with CRS there. Bonaparte asked Thomas, who had worked with CRS in a number of situations in Rochester, to find a CRS conciliator.[18] Thomas later commented to a reporter, "The situation was escalating. We needed somebody from the outside that could command respect, pull the community together and generate dialogue."[19]

Thomas left a message at the CRS Southeast Regional Office in Atlanta, Georgia. Regional Director Thomas Battles returned the call later that day and connected Andrew Thomas with CRS conciliator Mildred Duprey de Robles, a longtime mediator with a military background who worked out of the Miami CRS office. Robles immediately began meeting with Sanford police, activists, community members, and pastors to better assess the situation.

Sanford mayor Jeff Triplett admitted to being initially skeptical of CRS, but he knew he needed help. He explained, "These guys [CRS conciliators] have been there, done it, they're very astute. We on the city side, we fix roads. We make sure your lights turn off and on. We make sure your toilets flush. We cut ribbons for new businesses. So you've got to rely on those that know [how to engage with movements and protesters]." With Triplett's support, Battles made introductions between Sanford officials and CRS personnel in addition to reaching out to civil rights leaders Al Sharpton and Jesse Jackson and their respective organizations.[20]

CALLS FOR ZIMMERMAN'S ARREST

Crump, Tracy Martin's lawyer, publicly called for release of Zimmerman's calls to police dispatchers that fateful night, and Mayor Triplett ordered their release on March 6. The tapes were then played in local and national media. The Trayvon Martin story would become the most reported story in the United States in 2012, surpassing even that year's presidential election. Over 2.2 million people signed the Change.org petition calling for Zimmerman's arrest, which was the largest collection of signatures ever on that website. To honor Martin's life, professional sports superstars like basketball player LeBron James wore "hoodies"—hooded sweatshirts like Trayvon's. Sharpton and Jackson called for full investigations. Thousands of people protested throughout the country.

On March 10, City Manager Bonaparte called Mayor Triplett, who was away in Tampa watching his young son's football game, to warn him that the story was ricocheting through worldwide media.[21] On March 14, approximately four hundred people came to the Allen Chapel African Methodist Episcopal (AME) Church in Sanford demanding Zimmerman's arrest. A number of local civil rights leaders and a few prominent out-of-town advocates were involved, including Baltimore activist and pastor Jamal Bryant. Robles and Thomas were also present, with the goal of observing the scene.

The group made what seemed to be an impromptu march to the Sanford police building. A police officer came up to Thomas and asked if he was doing alright, and Thomas responded, "I was until you came up to me," indicating that the exchange had exposed him as a city employee. Soon afterward, protesters began "raining Skittles candy" on Thomas and others.[22]

The calls for Zimmerman's arrest were soon joined by calls for the firing of Sanford police chief Bill Lee for his refusal to arrest Zimmerman. Battles provided assistance in convening a meeting with Chief Lee, the National Association for the Advancement of Colored People (NAACP) Seminole County chapter president Turner Clayton, Mayor Triplett, and City Manager Bonaparte. After the meeting, Lee announced he would remove himself from office temporarily.

Sanford police turned the case over to the Florida state attorney, Norm Wolfinger, so that state officials could make the difficult decision of whether or not to arrest Zimmerman. After Wolfinger recused himself due to outcries of moving too slowly, Florida governor Rick Scott then appointed Angela Corey as state attorney in charge of the investigation in place of Wolfinger.

On March 20, Battles convened a town-hall meeting at which he first met Pastor Valerie Houston of the Allen Chapel AME Church. The Allen Chapel would become a significant center for the local protest movement, and Reverend Houston emerged as a key leader in both pursuing justice for Trayvon Martin and peace-building and coordinating efforts toward concrete change for the Sanford community.[23] CRS conciliators went to numerous protests, meetings, and marches with Allen Chapel congregants to help keep them safe and strategize a constructive and nonviolent path forward. As the saga continued and the demand for Zimmerman's arrest grew, protest groups planned a large rally.

PROTESTING SAFELY

What distinguished Sanford from many other cities that have experienced mass protests is that Sanford officials consciously and proactively welcomed the busloads of arriving protesters. Conciliators Battles and Robles connected numerous civil rights groups to Sanford in advance of the gathering and facilitated the process of obtaining permits to hold a public rally. Additionally, knowing that protesters who planned to attend a Sanford City Council meeting would overwhelm the small meeting space, Thomas and the city of Sanford rented a jumbotron screen so that people outside could see what was happening. The city also rented golf carts to transport older protesters and others who were physically challenged from the parking lots to the park outside the city council meeting.

For this event and for many other rallies and protests in Sanford, a CRS team member was assigned to train protest groups in self-marshaling, which helps the group stay safe while it protests. Self-marshaling involves designating and training individuals to be chaperones for the group and to be responsible for keeping the group together, remaining alert to individuals who might be using the event to cause violence or trouble, and learning steps to take in case of medical and other emergencies. The goal of such training is to keep everyone safe and to prevent protests from escalating into dangerous situations, and to ensure that free speech remains protected.

Mayor Triplett was initially wary of the CRS conciliators' advice. At a rally in a downtown Sanford park, Battles suggested to Triplett that he address the demonstrators. Triplett would thus be sharing the stage with Jesse Jackson and Al Sharpton. Initially, Triplett was booed off the stage. However, Florida congresswoman Corinne Brown called him back to the stage and thanked him for welcoming the Justice Department Civil Rights Division investigation. This time, there was applause for Triplett. "She totally took that crowd in a different direction. I called her the next day and couldn't thank her enough," he said.[24] Afterward, the mayor noted that Brown's acknowledgment of his cooperation with investigations "really subsided the animosities out there." The congresswoman's statement was "absolutely a key moment" in supporting Sanford in initiating the healing process.[25]

Acting CRS director Becky Monroe came to Sanford during this period and observed a high level of tension at the rallies. Further complicating the scene were new arrivals from extremist organizations including both white and Black nationalist groups. Monroe recalled that Sanford police officers were particularly on edge when the New Black Panthers arrived. One officer anxiously talked to Conciliator Robles, expressing that he didn't know what that group was trying to accomplish. Robles calmly said, "We should just ask them," and proceeded to do so. They quickly learned the group was trying to determine where to protest, so the CRS representatives provided them with the information they were seeking.[26]

FEDERAL INTEREST

On March 23, after the Justice Department opened an investigation into the case, President Barack Obama opined on the case for the first time. He stated, "When I think about this boy, I think about my own kids, and I think every parent in America should be able to understand why it is absolutely imperative that we investigate every aspect of this. . . . If I had a son, he would look like Trayvon."[27] The president's public statement became a flashpoint and an inflection point, as many viewed it as a president who was African American speaking directly to the racial aspect of the case. Some viewed this perspective in a positive light, while others—including many in the Republican Party and conservative media—criticized his comments as meddling unnecessarily in a local matter.

Numerous members of Congress requested to hear from Martin's parents, but Republican congressional members did not agree to an official subcommittee session. Instead, on March 26, Trayvon Martin's parents, Sybrina Fulton and Tracy Martin, came to Washington, D.C., to speak at a congressional forum. CRS Acting Director Monroe was seated next to them and also testified regarding CRS's role. Numerous Democratic congressional members criticized both Sanford police and the Stand Your Ground law.[28] However, no legislative action was taken.

THE DREAM DEFENDERS

Organizers from outside Sanford likewise became involved with the case. Phillip Agnew, Ahmad Abuznaid, and Gabriel Pendas were three friends who had met while college students in Florida and who shared both a passion for politics and a high level of anger over Martin's death. Talking to one another, they decided to initiate an organized response. Abuznaid explained, "We thought we'd like to start a movement reminiscent of the civil rights movement of the past, but in our generation."[29] The three young men crafted a Facebook invitation for a conference call. The name "Dream Defenders" came from a young woman on the call, who observed, "You all are defending the dream. You should call yourselves the dream defenders." From that call came the plan for a forty-mile march from Daytona Beach to Sanford. The march would honor Trayvon Martin and protest the Stand Your Ground law and racial profiling.[30]

Battles and Robles worked with Florida police to ensure the Defenders' safe passage. Battles recommended to Andrew Thomas that he first come to Daytona to meet the Defenders, not in his role as a Sanford city employee but as a private individual. Thomas followed this advice. On the other end of the march, as the Defenders arrived, Bonaparte took a welcoming stance: "The city of Sanford hopes the actions of the students will be as peaceful and orderly as the previous rallies and marches have been. We want to be accommodating to all our visitors [provided] they act in a manner that is respectful to the people of the city."[31]

When the approximately sixty Dream Defenders arrived in Sanford after three days of marching, they positioned themselves at the doors leading to the main entrance to the Sanford Police Department, blocking the building for five hours.[32] Thomas remembered meeting the Dream Defenders outside. He remarked, "They were surprised to see me again and as an employee of Sanford."[33]

With the help of the CRS conciliators, both Sanford city officials and the Dream Defenders agreed to meet inside the building. There had been a city commission meeting scheduled for that day, and rather than going forward with the preset agenda or postponing the meeting, city officials used the opportunity to work with the activist group. CRS facilitated a conversation around issues including racial profiling, the Stand Your Ground law, and other concerns related to racial minorities and law enforcement. Several Dream Defenders agreed to continue meeting with Sanford officials.

In the regular meetings that ensued, the group discussed the high number of murders in Sanford of young Black men; the African American community's distrust of the police department; the county's noncompliance with a 1970 consent decree to desegregate its public schools; and the housing, unemployment, and infrastructure problems facing Sanford's African American community.[34] Together, the Dream Defenders and city representatives drafted a plan to address these problems.

The "Nine-Point Plan" that followed illustrates several principles of effective engagement between community members and city government:

1. "Request the Department of Justice–Division of Special Litigation and Civil Rights Patterns and Practice Program to conduct an investigation of the Sanford Police Department's overall pattern and practice for civil rights violations."

This point was a primary demand of many community members, particularly given their distrust of local and state officials. Acceptance of this demand is an example of city officials being proactive rather than defensive in dealing with a tragedy.

2. "Explore with the City Commission the creation of an Office of Community Relations and appointment of a Community/Human Relations Commission."

Andrew Thomas explored and then created a Community Relations Unit as part of the city manager's office in 2015.

3. "Explore with the City Commission the creation of a Director of Community/Human Relations staff position to be responsible for follow through, coordination and implementation of the next step action plans."

In 2015, the city created a staff position to head the Community Relations Unit.

4. "Explore with the Commission the creation of a 'Police-Community Relations Blue Ribbon Panel' to assess and suggest strategies to strengthen police-community relations. This panel should represent a diverse broad cross section of the community."

The panel was created in 2015 and co-chaired by Reverend Valerie Houston and retired Judge O. H. Eaton. Thomas worked with Sanford interim chief Richard Myers to launch the panel of twenty-five members. Top recommendations were increased Sanford police funding, raising police salaries, more focus on crime on the street, and enhanced community police. Battles made a presentation as part of the assessment process.

5. "Explore with City Commission the Establishment of an Inter-Racial Interfaith Alliance, to concentrate on moving forward and strengthening race relationships in the community."

Battles convened the "Sanford Pastors Connecting" group, discussed in the following section, which played a substantive role in race relations and a mediative role with city officials, community, and police.

6. "Explore with the City Commission the establishment of an Anti-Violence Campaign: Create a Task Force that's representative of a broad diverse cross section of law enforcement, criminal justice and human services agencies to propose projects and/or strategies to increase the community's awareness of the impact of violence on community stabilization. The Task Force will suggest best practices for the reduction of violence in Sanford Communities."

   Sanford officials worked with central Florida government officials and workers and ran numerous collaborative events to focus on crimes committed against people of color, decreasing youth and young adult violence and crime, increasing use of conflict resolution strategies, and other crime prevention issues.

7. "Reactivate Sanford Neighborhood Action Partnership (SNAP)."

   This step was placed on hold. City Manager Bonaparte instead utilized homeowners' associations to monitor neighborhood concerns.

8. "Request the continued support and assistance of the Department of Justice Community Relations Services."

   Conciliators Battles and Robles remained involved with the city and played a key role in designing and implementing the nine-point plan as a whole.

9. "Increase Youth Training and Employment Opportunities: Look for partners to collaborate with the City of Sanford to increase employment opportunities for the youth."

   Sanford found a partner to reestablish its youth employment training program.[35]

FAITH AND PEACEKEEPING

Forty-four days after Trayvon Martin's death, Acting State Attorney General Angela Corey charged George Zimmerman with second-degree murder. A significant concern for CRS and other peacekeepers was how the trial could further divide the Sanford community and potentially lead to rioting and violence, depending on the verdict.

Battles saw the city's well-established faith traditions as a foundation for peace. If the city's ministers were well informed about the trial, he reasoned, they could help keep the community together no matter the verdict. He hoped that ministers would work with their congregations to prevent unfounded rumors and correct factual misrepresentations as well as urge Sanford unity.[36]

Although Sanford had strong Christian congregations, and some pastors and congregational members had cordial relationships with their counterparts in other organizations, a network across congregations was lacking. In particular, the city did not have strong ties established between African American churches and those that were predominantly white.

This lack of interethnic faith community ties was evident when tensions grew after Harry Rucker, an African American pastor, began leading local rallies and protests. Rucker was well known locally for his militarism, having publicly stated in the 1990s, "The worst thing that happened to us when they changed our schools [through desegregation], there went our leaders, there went our teachers. We never asked for integration. We asked for equality."[37] Accordingly, Rucker did not appear interested in collaborating with white congregations. Nonetheless, a white pastor, Jeff Krall, attempted to convene a prayer ceremony in the city. He was dissuaded by Trayvon Martin's family, who had spoken with several local African American preachers and agreed not to support Krall's plan due to the lack of diversity in his fellowship.[38]

Thomas Battles spoke separately with Rucker and Krall to see if they would be willing to share a meal at the local Cracker Barrel restaurant. Two weeks after that initial conversation, more than a dozen local ministers came to the same restaurant, forming a group that became Sanford Pastors Connecting.[39] This group would play a strong role in both advocacy and peacemaking throughout the months leading to and following the Zimmerman trial. Battles and his team also began holding workshops for local ministers and organized a ministers' trip to the court. Importantly, CRS was able to reserve four courtroom seats in the trial of George Zimmerman for clergy. This direct observation enabled faith leaders to keep their congregants informed as the trial progressed and dispel false rumors.

The alliance would eventually include more than forty African American, white, and Hispanic ministers and pastors. Krall and Houston served as co-chairs. Sanford city and law enforcement public information officers trained the ministers for media interviews. The pastors held a prayer meeting for Sanford police. Several offshoot groups formed to increase reconciliation and positive law enforcement–community relations, including a team of white pastors who attended African American worship services each week, and pairs of ministers from different racial backgrounds who met over meals to build relationships.[40]

Krall observed of the interfaith alliance, "After 30 years of ministry in Sanford and after 24 years of leading the Sanford Ministers Fellowship, I have never seen such a positive atmosphere in Sanford. It seems almost every week we hear of another group wanting to build bridges and establish long term relationships between the races and the churches in our 'friendly' city."[41]

MISINFORMATION CAMPAIGN TARGETS CRS

In the days between closing arguments and the announcement of the verdict, CRS was more visible in the public domain than it had arguably ever been before.

With Trayvon Martin's killing capturing the attention of the country, the politicization of the event, and the rise of new cable channels and the internet, CRS found itself in the crosshairs of conservative media. The earliest evidence of this new interest on the part of conservative commentators came on April 17, 2012, when two conservative sites questioned or accused CRS of bias. Both *White House Dossier* and the *Conservative Treehouse* published the following passage: "It appears that in carrying out their duties, [CRS representatives] have provided significant assistance to those protesting the killing of Martin, who [is] black, by George Zimmerman, who is half white and half Hispanic."[42]

On April 24, Judicial Watch, a conservative watchdog organization, made a Freedom of Information Act request concerning documents related to CRS's work in Sanford.[43] It received the material from the Justice Department on May 30, 2012, and March 8, 2013. On July 10, 2013, two days before the closing arguments, Judicial Watch released the documents, providing selective evidence for its president, Tom Fitton, to conclude, "These documents detail the extraordinary intervention by the Justice Department in the pressure campaign leading to the prosecution of George Zimmerman. My guess is that most

Americans would rightly object to taxpayers paying government employees to help organize racially-charged demonstrations."[44]

Over the ensuing days, numerous posts appeared on conservative websites and the story was picked up by larger and more prominent conservative media outlets and personalities, including radio talk-show host Rush Limbaugh and Fox television hosts Sean Hannity, Lou Dobbs, and Bill O'Reilly. The Fox Network as a whole gave the story significant coverage as closing arguments were made and during the lull of jury deliberations.[45] Mainstream and liberal media outlets then responded, challenging these portrayals as inaccurate.[46]

As CRS director at the time, I knew our staff took great care in maintaining an impartial approach to mediation. Our conciliation specialists were extremely focused on their behavior and actions with all involved parties. We tried hard to keep morale up and stay focused on the important work we were doing. I did my best to convey how critical it was to not let the negative and untrue noise impair us, and that the best thing we could all do was continue the mediation and conciliation efforts that we all knew mattered even more now, as the peacekeeping effort was under attack.

We shared our information with management at the Department of Justice, which worked to correct the misrepresentations being aired publicly. Most troubling was a site that misled the reader to think that audio being played was the voice of a CRS conciliator, when it was in fact the voice of a Dream Defender protester.[47]

This incident was the first time CRS had to deal with this type of public attack, a result of a combination of technology and the hyper-partisanship of this new era. For an agency that holds fairness, balance, and neutrality as central principles of action and behavior, it was an important reminder of the need to continue to practice these values in the face of such blatant falsehoods.

For the most part, Justice Department spokespersons stayed silent regarding media attacks and referred reporters to the CRS website. I agreed this was the best strategy. If reporters spoke to law enforcement and government officials, they would hear reinforcement of the role described on our website: that we provided mediation, dialogue facilitation, training, and technical assistance for the purpose of helping resolve community differences.

On the night of the verdict, there were many fears in the Sanford community—especially of a "not guilty" verdict. At CRS, we had set up our "peace room"—our version of a "war room"—in my office. I had Chief of Staff Daphne Felten-Green and Deputy Director Gilbert Moore with me. We were in communication with the CRS team on the ground, led by Thomas Battles and Mildred Robles. For months, the CRS team had been working with community leaders and had helped protesters raise their voices without major incident. Still, we were all unclear as to exactly what would happen if Zimmerman were found not guilty.

When that not-guilty verdict was announced, it did lead to protests locally and nationally. However, the fact that there was no rioting and no looting was a testament to the hard work of Sanford officials, employees, and community members. Protesters made their voices heard but did so without violence. CRS clearly had a role in achieving this peace.

DREAM DEFENDERS CONTINUE FIGHTING FOR CHANGE

Following the verdict, the Dream Defenders continued their work fighting against racial profiling and Florida's Stand Your Ground law. In July 2013, the group took over the Florida statehouse. They demanded that the state legislature hold a special session to overturn the law, ban racial profiling, and end the school-to-prison pipeline. Students from throughout the country joined them. Buses came from several East Coast cities including Washington, New York, and Philadelphia. Individuals came from as far away as California. The singer and activist Harry Belafonte joined the group. Florida house speaker Wil Weatherford committed to hold fall hearings on "Trayvon's Law," legislation proposed by the Dream Defenders and the NAACP to address racial profiling, repeal the Stand Your Ground law, and ensure data collection on homicides involving racial minorities.[48]

Battles and Robles played a mediator role, shuttling back and forth between the Dream Defenders and Florida governor Rick Scott's chief of staff. As CRS director, I was on the phone with both sides helping to determine what solutions might be possible while remaining mindful of the Dream Defenders' passion for change as well as the governor's interest in resolving the situation. We were able to help arrange a face-to-face meeting between the Defenders and Governor Scott in which the protesters shared both their anger with the Stand Your Grand law and the value to society of changing it.

After more than a month's standoff, the Dream Defenders decided to end their occupation of the statehouse on August 11. They then marched to the governor's mansion, declaring their demonstration "an eviction notice" for Scott. "We're coming for his job . . . the young people of Florida are coming for his job," Dream Defender Eric Maye promised. In a CNN interview, Maye stated, "We feel we've done all we could. We asked for the special session. We're not getting it and now we're going to the individual districts to lobby lawmakers and to register voters. We're going to take it to the streets."[49] As the Defenders departed the statehouse, famed civil rights leader Julian Bond affirmed, "You're ending a protest because you've started a movement."[50]

Despite the public outrage that followed Zimmerman's criminal acquittal, on February 24, 2015, the Justice Department announced that, following their own investigation, they would not be pursuing federal civil rights charges against Zimmerman. Attorney General Eric Holder stated,

> The death of Trayvon Martin was a devastating tragedy. It shook an entire community, drew the attention of millions across the nation, and sparked a painful but necessary dialogue throughout the country. Though a comprehensive investigation found that the high standard for a federal hate crime prosecution cannot be met under the circumstances here, this young man's premature death necessitates that we continue the dialogue and be unafraid of confronting the issues and tensions his passing brought to the surface. We, as a nation, must take concrete steps to ensure that such incidents do not occur in the future.[51]

This decision was not a surprise to most observers, given the high bar for such prosecution. Still, Justice Department officials took care in meeting with Trayvon Martin's parents and informing them of the outcome. CRS regional director Thomas Battles, who had earned the trust of Martin's parents, was in the meeting as well.

A region's history of discrimination against African Americans, the pursuit of the American dream, the foreclosure crisis, changing gun laws, the new technology of omnipresent smartphones with high-definition cameras, the viral nature of the internet's social media, and racial profiling all came together in Sanford and played their individual roles in the tragic death of Trayvon Martin. It was a potent mixture that rocked the nation and reverberated around the world.

Sanford was the starting point of a new civil rights movement centered on the mistreatment of African Americans by law enforcement. Angered by Zimmerman's verdict, three friends—Alicia Garza, Patrisse Khan-Cullors, and Opal Tometi—created the social media hashtag #blacklivesmatter. The three African American women coined what would become the name of a movement. A number of other high-profile incidents followed soon thereafter, and the Black Lives Matter movement would play a significant role in responding to those events and awakening the country's consciousness. In 2014, eighteen-year-old Michael Brown was shot to death by a police officer in Ferguson, Missouri, which led to unrest and a militaristic police response that gripped the nation. In Brooklyn the same year, Eric Garner died in an improper chokehold by a police officer after repeatedly exclaiming, "I can't breathe." In 2015, Freddie Gray died in a police vehicle and Baltimore experienced days of protests, unrest, and looting.

In contrast to the responses to these other incidents, in Sanford—despite more than eighty rallies and thousands of protesters—not a single rock was thrown nor a single arrest of a protester was made. Mayor Jeff Triplett, City Manager Norton Bonaparte, Reverends Valerie Houston and Jeff Krall, city employee Andrew Thomas, Interim Police Chief Richard Myers, and many others were committed to recognizing past and present problems, working closely with protesters such as those from the National Action Network and the Dream Defenders to ensure their voices were heard, and inviting and collaborating with CRS conciliators.

Al Sharpton remarked of the civil rights work in Sanford, "The beauty of that moment was the non-violence, was Blacks and whites together, was generations together. It showed the protest movement at its best."[52]

FACING FERGUSON, MISSOURI, AND
THE MICHAEL BROWN TRAGEDY

Attorney General Eric Holder faced what many considered the most challenging time of his tenure in the Obama administration when rioting worsened after Michael Brown was killed by a Ferguson policeman on August 9, 2014.[53] In the ensuing days, looting, rioting, and police confrontations continued. Photos and streamed media of military-style vehicles and officers pointing long rifles at protesters spread throughout the world. Should the attorney general come to Ferguson? The risk was considerable. If the violence worsened, the attorney general and the president would be blamed. Bringing additional complexity to the situation was the fact that both the president and the attorney general were the first African Americans to hold their respective positions.

Ultimately, Holder decided that he needed to step into the fray to help bring peace and justice to the situation. On August 19, he released a letter to Ferguson residents calling for an end to the violence. He wrote, "The Justice Department will defend the right of protesters to peacefully demonstrate and for the media to cover a story that must be told. But violence cannot be condoned. I urge the citizens of Ferguson who have been peacefully exercising their First Amendment rights to join with law enforcement in condemning the actions of looters, vandals and others seeking to inflame tensions and sow discord."[54]

CRS was the first federal agency on the scene. Within hours of the shooting, local St. Louis area leaders who had worked with CRS in the past contacted CRS conciliators Rita Valenciano and Darryck Dean. I then strategized with Deputy Director Gilbert Moore and Regional Director Pascual Marquez and immediately approved dispatching Valenciano and Dean to Ferguson. On Sunday, the two conciliators drove from Kansas City to Ferguson, only to see memorials, protests, and a candlelight vigil turn from peaceful to dangerous. Some influential actors, including Missouri state representative Sharon Pace, blamed this turn on police for allowing a police dog to urinate on a memorial and for later destroying the memorial with their vehicles.[55] Stores were looted, private vehicles were totaled, and at least three businesses were set on fire. When the CRS conciliators arrived, law enforcement refused them access to the scene.

President Obama announced the decision to send the attorney general to Ferguson on Monday, August 18. At the same time, the president shared with the country, "We've also had experts from the DOJ's Community Relations Service, working in Ferguson since days after the shooting to foster conversation among local stakeholders and reduce tensions among the community."[56] The attorney general planned to meet with Ferguson residents in several settings: a town-hall meeting, a small faith-leader gathering, a conversation with local community college students, and a lunch with a group of citizens. Because CRS was the only agency that had connections with these Ferguson constituencies, it was up to the CRS team to identify and vet which individuals to invite to the various meetings and to scout possible locations—all within forty-eight hours. I personally flew in to help the team prepare, to join the attorney general, and to facilitate the town-hall meeting.

The entire CRS team worked incredibly hard to pull off the effort. Valenciano and Dean had been on the ground in Ferguson continuously since August 10 and led much of the work. As I moderated the Wednesday conversation between Holder and the Ferguson residents, what reverberated was the personal nature of the attorney general's words. He said, "I am the attorney general of the United States. But I am also a black man. I can remember being stopped on the New Jersey turnpike on two occasions and accused of speeding."[57] Holder spoke eloquently of how important law enforcement was to reducing tension, about his brother's career as a law enforcement officer, and of how police officers risked their lives daily.

I personally will never forget how anxious I was that day with my hopes for an end to the looting and destruction. Nor will I forget how quiet and peaceful Ferguson neighborhoods were that night. The visit accomplished the immediate goal of bringing peace to a neighborhood that had seen ongoing violence for eleven straight days. It also influenced later chapters to the story, including a Department of Justice consent decree in which Ferguson agreed to remedy the unconstitutional conduct of its police department. This mandate was based on a Department of Justice Civil Rights Division report that found patterns or practices of unlawful conduct, including conducting stops without reasonable cause and arrests without reasonable suspicion, engaging in racial discrimination, and violating individual due process and equal protection rights.[58]

On an attorney general's last day, there is a tradition in which Department of Justice employees line up in the hallways and stairways to offer farewells. The attorney general then says a personal goodbye to each person and continues down the line, speaking to each and every employee. Holder's departure in 2015 was the first and only time I took part in this ceremony. He was clearly appreciative as he came up to me, gave me a big hug, and stated, "Thanks for all you and CRS did at Ferguson. We made a difference there and we must continue that work."

NOTES

1. "History and Historic Preservation," City of Sanford, Florida, https://perma.cc/HW5T-G7MA.

2. Tom Brown, "Racist Past Haunts Florida Town Where Trayvon Died," Reuters, April 8, 2012, https://perma.cc/4ULP-Z7JT.

3. Altermese Smith Bentley, *Seminole County* (Charleston, SC: Arcadia, 2000), 9.

4. Mark Simpson, "Racial Tension Runs through Sanford's Roots," *All Things Considered*, NPR, March 22, 2012, https://perma.cc/35GB-BVMX.

5. Andrew Carter, "On March 4, 1946, JACKIE ROBINSON Broke Baseball's Color Barrier," *Orlando Sentinel*, March 4, 2006, https://perma.cc/PW4Q-GWPH.

6. Robert Perez, "Officer's Rehiring Spurs Outcry," *Orlando Sentinel*, December 4, 2005, https://perma.cc/P63B-PKRY.

7. Rene Stutzman, "Sanford Cop's Son Gets Probation for Punching Homeless Man," *Orlando Sentinel*, October 3, 2011, https://perma.cc/MZH9-T2JY.

8. Elizabeth Chuck, "Florida Had First Stand Your Ground Law, Other States Followed in 'Rapid Succession,'" NBC News, July 18, 2013, https://perma.cc/56IIP-8RH5.

9. Joe Palazzolo and Rob Barry, "More Killings Called Self-Defense," *Wall Street Journal*, April 2, 2013, https://perma.cc/TF4T-MQB9.

10. Lane DeGregory, "Trayvon Martin's Killing Shatters Safety within Retreat at Twin Lakes in Sanford," *Tampa Bay Times*, March 25, 2012, updated March 27, 2012, https://perma.cc/F873-TKUC.

11. Frances Robles, "Shooter of Trayvon Martin a Habitual Cop Caller," McClatchy, March 19, 2012, https://perma.cc/VP3T-ACQG.

12. DeGregory, "Trayvon Martin's Killing Shatters Safety within Retreat at Twin Lakes in Sanford."

13. Robles, "Shooter of Trayvon Martin a Habitual Cop Caller."

14. Lizette Alvarez, "Defense in Trayvon Martin Case Raises Questions about the Victim's Character," *New York Times*, May 23, 2012, https://perma.cc/6K5Y-5DWH.

15. Matt Gutman and Seni Tienabeso, "ABC News Exclusive: Zimmerman Medical Report Shows Broken Nose, Lacerations after Trayvon Martin Shooting," ABC News, May 15, 2012, https://perma.cc/F9RM-7TJN.

16. Madison Gray, "Report: Police Initially Wanted to Make Arrest in Trayvon Martin Case," *Time*, March 29, 2012, https://perma.cc/U5Y9-C9EQ.

17. Rogers "When Conflicts Polarize Communities," 173.

18. Andrew Thomas, interview with Grande Lum, May 24, 2019.

19. Audra D. S. Burch, "Federal Mediator Thomas Battles Serves as Peacemaker in Sanford," *Miami Herald*, July 4, 2013, updated July 8, 2013, https://perma.cc/R3TS-7SA9.

20. Evan McMorris-Santoro, "Sanford, Florida, Mayor Urges Ferguson to Welcome Obama Administration's Help," BuzzFeed News, August 20, 2014, https://perma.cc/8MRZ-EVJU.

21. Barbara Liston, "Trayvon Martin Shooting Transforms Part-Time Mayor," Reuters, March 29, 2012, https://perma.cc/4JPL-XVGQ.

22. Thomas, interview with Lum.

23. Arelis Hernandez, "DOJ 'Peacemakers' Helped Sanford Stay Cool Amid Rising Tensions," *Orlando Sentinel*, April 15, 2012, https://perma.cc /T6LF-AA46.

24. Liston, "Trayvon Martin Shooting Transforms Part-Time Mayor."

25. Grande Lum, "Trump Budget Would End Agency That Resolves Differences in a Time of Deep Divisions," The Hill, February 23, 2018, https://perma .cc/7D4C-97GS.

26. Becky Monroe, interview with Grande Lum, May 22, 2019.

27. Stacia Deshishku, "President Obama Statement on Trayvon Martin Case," *The 1600 Report*, CNN, March 23, 2012, https://perma.cc/4P78-3JUU.

28. Donna Smith, "Democratic Lawmakers Blast Police in Teen Killing," Reuters, March 27, 2012, https://perma.cc/5SW4-WG76.

29. Chabeli Herrera, "Who Are the Dream Defenders?" WUFT, October 15, 2013, https://perma.cc/9G67-G82A.

30. Vincent J. Intondi, "The Dream Defenders: Learning from History," HuffPost, September 27, 2013, updated November 27, 2013, https://perma.cc /RG4U-X2D9.

31. "'Dream Defenders' March to Sanford Police Dept.," WESH 2 News, April 9, 2012, https://perma.cc/9WMH-Z3D2.

32. "'Dream Defenders' March to Sanford Police Dept."

33. Thomas, interview with Lum.

34. Andrew Thomas, "Nine Point Plan: Action for Reuniting the Community," two-year progress report, City of Sanford, Florida, January 2015, https://perma .cc/V4GZ-4LEU.

35. Thomas, "Nine Point Plan."

36. Trymaine Lee, "'Peacemaker' Heals City in Wake of Trayvon Martin Killing," MSNBC, September 13, 2013, https://perma.cc/K3Y7-VXQE.

37. Adam Weinstein, "Trayvon Martin's Death Extends Sanford's Sordid Legacy," *Mother Jones*, March 28, 2012, https://perma.cc/7FMK-92YV.

38. Weinstein, "Trayvon Martin's Death Extends Sanford's Sordid Legacy."

39. Lee, "'Peacemaker' Heals City in Wake of Trayvon Martin Killing."

40. Thomas, "Nine Point Plan."

41. Thomas, "Nine Point Plan," 10.

42. Keith Koffler, "Little-Known DOJ Cell Watches Trayvon Martin Protests," *White House Dossier*, April 17, 2012, https://perma.cc/Q48Q-KLBQ; [Sundance], "The Department of Social Justice—The DOJ's Community Relations Service (Peacekeepers)," *Conservative Tree House*, April 17, 2012, https://perma.cc/3KWN-4M7Z.

43. Untitled documents related to requests for information from CRS by Judicial Watch, June 5, 2012, https://perma.cc/4UZ5-R7YE.

44. "Documents Obtained by Judicial Watch Detail Role of Justice Department in Organizing Trayvon Martin Protests," Judicial Watch, July 10, 2013, https://perma.cc/22V6-9QMX.

45. "Limbaugh: Media Invested in a Guilty Verdict for Zimmerman," Real Clear Politics, July 11, 2013, https://perma.cc/LV33-377A; "Explosive: Did DOJ Give Support to Anti-Zimmerman Rallies?" Fox News Insider, July 11, 2013, https://perma.cc/Y9NZ-ACSK; David Weigel, "The Newest Trayvon Martin Race-Baiting Theory from the Right," Slate, July 11, 2013, https://perma.cc/L3L3-74JR.

46. Katie Sanders, "Judicial Watch Says Department of Justice Unit Organized Protests against George Zimmerman," Politifact, July 12, 2013, https://perma.cc/FUG9-UNJN; Weigel, "The Newest Trayvon Martin Race-Baiting Theory from the Right"; Ryan J. Reilly, "No, Justice Department Unit Didn't 'Support' Anti-Zimmerman Rally," HuffPost, July 11, 2013, https://perma.cc/MG7M-QV5X.

47. [Sundance], "Federally Approved DOJ CRS Extortion—Dream Defenders and Thomas Battles Turn 'Justice' into 'Just Us,'" *Conservative Tree House*, July 17, 2013, https://perma.cc/4GGM-L9DR.

48. Jeff Schuhrke, "Dream Defenders Stand Their Ground," *In These Times*, September 17, 2013, https://perma.cc/TKF7-47ZK.

49. Rich Phillips, "Dream Defenders End Sit-In Protest of Florida's Stand Your Ground Law," CNN, August 15, 2013, https://perma.cc/R4DD-XUSD.

50. Schuhrke, "Dream Defenders Stand Their Ground."

51. U.S. Department of Justice, Office of Public Affairs, "Federal Officials Close Investigation into Death of Trayvon Martin," February 24, 2015, https://perma.cc/3YMV-9WGN.

52. *Rest in Power: The Trayvon Martin Story*, episode 2, "The Elephant in the Room," directed by Jenner Furst and Julia Willoughby Nason (Paramount Network, 2018), film, 23:40, https://perma.cc/HP7N-V6JR.

53. David Nather, "Holder's Real Legacy," Politico, September 25, 2014, https://perma.cc/4PBM-9K4G; Clare Kim and Nick Ramsey, "Top 5 Things Attorney General Eric Holder Will Be Remembered For," MSNBC, September 25, 2014, https://perma.cc/FL2Y-DR28.

54. Nia-Malika Henderson, "Attorney General Eric Holder Pens Open Letter to Ferguson," *Washington Post*, August 19, 2014, https://perma.cc/4CER-T72Z.

55. Henderson, "Attorney General Eric Holder Pens Open Letter to Ferguson."

56. "Full Transcript: Obama's Remarks on Ferguson, Mo. and Iraq," *Washington Post*, August 18, 2014, https://perma.cc/U5S5-WF8J.

57. "Full Transcript: Obama's Remarks on Ferguson, Mo. and Iraq."

58. U.S. Department of Justice, Office of Public Affairs, "Justice Department and City of Ferguson, Missouri, Resolve Lawsuit with Agreement to Reform Ferguson Police Department and Municipal Court to Ensure Constitutional Policing," March 17, 2016, https://perma.cc/66DX-UV6M.

CONCLUSION

SIXTEEN

The Quest for Value

THIS BOOK WAS written to tell two previously untold stories. The first is that of the handful of Community Relations Service specialists who, day after day and year after year, were charged with witnessing the details of civil rights conflicts and working for solutions. The second story, woven between the lines, depicts the life of a federal agency whose anonymity prevented the American people from being informed about the work it does and how it does it.

This final chapter looks into some of the nooks and crannies of that federal agency and considers some of the human factors that animated the organization. It attempts a composite personality sketch of the agency and discusses some of the influences that shaped its culture.

The data, drawn from a wide range of CRS activities and concerns, cluster into three themes: (1) the institutional culture of CRS and its effect on agency performance; (2) costs and benefits of the much vilified federal bureaucracy (as well as the CRS bureaucracy) and the administrative systems that make possible, provide daily nurture to, and magnify the effectiveness of the front-line service programs; and (3) the legacy of CRS in resolving racial conflict and advancing the art and science of community conflict resolution.

These themes are interlaced, often drawing substantiation from the same data. For example, the casework described illustrates how the freedom and trust needed by field representatives to be effective was buttressed by reporting requirements and accountability standards that pushed them to more thoughtfully and rigorously pursue their work. Similarly, without the requirements of performance and outcome measurements, and the documentation of case impact, the long-range

---

The first sections of this chapter are by Bertram Levine; the latter sections are by Grande Lum and so noted. The first sections by Levine have been updated by Lum as well to reflect events and trends since the first edition was written.

achievements of CRS as an agent for change could not be made apparent. So, too, the chapter notes the contribution of rank-and-file staff members to the development of programs of lasting value, as well as the contributions of conciliators and mediators who pioneered techniques that expanded the repertoire of the conflict resolution profession.

DEVELOPMENT OF THE AGENCY CULTURE

One of the elements composing the CRS ethos was the fact that many of its personnel harbored a penchant for social justice and social action. Sometime in the late sixties, when Martin Luther King Jr. and Andrew Young were discussing plans for the Poor People's Campaign with Roger Wilkins, Young said to Wilkins, "We regard your agency as the extension of the civil rights movement into the federal government." Recalling that conversation twenty years later, Wilkins said, "And that's what I tried to make it. That surely is how I viewed myself. I viewed us as a voice, inside the government, for the powerless. In the cities around the country, I viewed us as providers of technical assistance and legitimation for groups of powerless people . . . and people who were seeking to represent and to expand the interests of the powerless."[1]

While the impact of Wilkins's drive and focus on the program of the agency lessened with his departure, and as needs changed and as CRS capabilities grew, full recognition of the minority stakeholder as a major partner in the conflict resolution process and of the need for negotiation to take place on a level playing field remained as basic tenets of CRS operations.

A number of staff members, including leaders of the agency, had worked for civil rights organizations before joining CRS, or had been volunteer advocates of minority-centered issues. Among them was director Gil Pompa. Before entering federal service, he had been a city prosecutor in San Antonio, Texas, and president of the board of the Edgewood Independent School District, one of the poorest in the state. The district was plaintiff in a lawsuit he helped to initiate that ultimately resulted in a state supreme court decision equalizing state funding of school districts. Others served voluntary civil rights organizations during their CRS service. Associate Director Roscoe Nix, as president of the NAACP branch in Montgomery County, Maryland, for ten years, helped to build it into a major defender of minority rights; Regional Director Ozell Sutton, as president of Alpha Phi Alpha, the largest national Black fraternity, presided over the development of a major program in support of improved education and leadership development for Black youth; Regional Director Thomas Battles followed in Sutton's footsteps by heading the Southeast regional office and leading a national Black Fraternity; Leo Cardenas was a national vice president of the League of United Latin American Citizens; and Regional Director Ron Wakabayashi was national director of the Japanese American Citizens League during the successful passing of the Japanese American internment reparations legislation. Others worked in federal civil rights agencies or departments, like Daphne Felten-Green, who was special counsel in the Office of Civil Rights within the Office of Justice Programs at DOJ, and Senior Counsel Marlene Sallo, who was staff director at the U.S. Commission on Civil Rights.

It is also important to note that individuals with significant law enforcement backgrounds began to join CRS as well. They often had a community policing background or a passion for law enforcement community relations. Many were members of racial minorities who were pioneers in law enforcement organizations. Administration of Justice Specialist Dante Andreotti was a San Francisco police district commander who started the country's second police-community relations unit; Regional Director Robert Lamb was a police captain of Atlantic City's police community relations unit who, along with Lee Brown, helped found the National Organization of Black Law Enforcement Executives while at CRS; Regional Director Rosa Melendez was the first woman of color to be a U.S. marshal, serving in this capacity for the Western District of Washington after a pioneering career in the Seattle Police Department; Regional Director Philip Arreola was the first Latino police chief for the Milwaukee Police Department; Regional Director Francis Amoroso was police chief for Portland, Maine; and Associate Director Ben Lieu was the first Asian American captain of the Baltimore Homicide Division.

In the early years, some CRS workers were troubled by what they saw as an ethical dilemma. In a conflict between civil rights advocates, who demanded change, and those who resisted change, how could you be a neutral mediator if, deep down, you believed in racial justice?

In time they recognized that this was not a valid dilemma. Both parties expected CRS to be an advocate for compliance with the law. Neutrality had nothing to do with the mediator's feelings about civil rights; it had only to do with the peacemaker's objectivity, honesty, and fairness in guiding the process so that both parties in a conflict would be able to negotiate the best deal they could consistent with the law. Those CRS staff members who longed to be agents of change had to get their satisfaction from knowing that almost all settlements represented movement away from the status quo and toward a situation of greater equality.

The issue of neutrality burst into the public realm and took on a partisan tone when former CRS director Ondray Harris, the appointee of President George W. Bush, stated to Blaze, a conservative pay TV network founded by Glenn Beck, "I found that some of the employees of CRS talked neutrally in the tenor of mediators in public, but behind the scenes, when they talked to the civil rights groups or the perceived aggrieved parties, they'll say essentially, 'Don't worry. The Department of Justice is here and we're going to get to the bottom of it.'"[2]

While the early CRS pioneers often came from civil rights or law enforcement backgrounds, more recent conciliators received dispute resolution training in their undergraduate courses or obtained graduate degrees with a conflict resolution focus, reflecting the formalized dispute resolution education curriculum and degree programs that began in the 1970s and 1980s. Regional Director Thomas Battles took conflict resolution classes while pursuing his master's degree in applied social science from Florida A&M, Senior Conciliation Specialist Kenith Bergeron received his bachelor's degree from DePaul University in conflict resolution, Program Manager Kit Chalberg attained a master's in conflict resolution from the University of Denver, Conciliator Charles Phillips received his master's degree in peace and conflict resolution from Bradford University and ran a restorative justice program in the Texas courts, Conciliator Marquez Equilibria earned a master's degree in international peace and conflict resolution from American University and was a conflict resolution education program director, Conciliator Suzanne Buchanan received her master's degree in conflict analysis and resolution from George Mason University and was a student of former CRS conciliator Wallace Warfield, Conciliator Justin Lock studied alternative dispute resolution at Chicago-Kent Law School, and Conciliator Matthew Lattimer studied dispute resolution at Cardozo Law School and was a mediator at the Harlem Community Justice Center. Many in this generation of conciliators also studied race relations and civil rights while in college or graduate school.

When CRS first began, as a conciliator on a field assignment, you were on your own in a troubled and bitter world. You could call on your training, a manual full of operational guidelines, the availability of technical support, and a phone line to regional headquarters. Later conciliators, like those mentioned in the previous paragraph, also had specialized education and other conflict resolution experience to leverage. But, essentially, you acted on your own initiative, largely dependent on your own resources. It took more than professional skill to carry the load. It took a sturdy ego to venture daily into troubled communities, often as an outsider, to help the conflicting forces calm the raging waters and to work out a resolution for deeply rooted problems.

But the outcome was not always one for the trophy room. The CRS field practitioners knew very well that the resolution of community problems is complex, often involving the interplay of scores of factors: history, public attitudes and opinions, politics, community rivalries, as well as institutional and personal agendas. The task of helping to restore even short-range harmony requires the give-and-take of scores of players. While clear-cut instances of decisive improvement attributable primarily to CRS came often enough to reward the agency's labors, other cases could lead one to wonder: "How much of a difference did we really make?"

Wallace Warfield, an up-through-the-ranks veteran mediator who served as acting director of CRS during the latter part of the Reagan administration, would refer to some conciliation cases as requiring the mediator to "run alongside the case." By that he meant that CRS might participate in a case for weeks or months without finding the opportunity to make a distinctive contribution—until the magic moment when the conciliator's long-cultivated contacts, special skills, and careful trust building enabled him or her to become the critical agent for working out a solution. But sometimes a case might run its full course without that magic moment ever coming.

Two questions were always on the mind of CRS's leaders and employees in the field: "Did our intervention do any good? How do we know?" Over time, a variety of approaches would be used to find the answers.

The concern of CRS staff members that their work "make a difference" was also reflected in the informal culture of the conciliators who continually stretched the operational guidelines when they thought it would help them to do a better job. To supplement the flow of technical assistance and training from headquarters, individual conciliators developed their own direct peer networking. Through this one-on-one give-and-take among fellow professionals across regional lines, they sought and offered solutions for thorny problems by informally sharing methods and contacts. This back-channel network also helped to cement fraternal bonds and maintain a high esprit de corps.

The small size of the agency permitted wide participation in its leadership. The ten regional directors routinely served on or chaired committees and task forces dealing with the most critical problems. Journeyman field representatives also were called upon for input. Regional directors, on many occasions, operating via their own back channels, initiated proposals that became important agency policies or programs.

Like most national organizations with local operations, CRS had to deal with the dynamic tension between the need of headquarters to provide oversight and the insistence of regional offices on maintaining the freedom to manage their own operations.

Field staff often felt overburdened by what they saw as Washington's incessant demand for information. They believed that headquarters just didn't appreciate the pressures on an overworked staff member operating in an atmosphere of continuing crisis, where solving the problem was more important than taking time out to write about it. Moreover, conflict resolution was so complex, and community situations so unique, that the conciliator had to ply his craft with unfettered flexibility. Headquarters, in turn, tried to point out that the very flexibility the conciliator enjoyed was a grant in trust to make good and proper use of the influence that flowed from Washington. Such trust could not be possible without a reliable accountability system involving disciplined operational controls and reporting systems. Differences were reconciled, in part, by including members of the field staff in the design and updating of operational policies and guidelines.

In the mid-1980s, director Gilbert Pompa set the performance bar even higher, introducing a quality assurance program to systematize the inquiry into the question of "did we really make a difference," as well as to test the reliability of case reporting. A peer-review process was initiated in which teams of mediators and conciliators were sent into the field to review a sampling of cases closed the previous year. Evaluation interviews were conducted with participants on both sides of the conflict as well as with qualified observers. A critical question when evaluating closed cases was, "Without CRS intervention, how would the outcome have been any different?"

The quality-assurance program succeeded in validating, through the eyes of people in the community, the extent of CRS's contribution to the solution of the conflict. It also certified the reliability of the case reporting system. While the idea of built-in case evaluation generated a measure of anxiety among members of the field staff, the knowledge that their own colleagues were doing the review of their casework provided reassurance as to the fairness of the process. There were other benefits. Some of the mediators found that in evaluating the work of others they acquired insights useful in improving their own case practice; some of the case reviews revealed findings that could be factored into ongoing staff development.

RUNNING THE BUDGET GAUNTLET

Even before the agency was out of swaddling clothes, President Johnson's own Bureau of the Budget as well as congressional watch-dogs of the public treasury were demanding a show of evidence as to the need for the existence of CRS as well as the necessity for every dollar of requested program growth. For a while—during the directorships of LeRoy Collins and Roger Wilkins—anecdotal evidence presented with common sense (and a good deal of charm) was able to carry the day. Moreover, the case was made that the most significant accomplishments of CRS were imponderables. Roger Wilkins wrote, "While we can count the number of communities to which assistance has been given, it is impossible to measure the extent to which antagonisms, conflict and violence were restrained or the degree to which repair of the social fabric and the pace of social change were quickened by our efforts."[3]

The going got heavier after that, with an increasing demand for proof and quantification of achievement. Among the challenges: How to measure the success of a case whose outcome was a non-happening—a confrontation that didn't escalate to a major disorder? How to claim credit as the catalyst of a multi-causal event involving a variety of players?

The CRS staff felt that the agency's worth should have been obvious to any sensible observer, even from anecdotal evidence alone: the potential riots that never happened; the civil disturbances that ended days earlier than they might have; the school systems that desegregated without turmoil; the battles for racial equity and justice that were won just a little bit faster and sometimes a little more convincingly than might have happened otherwise; the return of fractured communities to stability a month, or a year, or several years sooner than might have occurred without CRS intervention. In addition, an untold number of communities gained something of lasting value by learning early on, thanks to CRS, to listen and negotiate across racial lines and thus to resolve many problems through their own resources.

But the system didn't work that way. At the annual running of the gauntlet by which agencies proved their worth to administration and congressional budget analysts, and ultimately to congressional appropriations and authorization subcommittees, more rigid measures of proof were often demanded.[4] Gradually, seat-of-the-pants program direction gave way to management via goals and objectives. Those staff members who in their hearts thought the worth of the agency should be measured solely by its "obvious" contributions to keeping the peace learned to talk the talk of the bean counters. It wasn't easy, but CRS ultimately learned how to count what had seemed to be uncountable and how to do program planning for activities that often were rendered on an ad hoc basis in response to emergencies.

Sometimes the answers were found by developing proxy measures of performance—like "objectives achieved." To a congressman's question as to how the agency judges if its case intervention did any good, a CRS director could reply with precise information such as: "We know that in 93 percent of the 243 cases involving police use of excessive force, one or more of our objectives was achieved." That kind of answer was usually enough. But when a skeptical legislator would follow up with, "What is an objective and how do you know when it has been achieved," the director was ready with a description of case process. He could explain that no case could be opened without the regional director's personal approval of the conciliator's assessment; that every assessment included the conciliator's "verifiable" objectives for resolving the conflict; and that no case was closed without a review of the "outcome" of each objective. Examples of such objectives might include: "to get the parties to the bargaining table"; "to gain a signed, written agreement"; "to bring about a study of the student discipline code and its implementation"; "to negotiate the creation of a minority advisory committee to the police chief"; or "adoption of police guidelines for the use of firearms."

In learning to satisfy the outside demand for tangible evidence of performance, the agency's advocates for social justice found tools to satisfy their own need for assurance that their work was furthering the cause.

Despite its microscopic budget, the CRS program was often stunted by funding reductions, and at times threatened with extinction. CRS administrators who struggled to keep the agency adequately funded believed that budget analysts in the administrative division of the Justice Department, and in the White House Office of Management and Budget (OMB), thought they won their stripes by recommending budget reductions.[5] These technicians had few opportunities to shine when dealing with the costly programs favored by the department or the administration, or by powerful committee chairs in Congress. It was the runts at the feeding trough, small agencies like CRS that lacked powerful sponsors, which were the easy marks on which a junior analyst might build his or her reputation.

The ultimate fate of the CRS budget depends on two subcommittees of the House of Representatives that decide each year whether to approve the level of funds requested by the administration. Consistent support has historically come from the Judiciary Committee's Subcommittee on the Constitution, Civil Rights and Civil Liberties, which has oversight authority over the agency's programs. In its annual reauthorization hearings, members of the subcommittee expressed familiarity and concern with the problems CRS addressed. They often challenged the agency to make even greater efforts and asked how they might be of help. The CRS budget team attributed this support to the pro–civil rights bias of many subcommittee members, which made them comfortable in accepting the worth of CRS achievements at face value. Particularly helpful were those congressional members whose hands-on involvement with civil rights issues in their own district had given them an insider's view of CRS services in times of crisis. Subcommittee Chairman Don Edwards, who presided for many years, and Congressman John Conyers, for example, would often raise questions about CRS's performance in San Jose, California, and Detroit, Michigan.

The defenders of the budget had a harder row to hoe in making their case before the Appropriations Committee's Subcommittee on Commerce, Justice, State, and the Judiciary (now called the Subcommittee on Commerce, Justice, Science and Related Agencies). This group, whose members had to examine the budgets of three large departments and more, tended to take a more dispassionate and more challenging view of the needs of CRS, whose operations laid claim to but a smidgen of the budget of just one of the three departments. CRS knew that the appropriations people had the final word on funding but always hoped that a good word from the reauthorization group would help in the formulation of the bottom line.

The agency became something of a political football during the budgeting process, when Democrats on the House Judiciary Committee would praise CRS to the heavens in such a manner as to embarrass a Republican administration for the inadequacies of all its other civil rights programs. At such times the CRS director, in testifying before the committee, would have to become an artful dodger to avoid being cast in the role of a critic of the department and of the president, whose budget he was there to defend. He would pass the ball, when possible, to an administrative official of the Justice Department for the more intricate phases of the repartee. All the players were familiar with the game, in which the congressmen would relent before going too far, since the last thing they wanted to do was to compromise CRS's relations with the department.

The lack of a constituency to lobby for an ample appropriation did not help the CRS budget process. The national civil rights organizations, which would appear to be a natural constituency, focused mostly on the need to defend and expand civil rights. They had little appreciation for the role that conflict resolution played in the cementing of hard-won gains all over the country. The CRS tendency toward self-effacement, resulting from the behind-the-scenes character of its casework, undoubtedly contributed to this low level of regard by those we had looked upon as friends.

During the critical battle for survival in the late 1970s, CRS organized a last-ditch effort to stay alive. Key staff members asked civil rights organizations for their help. Regional Director Bob Lamb and I (Levine) called upon Clarence Mitchell, the lobbyist for the NAACP whose leadership in the fight for civil rights legislation had won him the title "the 101st senator." We were greeted with the challenging remark, "Where have you guys been in the last fifteen years? We wrote you into the law, and then you vanished." After acknowledging the criticism of CRS's low profile, we presented him with a study, especially researched for the occasion, documenting 151 instances, in the previous eighteen months alone, in which CRS had been called on by local NAACP branches around the country to help resolve community civil rights conflicts.[6] Mitchell had no idea of the service CRS was rendering to local branches of his own organization.

Over the years, CRS became reasonably adept at explaining its work, although sometimes it would take more than paper and ink. On one early occasion CRS persuaded an OMB budget analyst to spend a weekend with a conciliator working a case in Baltimore. Afterward the analyst said, with some vehemence, "Now I understand what you were trying to get across in your budget. I kept looking for your 'product.' But it's not just any one thing. It's the process itself that's the product—that draws the parties into a collaborative effort."[7]

CRS learned early on that, in times of budget trouble, the best ally to have in your corner was the attorney general. With the attorney general's support, the full weight of the Department of Justice technicians and lobbyists would push the CRS case among the department's top budgetary priorities. Sometimes even that might not be enough. On several occasions, the agency was saved only by the attorney general's personal intervention at the White House and readiness to take the matter all the way to the president if necessary. During the Carter administration, when OMB came up with a two-year strategy to terminate CRS, Attorney General Griffin Bell personally had to go head-to-head with the budget agency's director to effect a compromise that assured the CRS's continued viability.[8] A few years later, when President Reagan's OMB slated CRS for elimination, it took the intervention of Attorney General Edwin Meese, who threatened to personally take the matter to the president, to assure the agency's continued operation.

WINNING THE CONFIDENCE OF THE ATTORNEY GENERAL

The confidence of the attorney general had to be won anew with each new incumbent. Only a few of the incoming attorneys general were familiar with CRS or had encountered anything quite like it. CRS didn't investigate, litigate, or incarcerate, so what was it doing in the Department of Justice? The very concept of community conflict resolution as an ongoing function of the federal government seemed strange.

Four attorneys general did have personal familiarity with CRS before becoming its boss. Ramsey Clark had worked well with Roger Wilkins in the aftermath of the Watts riot and understood the agency's role at the operational level. In later years, Janet Reno had worked with CRS on a variety of cases as the state prosecutor in Dade County, Florida. She had personally witnessed the performance of a succession of conciliators, including Fred Crawford, Bob Schroeder, and Tom Battles, at troubled street corners and rancorous conference tables across Dade County. As a longtime Justice Department employee, Eric Holder was familiar with CRS work, especially when he was deputy attorney general in the Clinton administration and played a lead role in the Elián González situation in Miami. Loretta Lynch worked well with Regional Director Reinaldo Rivera when she was U.S. attorney for the Eastern District of New York in both the Clinton and Obama administrations.

Attorney General John Mitchell thought it made sense to have a federal agency working to reduce the pressure of racial stress in local communities before they exploded. CRS director Ben Holman also felt that Mitchell valued CRS's social analysis of what was happening in the nation's poor urban communities, as a counterweight to the unevaluated raw data from informants that the FBI often used to depict a threatening and conspiratorial profile of various inner-city problems.[9]

Attorney General Griffin Bell especially valued CRS's ability to use mediation to keep conflict off the streets and out of the courts. Bell, as a federal judge, had been an influential intellectual force seeking to advance the use of alternative dispute resolution techniques to relieve the burden on America's overworked court system. As attorney general, he put the weight of the Justice Department behind that movement. Gil Pompa noted that Bell often teased him about the number of federal judges who wrote to the attorney general commending the work of a CRS mediator to whom he had referred a case that had stubbornly resisted a litigated solution. Pompa felt that while he and the attorney general both suspected that some of the letters may have been solicited, there was no mistaking the judges' enthusiasm for this new and unexpected resource.

William French Smith, early in the Reagan administration, had apparently been impressed with a briefing from Pompa on the work of the agency. Pompa had mentioned, in passing, that each year CRS conducted a review of tension levels in the most troubled cities. At an informal press conference at Kansas City's Union Station one morning, Smith had been asked whether he anticipated a long hot summer of racial violence. He replied that he wasn't worried because he had an advance warning system. Asked what that warning system was, he replied, "The Community Relations Service."

No one was more shocked than Pompa to read in the *Washington Post* the next day that he was running an early warning system. But the announcement did impel the agency to convert its highly informal, highly subjective system of tension-level assessments into a data-based, quasi-scientific process. While the agency was convinced that specific riots were unpredictable, it did believe it was possible to identify cities vulnerable to outbreaks of racial violence and to distinguish cities at high risk from those facing lower levels of risk. In subsequent years such risk estimates—always treated in the highest confidence—were used to help CRS sharpen the focus of its preventive programming.

LEGACY—WHAT LEGACY?

None of the congressmen who voted the Community Relations Service into existence—and nobody who worked for it in the years that followed—expected anything more of it than that it would do its job in moderating the turmoil resulting from resistance to the changes brought on by the civil rights laws. The agency was to be a problem solver, helping others to relate more peacefully as they worked out the social changes by which America would make the transition to a more equal society. No one expected the peacemakers to be change makers—to leave any footprints of their own in the sands of time.

Yet the federal troubleshooters, the hand-holders, the community problem solvers could not have done their job for more than half a century without having some impact on history. A review of the record finds presumptive evidence that had there not been a CRS, many changes that took place would have occurred more slowly, many would have been worked out less well, and some might never have occurred.

We have seen how CRS, in responding over decades to thousands of community conflicts involving police use of deadly force, became a catalyst for improved police practice in hundreds of cities. The resulting national change in standards has undoubtedly helped to bring about a qualitative change in how police relate to minorities. We have also seen that, without CRS assistance to thousands of school districts, the process of school desegregation would have been a far more violent chapter in American history than it has, in fact, turned out to be. In addition, CRS helped to sound the reveille that awakened the broadcast and print media to the need for opening economic opportunities to minorities and for a fuller and fairer portrayal of minorities in American life.

One of the rewards of being a CRS field representative was the latitude within the standard operating procedures to cultivate your own special talents and interests as problem-solving tools. Some of these methods became enduring techniques for conflict resolution. Joe Rodriguez, a Central Region conciliator, worked in Missouri, Iowa, Nebraska, and Kansas. During the period of rampant racial violence in the public schools, he was called on to help resolve a bitter and stubborn situation in a large technical high school in Kansas City, Missouri. Over time he was able to organize a program (subsequently to be known nationwide as "peer mediation") in which students themselves, including some who had been leading antagonists, were trained to be conflict resolvers. Within two years the climate of bitterness was gone. The school system then called upon Rodriguez to help introduce peer mediation in all its technical high schools. He used the approach in other high schools in the four-state region and was called upon to consult in other school districts around the country. Peer mediation eventually became a popular program in many American school districts.

Another approach that worked well in some schools experiencing violence was used by Arthur Peltz, a former media expert, who worked as a CRS conciliator in California, Arizona, and Nevada. Peltz taught students in racially troubled schools how to write, direct, act in, and produce videos in order to present their grievances with the school and with their fellow students. Rival groups were then helped to respond with videos of their own. The care and thoughtfulness required to state their own position and to understand the position of the other side in order to make an effective response sometimes revealed an identity of views and permitted the face-to-face discussions that followed to get off to a productive start. Peltz enlisted the local TV stations for facilities, equipment, and technical assistance. While the program was effective in reducing interracial friction, as well as enlarging the career interests of the students, CRS found it too time-consuming for widespread use.

Regional Director Julian Klugman encouraged the other troubleshooters of his Western Region to utilize the same principle of sharing grievances and responses between disputing groups in other violence-ridden school settings. CRS would meet separately with antagonistic groups of students, as well as with parent groups and faculty, to help them exchange grievances and responses. The process was successful in creating a less rancorous atmosphere before opening direct problem-solving sessions. Called the SPIR program (Student Problem Identification and Resolution), it provided a formula for approaching racial disputes in many schools for many years. Jonathan Chace, CRS's associate director, noted that the conciliators of the Western Region were still making good use of the SPIR technique in school cases in 2002. The program now named SPIRIT (Student Problem Identification and Resolution of Issues Together) remains one of CRS's most popular tools for racial issues and more recently for other identity concerns like sexual orientation, religion, and gender identity.

The technique of sharing grievances had been adapted by CRS from a program the National Labor Relations Board used in certain industrial situations to forestall labor disputes they might otherwise have had to mediate. Months in advance of contract renewal negotiations, mediators would meet separately with each group to identify grievances and study the other side's response. Later, workers and supervisors would meet to work out solutions.

Conciliator John Mathis, who had helped to resolve some thorny racial clashes in state prisons in Oregon, worked with the state corrections authorities to adapt the program as a preventive measure in troubled penal institutions. CRS would meet separately with prisoners and corrections officers to define problems and review the opposing side's perceptions. Then small groups consisting of both guards and prisoners would meet, with the help of a CRS mediator, to work together to define problems and find solutions they could jointly recommend to prison management.

THE ART AND SCIENCE OF
COMMUNITY CONFLICT RESOLUTION

The healing art of community conflict resolution has come a long way since its inception in the mid-twentieth century when a few pioneering practitioners arose to meet the need in multicultural urban areas. Since then, the primary development has been in two isolated environments: the Community Relations Service and academia. CRS was enveloped in conflicts that it sought to resolve with intelligence and goodwill. Its methodology grew inductively out of trial and error and developed through usage and pragmatic adaptation into a formal body of practice.

The theory and principles of community conflict resolution, on the other hand, were developed in university programs, where they derived from the world of diplomacy and commercial and labor mediation. A handful of private practitioners also made notable contributions to the development of standards and techniques. University-based clinical institutes that taught dispute resolution had only limited opportunities, compared to CRS, to test and develop the skills they taught in actual multiparty conflicts out in the community. CRS, on the other hand, started out with more cases than it could handle but little theoretical background.

In an early effort to bring the budding profession of community racial conflict resolution as practiced by CRS closer to the broader world of conflict resolution, Regional Director Martin Walsh brought in Harvard Law School professor and renowned negotiation expert Roger Fisher to present and dialogue with CRS staff.[10] CRS's national director in the early 1970s, Ben Holman, led a group of CRS staff to the annual conference of SPIDR, the Society of Professionals in Dispute Resolution, an association made up largely of labor and business mediators. At a workshop on the resolution of community disputes, conducted by CRS mediator Ed Howden, only a handful of non-CRS mediators were interested enough to attend. Holman later made a second attempt to bring about a blending of the two communities by developing a proposal for CRS to develop its own academy for the teaching of dispute resolution, but he was unable to win budgetary approval for it. It was only in later years that community disputes became a major focus of SPIDR meetings.

In the meantime, some blending did occur as men and women with formal dispute resolution training joined the CRS ranks and as some mediators trained via the CRS experience gravitated into private practice or university settings. A number of CRS veterans moved to leadership roles in the Association for Conflict Resolution (ACR), the successor organization to SPIDR. James Laue was among the first to straddle both worlds. Following his experience at CRS, he founded and directed a clinical institute for the study and practice of community dispute resolution at the University of Missouri–St. Louis. He later helped to organize the Institute for Conflict Analysis and Resolution (ICAR) at George Mason University, where, as Lynch Professor of Conflict Resolution, he established the first doctoral program in conflict resolution in the United States in 1987.

Laue's writings reflected his CRS experience; his humanistic attitude led to a passionate grappling with what it meant to be a mediator. He pondered the ethical implications of intervention and concluded that non-neutrality was appropriate. A fundamental question Laue posed was, "Does the intervention contribute to the ability of relatively powerless individuals and groups in the situation to determine their own destinies to the greatest extent consistent with the common good?"[11] Like President Johnson, Laue was a forceful advocate for people resolving their own community issues.

In 1987, CRS conciliator Richard Salem cowrote one of the very first mediation textbooks with law school dispute resolution pioneer Nancy Rogers of Ohio State University's Moritz College of Law.[12]

Wallace Warfield brought his twenty years of CRS experience to the George Mason faculty and ICAR in 1990. Like Laue, Warfield emphasized how community conflict resolvers could not be neutral bystanders. He was an advocate of the interest-based problem-solving approach popularized by Roger Fisher but was critical of its use in identity-based conflicts. Warfield emphasized the need to start with a value-based perspective that was "nonrational" because these highly emotionally charged conflicts were so rooted in identity. Warfield also advocated for transparency in working with groups where there was a power imbalance.[13]

A significant move to help make the CRS experience available to others via the internet occurred in 2001. Salem, in cooperation with Heidi and Guy Burgess of the Conflict Research Consortium of the University of Colorado, developed an oral history project to interview retired CRS veterans about techniques they employed in actual community conflict situations.[14] Questions focused on technical problems of interest to others in the profession. Problem areas explored included such matters as goal setting, trust building, identifying underlying issues, dealing with intractable demands, use of the caucus, balancing equity against the need for settlement, dealing with personal attacks, strategies for impasse resolution, maintaining neutrality, dealing with cultural and racial factors, use of outside resources, use of fact finding, handling power differentials between the parties, and so forth.

The interviews reveal the differences in individual style and emphasis that CRS practitioners brought to their casework. The interviewers went to great lengths to explore the situational context of the conflicts that drew forth specific techniques. One such interview is with Nancy Ferrell, one of the conciliators who represented CRS in the states of Texas, Oklahoma, New Mexico, and Arkansas.[15]

In opening a case, Ferrell would first look for case objectives that would involve lasting systemic change, as opposed to objectives designed primarily to resolve the immediate conflict. Among CRS's case selection criteria, problems involving violence or the threat of violence were accorded first priority. After that, high value was placed on case objectives that held out the hope for influencing long-lasting change. However, such objectives were time-consuming, and successful outcomes were by no means assured. They were a luxury CRS often could not afford. Ferrell was fortunate to have as a regional director John Perez, whose own zest for systemic change enabled him, on occasion, to give her latitude to take on such high-risk, high-potential cases.

Ferrell developed such a case at a large university, where the initial conflict was only the tip of an iceberg. She was drawn to it by a newspaper article describing the hijinks of a traditional fraternity/sorority caper—Plantation Day. Members of one fraternity, in blackface and each with a noose around his neck, placed themselves for a day at the beck and call of the sorority sisters, presumably to the great amusement of all. The newspaper indicated that African American students had protested and demanded that the fraternity be banned from the university. The Ku Klux Klan distributed flyers attacking the Black protesters.

The initial response among some on campus was that the incident was overblown. After all, Plantation Day was a tradition dating back many years, and no one had protested before. There was, these community members claimed, no deliberate meanness to it. The attempt of the Klan to exploit the situation was meaningless since it was not a part of the university community. The head of the fraternity couldn't understand why anybody would be offended by a bit of innocent fun.

In interviewing faculty members, administrators, and white students, Ferrell perceived an undefined uneasiness about race beneath a surface of goodwill, but no one seemed to know what to do about it. From African American and Hispanic students she got a different view. Practices of racial subordination were built into the system. Minorities were virtually excluded from all activities; there was no safe mechanism through which to present grievances and seek remedies. As a result, contrary to the university's intent, the percentage of African American students attending the school was decreasing, and the authorities seemed clueless.

Ferrell concluded that the fraternity incident was just a symptom, and resolution of that problem alone would have little impact on the pervasive institutional racism. Her first objective, therefore, would be to help the university recognize its own problems. If that could be done, work on solutions was likely to follow.

She found a nucleus of support within the administration and faculty. The problem was to get the go-ahead from a resistant university president. Ferrell, who tends to be analytic in her approach, sees her methodology as a dance with the client. You can't dance with someone if you're at one end of the floor and he's at the other. It's hard to dance if he thinks you're insensitive to his self-interest. For a time you follow his lead, until, in time, he's comfortable enough to follow yours. It's a matter of timing and trust-building. In meeting with the university president, Ferrell was guided by two axioms of human behavior she brought to all her cases: (1) no one can be expected to negotiate to the detriment of self-interest; and (2) all other things being equal, a person would rather think of himself as wanting to do good than as wanting to do bad.

Thus, she had to find a way to let each side understand that she would remain sensitive to its needs and that she appreciated any willingness to make an honest effort to work toward a solution. This belief enabled her to take other people at their word. Others, in turn, would be reluctant to break the bond of trust that she offered.

Ferrell said to the university president, "I'm here to see if there's any way you think the Community Relations Service might be able to help." With an eye on the board of regents, to whom he was accountable, the president indicated that he didn't want to be seen as "making a federal case of it" by involving the Justice Department. Ferrell responded that she understood how he felt, but then asked what would happen if there were another racial incident, and it was learned that a CRS offer of assistance had been rejected because the university thought it didn't need any help. Then, she tactfully provided him with two thoughts he could offer any detractors. The first was to point out that CRS was a confidential problem-solving arm of the Justice Department that had been created for the very purpose of lessening the need for the department to call on its investigative and prosecuting agencies. Her second thought was: "If you think there's room for improvement, we're here to help."

Before leaving she asked if he'd like her to stop back after completing her assessment, in case he would find in it any suggestions for improvement. He acknowledged, "Well, of course there's always room for improvement." That became her mantra for continuing her work. The president had set the tune to which they could dance.

Eventually, the president authorized one of the university vice presidents to work with Ferrell on the formation of a task force to look into the problem. Ferrell then found herself dancing with many at-first-reluctant parties. African American students balked at the inclusion in the task force of the offending fraternity, until they became convinced that was the only way to get at the root of the problem. Faculty members were fearful of giving more power to students. Minorities did not trust the student government, from which they felt excluded. Student organizations did not trust the administration. Some groups thought others might be troublemakers and should be excluded. Many individuals feared facing unfair accusations and angry confrontations. Ferrell made it clear to all groups that she would guarantee a safe environment for all to speak freely and expected in return that all would be heard in good faith.

It took three months of work before Ferrell felt that a representative task force was ready to come together. She then assisted the group for more than a year as it worked through its differences and developed into a cohesive entity that was united in its purpose. A major breakthrough came when the president of the fraternity announced to the group that *he* finally understood the enormity of Plantation Day, and he was ashamed that he had failed to see how hurtful and demeaning an event it had been.

By the time Ferrell closed the case, the task force had presented a set of recommendations for encouraging and safeguarding the participation of minorities in all aspects of university life. It had enlarged its scope to cover a wide range of relevant problems, such as availability of housing and access for disabled students. It became a mechanism for processing minority grievances and monitoring the remedy process. It was converted into a permanent body, reporting directly to the university president.

U.S. District Court Judge W. Arthur Garrity Jr. had a special relationship with the Community Relations Service. As related in chapter 7, they worked together for more than six years on one of America's most notorious episodes involving violent resistance to civil rights changes required by the Constitution. The school desegregation case in Boston drew the attention of the entire world, and the struggle over its resolution was helpful to many other cities in forestalling violent resistance to their own school desegregation.

In 1975, Judge Garrity endorsed the nomination of CRS mediator Silke Hansen for a Federal Woman's Award. His letter bore eyewitness testimony to some of the details of CRS case activity:

One of the principal stabilizing forces in the city during the present school year has been a network of racial-ethnic councils of parents and students at racially troubled schools. I sought and benefitted from Miss Hansen's advice in establishing these councils. . . . She, more than anyone else, was responsible for the functioning and progress of these councils. Her perseverance in initiating and promoting meetings of black and white parents after repeated rejections has been remarkable. . . . By way of illustration, there has been almost fanatical resistance to desegregation in South Boston, which has been a scene of violence and ugly confrontations. White parents and students at the high school there refused to participate in the formation of a biracial council for many reasons. . . . Only Miss Hansen remained undiscouraged. By patience and the force of her forthright personality and skill and judgement . . . she succeeded in organizing a biracial group there which has kept open lines of communication between hostile factions. . . . A city-wide parents' advisory group has been elected to assist local groups. . . . I attended and addressed one of its meetings. . . . It was readily observable that she enjoyed the confidence and trust of all fourteen members of the city-wide group. They obviously valued her suggestions and comments. Some of the members were at swords' points on various substantive questions, but they seemed disposed to discover peaceful resolutions under her influence.[16]

Three years later, Judge Garrity again evoked the CRS's role in the Boston school case, this time in a letter to President Jimmy Carter, in response to press reports that the administration was weighing the termination of CRS. The judge said: "At the outset of school desegregation here, and on several occasions thereafter, local officials simply didn't know which way to turn. CRS was able to . . . provide counsel and leadership not only to school officials but to the police and other municipal departments as well, and to avoid widespread violence." Calling the contemplated move penny wise but pound foolish, the judge went on: "According to the newspapers the annual budget of CRS is under $6,000,000. Why, the cost of police overtime at a single city high school during the first two years was over $10,000,000."[17]

On January 20, 1959, Lyndon B. Johnson, then majority leader of the Senate, introduced a bill to create a community relations service. The proposal was not acted upon, but its provisions ultimately became law as Title X of the Civil Rights Act of 1964. In his speech presenting the 1959 bill, Johnson said: "In any protracted controversy there is the stage of stalemate, a stalemate so bad that people cannot talk to each other. At this point . . . a conciliator would be worth his weight in gold. A man who could be trusted and who could come into the community and go back and forth between the leaders could break the log jam in communications. . . . And the people themselves would settle the controversy."[18]

Many objective observers reading that quote might salute Johnson's prescience—with due allowance, perhaps, for a bit of overstatement with regard to the weight-in-gold business. Judge Garrity, however, quite likely would have endorsed Johnson's valuation without qualification.

THE JOURNEY CONTINUES

Throughout its five-decade-plus history, CRS has had a unique role as a federal agency with the mandate to resolve conflict in civil rights matters.[19] The tension between impartiality and a commitment to upholding civil rights has played out over and over again. From its earliest work in Selma, preventing violence at the Pettus Bridge, to keeping protests safe in Sanford, Florida, CRS has toed that line. Protesters sometimes view consensual processes as antithetical to pressuring for change via demonstration and conflict. Local government players like law enforcement and city officials can view a small, federal civil rights–based agency as advocating for a specific outcome. Therein has always laid the challenge for CRS, but, as this book has hopefully shown, through the agency's work, it has created processes and outcomes that can allow both justice and peace to flourish.

Whether it was providing court-based mediation for integrating the Cook County Jail near Chicago, working at the local and state level to implement treaty rights for the Nez Percé tribe in Idaho, mediating with Coors Brewing Company and creating successive five-year agreements to improve Hispanic hiring and advancement, or helping Sikh American civil rights groups enhance the Uniform Crime Reporting Program to add several religious categories to more accurately reflect hate crimes in America, CRS has played a role in how governmental and corporate institutions systemically treat and interact with historically marginalized minority groups. Working at the intersection of neutrality and civil rights has reaped benefits in the service of justice.

Wallace Warfield's perspective on how conflict resolution and social justice can interact best is apt here. CRS work is not about removing the pressure of civil rights advocacy. The question is how to best work with that pressure to move toward a functional outcome for all parties that advances the situation toward justice and peace. This was true in CRS's attempt to mediate a peaceful handover of Elián González from his Miami relatives to his father in Cuba, and in Ferguson, working with Attorney General Holder to help bring respite to an area in crisis.

Working at that intersection has meant doing so with confidentiality and without publicity. While CRS has had success, in no small part due to relationships and credibility built over time by conciliators, its ability to make an impact has been hampered by its anonymity and lack of resources, notably staff and budget. Other Department of Justice agencies like the Civil Rights Division can tout blockbuster trials and go after wrongdoers and get its work known instantly across the country through the media. When CRS successfully helps communities avert violence and make change, it does so under the radar, as its name is rarely mentioned in press releases or media reports.

CRS does not hold press conferences or conduct interviews after its accomplishments.

For CRS, it has been difficult to prove a negative in order to increase budget, staff, and resources. Cases throughout CRS history have shown how situations would have turned out very differently had CRS not been there. For example, if CRS conciliators had not been engaged with the neo-Nazi organization in Skokie, Illinois, there would have been a high likelihood of violent confrontation. CRS's interventions are often about consensual processes leading to agreement, which removes situations from social media or the headlines.

THE DELIVERABLES

There are three concentric circles in the seal of the Community Relations Service forming a center and two outer rings. In the center is a drawing of the balancing scale representing justice, a concept that has its origins in the ancient Egyptian goddesses Maat and Isis. In the middle ring are the words "Educate Communicate Conciliate Mediate Facilitate," which describe the services of CRS. On the bottom of that second ring are the Latin words "Justicia Omnibus Gens," which mean "justice for all people." The outer ring contains the words "U.S. Department of Justice" and "Community Relations Service."

Having the scale symbolizing justice at the center is apropos for the goal of CRS's work. The target is not just about reducing violence or tension; it is ultimately about increasing fairness and equity. The service words in the middle ring convey the broad and varied ways in which CRS staff have been assisting people and communities for nearly two generations. The Latin words emphasize that all people are served, not just a subset. The CRS differentiation per the 1964 Civil Rights Act is the underlying philosophy that the resolution which impacts the people is crafted by those same people rather than imposed by a court or those with more power. The official CRS seal conveys the balancing act that CRS has deftly managed all these years.

At CRS, the term "conciliation" has been used as a comprehensive one to include all conflict resolution services the agency provides. The 2012 CRS annual report states, "Conciliation includes facilitation, mediation, training, and consulting through technical assistance."[20] As both its seal and its annual reports indicate, CRS's more measurable work can be seen through the lens of these four categories. They capture what has often been assessed for evaluation purposes and some of the most significant work CRS has done.

MEDIATION

According to the most recent CRS annual report (2018) available at the time of preparing this new edition, "As mediators, Conciliation Specialists assume the role of neutral third parties, who facilitate problem-solving discussions with parties in conflict. These mediation sessions are confidential, allowing for candid discussion of issues, interests, values, and, ultimately, sustainable solutions. . . . Frequently the results of a community's mediation will be memorialized in a document such as a Memorandum of Understanding, Mediation Agreement, Resolution, Proclamation, Collaborative Agreement, Community Pact or Ordinance."[21]

Chapter 8 of this book is devoted specifically to mediation and details the more formalized mediations that began in the 1970s, including prisoner civil rights cases in Louisiana; integration of the Cook County Jail; the Voting Rights Act in Cairo, Illinois; and the Hispanic coalition agreement with the Coors Company. As court-based mediation programs grew and as more lawyers became mediators, CRS conciliators ceased for the most part to do judge-ordered mediation. On occasion, CRS staff play a technical assistance role and provide facilitated dialogue services for a court-appointed special master, as it did in Tucson, Arizona, after the suspension of the district's Mexican American Studies Program.[22]

More recently, CRS conciliators continued to mediate between police departments and community and civil rights advocacy organizations, university administrators and professors, public school administrators and parents, tribal and white community members, and others. Over the years, specific conciliators developed an expertise in mediation and created a large portfolio of such work for themselves as individuals. These included Robert Greenwald, Richard Salem, Steven Thom, Silke Hansen, Thomas Battles, Kit Chalberg, and Kenith Bergeron. Some of the mediations are complex and lengthy, but increasingly, because of limited budget, training, and staff resources, the mediations have trended toward briefer duration. When CRS started in 1964, there were no court-based mediation programs and mediation did not exist as a profession or field, except in tiny pockets like the Federal Mediation and Conciliation Service for labor and management issues. CRS played a role as early pioneers and innovators of court- and community-based mediation.

The 2018 CRS annual report defines the purpose of facilitation as "to help communities open lines of communication by listening to the issues of each stakeholder group and learning from each party about the problem and underlying issues of the conflict."[23] When individuals and groups are in conflict, it can be difficult to be civil and productive in conversation, especially with increasing numbers of angry people in a meeting. Having a third party in the room, especially a conciliator trained to effectively run such meetings, can accomplish numerous goals. It can improve communication, create better group dynamics, create consensus, solve problems, and support healing. Facilitation methodology and training originates in what were called t-groups or encounter groups, developed by application to racial relations.

As communities requested CRS help, individuals and groups often were uncomfortable with the idea of being in a room with others with whom they were in conflict, or were concerned that the session would go badly. CRS conciliators could be a third party above the fray and be trusted to run the meeting, town hall, or group planning session and be perceived as impartial and fair. With factors such as its federal agency positioning, CRS also played a convener role, as the party who could invite parties in a conflict to a neutral territory, thus shortcutting power plays and drama. The Department of Justice's reputation for integrity and trust in the Community Relations Service, as well as the experience, training, and reputation of the individual conciliator, led to communities using this service more and more.

In Oak Creek, Wisconsin, right after the 2012 shooting, CRS, along with the U.S. Attorney's Office, quickly brought together leaders to problem solve, and then the larger community to begin healing and reassuring the community. In Baltimore in 2015, after the Freddie Gray tragedy, CRS conciliator Justin Lock facilitated a dialogue between Korean American merchants and African American residents to focus on next steps after rioting damaged businesses and conflicts came to the surface.

For community identity-based conflicts, having a facilitator can pay huge dividends in that the conciliator can be the peacemaker, bridge-builder, and referee, and help all parties advocate more constructively.

Even in the best of times, it can be challenging to juggle the desire to advocate for what one wants, make sure everyone at the table feels respected, divvy up opportunities to let everyone participate fairly, and run the session in an organized fashion. Especially in heated, difficult conversations, having a third party take on the responsibility of running the meeting results in an effectively facilitated dialogue and provides a key component to a better outcome.

TRAINING

Per the 2018 CRS annual report, "Conciliation Specialists provide an array of training programs to law enforcement groups and communities as a tool for cultivating understanding, building relationships, and conducting safe public events."[24] Over time, this form of education has become a popular CRS deliverable to users. It is easy to understand the goals, parameters, and format of training. Educational sessions can aid in prevention of conflict and are conducive to replication and measurement. Looking at what the trainings were and when they were developed is a window into the CRS priorities at a given time as well as what expertise CRS developed over time.

A number of CRS programs provide a more structured facilitation approach along with training. These programs are a hybrid of the facilitated dialogue and training services. Described in this book is the Student Problem Identification and Resolution of Issues Together program (SPIRIT). Currently there is also a Dialogue on Race program, which focuses on increasing understanding and finding commonality. In 1997, Director Rose Ochi initiated a similar program called One America Dialogue as part of Bill Clinton's America in the 21st Century: The President's Initiative on Race, which was created by Executive Order 13050. In 2018, CRS created Strengthening Police and Community Partnerships (SPCP),which brings together law enforcement and community leaders to problem solve and focus on overcoming historic barriers, improving trust, and developing partnerships.

Another category of training is cultural competency programs. Discussed in this book were the Law Enforcement and Transgender training as well as the currently titled Engaging and Building Partnerships with Muslim Americans and Engaging and Building Partnerships with Sikh Americans. CRS created a video for each of these programs, reflecting the importance of that medium. All of the trainings were developed with a coalition of national civil rights organizations within each identity group. Having their engagement was critical to the viability of these programs. Oftentimes, the programs were cotaught with individuals affiliated with the respective civil rights organizations. To have the Community Relations Service as a Department of Justice agency created credibility to law enforcement and governmental bodies as a seal of approval for the programs' contents. For civil rights and community groups, such trainings and videos represented an important step in righting or preventing wrongs. They also symbolized a validation that CRS, the Department of Justice, and the federal government cared about their critical issues and demonstrated that commitment through time, resources, and budget.

A third category of training programs is one that imparts advice and skill for managing marches, rallies, and demonstrations to give voice and prevent violence. These programs were provided in a number of the cases described in this book and many others, including Sanford, Ferguson, Baltimore, and political parties' national conventions.

One training program is Contingency Planning: Reducing Risk during Public Events, which enhances a group's ability to plan for safe public events, such as protests or rallies, and reduces the likelihood of violence. Another is the currently titled Event Marshals: Supporting Safety during Public Events, in which "Event Marshals support a safe and successful public event by being the primary point of contact with event participants."[25] This is a direct product of CRS's many years of expertise at protests against law enforcement, Ku Klux Klan rallies, commemorative civil rights events, political conventions, and impromptu rallies.

Also within the training category is education focused on critical information sharing. Since the Hate Crimes Prevention Act passed in 2009, CRS has and continues to do hate crime forums, educating people on the law, their rights, and resources. Doing so entails reaching out to interested stakeholders, partnering with experts, and planning and preparing events, which tend to be panel discussions. Another example is forums on protecting houses of worship given the long involvement of CRS in these issues.

CONSULTATION

Another way that CRS shares its expertise with communities is via consultation or what is often called "technical assistance" in government. Per the 2018 CRS annual report, "Conciliation Specialists offer consultation services to help educate and empower communities, as well as to refine conflict resolution strategies and improve their ability to address underlying sources of tension. Through consultation, CRS provides technical assistance, as well as information on best practices. This service also includes giving advice, sharing insight, and referring communities to available resources."[26]

A prime example is Richard Salem's work in the Skokie situation where a neo-Nazi group was pulling an entire community toward violence and mayhem. By skillfully providing the consequences of different scenarios and offering face-saving options to the Nazi leader and others, a potential disaster was averted.

Another instructive example from the book is the advising that Regional Director Thomas Battles provided to Mayor Jeff Triplett and City Manager Norton Bonaparte in Sanford, Florida. Battles built bridges by introducing them and bringing them together with Jesse Jackson, Al Sharpton, and their respective organizations. Battles advised Triplett to speak at a rally. Triplett noted that CRS's rolodex and its know-how from dealing with these situations hundreds of times basically saved Sanford from a much worse fate.

That source of institutional knowledge and the personal networks enable CRS conciliators to play the bridge builder—the "glue guy" or "glue gal" in basketball parlance, meaning the players who contribute to winning but whose contribution is not easily quantifiable. CRS conciliators play a public stewarding role to increase the likelihood of success, by using analysis gleaned from years of similar situations, a familiarity with the players and dynamics, and the ability to see several moves ahead.

MULTIPLE ROLES OF THE CONCILIATOR

Throughout its history, CRS conciliators have played different roles in their mission to resolve conflict. The originating language of the 1964 Civil Rights Act is broad as to what CRS's function is, that is, "to provide assistance to communities and persons therein in resolving disputes, disagreements, or difficulties relating to discriminatory practices based on race, color, or national origin which impair the rights of persons in such communities under the Constitution or laws of the United States or which affect or may affect interstate commerce."[27] It does not spell out limitations as to specific services, for example, mediation, training, coaching, consultation, and so on. As such, CRS as an organization and its conciliators have played multiple conflict and dispute resolution roles through the decades.

In cases throughout this book, there are numerous roles that conciliators take which go beyond the archetypal roles most have associated with mediators. Given that CRS has been providing "assistance" for over fifty-five years, it has done so in a variety of ways. The first examples of CRS work cited in this book provide exemplars. A single call from a CRS conciliator caused a southern, rural sheriff to provide squad patrols to protect an African American family targeted for harassment and vandalism—an example of an equalizer role by bringing the federal government's power to assist a family with little leverage. When the comedian and activist Dick Gregory came to Selma to demonstrate and was denied a room at the local Holiday Inn, the conciliator called the Holiday Inn board chair, who was on the National Citizens Committee for Community Relations, and the discriminatory policy was reversed in minutes, providing another example of the equalizer role played by CRS.[28]

When Rosa Melendez became regional director and was headquartered in the CRS Seattle office, she brought with her a huge network of trusted partners and allies, having risen in the ranks of the Seattle police and served as the first Latina to be a U.S. marshal. In 2012, she convened a meeting between local Latino leaders, clergy, immigrant rights groups, and Port Arthur and Bellingham officials and Department of Homeland Security officials concerning allegations of overreach by the U.S. Border Patrol. Melendez's relationships with those in various stakeholder groups enabled her to play a strong bridge-builder role.[29]

Many CRS conciliators before and after they joined the agency built strong relationships with activists, community leaders, law enforcement, politicians, and career government employees. In times of crisis and conflict, this network has provided many conciliators with a glide path to get engaged quickly and positioned them to help contain, prevent, and resolve conflict. The conciliator can make the introduction, bring individuals together over a meal, clarify miscommunications, and offer a host of other positive benefits.

When Regional Director Ozell Sutton testified at a House Judiciary Subcommittee on Civil and Constitutional Rights in Jackson, Mississippi, to share his perspective on the Sister Spirit Camp issues, he was in the role of witness, discussing how the conflict had worsened and how the parties were not talking directly to each other, instead waging their battle in the media. Pointing out conflict on a platform like a powerful congressional committee hearing can shine a light for many more people to pay attention to a potentially explosive situation and can be a means to a safer and saner outcome.

When Regional Director Ron Wakabayashi resolved a dispute between a protester against Arizona's SB 1070 and a Maricopa County sheriff's deputy, he played referee by officiating what comprised legal access to an area. Sometimes what is needed is a third party who can credibly communicate the rules and regulations and cajole the parties to stay within them in order to keep a conflict from escalating.

When Conciliator James Williams stood between J. T. Ready's neo-Nazi group and protesters against Arizona's SB 1070 at that same rally, he played a peacekeeper role by doing what was minimally necessary to lessen the tension and reduce the possibility of a conflict turning violent. CRS continues to play this role at large-scale rallies and protests. Other examples include protests over the death of Trayvon Martin in Sanford, protests over the death of James Byrd Jr., and Ku Klux Klan demonstrations.

When Conciliator Nancy Ferrell worked with a university task force composed of various stakeholders, including Black and Latino students, white fraternity members, and administrators, she played a healer role in dealing with the Plantation Day ritual in which fraternity members wore blackface and nooses around their necks and did a sorority sister's bidding. Ferrell created a safe environment where the white fraternity president was able to admit his shame for his failure to see the harm of Plantation Day. While conflicts can seem to be resolved, emotional injuries may not be and may also need to be mended. Ferrell's skill in handling a difficult conversation reflects the recognition that feelings and identity are at risk, and conciliation is not just about the facts of any given situation.

After the tragedy at Oak Creek, CRS worked with the Civil Rights Division and the FBI to add the Sikh category to the Uniform Crime Reporting Program, an example of CRS playing the provider role. There are numerous times where CRS works on a solution that pinpoints a specific need, here a desire to be counted in order to get better data to help prevent future hate crimes.

CRS conciliators offer a variety of assistance within the conflict process. Through this assistance, they are helping to find resolution, but often many of these situations contain intractable circumstances as well. As director, Roger Wilkins was supportive of programs that focused on reducing poverty, increasing employment, and improving housing. He was wary of bouncing from crisis to crisis. Director Ben Holman focused more on the dearth of minorities in media and improving the coverage of minority issues. As the second and third director during the 1960s and early 1970s, Wilkins and Holman were able to direct significant budget and staff toward impacting the underlying causes for conflict.

Throughout the last half century, CRS has consistently assisted in helping parties engage better in conflict. Much of what conciliators have been doing fits Bernard S. Mayer's thesis in *Beyond Neutrality*, as they have been coaching, consulting, and referring. They understand that these are approaches to conflict that serve individual parties better as well as all the stakeholders involved. The self-marshaling described in this book is about helping the parties advocate more effectively by staying safe and not being goaded into physical violence by the other side. Much of CRS's success can be attributed not just to the more archetypal roles we associate with third-party intervenors, that is, mediation, facilitation, and training, but also to playing the roles of bridge-builder, provider, equalizer, referee, witness, and healer.

WORKFLOW

In 2013, CRS was updating its case management technology system and performance evaluation system. I used the opportunity to enhance the underlying case management methodology in order to build a common framework throughout the agency. The goal was to make it easier for conciliators to document their work, learn from each other, and create consistency from region to region. The five steps of any CRS case were identified as (1) monitoring and outreach, (2) assessment and engagement, (3) service selection, (4) service delivery, and (5) evaluation and closeout.

Step one begins with the conciliator monitoring the situation, gathering information, and conducting outreach with various stakeholders. Fundamental questions to be answered include, "What are the potential flashpoints?" and "Is there potential for escalating tension and violence?"

Step two is an assessment wherein the conciliator processes the information and makes a recommendation to the regional director, who decides whether or not to open a case. Engagement then entails notification of key stakeholders such as the U.S. Attorney's Office and relevant congressional representatives. The conciliator subsequently initiates contact with potential parties to the conflict. Fundamental questions to be answered in this step include, "How might CRS play a meaningful role?" and "Does CRS have the capacity and resources to engage all the relevant parties to this conflict?"

In step three, the conciliator and the identified parties to the conflict collaboratively determine the CRS services to be utilized. The four services available are mediation, facilitation of dialogue, training, and consultation/technical assistance. A case can close here if the services are not accepted.

Step four consists of the conciliator performing the services. Fundamental questions to be answered here include, "Were the services delivered as planned?" "What is the impact of the services?" and "What else is needed?"

Step five is evaluation through collection of feedback, both formally and informally. Fundamental questions to be answered include, "What did CRS do effectively?" "How could CRS have been more effective?" and "What is the new tension level?"

Analyzing evidence to enhance service is strongly related to the truism that the amount and quality of the data are critical for analysis and improvement. This initiative was key to moving the agency forward in a time when data analytics had moved to the forefront of public service.

THE NEW DIGITAL FRONTIER

The rise of smartphone technology, social media, and a change in presidential administration led to increased scrutiny of the Community Relations Service. When Barack Obama became president in 2009, new tools were available for partisan warfare. More and more citizens had portable video and audio recording ability in their smartphones following the release of the iPhone and similar technology in 2007. Partisan cable television and radio talk shows had grown dramatically. A new conservative blogosphere proliferated, including the popular Breitbart site, which has been highly, loudly, and often misleadingly critical of CRS.

In this new digital media landscape, CRS, which had largely been anonymous, received more media coverage than ever before—with some significant consequences. For example, on April 18, 2012, a Breitbart headline read, "Spies and Muscle: Holder, Secretive DOJ Group Helped Oust Sanford Sheriff." The article pointed to an *Orlando Sentinel* story that articulated how CRS helped bring together Sanford-area elected officials and local NAACP leaders, which preceded the temporary resignation of the Sanford police chief.[30]

In addition to the provocative title of the article making a false statement that CRS employees were "spies" and that they "helped oust" a local law enforcement executive, the entire article makes several damning accusations with scant to no evidence. The article describes Attorney General Eric Holder as having a "cozy relationship" with civil rights leader Al Sharpton and indicates that in 2006, then-Senator Obama "was involved in a Florida case with [Trayvon] Martin's attorney Benjamin Crump and Rev. Sharpton." Although these connections have no clear relevance to the case, the article typifies the conspiratorial racial dog-whistle line of attack on CRS. The agency is described as a "secretive" group of "spies" doing the bidding of an attorney general and president in cahoots with African American civil rights leaders.

While one might dismiss such stories as extremist right-wing conspiracy mongering, it is important to recognize that Breitbart was run by Steve Bannon, later a senior advisor to President Donald Trump. A conservative activist group, Judicial Watch, made accusations along the same lines, suggesting that CRS was fanning the protests rather than reducing the tension. This line of accusation reached a crescendo after closing arguments in the George Zimmerman case. Conservative talk radio host Rush Limbaugh raised the topic of CRS's involvement on his show, and numerous hosts on the Fox News channel followed with similar segments denigrating CRS's integrity and mission.

Given CRS's legislative mandate to maintain confidentiality and shun publicity, its leadership and staff declined to respond in the media. There was some counterbalancing by liberal cable shows and media outlets like MSNBC's *The Rachel Maddow Show* and the Huffington Post. Nonetheless, it has been difficult to correct misperceptions and false depictions given CRS's mandate to stay out of the spotlight.

But this is the new reality of mass communication. While viral social media can shine a light on the realities experienced by communities, such as racial profiling and law enforcement treatment of minorities, it also enables unsubstantiated partisan attacks on a small federal agency that does not seek the limelight in order to do its work effectively. Underlying this digital weaponization is the increased political polarization in the United States, which CRS must navigate effectively regardless of who holds the position of president and the composition of the Congress.

In February 2018, the Trump administration proposed to eliminate CRS in the FY2019 budget.[31] The proposal closely followed the conservative Heritage Foundation's recommendation for doing away with the agency. The administration proposed to move the duties of the office to the Civil Rights Division. Former CRS acting director Becky Monroe criticized this decision in a blog post, explaining, "One of the reasons CRS is effective is because it is not an investigative nor prosecutorial component of the DOJ. Instead, it works through regional offices [to] deliver services tailored to community needs. For mayors, chiefs, sheriffs, and community leaders alike, the fact that CRS is not involved in prosecutions or investigations makes it possible for leaders to ask for the assistance without fear of facing a lawsuit."[32]

Todd A. Cox, NAACP policy director, came to the agency's defense, saying that the elimination of CRS, "by callously draining it of the resources [it needs,] is yet another move by this Administration to circumvent their legal obligations and strip minority communities of federal protections." He went on to say, "We need the Justice Department's 'peacemaker' now more than ever, and cutting off funding for the CRS—like so much of Trump's proposed budget—is irresponsible and shameful."[33] Thanks to Cox, other civil rights advocates, and congressional members, CRS was fully funded for fiscal year 2019.

RECOGNITION

In 2013, CRS received the Association for Conflict Resolution Peacemaker Award. The award acknowledged the significant and sustained contributions by CRS to the cause of peace. ACR makes the award based on a criteria of bringing of peace to troubled relationships, whether domestic, organizational, environmental, or international. This award is meant to recognize efforts to bring peace through various conflict resolution approaches to ethnic, religious, and civil conflicts that have raged domestically and outside the United States. Other awardees include Nobel Peace Prize winner Leymah Gbowee and Senator George Mitchell.

In the acceptance speech, I stated that I accepted the award "on behalf of the committed individuals who served at CRS for the last half-century and who did so often anonymously, with little fanfare or recognition."[34] In 2014, Richard Salem won the same award posthumously, which was fitting given his contributions in forty years in the field and his active role in ACR.

In 2014, the American Bar Association's Section of Dispute Resolution presented CRS with its John W. Cooley Lawyer as Problem Solver Award, which recognized CRS for its skills in forging creative solutions for resolving community problems. The bar association honored CRS for its ability to analyze situations from a multidisciplinary perspective, taking into account the broad array of interests and multitude of factors that impact the problem presented. In addition, CRS was recognized for its ability to translate positions into interests and build consensus around an option that best addressed the goals of the involved participants.

For over half a century, CRS conciliators have served in communities across this nation, without fanfare and without publicity, in some of the most significant civil rights events over those fifty-plus years, helping to keep people safe, to open communication channels, and to problem-solve. The agency's differentiation stems from, as Lyndon Johnson framed it, the goal that the people themselves would settle the controversy. CRS reflects its 1960s civil rights–era creation in the belief that communities themselves should have a voice in resolving their own conflicts, rather than having solutions imposed upon them. That desire by communities of color, other historically marginalized groups, and all Americans for self-determination is as strong now as it was then.

Throughout CRS's history, the themes of justice and peace have been intertwined. CRS has had a focus on bringing people to the table who had not been there before, or where there was a power imbalance, and resolving differences with those in positions of authority—the mayors, city council, police, corporate executives, and other civic leaders. The goal has been to find resolution while preventing serious physical and emotional injury. Whether it was the Southern Christian Leadership Conference, the Nez Percé tribe, La Raza, Camp Sister Spirit founders, Seadrift's Vietnamese fishermen, Sikh leaders after the Oak Creek tragedy, the National Center for Transgender Equality, or Black Lives Matter, CRS conciliators applied pressure and generated conflict to right or prevent a wrong. They worked with that pressure to prevent violence while moving the community as a whole toward desegregation, treaty implementation, legislation, or other progression. Sustainable peace requires just outcomes for all communities and hard work in the trenches to assist all the people involved. Impartiality, confidentiality, and discretion matter for CRS in getting this job done.

From Selma to Skokie to Sanford, CRS conciliators have been in the trenches and played a monumental role in increasing everyday people's voices and reducing violence. Its staff has worked, usually behind the scenes, in a myriad of situations that never made headlines or went viral, helping communities to collaboratively resolve their own problems and move forward toward a more just and fair society. In polarizing times, these individuals, "worth their weight in gold," have played a critical role in advancing the vision of our founders and the country's citizens in maintaining domestic tranquility and facilitating the pursuit of happiness. The Community Relations Service has and will continue to be America's peacemakers.

NOTES

1. Roger Wilkins, interview with Bertram Levine.

2. Erica Ritz, "Former Director of DOJ Army Sent to Monitor Zimmerman Protests Makes Shock Admission about Agency," The Blaze, July 22, 2013, https://perma.cc/S3RL-7LYJ.

3. U.S. Department of Justice, Community Relations Service, Annual Report, 1965, vi.

4. U.S. Department of Justice, Community Relations Service, "Operational Planning System Handbook," 1979.

5. OMB was the successor agency to the Bureau of the Budget.

6. Gilbert G. Pompa to Benjamin L. Hooks, December 7, 1978.

7. In budget issues during the Obama administration, a preeminent civil rights leader and then president of the Leadership Conference, Wade Henderson, reached out to Lum as CRS director to pledge his support and advocacy of CRS. To his credit and to the credit of CRS staffers, including longtime general counsel George Henderson, he was well-versed on CRS activity. (note by Lum)

8. *Washington Star*, December 5, 1978.

9. Ben Holman, interview with Bertram Levine.

10. Martin Walsh, interview with Grande Lum, 2013.

11. Laue and Cormick, "The Ethics of Intervention in Community Disputes," 217.

12. Rogers and Salem, *A Student's Guide to Mediation and Law*. (note by Lum)

13. Pfund, ed., *From Conflict Resolution to Social Justice*. (note by Lum)

14. See www.civilrightsmediation.org.

15. See www.civilrightsmediation.org/interviews/Nancy_Ferrell.shtml.

16. Judge W. Arthur Garrity Jr. to Community Relations Service, March 31, 1975.

17. Judge W. Arthur Garrity Jr. to President Jimmy Carter, December 6, 1978.

18. S. 499, 86th Cong., 1st sess., 1959, *Congressional Record* 105, pt. 1:876.

19. This section and those that follow are by Grande Lum.

20. U.S. Department of Justice, Community Relations Service, Annual Report, 2012, 31–32.

21. U.S. Department of Justice, Community Relations Service, Annual Report, 2018, 15.

22. U.S. Department of Justice, Community Relations Service, Annual Report, 2013, 56.

23. U.S. Department of Justice, Community Relations Service, Annual Report, 2018, 15.

24. U.S. Department of Justice, Community Relations Service, Annual Report, 2018, 15.

25. U.S. Department of Justice, Community Relations Service, Annual Report, 2018, 17.

26. U.S. Department of Justice, Community Relations Service, Annual Report, 2018, 15.

27. U.S. Department of Justice, Community Relations Service, Annual Report, 2018, 10.

28. Ury, *Getting to Peace*, 154–61. Ury describes ten different roles third parties play to get to peace. That framework is utilized here for understanding the multiple roles that CRS conciliators play in containing, preventing, and resolving conflict.

29. U.S. Department of Justice, Community Relations Service, Annual Report, 2013, 59.

30. "Spies and Muscle: Holder, Secretive DOJ Group Helped Oust Sanford Sheriff," Breitbart, April 18, 2012, https://perma.cc/AQP5-WVVD; Arelis Hernandez, "DOJ 'Peacemakers' Helped Sanford Stay Cool Amid Rising Tensions," *Orlando Sentinel*, April 15, 2012, https://perma.cc/T6LF-AA46.

31. A.C. Thompson and Robert Faturechi, "How a Key Federal Civil Rights Agency Was Sidelined as Historic Protests Erupted," ProPublica, July 9, 2020. https://perma.cc/AT44-QAYZ.

32. Becky Monroe, "President's Budget Would Eliminate Important 'Peacemaker' Agency Created by the Civil Rights Act of 1964," Medium.com, February 12, 2018, https://perma.cc/YDA4-KEHW.

33. "LDF Statement on Elimination of DOJ's Community Relations Service in Trump Administration's Proposed Budget," NAACP Legal Defense Fund, February 12, 2018, https://perma.cc/5S4H-FBLQ.

34. U.S. Department of Justice, Community Relations Service, Annual Report, 2013, 29–30.

THIS COMPELLING STORY of the Community Relations Service quietly making a difference in this nation, narrated by Bertram Levine and Grande Lum with fascinating illustrations and thoughtful analysis, has influenced my story as well. In contrast to Levine's and Lum's views of CRS as key insiders, my story about CRS is as an outsider—as a law professor assigned a course in mediation to teach, as a state attorney general, as a university administrator, and as an author focusing on mediation. My experiences with CRS are consistent with the themes threading through the stories in *America's Peacemakers* and discussed explicitly in chapter 16. I have observed three of these themes particularly: the culture and techniques developed to enhance both peace and justice, the interplay between CRS and the emerging dispute resolution field, and the persistent challenges to gain the support and trust of an ever-changing cohort of federal and local leaders for a behind-the-scenes agency in the age of evidence-based budget analysis.

CRS faces dilemmas as it strives to encourage problem-solving and serve justice. I began to focus on the peace versus justice issue in 1982 when I met Richard Salem, who had joined CRS in its early days, directed its Chicago regional office, and recently retired. When he gave guest lectures in my first mediation and law class, Salem recounted an incident discussed in chapter 11—the talks he facilitated as a CRS conciliator when a neo-Nazi group sought to march through Skokie, Illinois, home to many Holocaust survivors. I had heard about the Skokie situation from another vantage point, that of David Goldberger, the American Civil Liberties Union lawyer who represented the neo-Nazi group in federal litigation to defend their First Amendment rights to march. The ACLU would not back away from defending First Amendment principles but did not try to dissuade its clients from participating in talks with Salem. He in turn encouraged the neo-Nazi group leaders to consider the likelihood of violence and suggested that there were ways to avert violence without compromising their First Amendment rights. That led to the neo-Nazi group leaders' voluntary change of the march location to avoid what threatened to be a violent and painful result in Skokie.

The problem-solving strategies that CRS refined over five-plus decades and that Levine and Lum document so vividly in this book contributed to the formation of the dispute resolution field for legal disputes. The legal and ethical issues raised by mediators in legal disputes were somewhat analogous to those that CRS had already faced and dealt with in community-wide civil rights matters such as the threatened Skokie march. As we discussed these issues, Salem and I decided to write *A Student's Guide to Mediation and the Law*, published in 1987. Dick's stories from his CRS days brought mediation to life for the student readers. Dick's CRS mediation experience contributed to the book's description of mediation techniques that remains a staple in at least one dispute resolution textbook today.[1] Dick's understanding of the dilemmas that emerge because of what Lum refers to as a CRS role in problem-solving that is consistent with justice led us to include exercises for law students to deal with analogous dilemmas in the mediation of legal disputes.

Having thus become an admirer of the unique and vital contributions that CRS was making both in communities and in the development of the new legal dispute resolution field, I later learned about the need for others to augment or assist CRS contributions in the community setting. In 2008, with a few days' notice, I became Ohio attorney general, serving for the nine months between the resignation of the previous attorney general and the election of the next. During this time, several white police officers in an Ohio city fatally shot an African American man—in fact, a member of a family that had called the police for protection from a drive-by shooter. Local authorities would sort through the legal implications of what had occurred, and federal officials would decide whether civil rights statutes were violated. Whatever was determined about the legality of the officers' actions, the shooting surfaced outrage about longstanding discrimination against African Americans. I worried that it would deepen the bitterness if key local officials continued to refuse to discuss what had occurred and if they would not openly deal with the root causes of concerns about equitable treatment. I called a CRS conciliator in Dick Salem's old office, the regional CRS office in Chicago, and a mediator immediately became engaged with community members. Although my office encouraged community leaders to accept CRS's help in talking with concerned members of the community, some refused.

I left office with that matter still pending but also with a general sense that there ought to be something more at a state or local level to assist in situations like this. In other words, while CRS was the gold standard, it was not always the silver bullet, to use an unpeaceful analogy. Such an initiative might establish trusted relationships with local leaders and facilitate acceptance of CRS. It could also augment CRS's work outside of crises—to help community leaders and residents to prepare ahead of a crisis and to deal with underlying concerns through long-term collaborative processes.

After returning to the Ohio State University law faculty, I studied Levine's first edition of this book, trying to read between the lines to tease out the elements of CRS's obvious success. I wrote an article suggesting how to translate those elements into some sort of local version.[2] In the meantime, I discovered that my Ohio State colleague Josh Stulberg already had the same idea for local versions of CRS. With the help of the Kettering Foundation, in 2015 Stulberg, my students in a dispute system design workshop, and I convened a meeting of about twenty-five people, including Grande Lum and Thomas Battles from CRS. That group helped to set out the outlines of what became the Divided Community Project, a national initiative housed at the Ohio State University Moritz College of Law.[3] The audience for the project's work would be local leaders across the nation. The goals would mirror those of CRS though with a broader purview that included any divisive incidents or conflicts (not solely civil rights and hate incidents). The project would focus on building community resilience and readiness and implementing processes to work over the long term on underlying issues.

The Divided Community Project's first challenge was to build a model for reaching local leaders with the information they needed in an increasingly polarized nation. After leaving CRS, Lum led the effort to establish what would work to achieve that goal, becoming the project's first director and then chair of its steering committee. Already,

Lum was working on the new edition of this book. He brought his insights about CRS to the design of the Divided Community Project. Another Ohio State colleague, Bill Froehlich, became assistant and then deputy director. Experienced mediators from throughout the nation joined an active steering committee. A series of grants from the Judicial Arbitration and Mediation Services Foundation, the Littlefield Foundation, and the American Arbitration Association/ International Centre for Dispute Resolution Foundation, and support from the Ohio State University and the Kettering Foundation, made it possible to establish the Divided Community Project as a valued asset for local leaders. By 2018, the American Bar Association Section on Dispute Resolution had awarded the project the Cooley Lawyer as Problem Solver Award.

About the time that we had established some workable strategies, another CRS development intervened. The budgetary worries discussed in *America's Peacemakers* became reality, and the number of CRS conciliators dwindled. Becky Monroe, Lum's predecessor as acting director of CRS, became the Divided Community Project's director. Monroe developed a one-on-one consultation arm for local leaders, augmenting the work of CRS and also supplementing the guides, tabletop simulations, and academies that had became the project's primary outreach tools. Later, Thomas Battles, previously director of CRS's southeast regional office, became active in running the consultation arm, now called the Bridge Initiative @ Moritz. The Bridge Initiative has worked with leaders in communities across the nation.

As the nation faces polarization, *America's Peacemakers* makes the case for federal support of the objective, honest, and compassionate work of the Community Relations Service and sets out a path for local leaders and mediators to take advantage of CRS's rich resources and learn from its approach. Recounting example after example, covering over a half century, Levine and Lum elucidate how an agency comprising mediators, facilitators, and trainers quietly made a positive difference in a nation grappling with its differences. They trace how CRS influenced the growth of mediation in the justice system and were influenced by it. Moreover, drawing on their knowledge as former leaders and their dispute resolution expertise, Levine and Lum extract the recipe for that success. In doing all of this, the new edition of *America's Peacemakers* makes a signal contribution to those who will seek to bridge differences over the next half century.

Nancy H. Rogers
Moritz College of Law
The Ohio State University

NOTES

1. See, e.g., Stephen Goldberg et al., *Dispute Resolution: Negotiation, Mediation, Arbitration and Other Processes*, 7th ed. (New York: Wolters Kluwer, 2020), 106.
2. Rogers, "When Conflicts Polarize Communities."
3. Divided Community Project, https://go.osu.edu/dcp.

THIS LIST IS meant to provide a timeline of some but not all noteworthy cases and significant milestones. Because of confidentiality, a number of high-profile cases CRS was involved in were not accessible in the CRS annual reports or elsewhere. The year noted is when CRS involvement began and not necessarily when it concluded. For a more comprehensive list and additional details, see the official CRS annual reports and cases covered in this book.

1964
— Civil Rights Act passed; Title X created the Community Relations Service
— LeRoy Collins confirmed as first director
— President Lyndon Johnson appointed 450 distinguished individuals to the National Citizens Committee for Community Relations to assist CRS

1965
— Provided significant conciliation services including mediation and direct liaison with President Johnson for civil rights marches from Selma to Montgomery
— Assisted the President's Task Force on Urban Problems in nine large cities
— Supported creation of local human relations commissions
— Mediated end of Black boycott of white merchants in Natchez, Mississippi, led by the NAACP's Charles Evers

1966
— Roger Wilkins confirmed as second director
— Moved from the Department of Commerce to the Department of Justice

Primary Source: CRS Annual Reports

— Produced *The Mercer Project*, a documentary film to help African American students enter previously all-white schools

1967

— Conciliated in numerous civil disturbances in communities throughout the country during what became known as the "Long Hot Summer of 1967"
— National Advisory Commission on Civil Disorders created
— Office of Community Action and Media Relations created within CRS
— Prevented escalation and enhanced safety when SNCC chairman H. Rap Brown was arrested in Cambridge, Maryland

1968

— Helped maintain calm in the wake of the assassination of Martin Luther King Jr. and subsequent riots
— Worked with SCLC to encourage nonviolent withdrawal and with law enforcement to use restraint in the Resurrection City protest
— Engaged in a case with allegations of discrimination against Mexican Americans at a U.S. Air Force base in the Southwest, resulting in the base undertaking an extensive equal opportunity program

1969

— Ben Holman confirmed as third director
— After the U.S. Supreme Court ordered school desegregation, developed and implemented what was known as the P81 plan for southern school systems desegregation
— Organized by programs: education, police-minority relations, economic development, housing and planning, communications

1970

— Prepared for school desegregation assistance by hiring thirty-seven temporary field representatives and creating media programs to work with school districts for the fall opening
— Liaised with local Black leaders and set up rumor control for a May Day rally in New Haven, Connecticut, for fourteen Black Panthers, including national chairman Bobby Seale, who were on trial for murder

1971

— Assisted in desegregation of San Francisco, Los Angeles, and San Bernardino, California, schools
— Worked throughout the South on school desegregation
— Assisted in forming and implementing plans involving Ourway, a national discount store that resulted in Houston's first joint venture with an African American businessperson

1972

— Conciliated between American Indian Movement leaders and the White House after the Trail of Broken Treaties takeover of the Bureau of Indian Affairs headquarters
— Mediated prisoner cases in Louisiana and settled civil rights complaints filed by inmates against prison authorities
— Worked with minority groups over three years to gain access to media and helped lead to a cable television agreement with McGraw-Hill with minority employment goals, as well as minority and public affairs programming

1973

— Extensively mediated issues of safety, necessities, and ending the American Indian Movement takeover of Wounded Knee
— Budget cut significantly, with staff reduced by two-thirds; media and conflict prevention programs largely eliminated
— Police shooting and death of twelve-year-old Santos Rodriquez in Dallas, Texas

1974

— Worked as court monitor to Judge W. Arthur Garrity for Boston Public Schools desegregation, created and maintained biracial councils, and provided conciliation services
— Budget for fiscal year 1974 set at $3.5 million, down from $6.8 million in the previous year. Authorized staff positions went down from 341 to 103

1975

— Mediated agreement on Port Arthur, Texas, police department issues, reducing use of deadly force, improving minority recruitment, and establishing a police community relations program

— Set up a temporary field office in Detroit to provide full-time assistance to Detroit desegregation and served as court monitor
— Completed closing of forty-six field offices and transitioned to ten regional offices
— Published "Guidelines for Effective Human Relations Commissions"

1976

— After the shooting of a man of Puerto Rican descent by a Springfield, Massachusetts, police officer and arrests of twelve protesters, mediated settlement including creating a reform advisory committee and a police internal review committee
— Mediated Flint, Michigan, police agreement that all police applicants would get new job examinations, psychological screening, and human relations training following a gun battle between two police officers, one white and one Black

1977

— Mediated with Nazi group to avert possible large-scale violence in Skokie, Illinois
— Mediated between prisoners from different races after two African American prisoners died following a fight in the Nevada State Prison in Carson City

1978

— Gilbert Pompa confirmed as fourth director
— Published "Police Use of Deadly Force"
— Brought together Texas police chiefs and Hispanic organizations to address the use of deadly force after the police killing of sixteen Mexican Americans and subsequent Brown Berets protest
— Helped Los Angeles Schools with 51,210 students desegregate more effectively and safely
— Opened a temporary field office in Wilmington, Delaware, to help with a court-ordered desegregation plan merging 11 suburban and city school districts involving 65,000 students

1979

— Mediated a Texas Gulf Coast shrimping conflict between Vietnamese and white fishermen and arrived at a resolution that allowed all to resume shrimping without outbreaks of serious violence

— Mediated integration of five thousand inmates in the Cook County, Illinois, jail
— Mediated a voting rights class-action suit in Cairo, Illinois, where Blacks, who were one-third of the population and had been barred from city council, gained representation
— Mediated conflict between the Nez Percé tribe and Idaho state fish and gaming agencies that led to development of an improved formula for tribal fishing of salmon

1980

— Assisted in resettlement of immigrants from Southeast Asia, Haiti, Cuba, and other countries, including from the Mariel Boat Lift
— Temporarily opened an office in Miami, established a citizens' complaint process, and reviewed firearms policy following the police custody death of Arthur McDuffie and resultant rioting

1981

— Mediated a negotiated agreement of civil suits with the Richmond, California, police on employment discrimination and excessive use of force against African Americans, resulting in revised use of force policies

1982

— Provided conciliation services after the murder of Vincent Chin and resulting protests and assisted in pursuing federal involvement of the U.S. attorney and the deputy attorney general
— Published "Deadly Force Handbook"
— Successfully closed the last of twenty-four cases referred to a regional office by U.S. District Court judges of the Seventh Circuit under a pilot project
— Reopened Miami field office permanently due to refugee-related cases and serious racial-ethnic challenges

1983

— Partnered with the National Urban League to develop community anticrime programs
— Attorney general transferred the Cuban/Haitian Entrant Program from the Department of Health and Human Services to CRS
— Successfully mediated a federal suit in which Hispanic parents charged that the schools were failing to provide adequate instruction for children with limited English proficiency

1984

— Provided services in a conflict between Native Americans and hunters over treaty rights usage for fishing and hunting off-season in numerous states including California, Minnesota, Oregon, Washington, and Wisconsin

— Mediated agreement between Coors and a coalition of Hispanic organizations on hiring and promotional practices

1985

— Convened sessions of community leaders and police to deal with escalating problems between Black and Vietnamese gangs in the eastern section of New Orleans

— Facilitated greater police awareness of Cape Verdean concerns and opened communications due to increase in complaints alleging police brutality against Cape Verdeans in Pawtucket, Rhode Island

— Developed Student Problem and Resolution program, a facilitated problem-solving technique, in the Western Regional Office

1986

— Defused tensions between Korean merchants and African American residents in Washington, D.C., enflamed by the brandishing of a gun at a Black woman customer. This prompted a local dispute resolution center to help develop a mediation program for disputes between merchants and residents

— Obtained a negotiated settlement in a dispute involving the Navajo Nation of Window Rock, Arizona, and the Winslow, Arizona, Municipal Court and Police Department alleging the police department discriminated against Navajos

1987

— Brought together four preeminent law enforcement executives, published "Principles of Good Policing: Avoiding Violence between Police and Citizens," and used it to train police departments

— Met extensively with youth and organized a teacher-student group to conduct conferences in response to an attack on two African American brothers by a group of whites in Bensonhurst, New York

— Provided conciliation services in response to racial violence on college campuses including the Citadel, University of Michigan, and Penn State

— Assisted in establishment of the Northwest Coalition against Malicious Harassment in response to high incidence of hate group activity

1988

— Grace Flores-Hughes confirmed as fifth director
— Mediated a plan for Smith College to deal with complaints of historical racism called the Smith Design for Institutional Diversity, which became a blueprint for other universities dealing with similar issues

1989

— Supported resettlement of Central American families and unaccompanied minors in Texas, including opening two new facilities in the state
— Created special initiative Youth, Gangs, and Drugs, which handled casework and cooperative efforts with the FBI, Drug Enforcement Agency, and Department of Housing and Urban Development
— Expanded the Unaccompanied Minors Program through a memorandum of agreement with the Immigration and Naturalization Service and provided foster care, education, counseling, and other services
— Mediated the return of Ohlone human remains from Stanford University to Ohlone representatives

1990

— Created a task force that published "Avoiding Racial Conflict: A Guide for Municipalities"
— Initiated a national toll-free hotline telephone service to receive calls reporting hate violence and harassment based on race, color, or national origin; 2,140 calls were documented in the first six months
— Signed a memorandum of understanding with the U.S. Coast Guard to advise them on handling discrimination complaints and mediate disputes between the coast guard and community agencies

1991

— Worked with the FBI's Uniform Crime Report Unit to develop a model training program on reporting of hate crimes
— Mediated an agreement with the American Indian Movement minutes before a protest was to end, averting serious violence on the five hundredth anniversary of Christopher Columbus's arriving in the Americas
— Provided placement and resettlement assistance to an unprecedented number of Haitians leaving Haiti after the September coup

1992

— Developed a nationwide crisis response plan to address issues involving police use of force in the aftermath of the Rodney King trial verdict

— Mediated with Korean American groups and federal agencies in the aftermath of the destruction of Korean-owned businesses in Los Angeles

— Helped bring together a series of meetings on how to combat hate crimes in response to a Ku Klux Klan rally during observance of Martin Luther King's birthday in Denver

— Southwest regional office mediated five court-referred voting rights cases in Texas, Arkansas, and Louisiana

1993

— Provided mediation services to a conflict over Camp Sister Spirit, a feminist and lesbian retreat in Ovett, Mississippi

— Developed recommendation for bridging the gap between the all-white police department and the 99 percent Aleut community of St. Paul Island, Alaska, where the chief of police shot and killed a young Aleut

1994

— Provided additional conciliation services in response to heightened community tension during the Cuban and Haitian migrant influx, in which thousands of migrants were provided temporary shelter at the Guantanamo Naval Base in Cuba and other locations

— Signed a memorandum of agreement with the National Organization of Black Law Enforcement to jointly work to reduce law enforcement–citizen violence

1995

— Helped navigate planning and enhance communication for the Million Man March in Washington, D.C.

— Published "Police and Urban Youth Relations: An Antidote to Racial Violence"

— Mediated a dispute over ownership and tribal sovereignty on the Onondaga Reservation in New York

1996

— Established the Church Burning Response Team to deal with arson and desecration of African American churches

— Provided pre-event and onsite assistance to the Republican National Convention in San Diego and to the Democratic National Convention in Chicago
— Office of Immigration and Refugee Affairs transferred to the Office of International Affairs at the Immigration and Naturalization Service
— Staff reduced to forty-one employees: seven at headquarters and thirty-four field staff

1997
— Rose Ochi confirmed as sixth director
— Mediated settlement to create a civilian oversight board, computerized tracking system, and civilian training academy in Cincinnati after a series of use-of-force incidents

1998
— Served as the court-appointed mediator for Little Rock, Arkansas, desegregation and produced a settlement
— Supported contingency planning for protests after the murder of James Byrd Jr.

1999
— Began notifying congressional members when conciliators do conflict resolution work in their district or state, per appropriations report requirements
— Initiated One America Dialogue in St. Louis to improve race relations; the mayor created a task force to implement the dialogue recommendations
— Provided conciliation services over a year's time after Riverside, California, police shot and killed Tyisha Miller, resulting in protests

2000
— Provided mediation and other conciliation services when five-year-old Elián González was found at sea after leaving Cuba and his Miami relatives fought to keep him
— Trained more than six hundred law enforcement officers in conflict management and created teams of welcoming ambassadors for a "Black Bike" Memorial Day weekend event in Myrtle Beach, South Carolina

— Provided a team of fifteen mediators for protests organized by an umbrella organization of two hundred activist groups at the Democratic National Convention in Los Angeles
— Deployed conciliators to help manage protests at the Republican National Convention in Philadelphia

2001

— Sharee Freeman confirmed as seventh director
— Created organizational response to deal with post-9/11 terrorist attacks backlash against Arab, Muslim, and Sikh communities

2002

— Continued sustained response to 9/11 aftermath included conducting hate crimes training as well as establishing working groups with U.S attorneys and state attorneys general focused on backlash issues
— Responded to threats and attacks on houses of worship in seventeen states and provided prevention and conflict resolution assistance
— Introduced Law Enforcement Mediation Program to provide mediation training to police officers
— Defused tensions in the community when a coalition of groups including the American Indian Movement, members of the Hispanic community, the NAACP, and the Urban League demonstrated against Columbus Day in Pueblo, Colorado

2003

— Provided services after riots in Benton Harbor, Michigan, following the death of an African American male during a police pursuit, including serving as technical advisor to Michigan governor's task force that resulted in a plan of action
— Created video *The First Three to Five Seconds* to help police officers differentiate between threats and cultural norms surrounding Arab, Muslim, and Sikh issues
— Created the Arab, Muslim, and Sikh Awareness and Protocol seminar to educate law enforcement and government officials on customs and culture

2004

— Involved in several cases in which articles of faith worn by Sikh Americans were mistaken to be weapons by the police; provided training and other conciliation services

— Mediated an eighteen-point agreement to improve relations between the police department of Randolph, Massachusetts, and its minority and mostly African American community
— Helped organize a community-wide discussion that resulted in recommendations to improve relationships between the city of Lewiston, Maine, and its new Somali American residents

2005

— Provided sustained support to recovery efforts following Hurricane Katrina including resolving race-based conflicts in housing, education, employment, and contracts
— In Katrina aftermath, worked with school officials; Mississippi Band of Choctaw Indians in Philadelphia, Mississippi; and Vietnamese Americans in New Orleans
— Supported development of a planning committee, facilitated community dialogues, and provided a structured forum after a white supremacist group distributed thousands of racist and anti-Semitic fliers in two Charles County, Maryland, communities

2006

— Ondray Harris confirmed as eighth director
— Mediated with the New Orleans police chief, the human relations commission director, and community members on purpose, types of cases, and other provisions to create the New Orleans Police Community Board
— Provided contingency planning and self marshal training for a League of United Latin American Citizens–sponsored march and rally in support of the federal immigration reform bill

2007

— Provided contingency planning, self marshal training, and on-site conciliation for a protest over the treatment of the Jena 6, six African Americans convicted of beating up a white classmate in Jena, Louisiana
— In Baltimore, mediated a twenty-seven-point campus plan to improve racial tolerance at Johns Hopkins University following an off-campus fraternity "Halloween in the Hood" party that featured a theme using racial stereotypes
— Mediated an agreement in Crowley, Texas, resolving complaints from African American parents of racial discrimination by white teachers and administrators

— Mediated Navajo and white student diversity issues between the Page Unified School District and the Dine Committee for Equal Education in Page, Arizona

2008

— Facilitated dialogue between African American and Hispanic community leaders and the New York City Police Department after three white officers were acquitted of manslaughter in the fatal shooting of Sean Bell, a twenty-three-year-old African American man on the eve of his wedding
— Provided marshal training, law enforcement–protest group liaison program creation, technical assistance, and onsite conciliation for protests at the Republican National Convention in St. Paul, Minnesota, and the Democratic National Convention in Denver

2009

— The Matthew Shepard and James Byrd Jr. Hate Crimes Prevention Act (HCPA) passed, increasing CRS's jurisdiction for the first time to broaden beyond race and ethnicity and focus on the prevention of and response to hate crimes on the basis of race, national origin, sexual orientation, gender, gender identity, religion, and disability
— In the aftermath of the shooting of Oscar Grant at the Bay Area Rapid Transit Fruitvale Station in Oakland, California, provided conflict resolution services to community leaders, law enforcement, and government officials

2010

— Provided contingency planning, technical assistance, and onsite conciliation for protests against the passage of Arizona SB 1070, a strict anti-immigrant bill, in Phoenix and across the country
— Conducted 130 presentations in support of community outreach under the newly passed HCPA
— Facilitated a community dialogue in response to tensions following reports of antigay violence in Chicago

2011

— Convened dialogues that led to increased LGBTQ cultural awareness training for law enforcement and LGBTQ representation on the police chief's advisory council after Chrissie Bates, a transgender woman, was murdered in Minneapolis

— Facilitated dialogue between Amish leaders and local law enforcement after an Amish barn burning in Fertile, Minnesota, to help prevent future bias crimes
— Mediated an agreement after a series of African Muslim hate-based robberies in Bronx, New York; the agreement included action items on violence reduction, police-community relations, housing, and youth development

2012

— Grande Lum confirmed as ninth director
— After the shooting of Trayvon Martin, provided substantial services including contingency planning, creation of a faith leader coalition, and technical assistance
— Convened problem-solving sessions, hosted dialogues, provided technical assistance, and worked on amending hate crimes reporting after a mass-casualty shooting at a Sikh gurdwara in Oak Creek, Wisconsin
— Worked with members of the LGBTQ community, law enforcement, and prosecutors to provide hate crime prevention training after numerous murders of LGBTQ individuals in Puerto Rico
— Convened a series of meetings and helped parties develop a community action plan after a seven-year-old boy who had been bullied on the basis of gender committed suicide in Detroit

2013

— After the Boston Marathon bombing by two brothers of Muslim faith, provided technical assistance to Muslim and Sikh houses of worship throughout the country to prevent backlash violence
— Received Association for Conflict Resolution Peacemaker Award
— Convened dialogues on poaching, licensing requirement, and fishing safety after harassment, intimidation, and threats directed at Hmong hunters and fishermen in Appleton, Wisconsin

2014

— Following the shooting of Michael Brown by police officer in Ferguson, Missouri, convened dialogue sessions, established a coalition, and provided onsite conciliation
— Released video *Law Enforcement and the Transgender Community*, the first federal agency video of its kind, and created training program

— After the death of Eric Garner in Staten Island, New York, provided onsite mediation, marshal training, and train-the-trainer sessions to improve racial dialogues
— Received American Bar Association Section of Dispute Resolution Problem Solver Award

2015

— After the death of Freddie Gray while in police custody in Baltimore, provided onsite conciliation and marshal training; convened governmental, community, and law enforcement leaders; and deployed more than fifteen staff
— Provided technical assistance and other conciliation services after the shooting of Antonio Zambrano-Montes in Pasco, Washington
— Following a mass casualty shooting at Emanuel African Methodist Episcopal church in Charleston, South Carolina, provided onsite conciliation and contingency planning

2016

— After the police shooting of Philando Castile in Falcon Heights, Minnesota, convened and facilitated numerous community dialogues, mediated a protest occupation, and established a community command center
— Met with the district attorney and activists, and convened and facilitated meetings with civil rights leaders, the governor, mayor, and state representatives following the police shooting of Alton Sterling in Baton Rouge, Louisiana
— After a mass shooting in the Pulse nightclub, an LGBTQ gathering space, in Orlando, Florida, facilitated community access to essential resources and services and reached out across the country to LGBTQ groups on prevention of further violence
— Provided onsite conciliation and mediation for protests in Standing Rock, North Dakota, over plans to build oil pipeline
— In Pontiac, Michigan, provided consultation and mediation after a man with cerebral palsy was brutally beaten by two men who used the victim's cell phone to record the assault and post it on social media

2017

— Supported deployment of staff who volunteered to join the FEMA Surge Capacity Force program in response to Hurricanes Harvey, Irma, and Maria

— Created Muslim, Arab, Sikh, South Asian, and Hindu Communities Program and appointed a national program manager
— Trump administration proposed to eliminate CRS
— After the Unite the Right Rally in Charlottesville, Virginia, convened and facilitated the first public meeting after the rally and facilitated a community leadership council for several months

2018

— Provided contingency planning and technical assistance for a neighborhood engagement program following the shooting of Stephon Clark by police officers in Sacramento, California, which helped lead to new policies on officer body cameras and foot pursuits
— Piloted the Strengthening Police and Community Partnerships Program, focused on building trust and addressing historical barriers that prevent positive law enforcement–community relations
— Provided training on how to prevent and respond to hate crimes following heightened concerns about the possible resurgence of neo-Nazi activity in Whitefish, Montana, where there was an onslaught of social media attacks against local Jewish business owners
— After the Tree of Life Synagogue shooting, conducted a national webinar "Responses to Hate Crimes and Community Conflict"

2019

— After shooting at a Poway synagogue that left one worshipper dead, convened an interfaith coalition and facilitated a Bias Incident and Hate Crimes Forum to enhance local capacity to prevent and respond to hate incidents
— Developed community-facing guides for planning and conducting Hate Crimes Forums and Protecting Places of Worship forums.
— Developed and provided resources to launch and maintain the Department of Justice's Hate Crimes website
— After threats to a LGBTQ group's placing a float in Independence Day parade in Sparta, North Carolina, provided conciliation services so that parade took place safely and mediated among numerous stakeholders to allow for establishment of local LGBTQ chapter
— Piloted revised training programs: Engaging and Building Relationships with Transgender Communities; Reducing Risk During Public Events: Contingency Planning, and Event Marshals; and Maintaining Safety During Public Events

SELECTED BIBLIOGRAPHY

Adams, John P. *At the Heart of the Whirlwind*. New York: Harper and Row, 1976.

Amsler, Lisa Blomgren, Janet Martinez, and Stephanie Smith. *Dispute System Design: Preventing, Managing, and Resolving Conflict*. Palo Alto, Calif.: Stanford University Press, 2020.

Branch, Taylor. *At Canaan's Edge: America in the King Years, 1965–1968*. New York: Simon and Schuster, 2007.

———. *Parting the Waters: America in the King Years, 1954–1963*. New York: Simon and Schuster, 1988.

———. *Pillar of Fire: America in the King Years, 1963–1965*. New York: Simon and Schuster, 1999.

Burns, James MacGregor, ed. *To Heal and to Build: The Programs of President Lyndon B. Johnson*. New York: McGraw-Hill, 1968.

Carpenter, Susan L., and W. J. D. Kennedy. *Managing Public Disputes: A Practical Guide for Government, Business, and Citizens' Groups*. San Francisco: Jossey-Bass, 1988.

Chestnut, J. L., Jr., and Julia Cass. *Black in Selma: The Uncommon Life of J. L. Chestnut, Jr*. New York: Farrar, Straus and Giroux, 1990.

Clark, Ramsey. *Crime in America: Observations on Its Nature, Causes, Prevention, and Control*. New York: Simon and Schuster, 1970.

Davis, Albie, and Richard A. Salem. "Dealing with Power Imbalances in the Mediation of Interpersonal Disputes." *Mediation Quarterly* 1, no. 6 (December 1984): 17–26.

Dawidowicz, Lucy S. "Civil Rights and Intergroup Tensions." In *The American Jewish Yearbook, 1965*, 155–93. New York: American Jewish Committee and Jewish Publication Society of America, 1965.

Deloria, Vine. *Behind the Trail of Broken Treaties: An Indian Declaration of Independence*. New York: Dell, 1974.

Dibrell, George. "Mediation in Civil Rights Issues: The Port Arthur Experience." *Police Chief Magazine*, November 1976.

Downs, Donald A. *Nazis in Skokie: Freedom, Community, and the First Amendment*. Notre Dame, Ind.: University of Notre Dame Press, 1985.

———. "Skokie Revisited: Hate Group Speech and the First Amendment." *Notre Dame Law Review* 60, no. 4 (1985): 629–85.

Edwards, George. *The Police on the Urban Frontier: A Guide to Community Understanding.* New York: American Jewish Committee, 1968.

Evans, Rowland, and Robert Novak. *Lyndon B. Johnson: The Exercise of Power.* New York: New American Library, 1966.

Examples of CRS Aid to Communities: Community Relations Service United States Department of Justice. Washington, D.C.: U.S. Government Printing Office, September 1977. https://perma.cc/RA5Z-95W5.

Finney, Graham S. "Desegregating the Schools in Dayton." In *Roundtable Justice: Case Studies in Conflict Resolution*, edited by Robert B. Goldmann, 181–201. Boulder, CO.: Westview Press, 1980.

Fisher, Roger, William Ury, and Bruce Patton. *Getting to Yes: Negotiating Agreement without Giving In.* 2nd edition. New York: Houghton-Mifflin, 1991.

Fleming, Harold C. *The Potomac Chronicle: Public Policy and Civil Rights from Kennedy to Reagan.* With Virginia Fleming. Athens: University of Georgia Press, 1996.

Flores-Hughes, Grace. *A Tale of Survival: Memoir of an Hispanic Woman.* Bloomington, Ind.: Author House, 2011.

Good, Paul. "A White Look at Black Power." *Nation*, August 8, 1966, 112–17.

Greenwald, Robert F. *Conflict without Chaos: A Look Back at Conflict Intervention Initiatives during the Nation's Early Civil Rights Era.* New York: Hampton Press, 2008.

———. "CRS: Dispute Resolution through Mediation." *Journal of the American Bar Association* 64, no. 8 (August 1978): 1250–54.

Halberstam, David. *The Children.* New York: Random House, 1998.

Hamlin, David. *The Nazi/Skokie Conflict: A Civil Liberties Battle.* Boston: Beacon Press, 1981.

Hampton, Henry, and Steve Fayer. *Voices of Freedom: An Oral History of the Civil Rights Movement from the 1950s through the 1980s.* New York: Bantam Books, 1990.

King, Martin Luther, Jr. *Where Do We Go from Here: Chaos or Community.* New York: Harper and Row, 1967.

Klugman, Julian. "Negotiating Agreements and Resolving Disputes across Cultures." *Mediation Quarterly* 9, no. 2 (Summer 1992): 387–90.

Klugman, Julian, Stephen Thom, and Larry Myers. "Mediation and Native American Repatriation of Human Remains." *Mediation Quarterly* 10, no. 4 (Summer 1993): 321–25.

Kotz, Nick. "The Minority Struggle for a Place in the Newsroom." *Columbia Journalism Review* 17, no. 6 (March–April 1979): 23–31.

Laue, James H. "The Emergence and Institutionalization of Third-Party Roles in Conflict." In *Conflict: Readings in Management and Resolution*, edited by John Burton and Frank Dukes, 256–74. London: Palgrave Macmillan, 1990.

———. "Ethical Considerations in Choosing Intervention Roles." *Peace and Change* 8, nos. 2–3 (July 1982): 29–41.

Laue, James, and Gerald W. Cormick. "The Ethics of Intervention in Community Disputes." In *The Ethics of Social Intervention*, edited by Gordon Bermant, Herbert C. Kelman, and Donald P. Warwick, 205–32. New York: Halsted Press, 1978.

Lazarus, Edward. *Black Hills, White Justice: The Sioux Nation versus the United States, 1975 to the Present.* New York: HarperCollins, 1991.

Lewis, John. *Walking with the Wind: A Memoir of the Movement.* New York: Simon and Schuster, 1998.

Lukas, J. Anthony. *Common Ground: A Turbulent Decade in the Lives of Three American Families.* New York: Vintage, 1986.

Lum, Grande. *The Negotiation Fieldbook: Simple Strategies to Help You Negotiate Everything.* New York: McGraw-Hill, 2005.

———. *Tear Down the Wall: Be Your Own Mediator in Conflict.* Boston: Optimality Press, 2013.

Lynch, Thomas P. "Camp Sister Spirit: A Retreat under Siege." *Mediation Quarterly* 13, no. 2 (Winter 1995): 151–63.

Mayer, Bernard S. *Beyond Neutrality: Confronting the Crisis in Conflict Resolution.* San Francisco: Jossey-Bass, 2004.

McClure, Edward D. *Police/Community Relations.* With Diana L. McClure. Brookline, Mass.: N.p., 2009.

Means, Russell, and Marvin J. Wolf. *Where White Men Fear to Tread: The Autobiography of Russell Means.* New York: St. Martin's Press, 1995.

Menkel-Meadow, Carrie. "Why We Can't 'Just All Get Along': Dysfunction in the Polity and Conflict Resolution and What We Might Do about It." *Journal of Dispute Resolution* 1, no. 5 (2018): 1–21.

Monroe, Becky. "An Attack on America's Peacemakers Is an Attack on All of Us: On the Importance of Embracing Power of Communities and Rejecting the Trump Administration's Attempt to Eliminate the Community Relations Service." *Yale Law and Policy Review* 37, no. 1 (2019): 299–343.

National Advisory Commission on Civil Disorders (Kerner Commission). *Report of the National Advisory Commission on Civil Disorders.* Washington, D.C.: U.S. Government Printing Office, 1968.

National Citizens Committee for Community Relations, Community Relations Service, U.S. Department of Justice. *Putting the Hard-Core Unemployed into Jobs.* Washington, D.C.: U.S. Government Printing Office, 1968.

Oswald, Ramona Faith. *Lesbian Rites: Symbolic Acts and the Power of Community.* New York: Routledge, 2014.

Pfund, Alicia, ed. *From Conflict Resolution to Social Justice: The Work and Legacy of Wallace Warfield.* New York: Bloomsbury, 2013.

President's Commission on Law Enforcement and Administration of Justice. *Commission Report: The Challenge of Crime in a Free Society.* Washington, D.C.: U.S. Government Printing Office, 1967.

———. *Task Force Report: The Police.* Washington, D.C.: U.S. Government Printing Office, 1967.

Raines, Howell. *My Soul Is Rested: Movement Days in the Deep South Remembered.* New York: G. P. Putnam's Sons, 1977.

Rogers, Nancy H. "When Conflicts Polarize Communities: Designing Localized Offices That Intervene Collaboratively." *Ohio State Journal on Dispute Resolution* 30, no. 2 (2015): 173–232.

Rogers, Nancy H., and Richard A. Salem. *A Student's Guide to Mediation and Law.* New York: Matthew Bender, 1987.

Rustin, Bayard. "Black Power and Coalition Politics." *Commentary*, September 1966, 35–40.

Salem, Richard A. "Community Dispute Resolution through Outside Intervention." *Peace and Change* 8, no. 3 (Summer 1982): 91–104.

———. "Mediating Political and Social Conflicts: The Skokie-Nazi Dispute." *Sociological Practice* 10, no. 1 (January 1992): 151–63.

Scott, Danielle. "All Opinions Matter: Breaking Down Assumptions about the Community Relations Service." *American Journal of Mediation* 9 (2016): 83–102.

Selden, Willis A. "Employment and Retention of Black Journalists by Michigan Daily Newspapers." M.A. thesis, Michigan State University School of Journalism, 1980.

Sorensen, Theodore C. *Kennedy.* New York: Harper and Row, 1965.

Stone, Douglas, Bruce Patton, and Sheila Heen. *Difficult Conversations: How to Discuss What Matters Most.* New York: Penguin, 2010.

U.S. Department of Justice, Community Relations Service. Annual Reports for Fiscal Years 1965–2018. https://www.justice.gov/archives/community-relations-service-publications-archive.

———. *Police Use of Deadly Force: A Conciliation Handbook for Citizens and Police.* Washington, D.C.: U.S. Government Printing Office, 1982. https://perma.cc/7LQD-HW9F.

Ury, William. *Getting to Peace: Transforming Conflict at Home, at Work, and in the World.* New York: Viking, 1999.

Whalen, Charles, and Barbara Whalen. *The Longest Debate: A Legislative History of the 1964 Civil Rights Act.* Washington, D.C.: Seven Locks Press, 1985.

Wilkins, Roger. *A Man's Life: An Autobiography.* New York: Simon and Schuster, 1982.

Williams, Juan. *Eyes on the Prize: America's Civil Rights Years, 1954–1965.* New York: Viking, 1987.

Wofford, Harris. *Of Kennedys and Kings: Making Sense of the Sixties.* New York: Farrar, Straus and Giroux, 1980.

Woodhead, Henry. "Red-Neck at the Bridge." *Atlanta Journal and Constitution Magazine*, May 12, 1974.

Young, Andrew. *An Easy Burden: The Civil Rights Movement and the Transformation of America*. New York: HarperCollins, 1996.

ANNOTATED TABLE OF CONTENTS

The introduction and chapters 1–10 are by Bertram Levine, the author of the original edition. Chapters 11–15 are by Grande Lum. Chapter 16 has sections by both authors.

INDEX

Figure numbers in italics refer to photographs.

PERMISSIONS

Passages from the following works are used by permission, as indicated:

From *Crime in America*, by Ramsey Clark. Copyright © 1970, 1971 by Ramsey Clark. Used by permission of Simon and Schuster.

From *My Soul Is Rested*, by Howell Raines. Copyright © 1977 Howell Raines. Used by permission of G. P. Putnam's Sons, a division of Penguin Group (USA), Inc.

From *Of Kennedys and Kings: Making Sense of the Sixties*, by Harris Wofford. Copyright © 1980 by Harris Wofford. Reprinted by permission of Farrar, Straus and Giroux, LLC.

From *The Potomac Chronicle: Public Policy and Civil Rights from Kennedy to Reagan*, by Harold C. Fleming with Virginia Fleming. Used by permission of the University of Georgia Press.

From *Where Do We Go from Here: Chaos or Community*, by Martin Luther King Jr. Reprinted by arrangement with the Estate of Martin Luther King Jr., c/o Writers House as agent for the proprietor, New York, N.Y. Copyright © 1968 Martin Luther King Jr., copyright renewed 1996 Coretta Scott King.

From "A White Look at Black Power," by Paul Good. Reprinted with permission from the August 8, 1966, issue of *The Nation*.

From "The Minority Struggle for a Place in the Newsroom," by Nick Kotz. Reprinted from *Columbia Journalism Review*, March/April 1979, © 1979 by *Columbia Journalism Review*.

From "Black Power and Coalition Politics," by Bayard Rustin. Reprinted from *Commentary*, September 1966, by permission; all rights reserved.